The Ad Men
and
Women

The Ad Men and Women

A Biographical Dictionary of Advertising

Edited by EDD APPLEGATE

GREENWOOD PRESS
Westport, Connecticut • London

HF
5810
A2
A3
1994

Library of Congress Cataloging-in-Publication Data

The Ad men and women : a biographical dictionary of advertising /
  edited by Edd Applegate.
      p.   cm.
    Includes bibliographical references and index.
    ISBN 0–313–27801–6 (alk. paper)
    1. Advertising—United States—Biography—Dictionaries.
  I. Applegate, Edd.
  HF5810.A2A3   1994
  659.1′092′273—dc20
  [B]   93–28040

British Library Cataloguing in Publication Data is available.

Library of Congress Catalog Card Number: 93–28040
ISBN: 0–313–27801–6

First published in 1994

Greenwood Press, 88 Post Road West, Westport, CT 06881
An imprint of Greenwood Publishing Group, Inc.

Printed in the United States of America

The paper used in this book complies with the
Permanent Paper Standard issued by the National
Information Standards Organization (Z39.48–1984).

10 9 8 7 6 5 4 3 2 1

Copyright Acknowledgments

August 4, 1981 and various J. Walter Thompson newsletters are printed with permission of the Special Collections Library, Duke University.

Extracts from Robert Glatzer's "Listen to Angry Young Voices in Ad Field, DDB's Phyllis Robinson Says," *Advertising Age* (June 3, 1968) appear courtesy of *Advertising Age*.

Material appearing in the Jane Trahey chapter courtesy of interviews with Jane Trahey by the author.

Quotes made by James Webb Young and appearing in the *New York Times* on Nov. 19, 1943, Nov. 1, 1945, and June 13, 1951 are printed copyright © 1943/45/51 by The New York Times Company. Reprinted by permission.

Every reasonable effort has been made to trace the owners of copyright materials in this book, but in some instances this has proven impossible. The author and publisher will be glad to receive information leading to more complete acknowledgments in subsequent printings of the book and in the meantime extend their apologies for any omissions.

CONTENTS

PREFACE

This reference volume is a result of the editor searching for a book on the lives of copywriters, art directors, and others who have contributed significantly to advertising. The editor believed that if readers were familiar with the lives of creative personalities they would be in a position to understand more fully how (and why) creativity occurs. Only four books were found. One was *Masters of Advertising Copy: Principles and Practice of Copy Writing According to Its Leading Practitioners*, edited by J. George Frederick. Unfortunately, the book contained very little information on the lives of the copywriters. Rather, copywriters of merit had merely contributed chapters on how they wrote copy. Furthermore, the book was published in 1925. Therefore, more recent copywriters, art directors, and others in advertising were not mentioned. Another book was *100 Top Copy Writers and Their Favorite Ads*, edited by Perry Schofield. This book, although worthy in the sense that 100 copywriters were featured, focused primarily on the advertisements, not on the lives of those who had created them. Also, it was published in 1954; more recent personalities were not included. The third book, *The 100 Greatest Advertisements—Who Wrote Them and What They Did*, by Julian Lewis Watkins, was published in 1959. This book discussed the advertisements briefly and mentioned the individuals responsible. It, too, failed to discuss in depth the lives of those who had created the advertisements. Unlike the other three, the fourth book allowed certain major players in advertising to discuss themselves and their advertising. This book, *Advertising's Benevolent Dictators*, by Bart Cummings, contained interviews with 18 personalities. Although insightful, the book was restricted in the sense that the author could interview only those who were alive. Some of the greatest advertising personalities were left out because they were deceased.

This reference includes more than 50 biographical entries by more than 30 scholars, researchers, and professionals. These entries discuss some of the greatest creative minds in advertising. The dictionary is not restricted to any particular period of time. Indeed, it contains biographies of those who lived in the 19th century as well as in the 20th century; it even includes biographies of some who are working in advertising as this is being written. As the reader learns about these practitioners, it is hoped that he or she will learn how and why they succeeded. Certain traits such as confidence seem to be common among many of them. Also, many, if not all, realized that advertising had one primary purpose: to sell goods and services. The reader should also note that most of these personalities were disciplined—that is, they were not afraid to work 12- or 16-hour days. In fact, if the puritan work ethic pertains to any group or profession in this country, it pertains to these men and women. Of course, as the individuals herein would testify, creativity (and greatness) does not come easy.

ACKNOWLEDGMENTS

This volume would not have been possible without the help and cooperation of various individuals. The editor and contributors wish to thank the following for their invaluable insights: Mary Edith Arnold, archivist, Leo Burnett Company, U.S.A.; Vicky (Schwab) Aronoff; Leandro Batista; Tom Burrell; Tom Collins; Father Michael Crosby, O.F.M., St. Peter's Church, Chicago; Vicki Cwiok, Department of Public Affairs, Sears Archives; Darcy DeWolfe, Foote, Cone, and Belding; Emerson Foote; Jarlath Graham; Paula Green; Joan Hafey, Vice President and Associate Director of Corporate Relations, Young and Rubicam, Inc., New York; Susan Hockaday Jones; Peggy Kreschel; John Leckenby; Michael McBride; Barrows Mussey; Ed Nash; David Ogilvy; John R. Osborn; Dick Porter; Thomas Randolph, Foote, Cone, and Belding, San Francisco; Leonard J. Reiss; Neil M. Sackheim and members of the Sackheim family; Philip W. Saywer, Director of Communications, Starch, INRA and Hooper; Ms. Bert Schachter, Vice President and Information Center Director, Backer Spielvogel Bates, Inc., New York; Bill Scherman; Frank Vos; Walter Weintz; and the reference librarians of Loyola University of Chicago, Texas Tech University, the University of Georgia's Main Library, the University of Illinois, Urbana-Champaign, and the University of Southern Mississippi's Cook Memorial Library. The editor and contributors also wish to thank Betty McFall of the Todd Library at Middle Tennessee State University, Bill Palzer of the Maxwell Library at Winona State University, and the staff at BBDO's library in New York for their help.

The editor and contributors are further grateful to members of the public relations and other departments of several advertising agencies for sharing information. These agencies include N. W. Ayer and Son; BBDO; Leo Burnett Company, U.S.A. Archives; D'Arcy, Masius, Benton and Bowles; DDB-Needham Worldwide; Della Femina, McNamee/WCRS; Foote, Cone, and Belding;

McCann-Erickson; Ogilvy and Mather, Houston; J. Walter Thompson; and Young and Rubicam.

Additional information for certain biographical entries was obtained from the following: the Belding Collection, Southwest Collection, Texas Tech University; the Walter Van Dyke Bingham papers at Northwestern University; the J. Walter Thompson archives at Duke University; and the Robert M. Yerkes papers at Yale University's Historical Medical Library.

INTRODUCTION

The purpose of this reference is to inform the reader about the lives of over 50 major personalities in advertising. Many of these men and women created some of the best campaigns in the history of advertising. Many were responsible for building large agencies. These major personalities include: Roy Sarles Durstine, who worked first for Calkins and Holden, then founded, with Bruce Barton and Alex Osborn, Barton, Durstine and Osborn (now BBDO), of which he was made president. In 1939 he founded an agency named for himself and worked until his death in 1962. Bruce Barton served as chairman of the board of Batten, Barton, Durstine and Osborn. He created Betty Crocker and a host of successful advertisements for such clients as General Electric, General Motors, and U.S. Steel. George Batten, who founded the George Batten Advertising Agency, believed in honest advertising and wrote copy that reflected this belief. He died before his agency merged with Barton, Durstine and Osborn. Alex Osborn, who was known for the creative process of brainstorming, was one of the founders of Barton, Durstine and Osborn, which handled such clients as McGraw-Hill, Condé Nast Publications, the General Baking Company, and the Wildroot Company. Osborn oversaw the agency's Buffalo, New York, office; Barton and Durstine handled the New York office.

One of BDO's (now BBDO) best copy writers was John Caples. Caples worked at various jobs before he entered advertising. He wrote copy for a leading mail-order advertising agency before he got a job with Barton, Durstine and Osborn, where he wrote copy until he was promoted to vice president. Caples wrote several books on advertising and researched several scientific methods of testing advertising's effectiveness.

William Benton and Chester Bowles are included here too. Benton worked for Lord and Thomas as an account executive, then for George Batten as a copywriter and later as a department head. He returned to Lord and Thomas as the assistant general manager in 1928 and conducted consumer research. In 1929 he and Chester Bowles opened an agency in New York. He retired in 1936 at the age of 36. Bowles also worked for George Batten as a copywriter, then, with Benton, founded the Benton and Bowles agency. Bowles was the creative force behind it; Benton was the businessman. Bowles was responsible for creating "slice-of-life" advertising, which appeared in comic strip formats.

Theodore (Ted) Lewis Bates worked for George Batten and Benton and Bowles before he formed the Ted Bates Company in 1940. The agency used the "unique selling proposition" concept that Rosser Reeves, one of the agency's most productive employees, coined. Reeves enjoyed "hard sell" advertising. A copywriter, he employed "reason why" copy that focused on his "unique selling proposition."

Three pioneers are discussed too: Volney B. Palmer, Francis Wayland Ayer, and George P. Rowell. Palmer was one of the nation's first advertising men to own an agency. He was responsible for introducing the commission system and the concept of media planning. Another early pioneer was Francis Wayland Ayer, who founded N. W. Ayer and Son in 1869. Ayer was responsible for modernizing the advertising agency by adopting the open contract system. George P. Rowell, also in the 1800s, forced publishers of newspapers to present circulation figures accurately when he began publishing a directory that listed them by name.

Two individuals who addressed the psychology of advertising are here as well. Walter Dill Scott wrote extensively about psychology and advertising, and informed businessmen that in order to convince the public to purchase goods, consumers needed to be understood. Daniel Starch followed in the footsteps of Scott. He contributed to the literature of psychology and advertising with articles and texts, including *Principles of Advertising* in 1923. Although he taught at several prestigious universities including Harvard, he established the research firm of Daniel Starch and Staff.

Another man who played a major role in advertising during the early- to mid–1900s was Albert D. Lasker of the Lord and Thomas agency. He was responsible for promoting several key copywriters, including John E. Kennedy, who informed Lasker that advertising was "salesmanship in print" and who pioneered "reason why" advertising, and Claude C. Hopkins, who employed "scientific" advertising. Lasker surrounded himself with some of the best minds in the business and consequently was admired for his ability to assemble as well as manage one of the largest agencies of its day.

Others who followed Lasker included Emerson Foote and Don Belding, two of the partners of Foote, Cone and Belding. Foote entered advertising when he went to work for the Leon Livingston agency. Later, primarily to work on the American Tobacco account, he went to work for Lord and Thomas. He became a partner in Foote, Cone and Belding when Albert Lasker dissolved Lord and Thomas in the early 1940s. Foote left the agency in 1950 because of illness. Two years later, after he had recovered, he found employment with McCann-Erickson, where he remained off and on for 13 years. Don Belding went to work for Lord and Thomas as a space buyer, then became a copywriter, manager, and later a partner of Foote, Cone and Belding. He retired in 1957.

Others who headed advertising agencies include Leo Burnett, Earnest Elmo Calkins, J. Stirling Getchell, and David Ogilvy, to name a few. Burnett headed the creative side of Erwin, Wasey in Chicago before he founded the company bearing his name in 1935. His agency created campaigns for Green Giant, Pillsbury, and numerous other clients. Calkins wrote copy for Charles Austin Bates before he and Ralph Holden founded Calkins and Holden in 1902. The agency created the first advertising plan for a campaign. He retired in 1931. Getchell wrote copy at Lord and Thomas, the George Batten Company, and J. Walter Thompson. In 1931 he established his own agency. He died nine years later. Ogilvy became a partner of Hewitt, Ogilvy, Benson, and Mather (later Ogilvy and Mather) and wrote copy, including the most famous advertisement for Hathaway shirts.

Among the women who played a major role in advertising, Bernice Fitz-Gibbon, Jo Foxworth, Paula Green, and Phyllis K. Robinson are given in-depth consideration. Fitz-Gibbon worked first for John Wanamaker, then Macy's, where she created advertisements. She moved to Gimbels, where she was given the freedom to create as she desired. In 1954 she started an agency that specialized in retail. She retired ten years later. Foxworth worked in the South for several years, then migrated to McCann-Erickson, where she worked as a copywriter. She had been promoted to vice president at Calkins and Holden before she left in 1968 to head her own agency. Green worked for Fawcett, the publishing company, then as a sales promotion copywriter for Grey Advertising. She moved to *Seventeen* magazine several years later, where she was eventually promoted to promotion director. She worked for other advertising agencies before she opened an agency. Robinson worked as a copy chief at Doyle, Dane, and Bernbach, creating advertisements for print and broadcast. She was eventually promoted to vice president at DDB, where she worked for 33 years.

Of course, there are others. However, the editor and contributors realize that it would require several volumes to discuss all the pioneers and/or those who have contributed significantly to American advertising's brief history. The purpose of this book is to present some of the greats.

The Ad Men and Women

FRANCIS WAYLAND AYER
(February 4, 1848–March 5, 1923)

John Vivian

Francis Wayland Ayer founded N. W. Ayer and Son in 1869, and it came to be recognized as the first full-service advertising agency. Ayer's services included counsel to clients on selling products and services; creative services, including advertisement and campaign design; and expertise on placing advertisements in advantageous media. These are sometimes called advertising's three Ps: planning, preparing, and placing. Ayer introduced the "open contract," which dramatically changed the advertising business by allying agencies closely to their clients' interests. He also began the *N. W. Ayer and Son's Directory of Newspapers and Periodicals*, which continued as a standard reference work in advertising. Ayer was a man of strong character and rectitude, and he prided himself in later years on operating an agency that refused unsavory clients.

Ayer was born on February 4, 1848, in Lee, Massachusetts, to Nathan Wheeler Ayer, whose puritan ancestors arrived in the colony eight generations earlier in 1636, and to Joanna B. (Wheeler) Ayer. His mother died when he was three, and his father married Harriet Post when he was six. Generally Ayer is remembered as going by his middle name, Wayland.

Ayer grew up in western New York, where he was schooled by his father, a lawyer who chose teaching over the bar. Beginning at age 14, Ayer taught school for five years. He attended the University of Rochester but ran out of money after one year. In June 1868 he moved to Philadelphia, where his father had opened a girls' school.

After a few weeks of part-time teaching, Ayer landed a job soliciting advertising for the *National Baptist* at a 25 percent commission. His first order, for $200, yielded him $50, and in less than 10 months he had earned $1,200. As a teacher back in New York, he had been paid only $20 a month plus lodging. Impressed at Ayer's enterprise, the *Baptist* offered him a $2,000-a-year position, but he declined, and in April 1869, with $250 in savings, he founded his own advertising company. Concerned that potential clients might not take him seriously because of his age—he had just turned 21—Ayer chose the name N. W. Ayer and Son, even though his father was chronically ill and not active in the company. Out of filial respect, Ayer gave his father 50 percent ownership.

Although N. W. Ayer and Son eventually became the prototypical modern agency, at first it was just another space brokering house, much like the older agencies of Volney B. Palmer and John L. Hooper. Ayer began as exclusive representative for 11 religious newspapers, including the *National Baptist*, and the agency listed itself as their advertising manager. These newspapers were pleased to be free of running their own advertising departments, particularly since the arrangement assured them of a steady customer, the Ayer agency, for their advertising space. Ayer assumed all the risk for selling the space. Because religious periodicals were popular at the time, young Ayer, a hard worker, was confident that he could sell the space.

In the start-up scramble, N. W. Ayer and Son derived revenue four ways. First, with the 11 religious newspapers for which he was exclusive representative, Ayer sold the space at a 20 to 30 percent markup, although space sometimes was unloaded at virtually no profit and on occasion the markup reached 70 percent. Second, Ayer negotiated to buy blocks of space wholesale from other publications, for which he was not exclusive representative, on speculation that he could sell the space at a profit. Third, he bought space for individual advertisements in publications in which he owned no space. The agency paid the publications' published rate and then charged advertisers a higher one. Fourth, Ayer accepted commissions from publications for placing ads in them. In these activities, Ayer and Son was much like competing agencies, distinguished only by the diligence with which the young proprietor went about his work.

Ayer was devoted to his father and stepmother, and he lived with them across the Delaware River in Camden, New Jersey. To work late and to get an early start, he rented a room in Philadelphia near his office and slept there weeknights.

The hard work paid off. Within a year, Ayer had outgrown quarters adjacent to the *National Baptist*, at 530 Arch Street, and moved to 719 Samson Street. By 1871, Ayer was placing advertisements in newspapers in 27 states, although mostly in Pennsylvania, New Jersey, New York, plus the District of Columbia. The volume reached $79,000 in 1873, and the agency, with a staff of seven, moved to larger quarters at 733 Samson Street. There would be two further moves during Ayer's lifetime, also for more space: to the Philadelphia *Times* Building, at Eighth and Chestnuts streets, in 1876, and to the Mariner and Merchant Building, at Third and Chestnut, in 1902.

Ayer's father, whose health had been deteriorating, died on February 7, 1873, and left his one-half interest in N. W. Ayer and Son to his wife. Although Wayland Ayer had a good relationship with his stepmother, he was concerned that her interest in the agency could be passed on to absentee owners, who might ruin it by pressing for immediate profit rather than the long-term growth to which he was committed. So, he bought his stepmother's share, becoming sole owner.

Later in 1873, Ayer took in a faithful employee, George O. Wallace, as a partner with a one-quarter interest in the agency.

Ayer, like other space brokers, had generally good relations with the periodicals in which he placed ads, but he did not escape the uneasiness that existed in relations between brokers and advertisers. Advertisers never were sure whether brokers were giving them space at a fair price or whether they were gouging. Until 1869, when George P. Rowell published a directory that estimated newspaper circulations and rates, brokers accumulated private lists of such data, and for competitive reasons they did not share the information. Because brokers negotiated privately with periodicals for special deals, unscrupulous brokers could easily misrepresent what a client's ad dollars were buying. Some periodicals, eager for national advertising, offered brokers extraordinary discounts which amounted, in effect, to under-the-table incentives to place ads with them. The result was that some brokers were more loyal to their periodicals than to their advertising clients. The publication of Rowell's directory probably reduced abuses, but advertisers remained suspicious.

Accounts vary about the date, but between the death of his father in 1873 and early 1875, an incident occurred that prompted Ayer to resolve the conflict of interest inherent in relationships between agencies and the periodicals in which they placed advertisements. As Ayer told the story, an older man whom he respected sat down with him, expressed his respect for Ayer as a person, and offered him a position in a company "of recognized standing." This mentor, whom Ayer never named, made clear that advertising had no such standing in his mind: "What is an advertising agent? Nothing but a drummer, and he will never be anything else!" (*Forty Years*, p. 11). Ayer said that the assault on his choice of vocation prompted him to make a radical change.

In 1875, N. W. Ayer and Son unveiled the open contract, declaring that the agency would charge its advertising clients the lowest rates that it could negotiate with periodicals—no rebates, no kickbacks, no covert special arrangements. Ayer would then charge a commission to clients, which would be negotiated with each individually. The commission originally ranged from 8 to 12 1/2 percent but eventually settled at 15 percent. With full disclosure of the agency's financial relationship to periodicals, clients could be confident that it would be motivated only by the client's welfare in placing ads. Henry Nelson McKinney, who promoted the new arrangement for Ayer, said clients who took advantage of the new service would know they were paying honest rates (Wright, pp. 129–30). In 1909 the agency recapped the advantages, saying that the open contract plan, by then dubbed "O.C. + 15," "pulled the advertising business out of the muck and mire of bidding and faking, and made the advertising agent an agent of the customer rather than an agent of any publication or group of publications" (*Forty Years*, p. 19).

Ayer's open contract precluded much of the corruption that had infected the space brokering business. Gradually, the open contract became an industry stan dard, and the space brokers disappeared or adapted to the new way of doing business. The transformation, however, was not immediate. Even Ayer eased into open contracts. Business historian Ralph M. Hower, who examined the agency's books for his 1939 history, said that less than one-half of the agency's business was by open contract in 1878, two years after the policy was announced (p. 68). The impact of the open contract on the rest of the advertising industry was not immediate either. According to historian Frank Presbrey, writing in 1929, agencies specializing in advertising were still mostly space brokers as late as 1890 (p. 348). Even so, N. W. Ayer and Son had a head start in building an image as a fair and honest agency.

Another Ayer innovation that inspired client confidence was the establishment of an in-house printing department in 1875. This gave the agency tighter control over typesetting and composition and reduced the chance that information in advertisements might be leaked to competitors before publication. The printing department offered no creative services beyond putting client instructions into type. At this point, Ayer was firm that decisions on advertising content should be made by the advertisers, who, he felt, were the people who knew their products and services best.

It was the open contract, however, that most visibly aligned N. W. Ayer and Son with client interests. Even so, Ayer's innovation still left open the possibility for abuse. In the interest of profit, agencies could recommend that clients spend more on advertising than necessary, with the effect of generating more agency revenue but there is no evidence that N. W. Ayer and Son engaged in such practice. Ayer undoubtedly was aware of this deficiency in the open contract system, yet he probably recognized that further reform was not practicable at the time. In fact, it was more than a century until the advertising industry began serious experimentation with a fee system by which clients paid the agency for services performed, instead of a commission based on the volume of advertisements placed.

A precursor of Ayer's open policy was the 1874 publication of N. W. Ayer and Son's *Manual for Advertisers*, which listed the periodicals with which the agency did business, including rates and circulations. Before 1874 space brokers had to create their own lists to supplement and update the Rowell directory, and these lists were treated like trade secrets. With the open contract in the offing, however, there was no further need for secrecy, and Ayer began publishing the manual annually. It was the predecessor of the *American Newspaper Annual*, which Ayer introduced in 1880, and *N. W. Ayer and Son's Directory of Newspapers and Periodicals*, which continues today as a standard reference in advertising.

In 1876 Ayer launched *The Advertiser's Guide*, a quarterly magazine edited for a general audience but distributed free to clients. The *Guide* carried short articles on business, odd bits of information, humor, and pieces extolling the virtues of advertising. Although N. W. Ayer and Son was not alone among agencies in producing promotional publications, the *Guide* represented the first of numerous Ayer publications, including books, pamphlets, and magazine advertisements, to win people over to advertising as a respectable, legitimate enterprise. One theme in the Ayer *Guide* was that advertising was effective. Another was that advertising had an important and moral role in business and American life.

Many periodicals in which N. W. Ayer and Son placed ads bought space in the agency's directory and the *Guide* to promote themselves as good advertising vehicles. These ads produced only modest revenue for the agency. Most significantly, they produced ongoing grief for Wayland Ayer, who was sensitive to grumbling among publishers of periodicals that they felt coerced to buy space in the publications as a quid pro quo for receiving insertion orders from the agency. This dissatisfaction was fueled by the fact that the agency solicited these ads. Finally, for the 1914 edition, Ayer decided to exclude advertising from the directory. The revenue, although amounting to several hundred thousand dollars a year by then, was not worth the trouble.

Although N. W. Ayer and Son was the first full-service advertising agency, historians quibble over who founded the first advertising agency. Many name Volney B. Palmer, a Boston space broker who set up shop in 1841. In 1877 N. W. Ayer and Son established a lineage to Palmer's agency by purchasing the floundering Coe, Wetherill and Co., which had succeeded Joy, Coe and Co., the agency that had bought out Palmer's. Ayer's purpose was not to establish any lineal claim. The fact was that Coe, Wetherill was an Ayer creditor, and Ayer took over the company to save it from dissolving.

N. W. Ayer and Son's claim as the first full-service advertising agency is rooted in several initiatives that began in the 1880s. Henry McKinney, who had just been named the agency's third partner, traveled to Battle Creek, Michigan, in 1880 to make a pitch for the Nichols-Shepard threshing machine account. The company was lukewarm to changing agencies but agreed to consider Ayer if the agency would generate a detailed proposal. McKinney returned to Philadelphia, wired every state agriculture department for county-by-county data on wheat, oat, rye, and other threshable grain production, then put every agency employee to work correlating the data with local newspaper circulations. After three days and nights, McKinney had assembled a heavy volume which listed the periodicals read by potential Nichols-Shepard customers. The volume, which McKinney carried back to Battle Creek on the next train, was the very first agency market analysis for an advertiser. So impressed were Nichols-Shepard executives that they immediately wired $18,000 to Philadelphia to assure the agency would take the account (Hower, p. 72).

Following up on McKinney's success, N. W. Ayer and Son set up a planning department to study periodicals to determine their value in reaching customers for specific products (Hower, p. 71). This established Ayer as the first agency to move beyond offering only one of the advertising agencies' three Ps, place ment, to become heavily involved in a second P, planning. Today, market surveys are a standard agency service to help clients decide where their advertising will be most effective.

It was with reluctance that N. W. Ayer and Son delved into the third P, preparation. Like most agency people, Ayer went along with the conventional wisdom of the time that the creation of advertisements, including writing and art, appropriately belonged to the clients, because they knew their products and customers better than anyone else. Advertisers were of the same mind and accepted responsibility for creating and preparing ads; some, like the John Wanamaker department store, hired their own copywriters and artists. The agency role in creating messages was limited to boiling down copy to fit and perhaps polishing a phrase. While this arrangement made sense to Ayer, he recognized that a lot of ads were poorly done by advertisers, which worked against their effectiveness. In 1884, in a break from existing practices, N. W. Ayer and Son took total responsibility for writing an ad for Police Plug Tobacco. The bold message, "Chew Police," attracted attention, and it established N. W. Ayer and Son as a pioneer in copywriting. Gradually the agency began doing more creative work. Not until 1892, however, did it hire a full-time copywriter, which historian Frank Luther Mott called "probably the first of his race" (p. 593), and not until 1898 did it hire an artist. Copy preparation was the responsibility of the agency's "business-getting department," as it was called, until 1890, when a separate department was established.

In the meantime, N. W. Ayer and Son was expanding beyond its initial specialty: newspapers. In 1883, when the J. Walter Thompson agency, which monopolized ad placements in magazines, branched into newspapers, Ayer responded by taking on magazine contracts (Fox, p. 31). It was not merely a competitive move. Ayer correctly foresaw great growth ahead in magazines as a national advertising medium (Hower, p. 80). In 1898 Ayer also began placing advertisements on billboards.

Ayer established the Keystone Type Foundry as a subsidiary in 1888 and encouraged the periodicals in which the agency placed ads to use its services. Keystone flourished—but at a price. Some periodicals felt they had to patronize Keystone to remain in N. W. Ayer and Son's good graces and receive the agency's insertion orders. This was much the same problem that Ayer had faced earlier with ads in his publications, and gradually he concluded that the taint could be eliminated only by selling the foundry, which he did in 1917. In the meantime, Keystone's capitalization had increased from an original $10,000 to $1.5 million, and the company had plants in nine cities. In his history of the agency, Ralph Hower says the sale of Keystone, following the earlier issue of ads in Ayer publications, was "the final step in divorcing the agency from all proprietary interests which might possibly color its judgment of advertising media" (p. 88). Hower also notes that the Keystone problem was one only of perception, explaining that agency people who placed ads had no access to information about Keystone's customers.

From the introduction of the open contract in 1876 to the Keystone sale in 1917, Ayer had moved his firm from being just another space broker beholden to the periodicals in which it placed ads to an agency above reproach in its commitment to its clients. This was a lengthy process, and Ayer felt his way gingerly with many innovations. Some came about despite Ayer's reluctance, like offering copywriting and design services. Others, like adding magazines to the agency's repertoire, were at least partly a response to competitive pressure. The 1876 open contract innovation in which Ayer prided himself was partly in answer to a policy of the Rowell agency, dating probably to 1872, of informing clients fully about the circulations, rates, and reputations of periodicals and leaving the decision about placements with them. Rowell made a public announcement of its policy in January 1875, and it was not until late in the year that Ayer tried his open contract ideas with Dinger and Conard, a rose-growing company in West Grove, Pennsylvania.

One N. W. Ayer and Son client was *Ladies' Home Journal*, an upstart magazine in the Cyrus H. K. Curtis empire. The circulation in 1884, after one year in publication, was 50,000. After a six-month Ayer campaign, the circulation doubled. The campaign continued, and the circulation doubled again and again, finally reaching 400,000 in 1889.

Ayer, who had counted Curtis among its clients since 1884, lent significant support to the magazine mogul in 1889 when Curtis expanded *Ladies' Home Journal* to 32 pages, added a cover, and, at considerable risk, doubled the price to $1 a year. Ayer gave Curtis a $200,000 credit in advertising and endorsed $100,000 in Curtis note to buy the paper he needed (Tebbel, p. 337).

Ayer's relationship with Curtis may have influenced him in refusing new accounts for alcoholic beverages and not renewing existing ones. *Ladies' Home Journal* allowed only "clean and safe" advertising which, to Curtis, excluded alcohol. By 1900 no brewers or distillers were among N. W. Ayer and Son clients, and in 1903 the agency also turned away accounts for medicinal port. Other factors that may have contributed to this decision were Ayer's personal moral code and the growing temperance movement (Hower, p. 91).

Patent medicines, however, remained an N. W. Ayer and Son mainstay until 1905, when the agency declined clients who gave their products extravagant claims. This new policy, aimed at patent medicines, may also have resulted from Curtis's influence, but the muckraking exposés against patent medicines, pending government regulation, and Ayer's own moral perspective probably contributed.

The 1905 policy that ended N. W. Ayer's relationship with patent medicine vendors was a sudden turnaround, considering the laxity with which claims had routinely been handled in even the recent past. For example, a 1903 claim for Dr. Davis' Compound Syrup, that it was a "sure cure for consumption," was expanded in 1905, on the eve of the new policy against hyperbolic claims, to include "all cases of consumption, coughs, asthma, influenza, bronchitis, croup, whooping cough, palpitations of the heart." Other accounts had included Oxygen

Compound, for almost any ailment; Rock and Rye, at $4 a gallon a "sure cure for lung diseases"; Kennedy's Ivory Tooth Cement, which made "everyone his own dentist"; and Pino-Palmine mattresses, whose aroma expelled rheumatic and neuralgic pains from the body (Hower, p. 44). Surrendering these accounts cost the agency significant revenue. Paine's Celery Compound was a $400,000-a-year account in the 1890s. In 1900 the Dr. Williams' Pink Pills for Pale People account was worth $216,000.

The incredible success of the newly formed National Biscuit Company in 1898 was due at least in part to N. W. Ayer and Son. Nabisco, as it later came to be known, went to Ayer for a campaign to promote its novel product: biscuits in an airtight package with a freshness and cleanliness not possible with the biscuits bought from most grocers' barrels. Henry McKinney came up with the brand name Uneeda Biscuit, a storm slicker–clad boy as a symbol to denote the moisture-proof quality of the product, and a slogan, "Lest you forget, we say it yet, Uneeda Biscuit." It was catchy, and it worked. Testimony to the name's success was its being widely imitated with product names like Uwanta Beer, Itsagood Soup, and *Ureada* magazine.

In the following years the agency prospered with a growing list of major clients: American Tobacco, H. J. Heinz foods, Simmons Hardware tools, Cluett Peabody collars and shirts, American Sugar Refining, International Silver, and Cadillac automobiles. To service the burgeoning client list, the agency's payroll grew to 160 employees by 1900.

At a time when many agencies were sweatshops, an attraction of N. W. Ayer and Son was that it was a pleasant place to work: no under-the-counter deals to plague employees and managers, friendly relations among employees, and appreciation expressed for good work (Fox, p. 130). The rewards, however, had a price, especially in the early days. Taking a cue from Ayer himself, employees routinely put in ten hours, six days a week, and often returned in the evening. Henry McKinney was an indefatigable dynamo. When George Wallace, whom Ayer had made a partner 14 years earlier, died in 1887 at age 37, overwork was blamed. The toll for being a member of "the family," as Ayer called his employees, was eased over time. In 1900 the agency shut down Saturday afternoons in the summer. In 1906 an employee summer camp was established at Meredith, New York, site of Ayer and McKinney's world-famous dairy and cattle-breeding Meridale Farms. In 1907 the half-day holiday on Saturdays was extended to the whole year, which put N. W. Ayer and Son in the vanguard of improving employee relations. Another new idea, group insurance, was extended to all employees in 1917.

Early in the new century, N. W. Ayer and Son established branches to service distant clients and increase its volume of business: New York, in 1903; Boston, 1905; Chicago, 1910; Cleveland, 1911.

During this period, N. W. Ayer and Son took on three accounts that gave advertising a dimension beyond selling goods and services. After scandal shook New York Mutual Life Insurance in 1905, Ayer undertook a campaign to restore confidence in the company. In 1908 the agency created campaigns to foster goodwill on behalf of American Telephone and Telegraph and Western Union (Griese, pp. 18–23). It was the beginning of "institutional advertising" and a precursor to Ayer's branching into public relations later in the century.

In 1908 the agency established a plans department, which centralized the research that had become a growing part of its work since McKinney's enterprise with the Nichols-Shepard company 30 years earlier. This department probably was the first of its kind at any agency, and its role was solely to study publications to determine their suitability as vehicles for reaching customers for specific products.

Worried that the agency had grown too large for him to manage effectively, Ayer attempted a major reorganization in 1912. He assumed that someone with his energy and drive but without his external commitments, which had become considerable, could do the job. Ayer considered McKinney, but he was not a detail person and his health was uneven. Other managers were good at their jobs, but Ayer doubted whether they could run the whole operation. Ayer hired a general manager from outside the agency and gave him great authority. The decision hurt morale, as did the new manager's approach to running the business. Twenty-four years later, in interviewing employees for his history of the agency, Hower found a reluctance to talk about the period, and Hower himself does not name the manager in his otherwise detailed account.

Over the next four years, the manager focused on improvements in some areas but neglected others, which disturbed Ayer. Ayer also was unsettled about subtle changes in the culture of the agency. The manager's dismissal of some key people encouraged employees to place loyalty in their superiors over loyalty to the agency, which struck at the heart of Ayer's idea of agency employees as "family." Why Ayer allowed the transformation to continue as long as he did might be explained by the agency's continuing prosperity. Ayer also valued being free to pursue newfound interests. Hower says Ayer may not have been able to articulate his own thoughts on what was happening and had therefore been reluctant to fire the man.

In 1916, however, Ayer found his reason in a turn of events that reveals a lot about how Ayer perceived his role as founder and chief executive officer of the agency. The manager, proud of an exceptionally profitable year, asked to be named a partner. Ayer was aghast at the request. Becoming a partner was an honor to be bestowed, not sought. The man resigned, and the agency's internal morale improved for a time with the announcement that Wilfred W. Fry, a junior partner who also was Ayer's son-in-law, would take over.

In the Ayer talent stable for a time was the young Raymond Rubicam, who joined the agency in 1920 as a copywriter. Rubicam was assigned to the Steinway piano account and came up with "The Instrument of the Immortals" slogan. Steinway sales increased almost 70 percent in the 1920s, despite the new home entertainment competition from radio and phonographs. Rubicam scored similar successes with the Rolls-Royce and International Correspondence Schools accounts. Soon he found himself also entrusted with the agency's own advertising and given a 50 percent raise, to $12,000 a year.

Francis Wayland Ayer died on March 5, 1923, at age 75, and the agency went to his son-in-law, Wilfred Fry, whom advertising historian Stephen Fox called "ignorantly complacent" (p. 132). Other observers, including N.S.B. Gras and Hower, have been less unkind to Fry (Hower, pp. xxxii–xxxiii, xxxv–xxxvii). Whatever Fry's competencies, talented people in the creative departments were passed over for partnerships, and morale slipped among artists and copywriters. In 1923 Rubicam, who had been with the agency three and a half years, and an Ayer account executive, John Orr Young, left to form their own agency, and they took some other Ayer talent with them. Young and Rubicam became the leading agency of the post-Ayer generation.

As N. W. Ayer and Son matured after 1900, Ayer spent more time on outside activities, and his presence at the agency became intermittent. Even so, the young Raymond Rubicam felt he knew Ayer well enough to characterize him as "autocratic but benevolent" (Fox p. 130). The model that Ayer gave agency employees was one of purposefulness, which had given the agency its initial successes in 1869. His contemporary George Rowell said Ayer "thinks of work all the time, eats little, drinks nothing but water; has no vices, small or large, unless overwork is a vice" (Fox, p. 21). The historian Fox called him "a paragon of sobriety" who did not participate in or enjoy small talk and displayed little humor (p. 21). This poorly developed sense of humor, combined with shyness, made him seem brusque. Ayer knew his limitations. When asked to be renominated for president of the Merchants National Bank, Ayer deferred to another candidate, saying: "The bank needs a man who can mix with people, and Mr. Law is popular—he goes to bankers' conventions and he meets people and makes friends easily. And you know I can't do that—I can't do that so well" (Cyrus H. K. Curtis, quoted in Hower, p. 119). Hower concluded that Ayer was a victim of his manner and "a comparatively lonely man" (p. 118).

Banking occupied Ayer in his later years. He was largely responsible for building up the Merchants National Bank of Philadelphia; he became a director in 1888 and president in 1895. When Merchants was merged with the First National Bank of Philadelphia, Ayer became chairman of the board.

Ayer also was involved in managing other companies. In the early 1890s the Brown Chemical Company, which made Brown's Iron Bitters, fell on hard times while owing a large sum to N. W. Ayer and Son. Ayer participated in the company's management until it was returned to profitability. He also became involved with the Saratoga Spring Water Company under similar circumstances until it also was turned around.

Ayer was an active Baptist. In 1869, when he was establishing himself in Philadelphia, he joined the North Baptist Church near his parents' home in Camden, and he was promptly named Sunday school superintendent, a position he held until he died. Over the years he became prominent as a Baptist layman and served for 25 years as president of the New Jersey State Baptist Convention and later of the Northern Baptist Convention.

Ayer married twice. He and Rhandena Gilman were wed on May 5, 1875, and they had two daughters: Alice Biddle, who married Hardin H. Wheat and who died in 1904, and Anna Gilman, who married Wilfred Fry. Mrs. Ayer died in 1914. Five years later, on April 21, 1919, Ayer married Martha K. Lawson.

Besides founding an agency that pioneered services that are the bedrock of modern agencies, Wayland Ayer left a respectability to advertising in his legacy. His open contract inspired client confidence. In later years he held to firm standards on accounts his agency would accept. On the 50th anniversary of the agency, ex-President Taft paid this tribute to Ayer: "We are honoring a man who has made advertising a science, and who has robbed it of many evil tendencies, and who has the right to be proud of the record he has made" (quoted in Ayer's *New York Times* obituary, March 6, 1923, p. 21).

Ayer worked hard at spreading the word about the importance of advertising. In 1919 the agency launched a campaign of essays in the *Saturday Evening Post*, the *Literary Digest*, and other publications "to increase public understanding of advertising and enhance its value as a business tool" (*In Behalf*, p. xi). Ayer was convinced that advertising was essential in the national economy. In 1893, writing in a book on modern commerce, Ayer had said: "The development— yes, even the continued existence of every industry described in this work depends upon the dissemination of information concerning it and the resulting knowledge of what it is and what it is doing. Such dissemination of information is advertising" (quoted in Presbrey, p. 341). By 1929, after Ayer's death, the agency reported it had spent $2 million buying space for the essays over ten years, and it reprinted them, all 68, in the book *In Behalf of Advertising*.

George Genzmer, writing in the *Dictionary of American Biography*, summed up Ayer's life, after the founding of the agency in 1869, in this way: "The remaining fifty-four years of Ayer's life saw American advertising grow from a small unintelligent, less than reputable craft into a well organized business that exerted a powerful influence on the national life. To that growth Ayer probably contributed as much as any one man."

FURTHER READING

Works by Ayer:

"Advertising in America." In *One Hundred Years of American Commerce*, edited by Chauncey M. Depew. 1893. Reprint. New York: Greenwood Press, 1968.

Works about Ayer

Appel, Joseph. "A Case Study of an Advertising Agency and Some Observations on Advertising in General." *Bulletin of the Business Historical Society* 13 (October 1939): 49–57.

Barbour, C. A. "F. W. Ayer: An Appreciation." *Watchman Examiner* (March 22, 1923): 361–362.

Cahn, William. *Out of the Cracker Barrel: The Nabisco Story from Animal Crackers to Zuzus.* New York: Simon and Schuster, 1969.

Forbes, B. C. "The Man Who Led Advertising out of Darkness." *Forbes* (July 21, 1923): 475–477, 500–501, 503.

Forty Years in Advertising. Philadelphia: Ayer, 1909.

Fox, Stephen. *The Mirror Makers: A History of American Advertising and Its Creators.* New York: William Morrow, 1984.

Genzmer, George H. "Francis Wayland Ayer." In *Dictionary of American Biography,* edited by Allen Johnson. New York: Charles Scribner's Sons, 1928.

Griese, Noel L. "AT&T: 1908 Origins of the Nation's Oldest Continuous Advertising Campaign." *Journal of Advertising* 6 (3): 18–23.

Hower, Ralph M. *The History of an Advertising Agency: N. W. Ayer and Son at Work, 1869–1949.* Rev. ed. Harvard Studies in Business History, no. 5. Cambridge: Harvard University Press, 1939.

In Behalf of Advertising: A Series of Essays Published in National Periodicals from 1919 to 1928. Philadelphia: N. W. Ayer and Son, 1929.

Mott, Frank Luther. *American Journalism: A History: 1690–1960.* 3d ed. New York: Macmillan, 1962.

Pollay, Richard W., ed. *Information Sources in Advertising History.* Westport, CT: Greenwood Press, 1979.

Presbrey, Frank. *The History and Development of Advertising.* New York: Doubleday, 1929. Reprint. New York: Greenwood Press, 1968.

Rowell, George Presbury. *Forty Years an Advertising Agent, 1865–1905.* New York: Printer's Ink, 1906.

Sandage, C. H., Vernon Fryburger, and Kim Rotzoll. *Advertising Theory and Practice.* 11th ed. Homewood, IL: Richard D. Irwin, 1983.

Tebbel, John. *The Media in America.* New York: Thomas Y. Crowell, 1974.

Wood, James Playsted. *The Story of Advertising.* New York: Ronald Press, 1958.

Wright, John S., and Daniel S. Warner. *Advertising.* New York: McGraw-Hill, 1962.

NOTABLE CLIENTS/CAMPAIGNS

Allen's Anti-Fat Pills (1870s)

Blackwell's Durham tobacco ("See that it bears the trademark of the bull," 1870s)

Bradstreet's reports (1870s)

Burnett's flavoring extracts (1870s)

Ferry seeds (1870s)

Incino ("Guaranteed to grow whiskers on the smoothest face in weeks," 1870s)

John Wanamaker (1870s)

LeFevre diamonds ("The only perfect facsimile of real diamonds in the world," 1870s)

Lewis perfumed lye (1870s)

Lippincott's books (1870s)

Mason and Hamlin organs (1870s)

Montgomery Ward (1870s)

Pond's Extract (1870s)

Psychomancy ("How either sex may fascinate and gain the love and affection of any person they choose, instantly," 1870s)

Singer sewing machines (1870s)

Whitman's chocolates (1870s)

Jay Cooke (1871)

Dinger and Conard (first open contract, 1875)

Burpee seeds (1880s)

Curtis magazines, including *Ladies' Home Journal* (1880s)

Henry Timken machinery (1880s)

Hires root beer (1880s)

J. I. Case threshers (1880s)

Nichols-Shepard threshers (first agency research, 1880s)

Procter and Gamble (1880s)

Police chewing tobacco (first agency-created advertisement, 1884)

Dr. Williams' Pink Pills for Pale People (1890s)

Mellin's baby foods (1890s)

N. K. Fairbanks (Fairy Soap, Cottolene, Gold Dust, 1890s)

National Biscuit Company ("Uneeda Biscuit," 1898)

Standard Oil (and several subsidiaries, including Mica axle grease and Glucose Sugar Refining Company, 1898)

American Sugar Refining Company (1900s)

American Tobacco (1900s)

Cadillac (1900s)

Cluett Peabody collars and shirts (1900s)

H. J. Heinz (1900s)

International Silver Company (1900s)

Simmons hardware (Keen Kutter tools, 1900s)

Dr. Davis' Compound Syrup ("Sure cure for consumption," 1903)

New York Life Insurance (1905)

American Telephone and Telegraph (1908)

International Correspondence Schools (1920s)

Rolls-Royce (1920s)

Steinway pianos ("Instrument of the immortals," 1920s)

BRUCE FAIRCHILD BARTON
(August 5, 1886–July 5, 1967)

Donald L. Thompson

Bruce Barton, by his own admission, never looked at advertising as his life's work. Even though he was a founding partner of one of the country's largest advertising agencies, his main focus was on his free-lance literary endeavors. Nevertheless, Barton's flair for copywriting made him a strong creative influence in his agency, which built an impressive list of clients largely on the basis of its copy strength. A man of many talents, Barton's main contribution to the advertising field was his ability to develop creative and effective advertising and image-building campaigns, and to communicate those talents to those who worked in the agency he helped found.

Barton was born in Robbins, Tennessee, on August 5, 1886, the son of William Eleazer Barton and Esther Treat (Bushnell) Barton. His earliest years were spent in rural Tennessee, where his mother was a schoolteacher and his father a circuit-riding preacher. One biographer suggests that in later life Barton tended to exaggerate the impact that rural poverty had on him during his formative years (Fox, p. 102). In fact, his father soon moved on to a comfortable suburban Chicago ministry in Oak Park, Illinois. And, at an early age, Barton's entrepreneurial proclivities were to manifest themselves. By age nine he had a paper route, and by the time he was 16 he was making $600 a year selling maple syrup from his uncle's farm.

After receiving his diploma from the public high school in Oak Park in 1903, he matriculated at Berea College in Kentucky. He later transferred to Amherst College, from which he was graduated with Phi Beta Kappa honors in 1907, being voted the most likely to succeed in his class. Despite his accomplishments, his postgraduate job search was made difficult by the fact that the country was in a severe recession at the time. The only employment he could find was as a timekeeper in a Montana railroad camp. After a few months he moved to Chicago, where he became managing editor of *Home Herald*, a small religious newspaper which failed in 1909. In 1910 he obtained a similar post at *Housekeeper* magazine, which also failed the following year.

Seeking to improve his luck, in 1912 Barton moved from Chicago to New York, where he obtained a job as assistant sales manager for the popular *Collier's* magazine, a muckraking journal which ran many attacks on advertising. More so than in his previous positions, Bruce Barton now found himself in the mainstream of print media advertising. One of his early challenges was to develop a direct-response ad campaign to sell the Harvard Classics, "Dr. Eliot's Five-Foot Shelf of Books." (The collected classics selected by Harvard President Charles W. Eliot had not been selling too well.) To fill a vacant quarter-page, Barton opened one of the books "almost at random," tore out a picture of Marie Antoinette in a tumbrel, and dashed off an ad with this headline: "This is Marie Antoinette riding to her death. Have you ever read her tragic story?" (Fox, p. 103). Thus started a campaign that produced many ads which are classics in the history of American advertising, and which sold more than 400,000 sets of the books, making the claim that by reading them only 15 minutes a day one could "earn more and enjoy life more than many college men."

On October 2, 1913, in Oak Park, Barton married Esther Maude Randall. They later had three children: Randall, Betsey Alice, and Bruce Jr.

In 1914 Barton moved on to become editor of *Every Week*, a three-cent weekly published by the Crowell Publishing Company, to which he contributed an inspirational essay in each issue. He also collaborated with an aspiring young artist, Norman Rockwell, who did the illustrations for a campaign for Edison Mazda light bulbs. His first book, *More Power to You; Fifty Editorials from Every Week*, was published in 1917. In 1918 *Redbook* hired Barton to write editorials under an exclusive contract, and in 1920 he published another collection of his essays, *It's a Good Old World*.

Barton's later career was significantly influenced by the volunteer work he did during World War I for the United War Work Campaign, a consolidated fund-raising effort on the behalf of a variety of nonprofit organizations. For the Salvation Army Barton coined one of his most famous, widely remembered slogans: "A man may be down, but he is never out!"

Barton's wartime fund-raising activities, which were to raise some $220 million, also brought him into contact with two other ad men of the time, Roy Durstine from Buffalo, New York, and Alex Osborn, a former newspaperman who had worked briefly for Calkins and Holden. Late in 1918 Durstine and Osborn asked Barton to join them in organizing their own ad agency in New York, Barton, Durstine and Osborn, with Barton as president. At the time, Barton later recalled, "I had never thought of advertising as a life work, though I had, on the side, written some very successful copy" (Fox, p. 104). Barton looked on the agency as allowing him the time to write free-lance articles, and to make enough money in 15 years so that he could then pursue another career in teaching, politics, or whatever. In September 1928 the young agency merged with the George Batten Company to form Batten, Barton, Durstine and Osborn (BBDO), with Barton as chairman of the board. This agency, which was later to become one of the largest in the world, within four years of its founding had a distinguished client list including General Electric, General Motors, Dunlop Tires, Lever Brothers, and U.S. Steel. Unlike many agencies, BBDO favored college graduates who demonstrated writing ability and who could write the terse, powerful copy for which the agency became famous.

In the early years, Barton was a strong creative influence in the agency. He created the character Betty Crocker, and he sought to improve U.S. Steel's image with a series of ads that built up the personal accomplishments of its founder, Andrew Carnegie ("He came to a land of wooden towns and left a nation of steel").

As widely known as Bruce Barton became for his work as an advertising professional, in the 1920s he was to become a national celebrity with the publication of *The Man Nobody Knows* (1925). This book, which reflected his early background and personal religious beliefs, was based on serialized installments that had appeared in the *Woman's Home Companion*, and it portrayed Jesus Christ as a salesman and advertising man. Despite its controversial nature, the book was an instant success, topping the nonfiction best-seller lists for two years. In it, Jesus, a masculine, friendly man, used all the techniques of the adman: persuasion, recruiting followers, impassioned speeches, and the principles of applied salesmanship.

The book's immense popularity was based, in part, on the fact that it reflected a popular view at the time—that religious faith was not unrelated to success in business. In any event, the book does not bear up well when critically evaluated from the standpoints of literary style or historical accuracy. In 1927 Barton sought to capitalize on the success of his earlier book by publishing *The Book Nobody Knows*, a story of the Bible. This and two later books on religious themes were notably unsuccessful.

Despite his short-lived success as an author concerned directly with religious themes, during the 1920s Barton developed his literary talents in a number of different directions. He wrote syndicated newspaper columns and continued with the publication of his collected inspirational pieces: *Better Days* (1924) and *On the Up and Up* (1929). He was a frequent contributor to magazines such as *Good Housekeeping, Reader's Digest, Woman's Home Companion,* and *Cosmopolitan.*

As positive and upbeat as his writing might have been at the time, there is also the suggestion that the 1920s were a period of soul-searching for Bruce Barton, leading to his progressive disenchantment with the values and norms of contemporary American society. For example, in a 1926 letter to a friend, he wrote: "It seems to me that a very large percent of the current advertising is merely representative of the most wasteful phases of the competitive system" (Garraty and Carnes, eds., p. 27). In a definitive work on the role of advertising in the American economy, Barton is cited as having remarked upon observing a crowd of women shoppers at a sale how "dreadful" it was to see them wasting their husbands' earnings (Marchand, p. 159). The same author also reports on Barton's comments in 1934, at the height of the Great Depression, concerning "silly advertisements, dishonest advertisements, disgusting advertisements . . . which have turned advertising into a circus" (p. 317).

The 1920s were also a period of personal crisis for Bruce Barton. One biographer describes him in these terms: "He worked hard juggling his two careers, always pushing and driving himself forward. . . . Beneath the surface charm he was edgy, running on a tightly wound spring. For years he suffered off and on from insomnia" (Fox, p. 110).

In 1928, subject to extreme pressures, Barton checked himself into a sanitarium. One possible explanation for his mental state at the time came to light in a 1932 court case, in which Barton charged his former mistress, Frances King, with blackmail for her request for $50,000 to suppress publication of a novel she had written about the sexual exploits of an advertising man. Despite a noticeable lack of newspaper coverage of the trial, Barton's marital infidelity became common knowledge, which emerged as inconsistent with his public advocacy of Christian beliefs. Barton's wife stuck with him through the trial, which resulted in a guilty verdict for the defendant. The following spring Barton and his family went on an extended trip to the Far East and India, during which he contemplated his future.

Given his record of accomplishment and his willingness to act on the basis of his beliefs, Barton's decision to enter into the world of politics was not totally unpredictable. Indeed, on both a volunteer and paid basis, he was one of the first advertising professionals to apply his skills to nonprofit and political marketing. What was surprising, however, was the intensely emotional and personal degree of his espousal of conservative Republican views. The focal points of his attacks were liberal Democrats, as typified by President Franklin Delano Roosevelt, and liberal Democratic programs, such as the New Deal.

His disenchantment with liberal thinking is illustrated by a satirical 1931 article he wrote for *Vanity Fair*, "How to Fix Everything." His frame of reference was the fact that he had recently celebrated his 45th birthday. To solve the problems of the Depression, he argued, the federal government should retire everyone at 45 and pay them one-half of what they had been making at the time.

In 1936, representing Manhattan's affluent "silk stocking" legislative district, Bruce Barton was elected to the first of two terms in Congress. Questions have been raised concerning the wisdom and long-run effectiveness of his intensely personal political style. For example, in a 1932 letter to then President Hoover, he called F.D.R. "just a name and a crutch" (McElvaine, p. 313). Barton's elected political career ended in 1940 with his unsuccessful bid for a senate seat from New York. However, he was extremely active in his advocacy of Wendell Willkie as the Republican Party's standard bearer in the 1940 presidential campaign. More use was made of modern advertising and marketing techniques in this campaign than in any previously. In fact, it has been charged that Barton's media hype was the key consideration in swinging the nomination to Willkie, not originally a front-runner (McElvaine, p. 314). Barton's tactics also invited retaliation from the Democrats at their national convention, when F.D.R. himself introduced a slogan that was repeatedly chanted and later used effectively in the campaign—"Martin, Barton and Fish!"—derisive of what were portrayed as the three most arch-conservative backers of the Republican candidate (McElvaine, p. 319).

With the end of his political career and the Democratic victory of 1940, Barton's primary energies once again focused on the agency that bore his name. He served as chairman of the board until his retirement in 1961. During this period he developed a reputation for being somewhat autocratic and difficult to work with, to the point that every year at the annual BBDO stockholders' meeting, he reminded those present (including 250 of the agency's own employees) that they could throw him out anytime they wished. It is appropriate to the multifaceted contributions that Barton made to American society that they never took him up on his offer.

Despite his, at times, disenchantment with the world of advertising as he knew it, Barton never lost his fundamental faith in the free enterprise system and in the possibilities for improvement. Even though he was displeased with what he saw and experienced along the way, his overall view of advertising is best summarized in his own words: "Advertising has been 'voted' for, and elected as the method by which people want to learn what to buy" (*Advertising Campaigns*, p. 20). He looked on advertising agencies and copywriters as playing a facilitating role in that their ultimate responsibility was to "interpret, and cater to, the consumer viewpoint." The ultimate objective, he argued, was for people "to exercise the right of free choice—in their food, their clothes, their books, their homes . . . the very essence of Democracy" (Mayer, p. 321).

Throughout his life Bruce Barton gave much of his time and talents to charitable and civic organizations, helping them to use advertising and promotional techniques to raise funds and obtain public support for their programs. These included the American Heart Association, the United Negro College Fund, and the Institute for the Crippled and the Disabled. At the time of his death, he was active in a wide range of organizations, including the *New York Herald–Tribune* Fresh Air fund, the American Heart Association, the Columbia-Presbyterian Medical Center, the National Urban League, Deerfield (Mass.) Academy, and Berea College.

Printers's Ink awarded Barton the gold medal for advertising in 1960. His campaigns and ads have won too many awards to mention. He was awarded two honorary degrees during his lifetime, from Juniata College in 1925 and from Amherst College in 1957.

On July 5, 1967, exactly one month short of his 81st birthday, Bruce Barton died in New York, where he had first made his home some 55 years previously. He was buried in his adopted city.

FURTHER READING

Selected Works by Barton

Advertising Campaigns, with Bernard Lichtenberg. New York: Alexander Hamilton Institute, 1930.
Another Boy: The Story of the Birth at Bethlehem. Minneapolis: Buckbee-Brehm, 1930.
Better Days. New York and London: Century, 1924.
The Book Nobody Knows. Indianapolis: Bobbs-Merrill, 1926.
Business Correspondence, with Charles W. Hurd. New York: Alexander Hamilton Institute, 1921.
He Upset the World. Indianapolis: Bobbs-Merrill, 1932.
It's a Good Old World. New York: Century, 1920.
The Man Nobody Knows: A Discovery of the Real Jesus. Indianapolis and New York: Bobbs-Merrill, Review of Reviews, 1925.
The Man of Galilee: Twelve Scenes from the Life of Christ. New York: Cosmopolitan Books, 1928.
More Power to You: Fifty Editorials from Every Week. New York: Century, 1917.
On the Up and Up. Indianapolis: Bobbs-Merrill, 1929.
A Parade of the States. Forward by Alfred P. Sloan, Jr. Garden City, NY: Doubleday, Doran and Co., 1932.
The Resurrection of Saul as Described by an Eye-Witness. New York: Pilgrim Press, 1912.
What Can a Man Believe? Indianapolis: Bobbs-Merrill, 1927.
The Woman Who Came at Night: Being the Experiences of a Minister. Boston and New York: Pilgrim Press, 1914.
A Young Man's Jesus. Boston and New York: Pilgrim Press, 1914.

Works about Barton

"Bruce Barton." In *Who Was Who in America*. Vol. 4. Chicago: A. N. Marquis, 1968.
"Bruce Fairchild Barton." In *Dictionary of American Biography. Supp. 8: 1966–1970*, edited by John A. Garraty and Mark C. Carnes. New York: Charles Scribner's Sons, 1988.
Fox, Stephen. *The Mirror Makers: A History of American Advertising and Its Creators*. New York: William Morrow, 1984.
McElvaine, Robert S. *The Great Depression: America, 1929–41*. New York: New York Times Books, 1984.
Marchand, Roland. *Advertising: The American Dream*. Berkeley: University of California Press, 1985.
Mayer, Martin. *Madison Avenue U.S.A.* New York: Harper, 1958.
Schlesinger, Arthur M., Jr. *The Age of Roosevelt: The Politics of Upheaval*. Boston: Houghton-Mifflin, 1960.

NOTABLE CLIENTS/CAMPAIGNS

Alexander Hamilton Institute
American Radiator Company

Dunlop Tire
Edison Mazda
General Electric
General Mills
General Motors
Harvard Classics
Lever Brothers
Macy's
The Salvation Army
U.S. Steel
YMCA
YWCA

CHARLES AUSTIN BATES
(August 18, 1866–?)

Ted Curtis Smythe

Charles Austin Bates rose like a comet in the advertising field of late–19th-century New York, sputtered after attracting attention, then left the field to develop a career as a financier and promoter of businesses from mortgage offerings to marble quarries to railroad operations. But during his decade-long career in advertising, he was a persistent self-promoter, a prolific writer, enthusiastic if not fanatic about copywriting, and a proponent of trained artists in advertising layout. These skills, coupled with his training of several young men, gave him an impact on the field far beyond the reach of his own contributions to any particular company or product.

Born August 18, 1866, in Indianapolis and educated in the public schools of that city, Bates began work in a retail bookstore before starting his own printing business at age 20. He made a success of it for seven years, during which time he married Belle Brandenburg of Chicago. Three years after his marriage he moved to New York.

Bates had prepared himself, if we can call it preparation, for the move during the previous three years. He bought *The Indianapolis Leader*, a populist weekly, in 1890 and with it got a subscription to *Printer's Ink*. Reading there of John E. Powers's success with the Wanamaker department store, he began writing advertising for small accounts in his area, charging 25 cents per ad. He also became advertising manager for a local department store. He wrote copy for *Printer's Ink*, and when it was praised he was encouraged to see if the big city was too large for this Indianapolis neophyte. Placing five ads in the advertising trade paper, he received enough interest from potential clients to move to New York.

Upon his arrival, Bates began writing advertising copy for retail and manufacturers. He quickly connected with *Printer's Ink*, where he began publishing a "Department of Criticism." Some of these articles or comments appeared in *Good Advertising*, a 600-page book published in 1896, only three years after he arrived in the city. Bates was a prolific writer and self-promoter, though he considered himself first and foremost a businessman, never a literary figure (*Good Advertising*, p. 29).

Since copywriting was a growing field at the time, Bates naturally gravitated toward it. His work in *Printer's Ink* gave him the credibility his experience did not. He established an interest in Bates-Whitman, a general advertising agency, but he also wrote for other agencies when they needed his copywriting skills. Bates-Whitman appears to have been what we now would call an advertising boutique, in that Bates offered specialized services, in this case copywriting and illustrations. In 1903 he incorporated as the Bates Agency, although he sold his interest shortly after.

Bates never wrote an autobiography, but his philosophy of advertising as well as hints at his background appear in his published works on advertising. This is especially true of *Good Advertising*.

Frank Presbrey acknowledged Bates as one of the pioneer free-lance advertising writers of the 1890–1910 era, largely for his work on behalf of honesty in advertising and for his numerous books (pp. 309–11). Bates produced copy for national advertisers and retailers who would solicit his services through the mail. They would contract for $100 a day plus expenses, a large sum in this era, though he would also write advertisements for a fee per ad, much less than $100 daily. When one manufacturer claimed a specialist he had used was not worth his pay, Bates remarked that the manufacturer probably had not used his "expert" correctly. It was incumbent upon the manufacturer to provide copywriters—or "ad-smiths," as Bates sometimes referred to them—with all of the information possible about the product and previous advertising. Even for advertising written for retailers some distance from New York, Bates pumped for information about the media, the kind of customers the retailer was trying to reach, and his objectives—whether he wanted immediate sales or customer traffic (*Good Advertising*, pp. 31–33). In 1896, only three years after arriving in New York, Bates claimed one-fourth of his billings were in retail, the rest in general advertising, including trade papers.

More important, Bates firmly believed in truth in advertising. In this he followed John E. Powers, copywriter for John Wanamaker. Bates recognized the obligation he and other copywriters were under to Powers, writing at one time: "I think I may safely say that Powers's influence is responsible for honesty in advertising—not because we are inherently virtuous but because we have found that it pays. Powers did not fail to consider fully the ultimate consumer; and there is where he founded the profession of advertising, as it likes to think itself today" (quoted in Presbrey, p. 310).

Bates promoted his views in his columns, books, and speeches. Writing in 1895, he asserted that "advertisements represent goods," and because they do, the best advertisement is the one that most accurately represents the goods.

Advertising which misrepresents, either by exaggeration or by inadequacy, is bad advertising. . . . Real, honest, scrupulous truthfulness in advertising becomes more and more prevalent as the years go by. . . . It was so uncommon [five years ago] that even now there are many people who believe that all advertising is more or less disreputable and dishonest. . . . There are still many inaccuracies in advertisements. There is still much exaggeration. (*Good Advertising*, p. 2)

If he was not ahead of his time, Bates certainly was in the vanguard of those advertising agents who understood the fundamental characteristics of the craft. He recognized that the first duty of an advertisement was to attract the attention of the reader. The headline was integral to the ad, both to capture attention and to get the reader into the advertisement itself. Writing was to be spare and to concentrate on the salient features of the product that were most attractive to the reader. Early in his career he favored the ad that concentrated on copy rather than display; before he left the field he seems to have shifted his emphasis to display advertising, showing he was capable of learning and adapting to a changing field. In fact, his agency was one of the first to have an art director or artist on staff.

He was progressive in certain business practices too. He would not accept competitors' clients, arguing it would not be fair to either. Nor would he mention a competitor in his ads.

Good copywriting was not that difficult, Bates believed, but he felt the attention given to technique (rules of measuring space, size of type, grammar, use of borders, etc.) reflected ignorance of what it was that set the good copywriter, or "advertising expert," apart from the "charlatan and ignoramus." He wrote: "The ability of the true advertising expert is founded on a lifetime study of human nature, a thorough knowledge of every department of the advertising business, and the power to express, in the right words, the message which the advertiser intends for the public" (*Good Advertising*, pp. 52–53). He backed up his belief by advertising himself and his agency extensively.

His business grew until Bates reportedly was earning well over $20,000 annually. Earnest Elmo Calkins and Ralph Holden, both of whom became important figures in New York advertising, started under Bates. Calkins, who was a copywriter whose work had caught Bates's attention, was hired in 1897 and worked for him for five years. Bates counseled the spare approach to writing, true to the Powers model, at a time when advertising was beginning to shift in emphasis to art and design. The Bates agency had George Ethridge as artist and layout designer, one of the earliest in the field, who remained in advertising for years.

In 1899 Bates bought controlling shares in a patent medicine, Laxacola, but he was unable to make it a success. This was the era of muckraking and vigorous attacks on the patent medicine industry. Other advertisers also entered this field and failed during the same period. It was, perhaps, a matter of poor timing rather than poor advertising.

Bates probably closed his agency late in 1903 and entered an entirely different business, forming the Knickerbocker Syndicate to promote and finance businesses. During the next several years he organized the Fidelity Bond and Mortgage Company, later becoming its president, was chairman of the executive committee of the Colorado-Yule Marble Company and the Rutherford Rubber Company, and was vice president of the Crystal River and San Juan Railroad, which served the marble quarry. His skills in promotion were used in his new enterprises just as he had used them in building a widespread reputation for himself as a copywriter.

Perhaps Bates's greatest contribution to the advertising field lay in his criticism and his publications, which broadened the literature in the field, such as it was, and allowed many businesses to improve their advertising. That, coupled with his incessant self-promotion, attracted attention to the copywriting side of the business, helping to make advertisers conscious of the need for general-service advertising agencies. His training of Calkins, Ethridge, and Holden bore fruit in the next several decades, especially as Calkins wrote extensively on advertising, having learned well from Charles Austin Bates.

FURTHER READING

Works by Bates

The Art and Literature of Business. 6 vols. New York: Bates, 1902.
"Department of Criticism," a regular column appearing in *Printer's Ink*, beginning sometime in 1896 or 1897.
Good Advertising. New York: Holmes, 1896.
Short Talks on Advertising. N.p., 1899.

Works about Bates

Fox, Stephen. *The Mirror Makers. A History of American Advertising and Its Creators.* New York: William Morrow, 1984.
The National Cyclopedia of American Biography. New York: James T. White, 1916.
Presbrey, Frank. *The History and Development of Advertising.* Garden City, NY: Doubleday, 1929. Reprint. New York: Greenwood Press, 1968.
Who Was Who in America. Vol. 4. Chicago: A. N. Marquis Co., 1968.

NOTABLE CLIENTS/CAMPAIGNS

Bates wrote for numerous retailers, national goods manufacturers, and other agencies.

THEODORE LEWIS BATES
(September 11, 1901–May 30, 1972)

Richard W. Easley, Marjorie J. Cooper, and
Charles S. Madden

Inconspicuous. Invisible. Publicity shy. Reserved. Retiring. Ironic as it may seem, these words are commonly used to describe one of the advertising industry's most well-known members. In an industry characterized (indeed *driven*) by flamboyance, Ted Bates was most certainly an anomaly.

Theodore Lewis Bates, born in New Haven, Connecticut, on September 11, 1901, was the only child of Vernal Warner (a wholesale distributor of poultry products) and Elizabeth Hailes Bates. His early schooling was in the public system in New Haven and at Phillips-Andover Academy in Massachusetts. After graduating with a bachelor of science degree from Yale in 1924, Bates began employment with the Chase National Bank in New York by doing such noteworthy tasks as cleaning desks and riding in the bank's armored cars. For his efforts, the company paid him the pricely sum of $80 a month.

In the early part of the century, advertising as a career was perceived very differently than it is today. Such was the case when the advertising manager at Chase National was stricken with double pneumonia, and the young, inexperienced Ted Bates was told by management to "handle" the position. This was quite a leap of faith for an employee whose only prior experience had been menial tasks within the organization. However, Bates was successful in the temporary position thanks, in large part, to the assistance provided by one of his female assistants in the department who had more experience. After a time it became clear that the original advertising manager would not be returning, and the young neophyte from Yale was named to his vacated post in the company, with a salary of $160 per month.

Ted Bates' rise from humble beginnings at Chase lasted only a little over a year when he was convinced, first by William H. Johnson, and later by George Batten, that, if he was serious about the advertising profession, he should work at a "real" full-fledged agency. He subsequently accepted a position at the George Batten Company (which eventually merged to become Batten, Barton,

Durstine and Osborn, or BBDO). In accepting the new job, Bates took a $60 pay cut per month and again began as a general assistant, doing menial work such as sweeping floors and keeping time sheets.

Bates progressed in the George Batten Company from general assistant to copywriter to a combination account executive and copywriter to vice president and account supervisor—a position he held until 1935. During his years at BBDO (the merger took place during his tenure there), he ultimately worked with the people at Continental Baking, a relationship which began as a result of another account executive's poor handling of the account. This fortuitous chance encounter would later prove to be pivotal in Bates's advertising career.

Benton and Bowles was the next stop on Ted Bates's career path when he became an account executive and copywriter there in 1935. His introduction to this agency was accomplished through his relationship with Chester Bowles, an old copywriting partner from the George Batten Company and one of the two principals in the agency. Bates's first assignment involved the Colgate-Palmolive account, and eighteen months later Continental Baking moved its account to his new agency.

During the next four years management at both Colgate-Palmolive and Continental Baking became increasingly frustrated at Benton and Bowles because the principals were not giving the accounts the attention that they felt was deserved. Both companies approached Ted Bates with an offer to give him their business if he would open his own agency. So, in December 1940, the Ted Bates Company opened its doors with $2.9 million in billings from only two accounts. These lucrative accounts were not the only defectors from Benton and Bowles: Thomas J. Carnese, Walker G. Everett, Clinton S. Ferris, Clifford N. Parsells, Rosser Reeves, and Edgar P. Small also jumped ship and became charter employees of the newly formed Ted Bates Company.

In the ten years that followed the opening of the agency, billings grew to over $25 million. This represented a 762 percent increase in billings for the agency when, during the same period, the industry average rose only 272 percent. Two factors are usually cited as the primary reasons for the phenomenal early successes of the Ted Bates Company: an intense dedication to teamwork and the "unique selling proposition" (USP). Ted Bates was a great believer in exploiting the potential of employees in his organization; a quotation of his from *Advertising Age* (June 5, 1972, p. 69) perhaps best illustrates the point:

Anybody who sits behind his desk and fears the next guy, or the man under him, is a fool. You should always remember that in a service business you must have the very best people you can get working for you. You have to know how to associate with your peers, so you can help them bring out their best. . . . Remember, if a campaign succeeds, there is plenty of glory for the whole agency—everybody in it.

In keeping with his philosophy toward the work environment and its effect on productivity, Bates converted his agency in 1948 into a 100 percent partnership, with 14 partners having equal control. Again, this step was taken to ensure the success of the company by assuring the new partners of their importance to the organization.

The second factor that contributed to the success of the Ted Bates Company was the unique selling proposition (USP)—a phrase coined by Rosser Reeves, who was a driving force in the company. The concept of the USP (many critics described the approach as "hard-sell") was especially timely in the field due to the concurrent and widespread adoption of a new technology—television, which was the ideal medium for the company's advertising philosophy.

Reeves was a firm believer that a product could not successfully be sold (over the long term) unless it was good. However, this was a necessary but not sufficient condition for the Ted Bates Company to sell a product. The company also had to find the USP for the product, which required three criteria: (1) a definite proposition (i.e., buy this product and get this benefit); (2) the proposition must be unique (competitors either cannot or do not offer the proposition); and (3) the proposition must sell.

Reeves correctly felt that criterion one was so basic to advertising that it should not even have to be spelled out. It is amazing, however, that to this day, this criterion is often violated in advertising.

Criterion two, in many cases, simply means being there first with a specific claim. For example, many of the agency's product classes (e.g., aspirin) are, in the eyes of many, commodities in that there are no "real" differences among them. Certainly, Rosser Reeves was expressing the Ted Bates philosophy concerning this when he stated: "Our problem is—a client comes into my office and throws two newly minted half-dollars onto my desk and says, 'Mine is the one on the left. You prove it's better' " (Mayer, p. 53). What the Ted Bates Company does frequently is imply "perceived" differences between their clients' products and those of competitors. Examples of this practice abound, with the Colgate toothpaste USP as a case in point. The original positioning statement for this product was that "it cleans your breath while it cleans your teeth." Now, it would be hard to argue that other toothpastes do not do the same thing, but Colgate was the first to be advertised with this USP. The Ted Bates Company, therefore, preempted the competition with respect to this claim. Another example is Anacin. The advertising for this product criticized "Brand X" (other brands of aspirin) while, at the same time, trumpeting Anacin for having the "pain reliever that doctors recommend most" (which is, surprise!—aspirin).

The Ted Bates agency was also well-known for its extensive repetition of advertisements. It spent large sums of money in developing its unique selling propositions; therefore, once developed, the ads (or slight derivatives) were very likely to be utilized extensively. As Ted Bates said, "It [an idea] will be good for an indefinite length of time. You might quibble with this, but I'd say it *never* wears out; you might put a new dress on it, that's all" (Mayer, p. 52).

However, this approach was not without its critics, most notably clients of the Ted Bates Company who were paying the agency a commission each time an ad was run. It is not hard to understand how a client could resent the practice of paying continuing commissions for work that, in their minds, was paid for months or even years prior to the multiple ad insertions. Rosser Reeves gave perhaps the best justification for this practice:

I had a client down in the Caribbean with me on a boat and he said to me, more or less joking you understand, "You have 700 people in that office of yours, and you've been running the same ad for the last 11 years. What I want to know is, what are those 700 people supposed to be *doing*?" I told him, "They're keeping your advertising department from changing your ad." ("Inside Ted Bates," p. 33)

There was also criticism from circles within the advertising industry. For example, George Gribbin, in a speech to the Advertising Writers Association of New York, noted that "Bates' Anacin 'fast, fast, fast' commercial belongs to the 'pneumatic-drill or nothing-succeeds-like-excess school of word-play.' " He also stated in the same speech that Rosser Reeves' book *Reality in Advertising* had "almost nothing to do with advertising" ("Inside Ted Bates," p. 31). Other criticisms directed at the agency include, "You can always tell a Bates ad by the white coat [of the expert]" and the Bates technique is "the philosophy of the uncheckable claim."

Though the tactics used by the agency were, without question, very successful for both it and its clients, Ted Bates was acutely aware of their contribution to the widespread criticism of the advertising industry. His feelings toward this criticism are best understood through the following quote: "Much of this criticism emanates from the academic community and comes from people who don't really understand advertising. They think of advertising as an added cost to products. They fail to understand that advertising creates sales volume that, in turn, lowers prices for the consumer. Advertising has become a convenient whipping boy for people who are suspicious of the free enterprise system" (Bart, p. 44). To help enhance the image of his industry, Bates was an active member of the Advertising Council, which promotes the use of advertising talents for public service projects.

Ted Bates died on May 30, 1972, of a heart attack, which occurred while playing bridge with friends. At the time of his death, he was a director and honorary chairman of the Ted Bates Company, which ranked fifth in the world with annual billings of $425 million (approximately $200 million from U.S. accounts). In 1982 the American Advertising Federation (AAF) elected Bates (along with Charles Brower and Bernice Fitz-Gibbon) to the Advertising Hall of Fame.

It is perhaps fitting that Ted's funeral service was held on Madison Avenue, at the St. James Church.

FURTHER READING

Works about Bates

Advertising Today/Yesterday/Tomorrow. New York: McGraw Hill, 1963.

Bart, Peter. "Advertising: An Interview with Ted Bates." *New York Times* (January 2, 1962): 44.

Buxton, Edward. *Creative People at Work.* New York: Executive Communications, 1975.

Fox, Stephen. *The Mirror Makers: A History of American Advertising and Its Creators.* New York: William Morrow, 1984.

Higgins, Denis. "Ad Business Is Pretty Human, Says Ted Bates." *Advertising Age* (December 20, 1965): 40.

"Inside Ted Bates & Co." *Printer's Ink* (April 20, 1962): 31–34.

Mayer, Martin. *Madison Avenue, U.S.A..* New York: Harper, 1958.

"Story of Ted Bates & Company." *Advertising Agency* 45, no. 11 (November 1952): 65–67, 100.

"Ted Bates & Company: A 10-Year Report." *Tide* (1950): 23–26.

"Ted Bates: A Quiet Adman, Is Dead at 70." *Advertising Age* (June 5, 1972): 8, 69.

"Theodore Lewis Bates." In *The National Cyclopedia of American Biography.* Clifton, NJ: James T. White, 1979.

NOTABLE CLIENTS/CAMPAIGNS

Anacin

Blue Bonnet margarine

Carter's Little Liver Pills

Colgate-Palmolive

Domino sugar

Fleischmann's gin

Hostess Cup Cakes

Kool cigarettes

Minute Maid orange juice

Viceroy cigarettes

Wonder Bread

GEORGE BATTEN
(1854–February 16, 1918)

Sammy R. Danna

George Batten founded the George Batten Newspaper Advertising Agency in 1891. He gained experience as an advertising manager working for Funk and Wagnalls publications and at N. W. Ayer and Son in Philadelphia. Unlike some other firms, he made sure that control of his company would never pass by inheritance but only via appointment of the firm's officers, raised from within the organization itself. He felt that his successor should uphold the beliefs on which his company was founded and built.

Batten was born in 1854 on a farm in Gloucester County, New Jersey, to Thomas G. Batten, a minister, and Emmeline Zane Batten. His American ancestry dates back to pre-Revolutionary times. He wore the ribbon of the Sons of the American Revolution (SAR) with a great pride almost bordering on fanaticism.

Batten was a tall man. He was described as "Lincolnesque" by his former secretary, Margaret Hopkins. He retained a relatively full head of hair through the years, and wore a brush moustache and steel-rimmed spectacles; in photographs he has a certain Teddy Roosevelt–like appearance.

On March 15, 1891, Batten opened an advertising agency in the Potter Building at 38 Park Row in New York. He had one employee, Miss Hopkins, but initially he had no clients. His principal asset appears to have been a "vast, mental storehouse of indignation." This was confirmed in a 1980 speech by retired BBDO chairman Tom Dillon to the international partners meeting.

First, let me tell you about George Batten. Many of his contemporaries believed he had not only one "bat" in his name, but a lot more of them flying in and out of his belfry.

The son of a minister, he was imbued with Christian principles and a clear mandate from the Lord to put them into practice . . . his humorless eyes peered through steel-rimmed glasses at a world that he generally found ignorant, incompetent, lazy, unpatriotic and dishonest. . . . His first ad [for the Macbeth Lamp Chimney Company] took pains to point out that if you dropped the glass chimney, it would break—a fact that must have been known to every child over four years old. . . . If your advertising was handled by George Batten, you were not going to fool the public. (Dillon, p. S–40)

Batten was "a stickler for doing things right, and at once. He had no use for words unless they meant something. He abhorred carelessness in others," notes Leon Kelly (p. 32). His message for advertising personnel of the future was as follows: "I have made it my business to be an advertising agent. . . . I conceive the advertising agent to have three clear duties: the first is to the advertiser, the second is to the publisher, and the third is to the consumer. There is no one of these duties more important than the others" ("What Agencies Were Like in 1891," BBDO Archives).

When Batten entered the advertising business, "price" was the sales appeal, not "service," as he often preached. Among his competitors selling "price" was the famed Albert Lasker, later sole owner of the notable Lord and Thomas agency.

At his 25th anniversary dinner celebration in March 1916, Batten gave the following account of his advertising career:

The advertising business did not command the respect that it now enjoys. In those days it was common practice for an agency to send an order to a newspaper for 10 lines, a cut measuring 12, and bill the advertiser for 14 lines. Newspapers were not particular about the class of advertising they admitted to their columns. There was scarcely a medical advertisement too rank or a financial advertisement too "fakey" to be accepted. . . . In making calls soliciting advertising, one was often confronted with a sign reading: "Beggars, Peddlers, and Advertising Men not admitted." ("Response—Twenty Five Years," p. 1)

Batten's idea of the value and importance of advertising was that it was "too vital a factor in the expanding economy of America not to be profitable to all who touched it; the three primary beneficiaries of advertising—the advertiser, the publisher and the reader." He felt that he had achieved true success upon "the discovery that he had a business that would survive himself" ("Notes for Account Executives Forum," p. 1).

Batten brought many talents to advertising. None, however, did he consider more valuable than honesty and good writing. He became a stickler for just the right word and would work until he got it. He was a rather stern man and was not only a good letter writer, but a good person-to-person communicator as well. One colleague who knew him well noted that you could not lie to him, nor could you intimidate him. His eyes seemed to penetrate the very soul of the person with whom he was talking. He was interested not only in advertising prose but also in literature, in Shakespeare, Ruskin, and Emerson.

Perhaps the best way to start the story of the origins of the George Batten Company is to cite the founder's notes from *Batten's Wedge*, a single-page report dated December 1905. He began:

We started business here [38 Park Row, New York City] in [March 15] 1891, in an office
12 by 14 feet, with one clerk who was a stenographer, bookkeeper, etc., and who still
"abides with us." The first year's business amounted to $25,000 in round figures. The
next employee was a bookkeeper who secured the position because he was willing to
come cheap. He, however, in a few weeks, told the stenographer that he thought they
had both better be on the lookout for new positions, because he thought the Saturday
when the concern would not be able to pay their salaries was rapidly approaching. *His*
salary did stop quickly; we dropped him. The first account secured was that of George
A. Macbeth—Macbeth's Lamp Chimneys—and it is one of the sources of greatest business
pride to us to say that we still retain this account [1905]. Mr. William H. Johns, now
vice president of this company, came in as assistant solicitor in 1892, and when later he
was admitted to an interest in the business, it was really to save fixed charges. The
success of our business is in no small measure due to his fidelity, energy and intelligence.
I question if ever two men have been as closely associated as we have been for fourteen
years with never a rub—not a particle of friction.

Batten went on to relate that the company grew from one employee to nearly
50 by December 1905, with an increase in annual expense from $1,500 to
$75,000. He felt that since his firm had paid all its bills, had established good
credit, and had a good reputation with clients that it was a success. He further
wrote that the agency's growth was due more to continuing accounts than to
new ones. For example, the National Cloak and Suit Company, beginning in
1895 with an advertising budget of $500, had increased that figure to $100,000
by 1905. Another source of pride to his firm was the refusal of a $50,000 order
because it was not the type of advertising he deemed proper to handle.

Batten was only 37 when he founded his company in 1891. However, by
1894, he had installed the first agency in-house printing setup. He advocated
the use of simple, plain type, which he claimed "stands out like a Quaker on
Broadway." In 1906 the agency boasted 50 employees and moved to the Metropolitan Annex building on East 24th Street, occupying the entire 5,000 feet
on the 11th floor. The Batten Company, as a rule, did increase billings over the
years, but the firm seemed to have fallen behind Barton, Durstine and Osborn
in the several years preceding the 1928 merger of the two agencies. The BDO
firm, organized in 1919, simply progressed considerably more rapidly.

When the agency was very new, Batten would often pace back and forth in
the little room at 38 Park Row. During one of these "walks," he told Miss
Hopkins, his only employee at that time, "If I live and have my health, we'll
make this business grow." He would describe in detail the future business he
hoped to build on the principle: "Be absolutely honest with client and publisher
and give good service." At first, he placed his clients' ads only in the many
religious papers of the time and wrote most of the copy himself. As noted, Batten
was a zealot for turning out precise copy, but he wrote a so-called "fist" like
Horace Greeley, the despair of many a typist. Sometimes when the manuscript

came back to his desk typed, he scarcely recognized it as his own (*Batten,
Biography #1*, p. 1).

Referring to the early period of his agency, Batten noted:

> It was uphill work during the early years, and there were times that tried men's souls. I
> remember one time when Mr. Johns was trying to close an order (and we needed that
> order). I wired him: "Get it into the advertiser's head that we want to *work for him*, not
> 'work him.'" We got the order in spite of the fact that our competitors were willing to
> take it at a smaller profit. [He continued] A man said to me one day: "I believe you
> people are honest." I replied: "Yes, I think we are; we try to be." And then he said:
> "Well, most of you are honest because you think it is the best policy, but Mr. Johns is
> innately honest." ("Response—Twenty-Five Years," p. 2)

Batten acknowledged that at the start of his general advertising firm, he received encouragement from only one man, John E. Powers. Here was a man
who was in his own right an early advertising great, the first ad manager of
Wanamaker's department store in New York. As a free-lance copywriter, he
commanded a fee of $100 a day, even in 1886. Powers was known as "the man
who tried out honesty," and also as the inventor of "reason why" ad copy.
Actually, his was likely the best type of encouragement Batten could have
received.

On one occasion, Batten called his entire staff together and adjured everyone
present to act on the principle of Marshall Field (Chicago department store giant):
namely, that "the customer is always right." This admonition was elaborated
upon in a half-hour lecture. Apparently, Batten had not thought out his advice
with customary thoroughness, for one young man spoke up somewhat timidly,
stating: "But Mr. Batten, Mr. Field was a merchant. We are advertising men.
Isn't it conceivable that the client of ours may be wrong to his own disservice?
If we think so, isn't it our plain duty to tell him?" Batten reflected for a moment
and replied, "You are right. I was wrong. What I spoke of is a wonderful policy
for a store, but no good for a business like this one" (Kelley, p. 32).

Kelley notes that if Batten had lived ten years longer, he would have been
"out fighting" against the frequent misstatements advertised in the latter 1920s.
Batten's fanaticism on copywriting was well-known, thus leading to the phrase:
"That's Batten copy." He was decidedly word-minded rather than eye-minded.
If handed a piece of copy already set up, he would read the caption before he
attempted to interpret the visual effect. His convictions gave him a steel confidence. He assured himself he was right, then he went ahead. He did not like to
be disagreed with unless substantial grounds were specifically presented. In fact,
he did not care very much for the opinions of others (Kelley, pp. 34, 73). Batten
had a "gift of seeing things in broad perspectives," but also a keen mind and
rigorous morals. His "great self-confidence opened before him the right-of-way
in practically every undertaking" he chose to follow (Kelley, p. 32).

Seemingly, Batten and Johns rose from lean years to great wealth. The founder owned a 400-acre cattle ranch in New Jersey, and Johns became commodore of the Bayside Yacht Club, frequently entertaining aboard his 72-foot steam yacht. By the time Batten died in 1918, the company, with branches in Boston and Chicago, was obviously well on its way to becoming an established success, with many of its mainstay employees and leaders such as Johns remaining in charge. By 1919 the George Batten Company was considered one of America's top agencies, with an increasing array of notable clients.

The Barton and Durstine Company agency opened on January 1, 1919, at 25 West 45th Street, with Bruce Barton as president and Roy Durstine as secretary-treasurer. In August Alex Osborn joined the agency, which was renamed Barton, Durstine and Osborn.

By 1924 BDO was the fourth largest U.S. agency. It aired its first national network radio program in 1925, an hour show for Atwater Kent. Also in 1925 BDO became the first agency to establish a radio department. Finally, in September 1928, the George Batten Company and BDO merged to form Batten, Barton, Durstine and Osborn. In fact, agency lore has it that the merger was the result of an elevator comment in 1928 from William H. Johns, head of the George Batten Company, to Roy Durstine.

By 1928 BDO was billing about $23 million, while the George Batten Company was billing about $8 million. In 1924, by coincidence, both had moved into the same building at 383 Madison Avenue. Actually, for years after the merger, the new name conjured up elaborate quips and jokes. Alexander Woollcott produced this gag: "Have you heard about the new advertising agency that sounds like a trunk falling downstairs? Batten, Barton, Durstine and Osborn." The gag spread when Fred Allen put it on the vaudeville stage. Newspaper columnists picked it up, cartoonists worked it into strips, and for 25 years, Jack Benny wove the name into comedy routines.

Batten died on February 16, 1918, at his Montclair, New Jersey home, leaving a widow, Lillie Shivers Batten, two sons, and two daughters. He was eulogized by his employees in these words:

There were changes in the advertising business between 1891 and 1918. There were changes in all businesses. Strange new currents began to run through the minds of men in those years. To be always out in front and yet remain clearly visible to those who followed was no task for a weak or narrow man, and George Batten was neither. . . . Batten was one of the leaders who made modern advertising the national force it is today. He brought dignity to his work and was instrumental in making the business of advertising a profession to which men became proud to say they belonged. . . . He worked always with the door of his office open. He was always accessible. He was interested in his associates and they were interested in him. . . . He was a man whose phrases or mannerisms were imitated, yet the mental processes of those who knew him became more and more like his own. He could abhor carelessness without creating punctilio. He could praise industry without condeming leisure. He could approve daring without causing a loss of faith in restraint. He could adhere to the old and still encourage the new. . . . Batten was active, especially active in the selection of people for his business family and in watching and helping these people grow. This kept him in close touch with everything. His strength permeated the whole organization. His goal was service; his reward, the respect of men. He made his institution a world in which we lived rather than an office to which we went. ("In Appreciation of George Batten," p. 1)

Batten often summarized his advertising acumen with this passage from Shakespeare's *Measure for Measure*:

> Our doubts are traitors
> And make us lose the good
> We oft might win,
> By fearing to attempt.

FURTHER READING

Works by Batten

Batten's Wedge. Agency report. New York: George Batten Company, 1905.
"Response—Twenty-Five Years." Speech at 25th Anniversary Celebration of the George Batten Company. New York: BBDO Public Relations, 1916.

Works about Batten

"BBDO on 75th Anniversary Plans for Further Advertising Innovations." *BBDO Newsletter* (February 1966): 1–9.
Dillon, Tom. "How BBDO Got That Funny Name." Speech of 1980. Reprinted in *Advertising Age* (September 30, 1991): 540.
George Batten (Biography #1). New York: BBDO Public Relations, n.d.
George Batten (Biography #2). New York: BBDO Public Relations, n.d.
"Highlights of the First 100 Years." BBDO 100th Anniversary commemorative section in *Advertising Age* (September 30, 1991): S1–S48.
"In Appreciation of George Batten." New York: George Batten Agency Employees, undated.
Kelley, Leon. "In Sharper Focus." *Advertising and Selling* (October 31, 1928): 32, 34, 73.
"Notes for Account Executives Forum." New York: BBDO Public Relations, 1946.
"Old Batten Office." New York: George Batten Company, 1910.
"What Agencies Were Like in 1891." New York: George Batten Public Relations, 1992.
Winski, Joseph M. "BBDO at 100: On the Right Track Again." *Advertising Age* (September 30, 1991): 54–55, 58, 510, 512, 514, 516.

NOTABLE CLIENTS/CAMPAIGNS

MacBeth Lamp Chimney (1891)

Zenith Horse Collar (1891)

Hammermill Paper (1912)

Armstrong Cork (1917)

DON BELDING
(January 23, 1897–September 16, 1969)

Billy I. Ross

Although one of the founders of Foote, Cone and Belding was called "Mr. Advertising of the West," many will remember Don Belding for his many years of public service to his country. His work in the founding of the War Advertising Council, now the Advertising Council, and the Freedoms Foundation at Valley Forge typified his many accomplishments in and out of advertising.

Belding was born in Grants Pass, Oregon, on January 23, 1897, to Mollie and W. P. Belding. His father was a miner, his mother cooked for mining crews. Roy and Earl were Don's half-brothers from their father's previous marriage.

One of Belding's first and most bitter memories was of his father and older half-brother, Earl, going East to look for work after the mines closed. The two never returned—leaving his mother solely responsible for Don's rearing. His other half-brother, Roy, left a few years later to join his father and brother.

The departure of Don's father and two half-brothers brought on a speech impediment that was never completely cured. His mother took him to a special school in Oakland that helped to control the stuttering in most situations. He improved so dramatically that while making a campaign speech for a friend running for high school senior class president, the class elected Don instead. This was one of his first accomplishments to give him self-confidence.

Don and his mother were very poor during his early school years. His mother became a teacher and had to move often to obtain positions. Because she taught Don to read at a very early age, he excelled in school.

He graduated from Grants Pass High School and went on to the University of Oregon in Eugene. A year before he was to graduate, he joined the Oregon National Guard (which would later serve in France during World War I). During his service he was accidentally exposed to nerve gas and spent nearly a year recovering in a veteran's hospital. He returned to the university and graduated cum laude in 1919 with a major in commerce.

Utilizing his army training, Belding's first regular job was as a telegraph operator for Western Union in Klamath Falls, Oregon. While working for the company he met and later married Eunice Hodges. They had two children, Don, Jr., and Barbara.

With two other men he bought the *Klamath Falls Record*, a weekly, and later developed it into a daily. The newspaper ceased publication, according to his September 1969 personal journal, after the local bank failed during a long lumber strike. He lost not only the newspaper but all his savings.

After the newspaper experience, he decided to make a career in advertising. With support from his army disability pension, he applied for a nonpaying job as an office boy with the Lord and Thomas advertising agency in Los Angeles in 1923. Within the first year, he was placed on the payroll.

According to his September 22, 1969, obituary in *Advertising Age*, Belding had followed the advice of his mother to "get with a company small enough to advance in, but big enough to offer security" (p. 8). Lord and Thomas fit that advice perfectly: It had been established in 1881 with headquarters in Chicago and became the first national agency to open an office in Los Angeles. It was run by Albert Lasker, one of the great advertising executives of the era, who took over the operations from the founders, D. M. Lord and Ambrose Thomas.

Belding's first paying job with the agency was ghost writing an article for Don Francisco, the agency manager, entitled, "The Agency's Relation to the Small Town Newspaper." After working as an assistant space buyer for a short period, he was promoted to space buyer at $75 per month in April 1924. While pleased to be with the agency, he wanted to become a copywriter. He spent many hours studying the work of the agency's copywriter, Bob Crane, who was a disciple of Claude Hopkins, the father of "reason why" copy.

Copywriting, however, was not his next job. Instead, at the end of his two-year training period, he became a space buyer and research manager. He finally became a copywriter and a junior account executive with an assignment to the Union Oil account, one of the agency's most important clients, in 1926. He later became the account executive.

After working with other accounts, Belding felt he had reached the peak when assigned the Sunkist account, but when Don Francisco was named agency president and moved to Chicago in 1938, Belding was named manager of the Los Angeles office. In 1941 he was named a vice president of the agency, along with Emerson Foote and Fairfax Cone. Another major event in his life came that year when he announced to his wife, Eunice, that he was in love with Albert Lasker's secretary, Alice Freter. Eunice and Don were divorced, and a year later he married Alice.

By 1942 Belding had already made a name for himself in advertising. However, a phone call from Lasker on December 15, 1942, launched new heights for Belding, Cone, and Foote. On that red-letter date, Lasker announced the dissolution of Lord and Thomas and his retirement from the advertising agency business. He asked that Belding, Cone, and Foote join him in New York to discuss the future of the three vice presidents of the agency. At the meeting,

Lasker said that he had decided to liquidate Lord and Thomas, and with the right financial agreement, he would give the agency to the three.

The new agency was incorporated as Foote, Cone and Belding on December 29, 1942, in Wilmington, Delaware, with January 2, 1943, the first day of business. Belding deferred to Foote the naming of the agency since Foote had convinced American Tobacco (Lord and Thomas's largest account) to remain with them.

The three new partners discussed many ways of organizing the agency. Since each of them had been the vice president of a different Lord and Thomas office—Belding in Los Angeles, Cone in Chicago, and Foote in New York—one thought was to have three independent subsidiaries. Belding objected to this suggestion. He wanted his accounts to have national representation and indicated he would withdraw if it did not go that way. The others agreed, and FCB became national with more than $20 million in billings.

In Jeanne M. Knapp's book *Don Belding*, she notes that Foote called the deal a ''bed of clover'' for the three partners and almost a gift from Lasker (p. 23). Foote was named president, Cone became chairman of the executive committee, and Belding became chairman of the board of what would become one of the world's largest advertising agencies.

In a draft copy of his autobiography, Belding wrote that when FCB took over the business, the principal accounts of Los Angeles were Union Oil, Sunkist, Southern Pacific, Pacific Mutual Life Insurance Company, Purex, and Security First National. Lockheed was the first account he obtained as manager of the office. The Pacific Coast operations of NBC was added in 1940 and, later, RKO Radio Pictures.

In his personal notes, Belding claimed that one of the hardest things that he did as manager of the office was to resign the Cole of California account to take on its competitor, Catalina. Catalina stayed with the agency for only six years, and Belding said that ''this experience proved to me that it's better not to resign a small account if you can make money on it.''

Belding also told of an experience that led to the resignation of a client, David O. Selznick Enterprises. Belding said that Selznick's advertising manager did not believe in the agency system and that some of his efforts did not meet FCB's ethical standards. He asked for a meeting with Selznick and told him that changes had to be made or they could no longer handle the account. Selznick moved the account.

United Artists was with the agency from 1944 to 1949, while Walt Disney Productions was added in 1946. Belding had high praise for Walt Disney. He wrote in his personal notes, ''One of the finest experiences I had in this business was the contact with Walt Disney.'' They had long conversations on many different topics. He admired Disney as a great patriot who believed in high moral and ethical standards. He was impressed that Disney would never allow anything in a film that could offend any member of a family. He referred to Disney as ''America's greatest ambassador.''

Hughes Aircraft came to the agency in 1951, one of the best accounts ever acquired by FCB. The agency also had other motion picture companies come and go during the 1940s and 1950s. Belding never thought of these companies as stable, long-lasting accounts.

Adding the Paper Mate Company in 1953 began a 16-year relationship with Patrick J. Frawley that lasted until Belding's death. Frawley organized Paper Mate with the $100,000 sale of his export business in San Francisco. He developed an ink that bankers would allow to be used on their transactions because it could not be transferred. Seven years later Frawley sold the company to Gillette for $15 million. Belding considered Frawley one of the great merchandising and marketing men of America.

In 1951 Belding took on added responsibilities when Emerson Foote resigned from the agency. In addition to handling West Coast operations, he took over the New York office, while Cone continued to head the Chicago office. While looking for a copywriter in the mid–1950s, Belding's wife, Alice, suggested that he offer the position to his secretary, Helen Gurley. He agreed that she was creative and decided to give her a chance. She was an instant success with the Catalina account. A few years later Max Factor moved from FCB to another agency with the understanding that she be hired to handle the account. She was offered $20,000 a year, which Belding could not match, so he advised her to ask for $25,000. She got the job and the salary. After leaving FCB she married a 20th Century–Fox story editor named Brown. She went on to become the very successful editor of *Cosmopolitan* magazine.

The last account that Belding secured for FCB was Trans World Airlines, to be handled in New York rather than Los Angeles.

On January 23, 1957, Belding reached his 60th birthday and retired from FCB. Many wondered why a person in relative good health making $100,000 a year should retire. As he related in his personal notes, $100,000 was a lot of money for a country boy who grew up in Oregon in near poverty, but there were three reasons:

First, I had enough money to keep me comfortable the rest of my life and to give my children a substantial inheritance.

Second, there were certain things going on inside the company which bothered me. One was it was getting more and more difficult to retain good people and this is a serious thing in our business as the main thing in a personal service business is what the people have in their heads and if the people who have the best ideas in their heads go someplace else you've lost half of your heritage. And, in order to hold key people it's necessary that they participate in the profits of the management in a way in which the tax situation will be more favorable than if they were just given bonuses at the end of each year. So, it was necessary to release a large amount of stock. Well, I was on the small end of FCB business . . . of course, there was more business in New York . . . more business in Chicago than there was on the coast and naturally I felt some obligation on this, that I should make this stock available.

Third, all of my life since I was made Manager of Lord & Thomas in '38, I'd been actively involved in civic affairs and the importance of them was growing in my mind because I could see things I was accomplishing from experience and dedication that hadn't been accomplished before and naturally I took these greatly to heart. I knew that sometimes it was the feelings of my partners that I was probably doing more of this than I should for the good of the business.

His daughter, Barbara Belding Richards, writes in her unpublished account of her father of one more reason why he retired so early: He had reached his goal of acquiring $1 million. In the November 23, 1953, issue of *Advertising Age*, he reflected on his long career in advertising and said: "Looking back, it had been 'fun' all the way. It had been a vigorous, vital and challenging business, that had changed a great deal" (p. 8).

In his agreement with FCB, Belding was to be retained as a consultant for a five-year period with office space and a secretary furnished to handle his mail. He was also entitled to travel expenses for any agency trips.

When asked about his retirement, Belding told a *Los Angeles Examiner* reporter, "I have elected to step aside in the business world so others of my younger associates may capitalize on the opportunities which have been my privilege to enjoy. But, being active, vigorous and in the best of health, I want to keep busy in civic affairs. I have found through life the thing which gives me the most pleasure is using what ability I have to serve others."

Although Belding was well-known in advertising, many will contend that he was better known for his many years of public service. According to Robert Koretz, Belding's work in public service stemmed from hospitalization as a result of accidental wartime gassing (later diagnosed as tuberculosis) (p. 31).

His public service to advertising started as early as 1940, when he was elected president of the Pacific Coast Advertising Clubs, later named the Advertising Association of the West. In 1942 he helped found the War Advertising Council, which became the Advertising Council after World War II. He directed its first campaign, which used Smokey the Bear to promote forest fire prevention. This campaign continues as the longest running campaign of the council. In 1946 he was named chairman of a joint committee of the American Association of Advertising Agencies and the Association of National Advertisers to promote the American economic system.

Belding chaired the Advertising Industry's Nationwide Committee on the Improvement of Understanding of Our Economic System in 1947–1948. His extreme interest in the American way of life led to his work with Dr. Kenneth Wells and E. F. Hutton in founding the Freedoms Foundation at Valley Forge. He later served as its chairman of the board, taking over from General Dwight D. Eisenhower. In his personal journal he wrote, "I consider the work of Freedoms Foundation to be my greatest contribution to improving the climate of the American economic and advertising system."

Other public service activities outside of advertising included: director of the Arthritis and the Heritage Foundations, chairman of the Small Business Advisory

Committee of the Department of Commerce, civilian aide to the Secretary of the Army for Southern California, chairman of the Los Angeles Airport Commission, national chairman of the Easter Seal Society, director of the Los Angeles Chamber of Commerce, director and member of the executive committee of the Merchants and Manufacturers Association of Los Angeles, vice-chairman of the Presidential Citizens Food Committee, trustee of the Association of the U.S. Army, president of the Defense Orientation Conference Association, president of the Crippled Children's Society of Los Angeles County, co-chairman of the Los Angeles Committee for the Handicapped, and state chairman of the Citizens Committee for Free-TV.

For four years Belding did a weekly radio program over many Mutual stations and the Armed Forces Radio network, with subjects about the American way of life and how it should be maintained. After his retirement he wrote a monthly personal journal for nearly 13 years and sent it to more than 400 friends all over the world. Belding gave hundreds of speeches and wrote many articles. Most of his speeches were on advertising and the American economic system.

His biggest day came on June 14, 1961, when the mayor of Los Angeles, the city council, and the board of governors proclaimed "Don Belding Day." Ronald Reagan was master of ceremonies. Belding's citation read: "For his many years of unselfish and unstinting devotion to his city and his nation." He also received the Distinguished Service Medal, the highest award given to a civilian by the army, on July 14, 1961.

In 1948 *Business Week* printed his picture on its cover and *Look* magazine also saluted him for his work in public service. *Sales Management* stated that he had become "Mr. Advertising of the West."

In 1973 Texas Tech University posthumously inducted Belding into its Mass Communications Hall of Fame. Before his death he had established the Don Belding International Grant-in-Aid fund to help students from other countries come to Texas Tech and study advertising and marketing. His 48 awards were donated to the university before his death, and his papers, photographs, recording tapes, phonograph records, and films were donated to the Southwest Collection at Texas Tech by his son, Don Belding, Jr. Of all his awards, the one he prized most was an encased section of an original rafter from the hospital at Valley Forge. A similar section was also presented to Dr. Wells for their work in founding the Freedoms Foundation.

Belding concluded one chapter that was to be in his autobiography, drafted six months before his death, in this way:

What I'm looking for now between the time I'm 75 and 80 if my health stands up, is some special project where I will just be doing one thing but something I hope to do well and something which will be extremely interesting and maybe a little off-beat. My future is uncertain because I have cancer. I licked it once, but it popped up again. As I write this my prognosis is unknown. I hope it is favorable and if I recover, which I expect to, I'll keep on doing what I am now doing until I am 75.

Don Belding died on September 16, 1969. His daughter, in her unpublished biography, had this description of her father:

Don was admired by many, for anyone with enthusiasm tends to be admired.

Moderately tall, a husky, cards-on-the-table westerner who never forgot his country boy origins, Don had a posture the Army never cured. Hands often jammed in his pockets, nervously jingling the coins and keys there, he had a lifetime habit of leaning back in his chair, which never quite lost its balance, but always seemed to.

He looked like a cross between Lionel Barrymore and Dwight Eisenhower, a silver fringe rimming a balding forehead. Horned rims of light plastic or metal framed his wide-set eyes, a soft friendly brown, which compliment his generous mouth that smiled easily. (p. 10)

Longtime FCB director and historian Robert Koretz ended his column for the agency magazine salute to Belding by writing: "One final thought. Don Belding was a man everyone at FCB can be proud of. Next time you hear someone carelessly refer to our firm as 'Foote Cone'—why not respectfully correct them and finish our name. It is 'Foote, Cone & *Belding*' " (p. 31).

FURTHER READING

Works by Belding

Many of Belding's personal papers are in the collection of Texas Tech University, Lubbock (Belding Collection, Southwest Collection).

Works about Belding

Belding, Mollie. *Mollie Belding's Memory Book*. Los Angeles: Ward Richie Press, 1945.

Brown, Helen Gurley. *Sex and the Office*. New York: B. Geis Associates, 1964.

Cone, Fairfax. *With All Its Faults*. Boston: Little, Brown, 1969.

"Don Belding, 71, Ad Industry Leader, FCB Co-Chief, Dies." *Advertising Age* (September 22, 1969): 8.

Gunther, John. *Taken at the Flood*. New York: Harper, 1960.

Knapp, Jeanne M. *Don Belding: A Career of Advertising and Public Service*. Lubbock: Department of Mass Communications, Texas Tech University, 1983.

Koetz, Robert. "Mr. Advertising of the West." *FCB Person to Person* (October/November 1983): 30–31.

Richards, Barbara Belding. "The Salesman of Freedom." Unpublished manuscript. Lubbock: Belding Collection, Southwest Collection, Texas Tech University, n.d.

Wakeman, Frederic. *The Huckster*. New York: Rinehart, 1946.

NOTABLE CLIENTS/CAMPAIGNS

Catalina

Cole of California

David O. Selznick Enterprises
Hughes Aircraft
Hughes Tool
Lockheed
MGM
Paper Mate
Purex
RKO Radio Pictures
Southern Pacific Railroad
Sunkist Growers
TWA
Union Oil of California
United Artists
Walt Disney Productions

WILLIAM BURNETT BENTON
(April 1, 1900–March 18, 1973)

E. R. Worthington

William Burnett Benton distinguished himself during the middle half of the twentieth century as an advertising executive and cofounder of the Benton and Bowles advertising agency. His advertising experience began at age 22 with the New York office of Lord and Thomas, he next joined the George Batten Company as a partner, then he returned to the Chicago office of Lord and Thomas before starting his own New York firm in 1929. At age 36 he retired from the world of advertising to become an educator, businessman, politician, publisher, international statesman, ambassador, and author.

On April 1, 1900, William Benton was born in Minneapolis to Charles William Benton, a college professor and Congregational clergyman, and the former Elma Caroline Hixson. His ancestors had arrived and settled in Connecticut 18 years after the Pilgrims' landing at Plymouth Rock, establishing a vocational family history of education and ministry.

Benton's father taught Romance languages at the University of Minnesota for 33 years, while his mother was initially a homemaker, then a college student, later an educator in public and private schools. Eighteen months after William's birth, his parents had a second son, Daniel, who died of encephalitis at age 18.

Elma Benton, who had married a man 23 years her elder, became a widow at age 39 in November 1913, when William was 13. The same month his father died William received financial aid to attend Shattuck Military School in Faribault, Minnesota.

Financial hardship upon her husband's death led Mrs. Benton to join her father and brother as a homesteader in Montana in 1913. She lived in a clapboard house she built with her meager savings while she tried to earn a living from the land. During the first summer his mother was on the homestead, young William became a last-minute replacement for a bicycle trip of England and Scotland, so he missed the first year of clearing the land. However, he spent the next three summers working on the homestead, which he viewed as depressing times in a depressing place.

While a student at Shattuck and at his mother's insistence, he took the entrance exams for Yale (his father's and grandfather's alma mater) but failed. In 1917, after graduating from Shattuck, he entered Carleton College in Northfield, Minnesota, where his late father's sister, Dr. Mary Benton, was dean of women.

At this time Elma Benton left the homestead to attend graduate school at Columbia University's Teachers College. The next fall she received a faculty appointment at Columbia, and William enrolled as a private in the U.S. Army Officer Training Program at Yale. Hardly had military training begun when the World War I Armistice was signed on November 1, 1918. The training unit demobilized in December after William had taken his second entrance exams for Yale. If he failed these exams again he could still be admitted to Yale as a freshman, which is what his mother demanded he do. William Benton had his own plan, which was to attend Williams College in Massachusetts as a sophomore, rather than repeat his freshman year, but he passed the Yale exams and entered as a sophomore in January 1919.

During his undergraduate days he achieved an excellent scholastic record, served as senior editor of the *Yale Record*, the school's humor magazine (increasing circulation and advertising revenues, resulting in a hefty profit), and was offered a Rhodes Scholarship, which he declined. Instead, after earning his baccalaureate degree in 1921, he entered the world of business with the National Cash Register Company—selling cash registers from the back of a truck.

Again it was his mother, now headmistress of a young women's finishing school, Hosmer Hall in St. Louis, who pressed him to take the NCR job (he was hired by his cousin). If that did not work out, she wanted him to enter Harvard Law School. Many of his decisions were not made without advice or counsel from Elma. For years he wrote her at least weekly, often daily, in his early years. In fact, the letters to his mother totaled over two million words.

In spite of earning $100 a week as a top salesman in pre-depression days, Benton felt he was in a rut. He was learning, but selling was hard work over long hours. Still, he was not enamored with three years of law school just to begin at the bottom again. Torn between the two choices, Benton opted to follow his mother's wishes and move to Cambridge to enter law school. Along the way, he again changed his mind, resisted his mother, and in 1922 took a job (at one-quarter his NCR income) with the New York office of the Chicago ad agency Lord and Thomas. At that time it was the largest agency in the United States, with accounts such as Pepsodent toothpaste, Palmolive soap, and Quaker Oats.

As personal assistant to Frank Fehlman, manager of the New York office, Benton's duties prepared him to be an account executive, learning how to manage an advertising agency. Fehlman was insistent that Benton remain on the administrative side as opposed to the creative; after all, copywriters did not make as much money as those getting and servicing accounts.

As an account executive Benton began to understand the value of an open and honest relationship with clients. This knowledge became a fundamental premise when he had his own agency. Benton's desire, though, was to be on the creative end of the business; he wanted to write copy, rather than find and service accounts.

Fehlman was transferred to Chicago but required Benton to remain in New York to work on projects arranged by him. The manager who replaced Fehlman also gave Benton assignments, which involved copywriting. Unfortunately, because of two bosses, he was unable to do as much copywriting as he wanted.

Caught between the two supervisors, unable to live on his income (in spite of a $10-a-week raise), and convinced the best way to learn advertising was by writing copy, Benton applied for a position in the number four agency, the George Batten Company, but was not accepted.

Having already given notice at Lord and Thomas, Benton was running out of time. When the Batten job did not come through, he accepted a position at the Charles W. Hoyt agency, run by a Yale classmate's father. Unfortunately, copywriting was not included in his duties; instead, his job was learning to sell the bathroom fixtures a client manufactured. A month later the George Batten Company offered Benton a copywriting job for $50 a week, which he immediately accepted.

Joining the staff of some 25 copywriters in late 1923, he became immersed in writing business-related copy for booklets, brochures, direct mail, and posters. Even though his salary was double that at Lord and Thomas, he still had trouble making ends meet, so he began to moonlight as a free-lance copywriter. His income was increased by 50 percent writing ads and direct-mail circulars for Robert Goldstein, publisher of *Juvenile Magazine*, which was distributed to department stores.

Disheartened by his self-perceived futile attempts at copywriting, he almost quit Batten because he did not feel he wrote convincingly. At the last minute he had the opportunity to address the staff in a weekly in-house training seminar. During his session he told everyone why and how his old firm, Lord and Thomas, was better at creating advertising than Batten. This talk brought forth both new friends in high places as well as enemies. Also, it gave him more confidence in writing consumer-related copy and paved the way for a managerial position.

After more administrative changes at Batten, Benton became the trade and industrial department head. His management philosophy involved a close working relationship with his subordinates, resulting in the creation of an on-the-job training program for new copywriters.

As Benton's responsibilities increased, he needed assistance. In early February 1925, for $25 a week, he hired a young Yale graduate, a man from an old New England family, Chester Bowles. Very quickly Benton and his new assistant began discussing the possibility of combining forces along with a more experienced partner and setting up their own agency. Instead, a friend and Yale alumnus offered Benton a $250-per-week contract to join a Miami ad agency working in real estate advertising. Benton almost left New York for Florida, but friends persuaded him to stay. When he decided to remain with Batten, he received a raise to $7,000 per year.

Among the new copywriters hired by Benton were Ted Bates and J. Stirling Getchell. Both men would go on to start their own highly successful firms.

In 1927 Benton was offered a partnership in Batten, a salary increase to $10,000, and shares of agency stock worth another $10,000. The caveat upon acceptance was a provision that if he left Batten, he would have to stay out of advertising for five years. He took the offer, becoming the youngest partner in the firm's history.

Since his days at Yale, Benton had dated Helen Hemingway from New Haven, Connecticut. During the previous several years she had alternated between living in Connecticut or New York and France. Twice she had indicated the possibility of marrying other men but never did. On a trip to Paris in 1928 she took a job in the fashion industry. Soon thereafter, in early May, Benton proposed marriage by mail and telegram, which she accepted.

That same week William Benton also lost his job at Batten. Recent client losses had prompted Benton to argue for the merger of Batten with Barton, Durstine, and Osborne, an agency in the same building. Benton felt Batten had strong creative talent but was unable to solicit and manage new accounts. On the other hand, the other agency was successful in landing new accounts but could not produce good ads. Being fired released Benton from the five-year restriction, so he did not have to leave the advertising profession. Ironically, the proposal that got him fired actually was consummated two months later, when the two firms became Batten, Barton, Durstine and Osborne.

Benton was immediately hired by his old firm, Lord and Thomas, to be assistant general manager of its Chicago corporate headquarters. On June 12, 1928, he married Helen. In July he assumed his new position; five years later he left.

In spite of his new job, Benton still had plans to form his own agency and corresponded with Chester Bowles (who remained with Batten, Barton, Durstine and Osborne) about a future partnership.

His first major Lord and Thomas assignment was to conduct a survey in an attempt to obtain the Colgate-Palmolive account. The two companies had just merged. Prior to the merger Lord and Thomas serviced Palmolive, and Colgate was a former Batten account. At this point it was not known whether the new company would use only one agency or continue to work with two. Lord and Thomas wanted it all and felt a large survey would convince Colgate-Palmolive to give them the account.

Albert Lasker, head of Lord and Thomas, put Benton in charge of conducting the project because the firm had no research department. The Colgate-Palmolive merger required more information than Lord and Thomas had, but Lasker had nothing but contempt for research and statistics. When Benton asked what kind of research Lasker wanted, he was told it really did not make any difference as long as it was the biggest research project ever done. Traditionally, research conducted in advertising agencies concentrated on collecting market data. Benton decided that, in addition to doing the largest research ever done, he would also concentrate on the consumer, rather than the market.

For two months Benton worked day and night overseeing the collection of data from consumers nationwide to ascertain which of the two firms' products were most preferred. Actually, the account was given to Lord and Thomas before the survey was completed. However, the information collected was used to prepare the campaigns for Colgate-Palmolive. This survey became a prototype for today's consumer research.

At the end of 1928 Benton's income (salary and stocks) equaled $22,000. He continually received offers to join other New York firms but declined, still hoping to start an agency with his good friend and colleague Chester Bowles. Before the agency could be formed, though, the team would first have to land accounts.

While listening to the 1926 Harvard-Yale football game radio broadcast, Benton recognized the possibilities of creating ad copy only for radio commercials. He drafted a radio ad plan concept while at Batten to no avail. Later, in 1929, a friend in the radio industry was putting together a $50 million merger and wanted Benton to head up advertising as manager. Benton wished to take on the project as an agency account, rather than as in-house ad manager. Unfortunately, while the deal was being consummated, the Depression and new management from the merger led the account to another agency.

In early 1929 Benton and Bowles met with Charles Mortimer. An ex-Batten man who had worked with the two, he was in the advertising department of the Postum Cereal Company. Mortimer agreed to talk to Postum's advertising manager on their behalf.

Postum was started in the early 1890s by Charles William Post. He had been a very sick, emaciated businessman who improved his health by eating nutritious foods. In 1896 he marketed a drink mix named Postum, followed by a granola-type cereal called Grape-Nuts, then Post Toasties. In 1925 Post initiated a series of mergers starting with Jell-O, then Swans Down Cake Flour, Minute Tapioca, Franklin Baker Coconut, Walter Baker Chocolate, and Log Cabin Syrup. In 1929 Postum was considering even greater growth through continued purchasing of other companies.

Another entrepreneur, Brooklyn-born explorer Charles Birdseye, was intrigued with the Eskimos' method of preserving food by freezing it in the dry Arctic air. Returning to the States in 1917, he formed the General Seafoods Company to utilize the quick-freeze method of preserving seafood. The General Foods Company was founded in 1924 by Birdseye, employing the same technology but for the large-scale fast-freezing of various food products. In 1929 Postum bought General Foods and retained the name for its entire combined operations.

Bowles prepared a presentation for the head of the firm's advertising department and was told he had a ten to one chance of getting at least one account from the new company, General Foods. Shortly thereafter two small accounts were given to Benton and Bowles. Informing his boss at Lord and Thomas of the possibility of forming his own agency, Lasker told Bill Benton his $25,000 annual income would double if he stayed. Benton declined.

While deciding to form a partnership with Bowles was one thing, financing the deal was another. Many friends offered Benton the capital for stock, but he was not inclined to let others share the potential results of his efforts. Bill and Helen Benton had only $6,000 in savings. In addition to the money for his partnership share, the couple needed money to live on until the new agency made money. Benton borrowed $1,000 from each of three friends and thus had $9,000: $5,000 for the agency and $4,000 for living expenses. Benton and Bowles was founded on $18,000 capitalization. Each cofounder invested $9,000, but because Benton had only $5,000, he borrowed $4,000 from Bowles. It is interesting to note that the original capitalization to create Benton and Bowles is remembered differently by each partner. Bowles states in his book *Promises to Keep* the amount was $12,000 (p. 7), while Benton, in Sidney Hyman's *The Lives of William Benton*, said it was $18,000 (p. 126). Gordon Webber, in his book on the Benton and Bowles agency, *Our Kind of People*, states the amount was $12,000 (p. 11).

On July 15, 1929, at Forty-second Street and Lexington Avenue in New York, Benton and Bowles opened its doors for business—three and a half months before Black Tuesday, October 29, 1929, the day the stock market crashed and the Great Depression began. Besides Benton and Bowles, the staff consisted of a secretary, an office boy, and a new college graduate. William Benton was to do account work and manage the business, while Chester Bowles was in charge of creative work.

The firm began with the two General Foods accounts, Hellmann's mayonnaise and Certo jelly preservative, totaling $60,000 for the rest of 1929. The consumer survey Benton did for Lord and Thomas became a stock-in-trade for the new firm. Benton and Bowles also was a pioneer in radio advertising. Other early accounts included the Adolph Goebel Meat Company, Helena Rubinstein cosmetics, and the Squibb Company.

When questioned about the decision to open an ad agency at the beginning of the Depression, both partners said it was actually a good time to start. Clients were desperate for new ideas that old-line agencies were not providing. Benton and Bowles was founded by young men with daring concepts.

While working on the General Foods Hellmann's mayonnaise account, Benton rode the firm's delivery trucks in Brooklyn. From this experience, he arrived at the decision that low sales volume and a poor distribution system were killing profits. Benton made a radical recommendation to the parent company—sell. Best Foods, a subsidiary of Gold Dust, had a profitable franchise operation and the marketing acumen needed to make a profit on Hellmann's. Benton believed Best Foods could do a much better job selling Hellmann's.

General Foods did indeed sell to Best Foods, and Benton and Bowles retained the account as well as getting Best Foods mayonnaise and Nucoa margarine for billings of $700,000.

In addition to his steady letter-writing to his mother, Benton wrote even more memos to his staff. Both at the office and at home, he constantly used dictating machines. He was a man who required only a few hours of sleep each night, and he dictated a dozen or more cylinders into the early morning hours. As the evening wore on, the memos on the machine became more critical and caustic. These memos were but another aspect of his almost obsessive attention to detail, his penchant for organization, and goal-directed behaviors.

William Benton wrote his mother at the end of 1930 predicting net earnings of $100,000 to $200,000 for the agency for 1931. Gross earnings, though, reached only $166,000, leaving a mere $28,000 profit. Benton and Bowles's 20 percent drop in net earnings compared to 1930 was not that bad when the advertising industry as a whole experienced a decrease in billings of over 50 percent.

In 1932, when Raymond Rubicam suggested General Foods seek another ad agency, Benton and Bowles was approached to see if it could handle half of General Foods' business. At the time General Foods was not entirely satisfied with the manner in which the ad firm of Erwin, Wasey was handling the account. Benton thought not, so General Foods suggested the firm bring in another partner, Atherton Hobler, a minor partner in the ad firm of Erwin, Wasey and the account executive for the General Foods account. Hobler joined Benton and Bowles with a one-third partnership. The firm got the $5 million General Foods account.

The agency's plans placed increased emphasis on radio. Such shows as Maxwell House "Showboat," Palmolive "Beauty Box," "Gang Busters," and Fred Allen's "Town Hall Tonight" were aired. William Benton advocated live studio audiences, radio commercials with sound effects, and studio applause signs. He also brought the Chicago-based "Amos 'n' Andy" show to national radio, sponsored by Pepsodent.

The firm's 1933 earnings doubled 1932's. Benton was president, with Bowles and Hobler vice presidents. The firm continued to grow, attract new clients, and hire the best creative talent in advertising. In 1935 Benton's annual salary was $250,000, with the firm having gross billings of $18 million. It was the sixth largest agency in the nation. That year Benton also decided to quit.

In 1929 William Benton and Chester Bowles verbally agreed that if or when Benton decided to leave the firm, Bowles would buy out his share on one condition—that Benton never return to advertising. When Hobler joined Benton and Bowles he was not told of Benton's verbal agreement, which required the company purchase his share. Benton first began to think of leaving at the end of 1933, but when he informed his partners, he was not taken seriously.

In 1934 William and Helen Benton purchased a country place in Southport, Connecticut, anticipating his retirement. Pressure from clients and partners delayed his departure. A major concern was the firm's ability to continue successfully if Benton left. To show his partners it could, Benton and his family took an extended vacation in 1935, and the business survived.

At the end of 1935 William Benton turned in his stock, and his resignation was official on April 1, 1936, his 36th birthday. His income dropped to investment earnings of about $15,000 per year. Stock buy-back payments would be made once a year over six years (1935–1940), estimated to be worth $1 million. He retained an office with the agency and continued to serve on the board until 1943.

An unconfirmed story has Benton declaring upon his graduation from Yale in 1921 that he would make a million by age 35 and retire (see *The Lives of William Benton*, p. 156). At 36 he, in fact, did quit the advertising business he cofounded to ''retire'' as a paper millionaire.

A Yale classmate, Robert M. Hutchins, president of the University of Chicago, convinced Benton to join the institution as vice president for special assignments. During his eight-year tenure with the school, he pioneered the use of radio and motion pictures for adult education. His interest in commercial broadcasting resulted in the creation of ''The University of Chicago Round Table,'' a radio show that won several national awards. While at the university Benton was active in other projects, until he left at the end of World War II to join the federal government.

Benton ventured into the public service field in 1939. Nelson A. Rockefeller, a Dartmouth graduate, was coordinator of Inter-American Affairs. William Benton became an adviser to Rockefeller and nurtured an interest in economic development.

In 1942 Benton helped found a nonprofit organization, the Committee for Economic Development (CED), which he served as vice-chairman. Within two years CED involved 50,000 businessmen and conducted research planning for postwar industrial conversion and production.

Sears, Roebuck had acquired *Encyclopaedia Britannica* from its British owners after they went bankrupt in 1920. A deal was made in 1943 by Benton for Sears to donate the *Encyclopaedia* to the University of Chicago. Benton in turn would provide working capital of $100,000, with the university obtaining beneficiary interest in the profits. Essentially, Benton would end up with two-thirds stock ownership and the university one-third. Benton chaired the board of *Britannica*'s American, Canadian, and English companies which published the *Encyclopaedia*, plus the *Britannica Year Book*, *World Atlas*, and *Britannica Junior*. The university faculty was involved in the publications as an advisory staff, supervising the constant updating of revisions.

Under Benton's management *Britannica* indulged in other educational endeavors. One was the *Encyclopaedia Britannica Collection of Contemporary Paintings*, a traveling exhibit of 117 paintings done by American artists. Another venture was the creation of Encyclopaedia Britannica Films, Inc., for the development of educational classroom films. Some critics, however, voiced concern that Benton's expansion into so many different areas diminished the informational quality of the *Encyclopaedia*. At least one editor quit for that reason.

As in his advertising days, Benton spent all day at the office or traveling around conducting business, then half the night dictating memos and orders to be sent to staff members. His CED work included trips to England to examine postwar industry and trade relations potential between Great Britain and the United States.

As a sideline venture Benton became a partner in 1939 in a firm called Muzak, in the business of providing piped music over a loudspeaker to people or offices (at that time radio transmissions had static and radio sets were expensive). While he originally perceived his involvement in Muzak as purely a financial invest-ment, Benton eventually became physically involved in various aspects of man-agement and strategic planning. He sold Muzak in 1958 for $4 million; he had purchased it for $132,500 in the late 1930s.

At the end of World War II Benton left academia, resigning from the University of Chicago to become Assistant Secretary of State for Public Affairs. During the two years he served in this public office, he helped establish UNESCO, the United Nations Educational, Scientific and Cultural Organization. He also re-organized the peacetime Voice of America radio broadcasts and established the U.S. Information Offices.

Tending his resignation to President Harry S. Truman effective September 30, 1947, William Benton found himself out of a job and out of a steady cash flow. The *Encyclopaedia Britannica* was also experiencing serious cash-flow problems. When Benton took over *Britannica* from Sears he had essentially assumed only the editorial and publishing functions. Marketing, collections, financing, purchasing, and legal services were provided by Sears until 1948. It was evident to Benton that his publishing company was not able to accomplish all these additional functions successfully. In the following year he devoted most of his time to reorganizing and refinancing *Britannica*.

Contributions for political candidates in the 1948 elections helped pay off some political debts incurred during his term in the State Department. One campaign Benton contributed to was that of his old advertising partner, Chester Bowles, who, as a Democrat, ran for and won the governorship of Connecticut. Bowles had resigned from the advertising agency at the end of 1941 to enter public service.

In late 1949 Governor Bowles had to appoint a senator to fill a vacancy. William Benton, a Connecticut resident, was seen as a viable compromise candidate.

The vacancy occurred when Bowles appointed Senator Raymond Baldwin to the Connecticut Supreme Court of Errors. A strong contender for the position was John M. Bailey, chairman of the Democratic Party of Connecticut. As a loyal political insider, Bailey believed Bowles had the potential for presidential nomination in 1952. As a U.S. senator, Bailey would be in a position to gain contacts and pave the way for Bowles's nomination.

The governor's appointment would last until elections were held in late 1950 to fill the remaining senate term. Bowles favored an appointee who had a national reputation and who would be able to win in the 1950 election, when Bowles would be seeking reelection. Bailey was, by his own admission, only a small-time politician. Ironically, John Bailey went on to national prominence as Democratic National Chairman. In spite of Benton's selection by Bowles, Bailey and Benton became long-time friends.

Benton accepted the appointment knowing he was expected to run for the office in 1950, which he did but won by only a handful of votes (Bowles lost). As a senator, Benton led the attack on Republican Senator Joseph R. McCarthy when McCarthy was at the height of his power in his obsessive drive to rid America of communists. He fought against the McCarran Immigration Act as being too restrictive and advocated the Fair Employment Practices Commission.

When up for reelection in 1952 Benton campaigned on his past record but was not very effective on television, a new campaign device. His wife, Helen, was very active in his campaign and, as in 1950, a helicopter was used to carry them around the state. His anti-McCarthy stance was not accepted throughout Connecticut, because some voters felt that being anti-McCarthy was also being soft on communism; in 1952 the United States was fighting communism in Korea. Benton lost his reelection bid.

After his senatorial defeat at age 52, William Benton devoted his time and energy to a variety of educational and public service interests and to writing numerous articles and books. He continued to work as the chairman and publisher of *Encyclopaedia Britannica* until 1967. During this time he also served as a U.S. member of the UNESCO Executive Board, with the rank of ambassador. At the 1968 ceremonies honoring *Britannica*'s bicentennial and Benton's 25th anniversary as its publisher held at the University of Chicago, he was the first recipient of the William Benton Medal for Distinguished Service.

William and Helen Benton had two sons and two daughters (one natural and three adopted). He died in his sleep on March 18, 1973, in his apartment in New York.

In February 1986 the two firms of Benton and Bowles and D'Arcy, MacManus, Masius merged to become D'Arcy, Masius, Benton and Bowles—today a major United States–based international advertising agency.

Author's Note: Newspaper stories and books offer different versions of events and circumstances regarding the founders of Benton and Bowles. Much of the information in this chapter reflects the recollections of William Benton. In the chapter on Chester Bowles, the facts may differ, in that case reflecting the information as recalled by Bowles.

FURTHER READING

Works by Benton

"The Teachers and the Taught in the USSR." In *1965 Britannica Book of the Year*. Chicago: Encyclopaedia Britannica, 1965.

This Is the Challenge. New York: Associated College Presses, 1958.

The Voice of Latin America. New York: Harper, 1961.

"The Voice of Latin America." In *1961 Britannica Book of the Year*. Chicago: Ency-
    clopaedia Britannica, 1961.

"The Voice of the Kremlin." In *1956 Britannica Book of the Year*. Chicago: Encyclo-
    paedia Britannica, 1956.

Benton also contributed over 100 articles to major magazines.

Works about Benton

Alter, Steward. "New Strengths Outweigh Mergers Cost: DMB&B Risks 'Minimal' $100
    Million in Bid to Build Global Network." *Advertising Age* (February 3, 1986):
    3, 66.

Bowles, Chester. *Promises to Keep*. New York: Harper and Row, 1971.

Current Biography 1973. New York: H. W. Wilson, 1973, p. 450.

Current Biography 1945. New York: H. W. Wilson, 1945, pp. 40–42.

Encyclopaedia Britannica. 15th ed. Chicago: Encyclopaedia Britannica, 1974, p. 986.

Hyman, Sidney. *The Lives of William Benton*. Chicago: University of Chicago Press,
    1969.

Lieberman, Joseph I. *The Power Broker*. Boston: Houghton Mifflin, 1966.

Ogilvy, David. *Ogilvy on Advertising*. New York: Vintage Books, 1985.

Webber, Gordon. *Our Kind of People*. New York: Benton and Bowles, 1979.

Whitman, Alden. "William Benton Dies Here at 72; Leader in Politics and Education."
    New York: *New York Times Biographical Edition*, March 1973, pp. 350–52.

Who's Who in America. Chicago: Marquis Who's Who, 1944–45.

Who's Who 1972. Chicago: Marquis Who's Who, 1972, p. 248.

Documents and information from the Benton and Bowles agency are on file at Duke
University (Durham, NC) in the Special Collections Library Center for Sales, Advertising,
and Marketing History.

NOTABLE CLIENTS/CAMPAIGNS

Elliott Fisher Machines (George Batten, 1920s)

Juvenile Magazine (Free-lance, 1920s)

Autostrop Razor (Lord and Thomas, 1923)

Blue Kitchens (Lord and Thomas, 1923)

Kotex (Lord and Thomas, 1928)

Colgate-Palmolive (Lord and Thomas, 1928–29)

Pepsodent (Lord and Thomas, 1928–29)

National Union Radio (Benton and Bowles, 1929)

General Foods (Benton and Bowles, 1929–30s)

Lehman Brothers (Benton and Bowles, 1929–30)

Adolph Goebel meats (Benton and Bowles, 1930s)

Gold Dust (Best Foods) (Benton and Bowles, 1930s)

Helena Rubenstein cosmetics (Benton and Bowles, 1930s)

Hellmann's (Benton and Bowles, 1930s)

Squibb (Benton and Bowles, 1930s)

International Silver (Benton and Bowles, 1931)

Bristol-Myers (Benton and Bowles, 1934)

Colgate-Palmolive (Benton and Bowles, 1934)

Ballentine (Benton and Bowles, 1935)

Drake's Cakes (Benton and Bowles, 1935)

Eastern Airlines (Benton and Bowles, 1935)

Standard Milling (Benton and Bowles, 1935)

WILLIAM BERNBACH
(August 13, 1911–October 2, 1982)

Sammy R. Danna

William Bernbach changed the face of advertising in America. He revolutionized "soft-sell" advertising with the use of suggestion or gentle persuasion rather than what could be called aggressive "hard-sell" pressure often used in sales promotions. He had a genius for enriching a sales message with sensitivity and humor. He was hailed as a creative leader who added much needed class and distinction to a profession often attacked as vulgar. "His creative philosophy was basic: find the simple story in the product and present it in an articulate, intelligent, persuasive way" (Marshall, p. 3).

Bernbach was born in New York on August 13, 1911, to Jacob Bernbach, a designer of women's clothes, and Rebecca (Reiter) Bernbach. After completing his public school education in New York, he was graduated from New York University in 1933 with a bachelor of commercial science degree. He married Evelyn Carbone in 1938, and they had two sons, John and Paul. He worked for the New York World's Fair as a writer and researcher during 1939–40, but his first, true advertising experience came when he joined William H. Weintraub, Inc. There, Bernbach became a close friend with Paul Rand, the agency's art director, who helped refine his interest in the fine arts. After serving two years in the army during World War II, Bernbach became director of postwar planning for Coty.

During the Depression, Bernbach had worked as an office boy for Schenley Distilleries in New York. This severely restricted his creativity, so he decided to write an ad for Schenley's American Cream Whiskey and send it to the company's advertising department. However, by the time the ad was published in the *New York Times*, the advertising department had apparently forgotten its source. Bernbach had this related to a Schenley official and was subsequently given a raise and a position in the advertising department.

Bernbach's first full-fledged advertising job was as a copywriter with Grey Advertising, where he later became vice president in charge of copy and art. It was here that he met Ned Doyle, a vice president of the firm. Both realized the importance of client opinion in the formulation of sales messages, but on the other hand, both men were tired of pandering to clients, often to the detriment of an ad's message. Thus, on June 1, 1949, Doyle and Bernbach joined Maxwell Dane, owner of a small advertising agency, and with less than $500,000 in billings formed Doyle, Dane, Bernbach (DDB). (By 1980, their billings had increased to $1 billion worldwide.) They seemed to complement one another quite well. Dane was the best organizer and ran the firm. Doyle took care of the finances and promotional work, and Bernbach's sole responsibility was "producing the show." The three were described as the most unassuming, unprepossessing men one would ever encounter. Legend has it that a coin decided the order of their names in the firm, and Bernbach was named president to compensate for his name being last.

From the start, clients flocked to DDB at a phenomenal rate. Bernbach kept his prize account from Grey Advertising, Ohrbach's, a New York and Los Angeles low-priced department store competing against stores with much larger ad budgets. "Rather than consuming space with item-by-item prices, Bernbach created a campaign that gave Ohrbach's a reputation for sophistication and, coincidentally, left the public with the impression that the store was expending as much or more on advertising than its more affluent competitors." Ohrbach's ads helped him achieve considerable advertising fame. For example, one ad featured a cat with a high-fashion hat and cigarette holder saying, "I found out about Joan," followed by text about a woman who had discovered the value of shopping at Ohrbach's. This ad became a pinup for copywriters all along Madison Avenue (*Current Biography, 1967*, p. 32).

DDB never tried to wow its clients or "snow" them. "The best way to get clients is to create good advertising, and I mean advertising that sells," Bernbach once asserted, because "too many clients are more interested in the manners of advertising than advertising itself. The client isn't God, but at the same time one should respect him. He may be right" (Bowen, pp. 24, 28). Bernbach's belief was that it was the ad agency's job to articulate the client's message in a fresh and imaginative manner. An ad must have energy "if it is to make itself felt, if it is to perform the first function of an ad—to stop the reader" (Bowen, pp. 28, 51).

With campaigns for Volkswagen, Avis, Polaroid, Levy's rye bread, American Airlines, Columbian Coffee, as well as Ohrbach's, Bernbach and his agency relied on humor and warmth. A good example of Bernbach's creativity was a full-page ad for Volkswagen in which a beetle was pictured on a sea of blank space with the words: "Think Small." One of his most famous campaigns was an Avis promotion countering no. 1 Hertz: "When You're Only No. 2, You Try Harder." DDB saturated the media with this slogan, and within two years, the distant second-place car rental firm's market share increased 28 percent. In 1966 even Hertz acknowledged the success of Avis's ads by instituting a retaliatory campaign. Under Bernbach's 25-year leadership, DDB was credited with upholding a creative revolution that changed the face of much of American advertising with ads that attracted the attention and sales dollars of readers, listeners, and viewers.

Bernbach would not handle a product that could not live up to its advertising because he felt "nothing makes a bad product fail faster than a great advertising campaign." As an example, before he undertook Calvert's campaign for its new "soft whiskey," Calvert had to remove every single bottle of its old whiskey from the market at a cost of $1 million. His favorite campaign was one DDB contributed to SANE (Committee for a Sane Nuclear Policy). Believing that previous SANE ads emphasizing fearsome mushroom clouds reached only those already converted, Bernbach developed a quieter approach. For example, Dr. Benjamin Spock was pictured holding a child on his knee with the caption: "Dr. Spock is worried." Another DDB piece, preparatory to a nuclear test-ban treaty read: "We now have enough atom bombs to kill every Russian 360 times. The Russians only have enough to kill every American 150 times. We're ahead, aren't we?" (*Current Biography, 1967*, p. 32).

Bernbach liked photographic images for their flexibility, their versatility, their realism, their special effects. He enlightened the advertising industry with his images, but they were never a trademark with him or even a focus of concentration. In reality, they were just something he thought seemed to work well.

Bernbach was willing to tackle impossible tasks in all his ads because he believed in the power of advertising to move people. His ad elements all worked together. The type was not merely set for maximum readability. It was designed to control the eye, and its boldness—or lack of it—was carefully chosen to steer one's attention to the proper emphasis. Dark shadows were another Bernbach innovation. They were the inevitable accompaniment to what is known in photography as high-key lighting. This technique provides a strong light source to highlight one side of a subject and lets the other side fall into shadow.

At times competitors chided Bernbach for making things look too real—which was precisely what this advertising genius desired to accomplish. This was clearly illustrated in his Levy's rye bread advertisement where teeth marks were pictured in a slice of bread with the caption: "New York is eating it up."

Bernbach respected the creative process above every other aspect of the advertising business and demanded that others respect it, too. He believed that advertising could be startling, as well as charming, interesting, persuasive, and inventive. This he proved time and time again, and the people he hired and inspired proved it countless times more. He believed that "it's a survival need of human beings to reach one another" because "our future depends on [communications]." When once asked, "Where does advertising fit?", Bernbach responded: "Morality doesn't come with communications expertise, it comes with the man. . . . The public believes the press, but they're not too sure about us. Ironic, isn't it? The public is protected against false advertising because in every buying-selling situation, they have a built-in suspicion, but they're vulnerable to the press. When the press lies to them, the damage is critical" (Hixon, p. 29).

Bernbach helped to open the ad industry to creative Jewish people, but "that had nothing to do with their being Jewish. I did the same thing for Italians and other minorities. My only requirement was that they be talented" (Hixon, p. 28). Bernbach defined a talented, creative person as one who does not follow but leads; one who gets his ads looked at; one who doesn't create at the expense of selling; one who establishes a personality for the client's product; one who stands up to the client when convictions demanded it; and one who has inventiveness but is disciplined. In short, he proclaimed: "Everything you write . . . everything on a page—every word, every graphic symbol, every shadow—should further the message you're trying to convey" (Marshall, p. 80). Some of those receiving Bernbach's creative training included George Lois of Lois Holland Callaway, Julian Koenig of Julian Koenig, Inc., and Ronald Rosenfeld and Leonard Sirowitz of Rosenfeld, Sirowitz and Lawson. These talents formed their own agencies, perhaps in much the same manner and circumstances as did Doyle, Dane and Bernbach.

In 1976, due to DDB's mandatory retirement age of 65, Bernbach stepped aside as chief executive officer of what was then America's 11th largest ad agency. He was succeeded as chairman by Joseph R. Daly, but upon the request of the board, he remained as chairman of the executive committee. In the early years at DDB, he wrote most of the ads himself, but as the agency grew, he edited ads and taught others—old and young—invaluable lessons in creativity.

The American Advertising Federation inducted William Bernbach into the Advertising Hall of Fame on February 9, 1977. Other honors received during his career included being voted "The One Person Who Did Most for the Progress of the Advertising Industry" in 1963, 1965, and 1966 (award made by the *Gallagher Report* via reader poll); Copywriters Hall of Fame, April 28, 1964; 1966 Man of the Year Award from Pulse, Inc.; 1968 Madden Memorial Award; "Top Advertising Agency Executive" in 1969 (by *Ad Daily* via industry-wide balloting); and the "1976 Recipient of American Academy of Achievement Award."

Bernbach was an officer and/or member of these organizations: Citizens Committee for New York City, Inc., board of directors; City Athletic Club, member; International Eye Foundation, board of directors; Lincoln Center Film Committee, vice-chairman; New York University, distinguished adjunct professor; New York University Alumni Club, member; Municipal Arts Society of New York, board of directors; Salk Institute for Biological Studies, board of directors; Urban Design Council of the City of New York, member.

Bernbach died of leukemia on October 2, 1982. *Newsweek's* obituary, like numerous others, was short, saying Bernbach was witty, low-key in his campaigns, but it noted how he subtly pitched products at what he called the "illogical passions" of shoppers (October 18, 1982, p. 112). *Time* reported that Bernbach preached that "honesty sells," noting too his wit and incisiveness (October 18, 1982, p. 100). *Current Biography* added that his notable campaigns "spearheaded the creative revolution on Madison Avenue" (Moritz, ed., 1982, p. 460).

In November 1983 George Lois, Bob Gage, Helmut Krone, and Bill Taubin presented Bernbach's wife, Evelyn, with a special award from the Art Directors Club of New York in honor of Bernbach's creative career. However, the best recognition of Bernbach's advertising career was given by Allan M. Kaufman in the October 1982 issue of *Madison Avenue*. The tributes to Bernbach upon his death "paint a picture of a man who left an indelible mark on almost everyone who knew him. They praise the brilliance of his contributions to advertising as a craft and a profession. They make it clear that he left a permanent vacancy in what is considered a large number of hard-boiled hearts." However, they did not explain the way he changed advertising, actually the nature of advertising itself. Bernbach's style in advertising was "wildly eclectic." He operated by "intuition and feel." Some of his best ads were done without him even having to pick up a pencil. "He knew when something was right or wrong long before he could explain why; sometimes he knew without being able to explain at all" (pp. 59, 60, 64).

Kaufman emphasized Bernbach's huge difference to the soul of advertising by comparing him with a great contemporary, David Ogilvy of Ogilvy and Mather. Kaufman described "the early '50s as fascinating years." Both Ogilvy and Bernbach were certainly "in their prime"; both used print brilliantly yet differently. Where Ogilvy's humor was almost always in the copy, Bernbach's might just as often be in the picture. Frequently, the joke was left out. Both men took themselves and their work seriously. Both were meticulously fussy in the pursuit of excellence. Ogilvy made rules, but Bernbach "ruled by the seat of his pants." Kaufman noted how neither Bernbach nor Ogilvy adhered to the then dominant myth that advertising must be geared to a 12-year-old's mind. While Ogilvy instructed his staff to think of the consumer "as your wife," Bernbach said that "it is impossible to *over*estimate the intelligence of your audience." Humor in print ads before Ogilvy and Bernbach came along was largely a matter of style rather than content. Ads were frequently illustrated with cartoons, though ad cartoons were seldom funny or expected to be. Kaufman characterized Bernbach's humor as quite different from Ogilvy's: The former was "as American" as the latter "was British" (p. 60).

Unlike industrial-heartland Americans such as Leo Burnett, Bernbach was melting-pot American. Regardless of how much money he made, Bernbach "never lost touch with whatever it is in this country that can take people as diverse as the Irish, Italians, Ethiopians, Slavs, Chinese, Cubans and Jews and turn them into card-carrying New York customers almost overnight" (Kaufman, p. 60).

Although he was a wonderfully articulate man in person, Bernbach did not say much about himself or his methods in writing. "Even his speeches—which leave no doubt about his fascination with the imaginative process and his abiding respect for the creative mind—give few clues to his own habits of thought or his own ways of working" (Kaufman, p. 59). "He considered research to be a major obstacle to creative innovation. 'I warn you against believing that advertising is a science,' " he once admonished an audience of advertising executives. "It is intuition and artistry, not science that develops effective advertising." Bob Gage, executive vice president of DDB at the time of Bernbach's death, 'noted: "If Bill liked it, he would make sure the client would buy it. Bill never had a lousy idea." Bernbach seemed to have an "ageless" mind, and his ideas remained as fresh as when he began (Marshall, p. 80). Another long-time DDB creative, Phyllis Robinson, stated: "I don't think Bill set out to make a revolution or a fortune. The whole idea was creative freedom. His ambitions were only large in terms of room to breathe. What excited him—and us—was the idea of running our own show and doing the kind of work we loved to do without having to filter it through a noncreative management." Bernbach asserted that the appeal to logic often fails because "the brain is not an instrument of logic at all. It is an organ of survival, like fangs and claws. So the brain doesn't search for truth, it searches for advantage" (Hixon, p. 28).

When Bernbach was director of the Harper's Magazine Foundation, it was noted that he "probably had a greater impact on American culture than any of the distinguished writers and artists who appeared in the pages of *Harper's* during the past 133 years" (Kinsley, ed., p. 11). "What Bernbach was looking for was uniqueness. He never worked on a campaign where a unique product quality wasn't discovered and entertainingly communicated." Bernbach once said: "The real giants have always been poets, men who jumped from facts into the realm of imagination and ideas" (George Griffin, "Find and Tell the Story," *Graphic Arts Monthly*, January 1983, p. 89).

FURTHER READING

Works about Bernbach

Bowen, Croswell. "Ned Doyle, Maxwell Dane, William Bernbach." *Madison Avenue* (August 1959): 23.

Cummings, Bart. "He Was Never a Slave to Rules, . . . " *Advertising Age* (November 8, 1982): M-4, M-5, M-46, M-49.

Hixon, Carl. "The Bernbach Fantasies." *Advertising Age* (August 11, 1986): 28.

Kinsley, Michael. ed. Untitled article. *Harper's* (January 1983): 11.

Marshall, Christy. "DDB Founder Bernbach Dead at 71." *Advertising Age* (October 11, 1982): 31, 80.

Moritz, Charles, ed. *Current Biography, 1982.* New York: H. W. Wilson, 1982, p. 460.

Moritz, Charles, ed. *Current Biography, 1967.* New York: H. W. Wilson, 1967, p. 32.

"William Bernbach" (Biography #1). Unpublished and unnumbered manuscript. New York: DDB, 1976.

"William Bernbach" (Biography #2). Unpublished and unnumbered manuscript. N.p., c. 1982.

Who Was Who in America. Chicago: Marquis Who's Who, 1982, p. 33.

NOTABLE CLIENTS/CAMPAIGNS

Avis

Levy's

Ohrbach's

Volkswagen

CHESTER BLISS BOWLES
(April 5, 1901–May 25, 1986)

E. R. Worthington

Chester Bliss Bowles's ambition was to be a diplomat; prior to reaching that goal he achieved other notable positions. He was cofounder and board chairman of the Benton and Bowles advertising agency, a high-ranking state official, a federal administrator, and a state governor before being appointed an ambassador at age 50.

Chester Bowles was born on April 5, 1901, to Charles Allen and Nellie Harris Bowles in Springfield, Massachusetts. Early schooling was in Springfield and at the Choate Preparatory School in Wallingford, Connecticut, prior to entering Yale, following a family tradition. At Yale he was an average student but a devoted golfer and captain of the golf team. He was graduated in 1924 from Yale's Sheffield Scientific School.

His grandfather Samuel had been owner and editor of the Springfield *Republican*, the local newspaper, which had been in the family over 100 years. His father was also in the paper business, not as a journalist but as a sales agent for wood pulp. After receiving his degree, young Bowles returned home to join the family paper as a cub reporter. Within a year he realized that there were too many relatives between him and the top; he also disagreed on editorial policies with his cousin Sherman, who controlled the paper, so he left. Another factor was his engagement to Julia Mayo Fiske, daughter of the vice president of the Fiske Rubber Company of Springfield. She was not inclined to marry a newspaperman who would spend his life working long hours into the night.

Attempting to begin a diplomatic career, he obtained a minor post at the American Consulate in Shanghai in 1925. Unfortunately, his father became ill before he could start, so Bowles declined admission into the U.S. Foreign Service. Next Bowles sought a job with the Department of Commerce, but none was available. His subsequent decision was to enter the business world; nevertheless, he solemnly promised himself to leave, successful or otherwise, at age 35. Moving to New York, he turned down a $12-a-week job at the *New York*

Times but was hired as a $25-a-week assistant copywriter by an earlier Yale graduate, William Benton, of the George Batten Company, in mid-February 1925. Within a few weeks Chester Bowles and Bill Benton were exploring the possibility of forming their own agency.

A proposal was put together in March whereby the two Yale men would be joined by an older Batten colleague, Maurice Collette. In April Benton and Bowles journeyed to Springfield to discuss with Bowles's future father-in-law the prospect of obtaining the Fiske account. Nothing came of the visit, so the ad agency plans were put on hold.

Bowles continued his involvement with golfing by joining the Baltusrol Golf Club in Short Hills, New Jersey. There he introduced Benton to the golfing clique, but Benton remained a duffer and was embarrassed to play with the more influential members, who were better golfers.

In 1925 Bowles finally married Julia (Judy) Fiske, and they began married life in New York as he continued his work writing copy for accounts such as Wonder Bread. Bowles's initial attempts at copywriting were seen as most elementary; his forte, however, was his imagination, and it did not take him long to master the technical aspects of writing ad copy.

Three years later, in 1928, Bill Benton advocated that Batten merge with another agency in the same building because Batten was not acquiring new accounts. Benton was fired. He rejoined Lord and Thomas in Chicago, a firm he had worked for previously. Ironically, the merger Benton proposed actually took place shortly after he was fired.

In early 1929 Benton returned to New York to meet with Bowles and Charles Mortimer, an old Benton colleague then in the advertising department at the Postum Company, maker of several food products. Mortimer agreed to talk to his boss, Ralph Starr Butler, Postum's advertising manager, about Postum's awarding an account to the proposed Benton and Bowles agency.

Because the Postum offices were in New York, as was Bowles, and Benton was based in Chicago, Bowles put together the presentation for Butler. Bowles promised the two young men could provide enhanced services with a fresh point of view. Collaboration by phone and mail polished the pitch, which was favorably received by Postum. Another meeting was held in Chicago between Benton and Butler. Butler said the duo had a ten to one chance of getting at least one account.

On the strength of the potential account from Postum (which was in the process of acquiring the frozen food company General Foods and retaining the GF brand for the parent company), Bowles and Benton decided to form their own agency in New York. On July 15, 1929, with an initial capitalization of $12,000, the men opened their firm in a two-room office on the 29th floor of the Chanin Building at Forty-second Street and Lexington Avenue. (The actual amount of capitalization for the creation of Benton and Bowles was not recalled similarly by the two partners. Bowles, in his book *Promises to Keep*, stated it was $12,000 [p. 7]. Benton, in *The Lives of William Benton*, remembers the sum as being $18,000 [p. 126].) Butler, now ad manager for the new General Foods, gave

Benton and Bowles two accounts, Hellmann's mayonnaise and Certo, a key ingredient for making jellies.

While at Lord and Thomas in Chicago, Benton had developed research techniques to conduct consumer surveys—questionnaires designed to capture the likes and dislikes regarding a particular product. Using these techniques, Benton and his wife, Helen, and Chester and Judy Bowles hit the streets, ringing doorbells to discover homemakers' jam- and jelly-making secrets. The survey results became the basis for a four-color, half-page magazine ad featuring various state fair jelly contest winners. The ad campaign increased Certo sales considerably.

Bowles was the creative force in the agency, while Benton handled the business end. The success of the Certo campaign was due solely to the creation of the ads. An ex-reporter was hired to cover state fairs and write feature stories for newspapers around the country. Each story included material about jelly contest winners and mentioned Certo.

At the end of 1929 Benton and Bowles had 17 staff members, billings of $40,000, and 10 accounts.

During the next five years the agency prospered in spite of the Depression. New accounts were added (and some such as Adolph Goebel meats and Helena Rubenstein cosmetics were just as quickly lost due to the Depression or ownership changes). These included National Union (producer of radio tubes), Squibb personal-care products, more General Foods products, International Silver, Gold Dust food products, Bristol-Myers, and Colgate-Palmolive.

Bowles believed the Depression actually helped the firm. As sales plummeted, businesses sought any possible means to shore up plunging profits. Thus, ad strategy usually called for a different agency. Firing an ad agency in the early 1930s was as common an occurrence as it is today. Benton and Bowles was young, eager, hungry, and creative; consequently, it was able to grow while other ad agencies were floundering.

During this time Bowles became aware of additional circumstances affecting his life. One was his own recognition that, in spite of a Yale degree, his formal education was lacking. History, geography, politics, economics, languages, literature, art, and music were topics with which he was not well acquainted. He developed a self-education program which took him a decade to complete. It consisted of studying the above topics as applicable to specific countries such as France, Germany, China, Russia, the United Kingdom, and others. Each country took a year of concentrated reading.

Further awareness involved his contact with low- and middle-income Americans while conducting consumer research. He discovered how they lived and what effect advertising did and did not have on them. Later, this knowledge served him well when he was a government official during World War II.

In 1930 the agency moved to larger quarters at 5 East Forty-fifth Street. Billings for 1931 were $166,000, with earnings of $28,000. By 1935, though, billings were almost $10 million, making Benton and Bowles the sixth largest advertising agency in the United States.

The firm's creative flair was founded on Bowles's talent for both copywriting and assembling and supervising a strong creative team. Some of the men and women hired in the early years included public relations man Norman Klein; copywriters Henrietta Owens, Walter O'Meara, Ted Bates, Duane Jones, Maitland Jones, Tom Revere, and Tom Carnese; general manager Jim Adams; account executives Bill Baker and Bob Lusk; and art directors Jim Balch, Walt Stocklin, and Charlie Faldi. Most either rose to top executive positions in Benton and Bowles, formed their own agencies, or left to assume senior positions in other companies.

In 1933 Bowles's marriage to Judy ended in divorce. He remarried in 1934 to Vassar graduate Dorothy Stebbins, a social service worker. His first marriage produced two children, Chester, Jr., and Barbara. Chester and Dorothy, affectionately called Steb by her friends and husband, had three children, Cynthia, Sarah, and Samuel.

In 1932 General Foods president Chester Colby was not happy with the Erwin, Wasey agency, which handled a $5 million, six-product GF account. Erwin, Wasey had taken on the $10 million Camel cigarette account, and Colby believed that it was paying more attention to the Camel campaign to the detriment of GF. The account supervisor at Erwin, Wasey was Atherton Wells Hobler, a partner in the agency. He also was not happy with the lack of attention paid to the GF accounts. One day General Foods ad manager Ralph Butler was invited to lunch by two principals of Erwin, Wasey. Butler, believing the three would be discussing the GF account, was dismayed when the two admen spent lunch worrying about the prices of stocks they owned.

Details of the lunch reached Hobler, who contacted Butler and asked if he would consider giving him the account if he left Erwin, Wasey to join another agency. Butler agreed. Hobler suggested Benton and Bowles.

First, Butler talked to Bill Benton, asking if his firm was big enough to take on the GF account handled by Erwin, Wasey. Benton said he did not think so. Butler then proposed inviting Hobler to become a partner in Benton and Bowles. Butler said even if the new partnership did not come about, GF would still give Benton and Bowles half the Erwin, Wasey account; the other half would follow Hobler, wherever he went.

In April Benton and Bowles welcomed a new one-third-share partner, who brought in the $5 million GF account of Maxwell House coffee, Post bran flakes, Post Toasties, Log Cabin syrup, Walter Baker's cocoa and chocolate, and Diamond Crystal salt. The creative work on these products was shared by Hobler and Bowles.

In the previous decade Maxwell House had been a best-seller. By 1932 sales had shrunk to 39 million pounds, compared to 40 million in 1928. Bowles conducted a consumer survey that revealed: (1) the product was seen as too expensive, and (2) its quality was not perceived to be as good as its competition's. Hobler recommended GF improve the blend, repackage the product in a vacuum pack, drop the price 5 cents a pound, reduce the ad budget from $3.1 million to $1.1 million, and increase brand awareness by sponsoring "Showboat," a one-hour radio variety show. GF agreed. "Showboat" was a success, and Maxwell House sales turned around.

Bowles had enjoyed earlier success creating radio shows and commercials (during the infancy of radio, ad agencies created entire radio shows as well as commercials) for Hellmann's mayonnaise featuring Morton Downey. The daytime radio soap opera "Young Doctor Malone" was created by Bowles as a vehicle to promote General Foods products. After writing the first several scripts, Bowles turned the chores over to a team of writers. Eventually, the show was sold to Procter and Gamble.

As writer and producer of "Showboat," innovator Bowles's ideas became standard procedures for radio and television shows of the future. The use of live audiences and cue cards to generate laughter or clapping and lifelike commercials using sound effects were Bowles's contribution to the new medium. Previously, radio ads had been read from a script by an announcer. Bowles had actors actually rattle their cups and spoons, sip, and sound out the appreciative responses one gets from savoring a delicious, hot cup of coffee. This led to more realistic settings and sound effects for other radio shows. Other Bowles radio firsts were the use of two sponsors for a single show and the creation of musical jingles.

By the mid–1930s Benton and Bowles created network shows that were rated first—"Showboat," second—Palmolive Beauty Box," and third—"Town Hall Tonight." Over 60 percent of its billings were from radio. Also, in 1932, the agency moved again, this time to the ninth floor of 444 Madison Avenue—the street that came to symbolize the home of the most creative advertising ideas in the world.

In the agency's sixth year, Bill Benton announced to his partners his desire to sell his share back to the firm and depart. Bowles and Hobler persuaded Benton to remain aboard a little longer; both worried that his departure would cause key clients to seek other agencies. This also was a personal setback for Bowles, since his 1925 plan called for leaving the business world in 1936. He was considering employment in either government or education. But the older Benton had declared his intention to leave first, so Bowles elected to wait.

The firm did run into some initial client problems related to Benton's formal resignation, which was effective on April 1, 1936. In time, though, the overall impact of Benton's leaving was insignificant, and the agency continued to grow and prosper. Bowles became chairman of the board, with Hobler as president.

The end of Prohibition in 1937 led to advertising opportunities from breweries and distilleries. Calvert Distilleries was one account Benton and Bowles received.

More radio shows, created by the firm's West Coast radio production office, became highly rated programs. These included Rudy Vallee's "Fleishmann Hour," the "Fanny Brice–Frank Morgan Show" (Baby Snooks), "Burns and Allen," and "Good News."

Bowles is also credited with creating the "slice-of-life" approach to selling products by showing how a product's usage benefits someone's life. In this case, though, Bowles used the comic strip format to present the story in print. Because he quite often used a story of a man put in the "doghouse" by his wife, his comic strip ads were called "doghouse strips."

The firm, seeking business from the Midwest, opened a Chicago office in 1937. Only moderately successful, it closed in two years. Benton and Bowles billings for 1937 reached $15 million.

Bowles was a tall, athletic man who enjoyed a vigorous life-style. Friendly, outgoing, and easy to be with, he was just the opposite of his detail-obsessed former partner, Bill Benton. An extremely skilled sailor, he and his wife built a 72-foot schooner, Nordlys, in 1935. Until World War II the family sailed to the Caribbean, Bermuda, Nova Scotia, Newfoundland, and all along the New England Coast. In 1939 Chester and Steb Bowles built a rambling, two-story, brick house on the banks of the Connecticut River in Essex at Hayden's Point.

By the end of the 1930s Benton and Bowles continued strong. Billings remained even at $15 million a year. New accounts added were Dr. Pepper, Prudential Life Insurance, Columbia Records, and Hudnut-DuBarry cosmetics.

In 1938 Bowles made plans to leave. When he announced his impending departure, two major clients voiced their objections, and one of the agency's executives left, taking the biggest account with him. Again Bowles felt obligated to remain with the company. The Colgate account was handled by vice president Ted Bates in late 1940. This account was $7 million, half of the firm's total billings. Bates decided to go out on his own, taking Colgate. Other key creative people also left—some with Bates, others to different agencies or businesses. Bowles approached Procter and Gamble and by mid–1941 had landed their Ivory Snow account, establishing a long-time and lucrative relationship for the agency and the advertiser.

As war clouds darkened Europe, Bowles was not an advocate of armed might to settle global disputes. On the other hand, he was not an isolationist; he did not believe the United States should divorce itself from the rest of the world.

When Bowles had contemplated leaving the agency in 1935 and 1938, circumstances prevented his departure. In early December 1941 Yale president Charles Seymour asked Bowles to consider joining the school in an administrative capacity. To Bowles the timing and position seemed ideal. He seriously considered the offer. The bombing of Pearl Harbor served as the impetus for Bowles finally to leave, but not to join Yale. He was appointed Connecticut State Tire Ration Administrator by the governor. The attorney for Benton and Bowles drew up a stock buy-back plan for Bowles to be paid over a period of years. The total sum he received was about $600,000, approximately $400,000 less than Benton.

During the remainder of his life, Bowles rarely discussed his years in the advertising world. In fact, all references he made to his time with Batten, Barton, Durstine, and Osborn and then Benton and Bowles were mentioned only as his early years in business. While professing a high regard for the people he had worked with, he firmly believed he would have been far happier if he had gone straight from college into public service. On the other hand, he admitted his years on Madison Avenue allowed him the financial freedom to pursue other careers and to travel and write as he saw fit.

In 1942 he was asked to be the Connecticut District Director of the Office of Price Administration (OPA). Since Pearl Harbor Bowles had considered joining the U.S. Navy, but an ear mastoid condition made him ineligible for sea duty. The navy did offer him a commission and the opportunity to teach officer candidates sea navigation courses. In comparison to the responsibility of the Connecticut OPA position, the commission was unattractive; he opted for the civil service post. He did such an outstanding job that in mid–1943 he accepted the position of general manager of the OPA in Washington, D.C.

As general manager and acting administrator of the federal wartime agency, he faced Congress, which complained that too many academicians were being hired as opposed to more desirable practical and applied people. Bowles responded by recruiting knowledgeable businessmen. A short time later President Roosevelt officially selected him to head the OPA, with later appointments to the War Production Board and Petroleum Council for War. His people skills and leadership talent overcame the problems and differences the agency had with Congress.

After the war, President Truman asked Bowles to be director of the new Office of Economic Stabilization. A major problem was coping with an inflationary economy causing high prices and a high cost of living for returning GIs. Outspoken in his support for "the people" and his attempts to control runaway prices, he began piling up enemies in Congress and various trade associations. The National Association of Manufacturers complained that the Price Control Act and Office of Price Administration, by requiring low prices, were not allowing manufacturers of food, appliances, and clothing to comply with market demands. Low prices restricted production and everyone lost, they claimed. Ironically, Benton and Bowles was writing ads for the National Association of Manufacturers, directed against Bowles and the OPA.

Tired of fighting manufacturers and Congress, and dissatisfied with the passage of a compromise OPA bill, Bowles turned in his resignation in mid–1946.

Friends discussed his running as Democratic Party candidate for governor of Connecticut following his return to Essex. Bowles decided he wanted to be the nominee and in the summer of 1946 began touring the state and meeting political leaders. During the summer and early fall much political infighting and maneuvering took place. An overconfident Bowles underestimated his opponents. At the State Democratic Nominating Convention he came in second.

In 1946 he was appointed an American delegate to the first UNESCO conference in Paris. The next year he served as special consultant to Trygve Lie, Secretary General of the United Nations.

By 1948 Bowles expressed renewed interest in being elected state governor and started to test the political waters again. This time Bowles was up against attorney Thomas Dodd, an Irish Catholic and former FBI agent who was an ardent anticommunist. By the end of the summer, though, Bowles was the party's choice when Dodd withdrew.

During the campaign the Republicans charged that the Democrats had an insider slipping them advanced copies of their candidate's speeches (this turned out to be true); otherwise, how was Bowles able to respond so quickly and eloquently to his opponent's charges? Moreover, using survey procedures developed and honed by Benton and Bowles, poll results predicted Bowles would lose. Bowles won the governorship.

A vacant senatorial seat gave Governor Bowles the opportunity for a temporary appointment until the 1950 election picked someone for the remainder of the unexpired term. Bowles wanted a man with a national reputation who had connections in Washington, D.C. The person selected also had to be willing to run in the 1950 election. Optimistically, the person would further be a desirable Democratic candidate for the regular senatorial election in 1952. Based on these criteria Bowles selected his ex-ad agency partner William Benton.

Off-year elections were tough on Democrats in Connecticut; because fewer people voted, most often the Republicans won. In 1950 Bowles and Benton ran as Democratic candidates for governor and senator respectively. Again Bowles employed his ad agency opinion poll techniques, which indicated he would win. But Bowles was fighting an uphill battle; both his record as governor (he failed to come through on a campaign pledge to slash prices) and his campaign were not vote-getters. Bowles lost and Benton won.

In spite of the feelings of some, while governor of Connecticut he accomplished several noteworthy achievements. He was the first governor to establish a State Commission on Civil Rights. As a part of his campaign against discrimination, he desegregated the state National Guard and named the first female and first black to his military staff. He also attended to problems in areas of welfare and child care, education, and housing.

The next year Bowles was appointed U.S. Ambassador to India and Nepal by his old friend President Truman. As a neophyte diplomat he faced the difficult task of creating stronger ties between the United States and Asian countries. India refused to honor the World War II peace treaty agreement with Japan and was opposed to U.S. intervention in Korea. As ambassador to India he immediately attempted to become a part of the country. He chose to live in a private residence rather than the embassy. His three younger children attended local public schools, a first for the United States diplomatic corps. A large, friendly, outgoing man, he traveled throughout India to study the country and its enormous economic problems.

Bowles's experience in business, government, and now foreign service led him to believe the United States needed to develop a bipartisan foreign policy that would meet the needs of countries around the globe. He felt the government was not doing enough to educate American citizens on what was happening in other nations. Too much energy was going into anticommunistic postures and behaviors, not enough into helping economically disadvantaged third-world countries. Nuclear weapons would not guarantee world peace. All countries and nations should put aside force as a means of settling international differences and use wisdom, understanding, and shared wealth and technology to help each other.

His tour terminated in two years, after which he wrote a best-seller, *Ambassador's Report*, an account of his experiences in India. This was followed the next year by *The New Dimensions of Peace*, an analysis of the course of communism and Asian countries and what it meant to Americans.

Returning to Connecticut in 1953, he began another drive for political office, seeking the Democratic nomination for governor. His polls showed strong support, and the state CIO was backing him. The Democratic power brokers, however, favored Abraham Ribicoff. With only organized labor's support, Bowles realized he had no chance for the nomination; in May 1954 he withdrew from the race.

In 1957 Bowles was a contender for the U.S. Senate, going up against his old partner Bill Benton; political foe Tom Dodd; and Dick Lee, mayor of New Haven. The mayor was cut out early in 1958, leaving a three-way race. This time the top Democratic Party leaders had no clear-cut candidate. It finally was settled at the State Democratic Convention in June, with the majority of the delegates opting for Dodd, with Bowles second and Benton last. Bowles finally declared party unity was most important and moved to nominate Dodd unanimously.

Bowles was persuaded to run in the 1958 election for Congress, representing Connecticut's Second District. He won, upsetting a Republican incumbent. As a congressman, he specialized in foreign policy and was a member of the Foreign Affairs Committee. He did not seek reelection in 1960.

As a supporter of John F. Kennedy for president in 1960, he became a key player in assisting the creation of the president's team after the election. Bowles was appointed Under Secretary of State, with Dean Rusk as Secretary of State.

Unfortunately, Kennedy's "new frontier" style of leadership rewarded people who were able to respond quickly, decisively, and aggressively. This conflicted with Bowles's slower, more speculative, and less aggressive manner. His personal tendency to avoid conflict and war found him opposing U.S. intervention in the Dominican Republic after President Rafael Trujillo Molina's assassination in 1961 and the Bay of Pigs incident in Cuba. As American involvement in Vietnam grew, it became apparent that Bowles's concept of foreign policy was no longer deemed acceptable. Moved out of the State Department position, he became special representative to the president for Asian, African, and Latin American affairs. This position included a pay raise and ambassadorial status.

In 1963 he was reappointed U.S. Ambassador to India. Initially, India felt he had little influence in the White House, but he won back the respect of those who saw him as ineffective and became popular by his opposition to the United States supplying arms to Pakistan. Throughout the Johnson administration he remained in New Delhi, resigning in 1969 when Nixon became president.

In 1964, while on his second tour to India, Bowles began to feel the effects of Parkinson's disease, a deterioration of the body's nervous system. Upon completion of his tour, he retired to his rambling, white brick home in Essex, until he died of complications from his disease and a stroke on May 25, 1986.

During his many years of government service and travel, Bowles had taken the time and effort to share his experiences, beliefs, and wisdom by writing books, beginning in 1946 with *Tomorrow without Fear* (a discourse on postwar production). His last book, *Promises to Keep*, concerned his years as a public servant.

In February 1986 the two advertising firms of Benton and Bowles and D'Arcy, MacManus, Masius merged to become D'Arcy, Masius, Benton and Bowles— today a major United States–based international agency.

Author's Note: Newspaper stories and books offer different versions of events and circumstances regarding the founders of Benton and Bowles. Much of the information in this chapter reflects the recollections of Chester Bowles. In the chapter on William Benton, the facts may differ, in that case reflecting the information as recalled by Benton.

FURTHER READING

Works by Bowles

Africa's Challenge to America. Los Angeles: University of California Press, 1956.
Ambassador's Report. New York: Harper, 1954.
American Politics in a Revolutionary World. Boston: Harvard University Press, 1956.
The Coming Political Breakthrough. New York: Harper, 1959.
The Conscience of a Liberal. New York: Harper, 1962.
Ideas, People and Peace. New York: Harper, 1958.
"The Makings of a Just Society." Series of lectures given at Delhi University, India, 1963.
The New Dimensions of Peace. New York: Harper, 1955.
Promises to Keep. New York: Harper and Row, 1971.
Tomorrow without Fear. New York: Simon and Schuster, 1946.
A View from New Delhi. New Haven: Yale University Press, 1969.
Bowles also wrote numerous articles on economic problems and foreign policy.

Works about Bowles

Alter, Steward. "New Strengths Outweigh Mergers Cost: DMB&B Risks 'Minimal' $100 Million in Bid to Build Global Network." *Advertising Age* (February 3, 1986): 3, 66.
Current Biography 1957. New York: H. W. Wilson, 1957, pp. 64–66.
Current Biography Yearbook. New York: H. W. Wilson, 1986, p. 629.
Encyclopaedia Britannica. 15th ed. Chicago: Encyclopaedia Britannica, 1974, p. 207.

Hyman, Sidney. *The Lives of William Benton*. Chicago: University of Chicago Press, 1969.
Lieberman, Joseph I. *The Power Broker*. Boston: Houghton Mifflin, 1966.
Webber, Gordon. *Our Kind of People*. New York: Benton and Bowles, 1979.
Who's Who 1980. Chicago: Marquis Who's Who, 1972, p. 277.
Documents and information from the Benton and Bowles agency are on file at Duke University (Durham, NC) in the Special Collections Library Center for Sales, Advertising, and Marketing History.

NOTABLE CLIENTS/CAMPAIGNS

Wonder Bread (Batten, Barton, Durstine and Osborn mid–1920s)

National Union Radio (Benton and Bowles, 1929)

Lehman Brothers (Benton and Bowles, 1929–30)

General Foods (Benton and Bowles, 1929–30s)

Adolph Goebel meats (Benton and Bowles, 1930s)

Gold Dust (Best Foods) (Benton and Bowles, 1930s)

Helena Rubenstein cosmetics (Benton and Bowles, 1930s)

Hellmann's mayonnaise (Benton and Bowles, 1930s)

Squibb (Benton and Bowles, 1930s)

International Silver (Benton and Bowles, 1931)

Bristol-Myers (Benton and Bowles, 1934)

Colgate-Palmolive (Benton and Bowles, 1934)

Ballentine (Benton and Bowles, 1935)

Drake's Cakes (Benton and Bowles, 1935)

Eastern Airlines (Benton and Bowles, 1935)

Standard Milling (Benton and Bowles, 1935)

Eno Effervescent Salt (Benton and Bowles, 1936)

Calvert Distilleries (Benton and Bowles, 1937)

Continental (Benton and Bowles, 1937)

Fleishmann Products (Benton and Bowles, 1937)

Swans Down Cake Flour (Benton and Bowles, 1937)

Columbia Records (Benton and Bowles, 1939)

Dr. Pepper (Benton and Bowles, 1939)

Hudnut-DuBarry cosmetics (Benton and Bowles, 1939)

Prudential Life Insurance (Benton and Bowles, 1939)

Procter and Gamble (Benton and Bowles, 1941)

CHARLES HENDRICKSON BROWER
(November 13, 1901–July 23, 1984)

Edd Applegate

Charles Brower worked for more than 40 years in advertising at the Batten, Barton, Durstine, and Osborn (BBDO) agency, now one of the three agencies that form Omnicom, one of the largest advertising agencies in the world. He was born on November 13, 1901, in Asbury Park, New Jersey. His father, Charles Hendrick Brower, was an insurance agent and the owner of two butcher shops. Brower, in his book, *Me and Other Advertising Geniuses*, referred to himself as coming from "a long line of New Jersey peasants" (p. 23).

In 1903 his father sold his two butcher shops and purchased a ranch near Pasadena, California, which turned out to be nothing more than acreage flooded with trees. The family moved and tried to live off of the ranch for a year. When that failed, they moved to Pasadena, where Brower's father sold burial insurance.

Young Brower's weeks were routine. As he put it, he went to the Brookside pool on Saturdays, he wore shoes on Sundays, and he attended the Columbia Grammar School Mondays through Fridays. Brower also worked as a paperboy for the *Los Angeles Examiner*. One customer, a wealthy woman, had been delinquent in her bill. One morning about five o'clock Brower stood on the sidewalk in front of her house and yelled, "This is where old Lady Tibbets lives, and she won't pay her *Examiner* bill!" (Brower, p. 26). He was jailed temporarily for disturbing the peace, then fired from his job.

Brower attended Pasadena High School for three years and specialized in agriculture, primarily to emulate his ancestors. During his junior year, his parents inherited enough money from an uncle to return to New Jersey.

The family settled in Freehold, and Brower attended the local high school, which had several hundred students. Brower, standing more than six feet, towered above the others, but he was not lanky; he weighed more than 200 pounds. Because of his size, he played center on the football team. He was elected secretary of his class and played the part of an English suitor in the senior play. He spoke on "Why I Will Never Leave the Farm" at commencement.

Perhaps because of the speech, Brower was determined to go to college. He won a state scholarship to study agriculture at Rutgers. His mother had died, but his aunt believed he was making a grave mistake. She told him that "college was right on the main highway to hell" (Brower, p. 28).

Brower attended Rutgers but within a short time changed his major to physics. Finally, he settled on English. In 1925 he was graduated with a bachelor of science degree in the latter. In an interview that appeared in *Printer's Ink*, Brower said, "I probably earned the distinction of being the only English major in Rutgers' 191–year history to get a B.S. degree" (p. 45).

After teaching at Middlesex County Vocational School, he was offered his first full-time position teaching at the Bound Brook High School in New Jersey. Brower enjoyed teaching, but not the salary. After considering several professions, he worked briefly in Boston as a trainee adjuster for a casualty insurance company. Brower was not suitable for this profession. He then worked as an assistant advertising manager at Pacific Mills. He enjoyed writing advertising copy, so he applied at the George Batten Company (later BBDO). Brower was not hired. Informed that he was not ready for a position in an advertising agency, he waited patiently for about 18 months before he approached the agency again. In 1928 he was interviewed by William Benton, who hired him. Benton later cofounded the Benton and Bowles agency.

When Brower reported for work on the agreed Monday morning, he learned that Benton had been fired and that he had not left anything in writing about having hired a person by the name of Brower. Brower reported to the company every day for three weeks, until Benton's successor finally asked him what salary had been offered. Brower raised the amount from $40 to $50 a week. As Brower put it, "Some say it was immoral, some say it was slick, but I say I deserved some recompense for the two years I had been kicked around and rejected" (Brower, p. 36).

About four months later the George Batten Company merged with Barton, Durstine and Osborn, and Brower worked as a copywriter; his salary was increased to $75 a week. To add to his salary, Brower wrote radio scripts for a friend. He earned $100 for each and averaged two a week.

The first advertisement he wrote at the agency was for Paniplus, a hygroscopic agent which drew moisture from the air and was used by industrial bakers to keep bread moist. The product was made by the Continental Baking Company. Brower's headline, "Cut Losses from Stales," was changed to "How to Cut Losses from Stales." Brower's ability to write, especially headlines and slogans, did not go unnoticed. Indeed, Richard Blackwell, who was in charge of the Armstrong Cork account, came across Brower's writing in a filing cabinet and requested that he be put on the account. He also worked on the Wonder Bread account, even though the client's sales manager suggested that Brower "be thrown to the lions" or "dropped out of the tenth-floor window" (Brower, p. 90) because Brower could not afford a new tuxedo.

Brower's experience as a copywriter broadened. For Hamilton, he wrote the first consumer advertisements that linked watches to the emotional—even sentimental—milestones in people's lives. Brower also wrote copy for the Electrolux refrigerator.

On July 8, 1930, Brower married one of the most influential women he had ever known, Mary Elizabeth Nelson. They had three children. For more than two decades they lived in a simple but pleasant white clapboard house in Westfield, New Jersey. Later, after Brower had received several promotions, they maintained an apartment in Manhattan too, primarily because of the hours Brower devoted to his work.

By the early 1930s he had been promoted to copy supervisor for several accounts, including Armstrong Cork, B. F. Goodrich, and Cellophane. He was earning $5,000 a year. In 1933, however, the agency's billings, which had been as high as $32 million, were about $17 million. Management asked personnel to cut their salaries 10 percent. Brower was no exception, even though he thought his big opportunity had arrived when Barton and Robley Feland asked him to lunch. In the interview that appeared in *Printer's Ink*, Brower said, "I kept planning little speeches of acceptance—what for, I don't know. But I needn't have bothered. They were fattening up the calf for the kill. Because of billings losses, I'd have to take a ten percent cut in salary" (p. 46).

Brower, however, blamed Roy Durstine for many of the agency's problems during the early 1930s because he subscribed to a belief in the "all-around" advertising man: "He abolished the copy department, and the art department, and scattered the people concerned throughout the contact groups. The result was thirty little agencies with nothing in common but the toilets. These little agencies in turn reported to three men of adequate incompetence" (Brower, p. 84). Brower claimed that it took the agency ten years to learn that the theory was faulty.

Brower, together with BBDO's art director and several others, directed the creative plans board when the agency decided to abandon decentralization in the mid–1930s. The plans board was involved in every campaign. Indeed, members decided whether a campaign worked or not; consequently, others in the agency questioned whether so few should have so much power. Finally, in 1939, the plans board was abolished. A copy department was created in its place and was headed by Brower.

In 1940 Brower was elected to the board of directors. During the early to mid–1940s, the agency's client list increased. Although liquor accounts had been forbidden, especially under Roy Durstine's reign, tobacco accounts had been acceptable. Viceroy, which was one of the first cigarette brands to have a filter, was one account. Brower wrote the copy, but sales refused to increase. Eventually BBDO lost the account. The agency continued to expand into the consumer and packaged-goods categories nonetheless.

In the late 1940s and early 1950s, the agency handled several campaigns for politicians, including the presidential campaigns for Thomas E. Dewey and Dwight David Eisenhower. Dewey lost, but Eisenhower won, and BBDO learned from both campaigns. Later, the agency handled Richard Nixon's presidential campaign against John F. Kennedy, which was successful in its own right. Nixon, who had been ill, appeared distraught during the televised debates. He lost the election, but the ad campaign could not be blamed.

In 1946 Brower became an executive vice president of creative operations, which included copy, art, radio, and television. In 1951 he finally became a member of the agency's executive committee. Ben Duffy, the agency's president and chairman of the executive committee, who had been instrumental in BBDO's becoming one of the biggest and most influential agencies after World War II, suffered a cerebral hemorrhage in December 1956, which left him handicapped. Brower was named general manager four months later. In December 1957 he was named president and chairman of the BBDO executive committee, while Duffy, who had partially recovered, was named vice-chairman of the board and vice-chairman of the executive committee.

Brower refused to move into Duffy's or the agency's presidential office. Instead, he remained in his small office, which he furnished "to look like an early-American living room," according to the interview in *Printer's Ink* (p. 44).

His first year as president was exciting, if not troubling. First, the agency lost the $7 million Revlon account. Then, the agency resigned the $1.5 million *Reader's Digest* account so as not to cause problems with its $17 million American Tobacco account. (*Reader's Digest* had published an article about the health hazards of smoking.) Brower also changed the internal structure of the agency by cutting 200 people from the staff. He reorganized the creative—art, copy, radio, and television—groups. He divided the account supervisors into eight groups, and they reported to eight management supervisors, who reported directly to the president. Brower created an office staff to help answer questions and/or solve problems usually brought to him.

Once he had solved these internal problems, Brower went after new clients. Schaefer pens, a $2.5 million account, was landed. Then, over the next several years, the agency landed Pepsi-Cola, a $9 million account; the Columbia Broadcasting System; the Book-of-the-Month Album Club; Coty perfumes; Valient automobiles, a $7 million account; Gallo wines; and the Dodge Motor Company, a $21 million account.

In 1960 the agency opened a branch office in London, which Brower inaugurated. In 1964 he was named chairman of the board of directors. By this time BBDO had about 150 clients. In addition to those mentioned, they included Campbell Soup, du Pont, Lever Brothers, Bristol-Myers, General Mills, U.S. Steel, and Continental Can. By 1965 BBDO had billings of almost $300 million. That year the agency merged with Clyne Maxon, another advertising agency. The merger brought an additional $50 million in billings.

Brower, the six-foot, four-inch man from New Jersey, was not the stereotypical advertising executive of Madison Avenue. Low-keyed, he preferred brown worsted to gray flannel and Rob Roys to Gibsons. He preferred New Jersey to Connecticut. Indeed, his philosophy of advertising even differed. Instead of perpetuating the concepts of hard sell and soft sell, he said, "There is only the smart sell and the stupid sell" ("The Smart Sell," p. 104).

Brower retired from BBDO in 1970. His book, which has been mentioned, was published in 1974, ten years before his death.

FURTHER READING

Works by Brower

Me and Other Advertising Geniuses. Garden City, NY: Doubleday, 1974.

Works about Brower

"BBDO's Charles Brower: The First Year Is Always the Hardest." *Printer's Ink* (December 26, 1958): 44–47.

Moritz, Charles, ed. *Current Biography 1965*. New York: H. W. Wilson, 1965, pp. 55–57.

"The Smart Sell: Charles H. Brower." *Time* (April 18, 1960): 104.

Spielvogel, Carl. "Advertising: The New Top B. at B.B.D.O." *New York Times* (December 22, 1957): 8.

NOTABLE CLIENTS/CAMPAIGNS

Continental Baking (1920s)

Armstrong Cork (1920s and 1930s)

B. F. Goodrich (1930s)

Cellophane (1930s)

Electrolux refrigerators (1930s)

Hamilton watches (1930s)

Wonder Bread (1930s)

Viceroy cigarettes (1940s)

LEO NOBLE BURNETT
(October 21, 1892–June 7, 1971)

Deborah K. Morrison

Most established American advertising firms owe their beginnings to some figurehead who, through either savvy business sense or raw talent, created a niche for his or her brand of advertising in the marketplace. Few agencies, however, keep the vision of those founders alive. In an era of corporate mergers and diminishing name recognition for company founders, one leading world-class agency still remains privately held by its employees and still pays daily homage to its visionary leader, though he died in 1971. The Leo Burnett Company, resolutely headquartered in Chicago since 1935, is one in spirit with Leo Burnett the man; his story gives the agency its inspiration.

Leo Noble Burnett was born in St. Johns, Michigan, on October 21, 1892, the son of a local merchant who intended to christen his son George but fell victim to poor penmanship. ''Geo'' was read as Leo in the birth certificate office, and a now famous moniker was thus created. Young Burnett was quick to learn, quick to show a way with words. His father's store windows proudly displayed the placards Leo lettered to announce sales and prices. In high school he wrote for several county publications and became a budding reporter. He studied journalism at the University of Michigan, graduating in 1914, then worked as a printer's devil and cub reporter at the *Peoria Journal*. His great plan, he later told a reporter, was to become publisher of the *New York Times*.

It was not until he moved to Detroit in 1917 to work for Theodore MacManus at General Motors that Burnett began to use his writing talent to sell. Just months before Burnett's arrival, MacManus had written ''The Penalty of Leadership,'' an advertisement that ushered in the first wave of image selling in American culture. Before this piece, advertising centered on exaggerated claims or dry listings of product benefits, including purchases with little regard to cultivating an actual relationship with the consumer. ''The Penalty of Leadership'' sought to establish that relationship by communicating in a friendlier voice than that of other advertising of its time. Though he was only a junior writer hired to work on an in-house publication in the MacManus shop, young Burnett took careful notes of his boss's method of courting the consumer with copy that befriended through shared experience. The first notion of a career in advertising had been planted.

Burnett married Naomi Geddes in 1918. Feeling the need for a career move that offered more opportunity and stability, they moved to Indianapolis in the early 1920s, where Burnett joined the advertising offices of the Lafayette Motor Car Company. From 1923 to 1930 he was a copywriter at the Homer McKee Company in Indianapolis, working his way up to creative vice president on the Stutz and Peerless automobile accounts. Though Burnett felt a special connection to Indianapolis—his three children were born there and his career became firmly established in that city—the 1929 stock market crash caused Homer McKee to lose major accounts. Realizing opportunity lay elsewhere, Burnett then moved to Chicago to head up the creative side of Erwin, Wasey. For those few years during the Depression, he and fellow writers and art directors watched as some of the most talented ad people in the Midwest moved to New York to create the best advertising. Because of this, Burnett's colleagues pushed him to start his own agency in Chicago. Ever cautious and even disinterested in such a commitment, Burnett held out until an Erwin, Wasey associate, DeWitt O'Kieffe (Jack to friends), threatened his own move to New York. Burnett finally agreed to the agency undertaking.

According to Stephen Fox in *The Mirror Makers*, Burnett gambled more than his good name on the agency opening. "I sold my house, hocked all my insurance and took a dive off the end of the springboard," Burnett recounted (p. 221). The shop was opened with $12,000 in capital, eight creative employees (no businessmen), and a few women's products accounts, among them Minnesota Valley Canning (later to be known as Green Giant), Hoover, and Realsilk Hosiery. On August 5, 1935, the Leo Burnett Company opened its doors with the simple mission to create superior advertising. Leo Burnett was 42 years old.

With the emphasis of his agency resting securely on high creative standards, Burnett and company set out to do advertising that spoke to people, or, in his own words, that used "the inherent drama of the product" to garner consumer attention. His memos on the subject would later be collected in *Leo* (1971). In one such memo, he explains his dedication to this dramatic proposition: "One of the basic concepts in our shop is that there is what we call 'inherent drama' in every product . . . and that [we should] capitalize on it rather than taking the easy way out and leaning on contrived devices and far-fetched associations. I don't think you have to be what they call 'off-beat' to be interesting. A truly interesting ad or commercial is 'off-beat' by it's rarity" (p. 23).

Burnett had a precise vision of what was to take place at his agency. The high standard for creative work would be ever present. His motto became one that would become a permanent fixture in every Burnett employee office and modeled a work ethic rivaling any in the industry: "When you reach for the stars you may not get one, but you won't get a handful of mud either." With Burnett's encouragement, a receptionist also took the concept of quality work—and empathy with the consumer—to heart. She began the tradition of bowls of bright red apples sitting atop her desk, a colorful offering in a bleak economy which represented the agency's commitment to simple, honest communication and an optimistic vision of the future. After all, people reminded Burnett and his new colleagues often, he was starting an agency during the Depression; few businesses could clear such an initial obstacle.

But Burnett's philosophy and business sense were sound, offering great promise to the clients who took that first leap of faith with him during the early years. He gave Green Giant, Pillsbury, the New York–based Tea Council, the American Meat Institute (Burnett's first $1 million client), and Kellogg's enduring appeal during the late 1930s and 1940s. (Indeed, the strategy worked so well that Green Giant, Pillsbury, and Kellogg's continue to be Burnett clients.) Throughout those first years for the agency, Burnett's passion for good advertising was nurtured by his insistence on quality relationships with both clients and his executive staff. Jack O'Kieffe remained his protégé and sounding board for decades, though Draper Daniels (*Giants, Pygmies, and Other Advertising People*) writes of O'Kieffe's disappointment that the company did not remain the "jewel box" small agency he first envisioned in 1935 (p. 206). Burnett found fresh management ideas in the likes of Dick Heath and Bill Young, Heath for his articulate salesmanship abilities, which Burnett himself lacked, and Young for his pool of fresh ideas and copy solutions. By the late 1940s, with Burnett serving as founder and president of the company, billings hit $18 million, reaching $22 million in the early 1950s, and forcing the New York advertising arena to admit Chicago's Leo Burnett Company was a formidable force with which to compete. With this, the "Chicago school of advertising" was recognized as having its own unique voice, reflecting the sensibilities of clients in that region from Green Giant to Pillsbury. Leo Burnett was the movement's strongest supporter.

Yet for all the millions of dollars in billings and the power associated with founding such a successful company, Leo Burnett was not the typical suave advertising man of the era. He was short, bald, and paunchy, smoked Marlboros incessantly, and wore the ashes about his chest and shoulders in a disarmingly frumpy manner, though he never lost the air of modest dignity he also wore so well. His face seemed to be a bit akimbo when one viewed him head on, with eyes peering beneath heavy glasses and a thick lower lip that protruded when he was excited, prompting some to recognize the Lip Protrusion Index evaluating Burnett's displeasure with a campaign idea. Indeed, Burnett was taken to downright earthiness whether he liked the work or not. Expletives peppered his famous creative review committees when he became excited about work that did its job well or he found weak in effort. He did not tolerate a sloppy work ethic from his employees; he himself was a tireless yeoman, scribbling away into the long hours with his trademark thick black pencil. This industry was not solely the prerogative of the young, he announced via memo, it belonged to those who worked the hardest.

These small affectations were part of the Burnett repertoire of working eccentricities. He always signed his name in green ink as a tribute to his first boss at Cadillac in Detroit, maintaining that it made business communication less dull, more spirited for the reader. He wore the same dark pinstriped suits throughout his career, always appearing rumpled and a bit ill-fitted, but suited, he thought, for the business at hand. He addressed his employees gathered to hear his critiques or speeches as "boys and girls" and, indeed, saw differences in how the sexes approached work. In keeping with the times, Burnett thought women generally less able to take on responsibility and emotionally less able to cope with the stressful day-to-day competitiveness of the industry, yet he threw them in the advertising trenches alongside the "boys," feeling the best would always perform. He was an outspoken consumer of his clients' products, often quoting some long-ago heard maxim: "There's no taste or aroma quite like bread and butter."

It was in 1955 that Leo Burnett introduced what has become one of the most famous concepts in advertising history: the Marlboro Man. Searching for a way to redefine the image of the cigarettes from one of tony elegance, Burnett and his team developed the iconographic image of the American cowboy as the quintessential rugged male. Using this as the visual linchpin in a campaign based on masculinity, Burnett developed an entire mystique connecting smoking and strength of character, rugged individuality. The campaign was an overwhelming success; advertising had succeeded in changing a product's image 180 degrees and did so with bravado. At the time, before smoking and cigarettes became topics of controversy and concern, the advertising was considered landmark in its smart relaunching of not only a brand, but a way of life. Burnett found an appeal greater than the product; his intuitive sense of what was believable to the American public made the advertising dramatic.

Throughout the 1960s Burnett remained active in the day-to-day management of the company, sitting in on creative review committees and demanding the work produced meet his standards. His writing brought awards: in 1961, along with David Ogilvy, George Gribbin, and the inimitable Bill Bernbach, Burnett was named a first inductee to the Copywriters Hall of Fame. In testimony to his brilliant career, his face—along with those of other advertising greats—graced the cover of a 1962 issue of *Time* magazine. In 1967 he retired, assuming the title of founder chairman and keeping his office in order that he be close to the work he knew so well. By 1969, after acquisition of accounts including United Airlines and Oldsmobile, the Leo Burnett Company had billings exceeding $200 million and, through acquisitions, maintained offices in 19 countries around the world. The agency was named *Advertising Age*'s "Agency of the Year" in 1976, though the late 1970s proved to be a lackluster creative period for the agency after Burnett's death in 1971. A turnaround occurred in the mid–1980s. Billings climbed to $1.116 billion, making Burnett the first domestic agency ever to exceed the $1 billion mark from a single office. In 1988 the Leo Burnett Company was named agency of the year by *Advertising Age* and *Adweek*.

Few other corporate cultures in the world have attributed their success so overwhelmingly to their founder, going so far as to build the corporate mission and agency standards around the writing and spirit of one man. Few other agencies have managed to keep over a dozen clients for more than 25 years, some remaining with the company for more than five decades. The Leo Burnett Company has accomplished those feats. Advertising great Jerry Della Femina tells the story of pitching the Sony account during the late 1980s. He delivered a powerful presentation to the Sony committee which dedicated his and his agency's efforts if they were given the account. After his pitch, the Burnett management walked in and quietly showed the Sony hierarchy a videotape of a short, gravel-voiced man explaining his philosophy of advertising. Almost 20 years after his death, Leo Burnett succeeded in winning a valuable account for his agency (Crump, p. 75).

In Burnett's memory, good advertising is produced daily in his agency. In his spirit, almost 500,000 apples per year are given out to employees and visitors to the Chicago office. As tribute to his simplicity and modesty, the agency gives Black Pencil Awards to the best Burnett creative work of each year, as well as keeping thousands of the thick pencils he brandished on hand for writers to wield with care.

Leo Burnett has been described by associates as both a dynamic perpetual motion machine and as a slow-walking, rather inarticulate curmudgeon who simply loved his work. Beyond all other descriptions, it seems he was a man passionately dedicated to his vision of advertising that did its job with simplicity and clarity. But, more important, it did this with a sense for what America was feeling at the time. The provocative messages offered by the Marlboro Man, the Green Giant, the Pillsbury Doughboy, Charlie the Tuna, and Tony the Tiger work their magic because they were based on a collective mythology and folklore Americans knew well, then re-created that mythology to sell products. They are comforting and friendly and give consumers visions of the happiness we might have in our daily lives. With these iconographic figures and the advertising that surrounds them, the Burnett style has evolved into a cultural phenomenon that touches the hearts of consumers, as well as reaches their brains. Burnett instinctively led his troops to that dramatic core of the product, perhaps tossing aside more sophisticated and trendy messages for those that came literally and figuratively from America's heartland.

To lead that march toward heartfelt advertising during his three decades as president, Burnett lovingly crafted memo after articulate memo to his vast corral of employees, reminding them that integrity must be the essential ingredient of their work, that the importance of client relationships is based on mutual respect, and that their inherent dedication to quality should push them to search for the superior idea, word, image. He often cited literary figures—Dickens, de Maupassant, Flaubert, Thoreau—to make his point about the quality of careful writing. His messages were sprinkled liberally with lists of how-tos and things to avoid, as if the paterfamilias of the Burnett clan always needed to refresh the memory of the youngsters in his charge. At his retirement from the day-to-day management of the agency in December 1967, Burnett wrote and delivered what possibly is his most eloquent legacy to his agency, "When to Take My Name off the Door." A videotaped version of the speech is shown to all new Burnett employees. In it, he explains his demand:

When you lose the restless feeling that nothing you do is ever quite good enough.

When you stop reaching for the manner, the overtones, the marriage of words and pictures that produces the fresh, the memorable and the believable effect.

When you stoop to convenient expediency and rationalize yourselves into acts of opportunism—for the sake of a fast buck.

When you lose your humility and become big-shot weisenheimers . . . a little too big for your boots.

When the apples come down to being just apples for eating (or polishing)—no longer a part of our tone, our personality.

Finally, when you lose your respect for the lonely man—the man at his typewriter or his drawing board or behind his camera or just scribbling his notes with one of our big black pencils—or working all night on a media plan. When you forget that the lonely man—and thank God for him—has made the agency we now have possible. When you forget he's the man who, because he is reaching harder, sometimes actually gets hold of—for a moment—one of those hot, unreachable stars.

THAT, boys and girls, is when I shall insist you take my name off the door. (*Leo*, pp. 86–87)

Leo Burnett died on June 7, 1971, at his beloved family farm in Lake Zurich, Illinois, after spending part of his day at the office. He was 78 years old.

FURTHER READING

Works by Burnett

Communications of an Advertising Man. Chicago: Leo Burnett, 1961.
The Good Citizen. American Heritage Foundation, 1947.
Leo: A Tribute to Leo Burnett through a Selection of the Inspiring Words He Spoke. Chicago: Leo Burnett, 1971.

Works about Burnett

Broadbent, Simon, ed. *The Leo Burnett Book of Advertising*. London: Business Books, 1984.
Crump, Joseph. "Top Guns: How Leo Burnett Became the Hottest Ad Agency in the Country." *Chicago Magazine* (August 1991).
Daniels, Draper. *Giants, Pigmies, and Other Advertising People*. Chicago: Crain Communication, 1984.
Fox, Stephen. *The Mirror Makers: A History of American Advertising and Its Creators*. New York: William Morrow, 1984.

Burnett was also the subject of articles in *Advertising Age*, *Printer's Ink*, and *Adweek* over a span of five decades.

NOTABLE CLIENTS/CAMPAIGNS

Green Giant (1935–present)

Pillsbury (1944–present)

Kellogg's (1949–present)

Procter and Gamble (1952–present)

Marlboro (1954–present)

United Airlines (1965–present)

THOMAS JASON BURRELL
(March 18, 1939–   )

Sharon S. Brock

Thomas Jason Burrell is chairman of the Chicago-based Burrell Communications Group (BCG), an integrated marketing consolidation of Burrell Advertising, Burrell Public Relations, and Burrell Consumer Promotions. In 1985 Burrell was named Advertising Person of the Year by the Chicago Advertising Club, and by the 1990s BCG was the largest minority-owned advertising agency in the country. Burrell previously worked as a copywriter and copy supervisor for Wade Advertising, Foote, Cone and Belding, Leo Burnett, and Needham Harper Worldwide.

A six-foot, four-inch, trim man, Burrell was born in Chicago on March 18, 1939. He and his sister grew up on the city's South Side. His father, Thomas, was a tavern keeper and his mother, Evelyn, cared for boarders in their home, where she also operated a small beauty salon. Burrell described his early high school years as unmotivated and troublesome. He realized in high school that if he wanted to change direction he needed to change schools and find a supportive peer group, away from his old trouble-seeking friends.

In his next high school, Burrell found friends who planned futures as doctors, lawyers, and corporate executives. He also enrolled in a career counseling program that administered aptitude tests. High scores on persuasive skills and creativity led him to consider a career as an advertising copywriter. However, none of his African-American friends knew any copywriters, nor had they heard of African-Americans becoming copywriters. Burrell's stirring for uniqueness manifested itself, and copywriting became his focus and special niche. within his group. The others talked about careers everyone understood, but he was the risk-taker. He wasn't sure what he would do with copywriting, but it was a goal that would exploit his talents.

Burrell enrolled in Roosevelt University in downtown Chicago as a psychology major. He changed to English and took advertising courses. Teachers mixed praise for his work with caution about the career toward which he was headed.

There were no role models, and agencies did not seem to welcome African-Americans on their staffs. Burrell began working in Wade Advertising's mailroom in 1961. After nine months he moved up to copywriter, and he continued to work at Wade after his college graduation in 1962.

Burrell opened his own agency in 1971, a particularly courageous business venture in the social climate of that time. His experience at general market agencies had taught him that while white advertising people understood how to develop campaigns, they did not understand the cultural differences between black and white consumers. Blacks are more complex and sensitive, Burrell said during a personal interview. If he could sell something to a black consumer, he could sell it to anyone. Burrell said black consumers act differently than whites. They were kept separate for so long that their behavior, attitude, and interests adapted to that separatism. White agencies saw blacks becoming lighter as they moved up the socioeconomic ladder, he said. It was hard for white people to see people of dark color as successful even in the early 1970s, when blacks became aggressively concerned about being black enough to be accepted by other blacks (Dates, p. 326).

Jannette Dates recounted in "Half a Loaf" (p. 424) that advertisers ignored the black market until the late 1960s, even though articles had reported the different spending habits of blacks and whites as far back as the 1930s and 1940s. These reports described the strong brand loyalty of black consumers and their particular concern for personal appearance and quality products. By the 1950s studies of the black market drew distinctions between the purchasing behavior of upper- and lower-class blacks, as well as between black and white consumers. Also during the 1950s advertisers exerted an enormous influence over television programming, and they were afraid to have their products associated with black consumers. The Nat King Cole variety show first aired in 1956 on NBC with no sponsors. When it drew high ratings, Rheingold Beer agreed to cosponsor it, but the lack of other sponsors caused the program to die after a year (Sherard, p. 386).

It was not until 1961 that Lever Brothers' Wisk laundry detergent ran the first general audience daytime TV commercial that included blacks. Two years later, with the trepidation of a sailor entering uncharted waters and the civil rights movement blowing gale-force pressure, Lever Brothers said it would use more blacks in its advertising, and it developed an All commercial with Art Linkletter interviewing a black housewife about her laundry problems. Over the next few months Lever received 64 letters from its millions of viewers and more than half were positive. Over the next few years, when Lever ran 167 integrated commercials, there was no positive or negative impact on sales (Fox, pp. 280–84).

Other studies showed that integrated commercials were important to African-American viewers but made little difference to whites (Dates, p. 327). In 1967 Foote, Cone and Belding put a black person in an ad for the first time. The ad was for the Buick Electra 225, a popular car in the black market. Martin Luther King's murder in 1968 created a surge of concern about the lack of blacks on

Madison Avenue, but even with scholarship programs and guaranteed jobs, few blacks felt welcome in the advertising field. White-owned agencies were not hiring blacks unless they sounded Anglo-Saxon, so the contribution of blacks to creative advertising for special markets was minimal. By 1970, however, the black cause had moved from integrationist to nationalist ideals, and special-markets advertising was unavoidable (Fox, p. 284).

It was in this environment that Thomas Burrell decided to start an agency and convince major companies that black consumers were not just dark-skinned white people. "They are a group with a unique heritage, distinctly different taste and formidable buying power. If behavior is different, and attitude is different and interests are different, that certainly translates into different buying habits, different brand preferences, different ways of looking at a particular product category" (McGeehan, p. 4). Furthermore, by 1971, 11 percent of the population, or 23 million Americans, were African-American, and they were spending more than $30 billion on consumer goods and services. Burrell and other early black agency owners like the late Frank Mingo, Carolyn Jones, and Vince Cullers knew that black American consumers would respond warmly to advertisers because "they wanted to be courted for their money as others were, and they would respond to the respect implicit in the courting process, when the advertisement was neither patronizing nor condescending" (Dates, p. 423).

Burrell started his agency in Chicago because the Midwest had a value system that included family involvement and an entrepreneurial spirit, he told E. E. Schultz of *Madison Avenue* magazine in 1986 (p. 40). Burrell's wife, Barbara, joined him in the agency in 1974 and was vice-chairman of BCG until their divorce in 1990. His sister worked at the agency in the 1980s and returned to the accounting department in 1992.

In Chicago, a person achieved success by owning a piece of land, a barbershop, a business, a bungalow, Burrell told Schultz. In New York, status was measured by a large office and affiliation with a large corporation. He thought this developed an employee mentality instead of an entrepreneurial spirit. Chicago also provided a hospitable environment for more than 10,000 minority-owned businesses, including some of the country's largest black-owned enterprises: Johnson Publishing, Soft Sheen cosmetics, and Burrell Advertising. Burrell believed that blacks succeeded in Chicago because they had developed a tradition of depending on each other to survive when they moved from the fields of Alabama and Mississippi to a segregated North. Blacks who moved to the East Coast were household servants or better educated and more assimilated into the white community, he told Schultz, and this weakened the support they gave each other.

Burrell started his business without bank loans. It took six months to win the first account, a $3,000 job from Philip Morris, but by 1972 Burrell had landed part of the Coke, Stroh's Brewery, and Ford Motors accounts. In the early 1970s it was fashionable for major corporations to award parts of large accounts to black agencies as a goodwill gesture. Eventually, however, McDonald's, Sony, Coca-Cola, K-Mart, Procter and Gamble and others sought creative black-owned agencies like Burrell's to reach a growing black middle class with billions of dollars to spend.

Burrell created advertising that had a special meaning for blacks but also appealed to whites. His black-oriented life-style ads for Martell cognac ("I assume you drink *Martell*") tested so well in the general market that the company dropped its "big bottle" campaign done by a competing agency and gave Burrell its first general audience account in 1984. When he won Procter and Gamble's general market Crest account the same year, Burrell used a scene with a black father teaching his son to knot a tie as the setting for a commercial. In another Crest commercial, a father was hurrying to his son's concert, speculating about his role as a parent, including choosing the best care for his son's teeth. These would be routine scenes for a white audience, but their meaning was poignant for black consumers about whom statistics documented a high number of families without live-in fathers (Tracy, p. 47).

The most effective way to reach a black consumer is to celebrate the people, not the product, Burrell said. Any time a black person appears in an ad, the black person is prepared to be offended. "How are they going to use us this time?" a black person wonders. White people don't have to go through that. After his agency won five of 42 Communication Excellence to Black Audiences (CEBA) Awards in 1987, Burrell said, "Black consumer advertising—its focus on playing back a positive reality, with themes of succeeding, surviving, overcoming, achieving and aspiring—has influenced what comes out of general market agencies." He said he could see influences of black culture, especially black music, on general advertising to the baby boomer generation. "Rap is excellent for advertising," he told a reporter in 1990. "With rap and its verbal emphasis, you can focus on the product message and disseminate all the information about the product and still be interesting" (Smith, p. 1).

Burrell deliberately uses emotion in ads (McGeehan, p. 5). He believes that before you can get to a consumer's purse strings, you have to touch the heartstrings. "You have to elicit some emotion, whether it's humor, warmth or fear. Into that emotional envelope, you put your message." Burrell advertising used high fashion and appealed to his market's affinity for high-end brands. African-Americans respond to status appeals, Burrell explained during an interview with the author, because they were stripped of their identity when they were brought to the United States. As they regain their place as intelligent, productive human beings, symbols of status are important. This means that African-Americans prefer visible and portable material goods, like cars and designer-label clothes. White consumers, who were not stripped of their status, can afford to have expensive houses which their work or social groups may never see. African-Americans want goods that can be seen by as many people as possible so they can establish their rank. Burrell estimates that this cultural difference will exist for a long time, until the country is many generations away from desegregation, poverty, and discrimination.

Burrell ads are in settings familiar to African-Americans, who usually live in cities, not along streams or on mountains. One of Burrell's TV spots for Coke showed five black kids on a Manhattan stoop singing the "Coke adds life" jingle. The commercial won a CLIO, the industry's top award. On the other hand, a Marlboro cigarette campaign created by Burrell modified "Come to where the flavor is" to "Where the flavor is" and featured the macho Marlboro Man in city scenes familiar to the African-American community. Apparently a citified, colored version of the outdoor, white Marlboro Man was perceived as threatening to the strong brand identification of the country's most popular cigarette, and Burrell's version of the campaign rests unpersuasively in the archives of the Smithsonian. Burrell said his agency instinctively "reads" the African-American community correctly, but it also uses research to track trends and changing values. Burrell Communications Group formed a partnership with research vendor Daniel Yankelovich to guarantee regular access to current data about its special audiences.

Coca-Cola acknowledged satisfaction with Burrell's work in 1983 when it awarded the agency all of its marketing effort in Africa, a large international account that Burrell was pleased to win. The marketing effort in Africa was put on hold when the continent's economy weakened, but with the recognition from that account Burrell became an international presence in a global company. Burrell Advertising opened a second office in Atlanta specifically to serve its Coke account.

Burrell's agency has won several CEBA Awards each year since that program began in 1977. The big winners were often black-owned agencies that specialized in advertising to black audiences. Young and Rubicam and Ogilvy and Mather are among the general market agencies that have won CEBA Awards for advertising for the Urban League, the United Negro College Fund, and Dr. Pepper. Burrell won a second general advertising CLIO Award, for a McDonald's commercial, in 1978.

Warren Berger wrote in *Advertising Age* in 1992, "Minority owned agencies don't do breakthrough creative work because they rely on old-fashioned formulas—warm, fuzzy family scenes and overly earnest testimonials" (p. 13C). Burrell said that positive social messages are what sell best to the African-American community, and his job is to sell products, not win awards. Black-owned agencies will make a stronger contribution to creative campaigns when they are brought in for the initial strategizing, he added. Frequently, minority agencies are asked to adapt an ongoing campaign to the nuances of the African-American culture, and that places restrictions on creativity.

While Burrell was building the billings of his agency to an estimated $60.7 million in 1991, he also served in leadership positions nationally and in Chicago. He was chairman of the Chicago Council of the American Association of Advertising Agencies, a member of the National Advertising Review Board, and on the National Board of Directors of AAAA. He serves on advisory councils for Roosevelt and Howard universities and is a member of the executive committee of Chicago United, the board of governors of the Chicago Lighthouse for the Blind, and the board of directors of the Lyric Opera of Chicago.

Burrell's effectiveness on many community governing boards was epitomized in November 1989 when he took charge of selling tickets for the Chicago Urban League's annual fund-raiser. At $250 a plate, the dinner broke all attendance records, with 3,354 guests seated everywhere the Chicago Hilton could find space. The Urban League filled its coffers with an estimated $568,151.

The Chicago advertising community awarded Burrell the Albert Lasker Award for lifetime achievement in advertising in 1985–86, and the University of Missouri gave him its prestigious Missouri Honor Medal for Distinguished Service in Journalism in 1990.

Vince Cullers, who started the first long-standing black-owned advertising agency in 1956, predicted to *Newsweek* magazine (Anderson, p. 60) that black advertising agencies might become victims of their own success. After playing a unique role in assimilating blacks into the general market, the agencies might become just American agencies, he said. Thomas Burrell assessed the future of black-owned agencies differently. He told the author that as markets become more segmented, he predicted that even the black market will segment as the middle class grows and African-Americans earn more positions of influence and power. "While social assimilation is happening very fast," he said, "the cultural differences are deep-seeded and it will take generations to change."

FURTHER READING

Works about Burrell

Anderson, Monroe. "Advertising's Black Magic." *Newsweek* (February 10, 1986): 60.

Berger, Warren. "A Different World." *Advertising Age* (July 6, 1992): 12C–16C.

City of New York Department of Consumer Affairs. "Invisible People: The Depiction of Minorities in Magazine Ads and Catalogs." New York, 1991.

Dates, Jannette L. "Half a Loaf: The Advertising Industry." In *Split Image: African Americans in the Mass Media*, edited by Jannette L. Dates and William Barlow. Washington, DC: Howard University Press, 1990, pp. 421–23.

Fox, Stephen. *The Mirror Makers: A History of American Advertising and Its Creators*. New York: William Morrow, 1984.

Lubell, Ellen. "More Advertisers Take the Rap." *Newsday* (August 5, 1990): 8.

McGeehan, Pat. "The Burrell Style." *Advertising Age* (December 19, 1985): 4.

Mahaney, Barbara. "Urban League Dinner Brims with Success." *Chicago Tribune* (November 6, 1989): 20.

Schultz, E. E. "Chicago: Windy, Toddling, and Black!" *Madison Avenue* (February 1986): 40.

Sherard, Regina G. "The Emergence of Blacks on Television." In *Impact of Mass Media: Current Issues*, edited by Ray Eldon Hiebert and Carol Reuss. White Plains, NY: Longman, 1985, pp. 384–93.

Smith, Lisa. "Still a Ways to Go." *BackStage* 28, no. 43 (October 23, 1987): 1.
Tracy, Eleanor Johnson. "Black-and-White Magic in Chicago." *Fortune* (September 2, 1987): 47.
Weingarten, Paul. "And Now, the Minority View . . . " *Chicago Tribune Sunday Magazine* (July 13, 1986): 8ff.

NOTABLE CLIENTS/CAMPAIGNS

Brown-Forman (Canadian Mist, Southern Comfort)

Coca-Cola

Ford Motors

General Foods

K-Mart

L'eggs hosiery

McDonald's

Martell cognac

Philip Morris, Marlboro

Procter and Gamble

Quaker Oats

Stroh's Brewery/Schlitz malt liquor

Sprite ("I like the Sprite in you")

EARNEST ELMO CALKINS
(March 25, 1868–October 4, 1964)

Arthur J. Kaul

Earnest Elmo Calkins, cofounder of the first modern advertising agency, was for decades the fledgling 20th-century advertising industry's influential spokesman for artistic, creative, and professional standards.

Born March 25, 1868, in Geneseo, Illinois, he was a son of Mary Harriet Manville and William Clinton Calkins, an attorney in Galesburg, Illinois, where young Calkins spent his youth. An attack of measles at the age of six caused a gradual loss of hearing that four years later resulted in deafness, a handicap that had a profound impact on his personality. "Deafness had produced in me what a more scientific age glibly describes as an inferiority complex," Calkins wrote in *"Louder Please!": The Autobiography of a Deaf Man.* "The world and I seemed so far apart" (p. 147).

His deafness isolated him in the world of books, pictures, and maps, and he became a prodigious reader, which offset the mediocre formal teaching he received in the public schools he attended. Nevertheless, he graduated from high school, working during the summer in the local newspaper's print shop. Calkins's first ambition was to become a printer and publisher, an interest kindled when he was 12 and acquired a hand press and type and set up a makeshift print shop in the woodshed of his parents' home. He entered Knox College in Galesburg, struggled through classes, and was elected editor-in-chief of the college magazine his senior year. The magazine experience, he recalled years later, was the most valuable aspect of his college education. He graduated with a B.A. degree in 1891.

After graduation Calkins went to work for the local newspaper, setting type and preparing crude advertisements for town merchants inspired by examples he had seen in *Printer's Ink.* An announcement in *Printer's Ink* of a carpet sweeper manufacturer's $50 prize for the best advertisement published in a local newspaper launched Calkins's advertising career. He submitted an advertisement for the sweeper as an ideal Christmas gift and won out over 1,433 entries. One of the contest's three judges was advertising pioneer Charles Austin Bates.

Calkins went to New York when he was 23 to launch a career with $28 and a union printer's card. He worked briefly as a compositor for Harper and Brothers, setting type for books by William Dean Howells and "touching with reverent fingers the hem of literature's skirts" ("*Louder Please!*", p. 129). Calkins was hired as the $12-a-week editor of a trade paper, *The Butcher's Gazette and Sausage Journal*, owned by an irascible German butcher. In an effort to find a better-paying job, Calkins answered a blind help wanted classified ad that turned out to be for his own job at *The Butcher's Gazette*. Calkins promptly returned home to Galesburg, where he spent a year barely scraping by, working as a printer, columnist, reporter, and advertising man. He took a job as advertising manager for a Peoria department store.

Five years after winning the advertising contest, Calkins sent a sheaf of his advertising copy to Charles Austin Bates in New York. Bates responded by telegram: "If you will work for fifteen dollars a week, more if and when worth it, come to New York" ("*Louder Please!*", p. 154). A few days later, Calkins arrived in Bates's office and began work as a copywriter. He succeeded and was given increasingly more important work. However, Calkins's zealous efforts to impress Bates and the agency's clients with his cleverness occasionally backfired. Across the top of Calkins's advertising jingles for George P. Rowell's *Printer's Ink*, Bates wrote: "Dear Mr. Rowell, here is some stuff one of my young men has written." Rowell responded: "Dear Mr. Bates, one of your young men has written some damned bad stuff" ("*Louder Please!*", p. 159).

Two discoveries during Calkins's five-year employment with the Bates agency had decisive impacts upon his career in advertising. An exhibition at the Pratt Institute School of Design introduced him to the world of art and design, a discovery that Calkins applied to advertising. "Here was what advertising lacked: form, visualization, the attractiveness of color and design to strengthen its appeal to the eye," Calkins wrote ("*Louder Please!*", p. 165). He enrolled in night classes in applied design to learn how he could apply art and design principles to advertising layouts. Calkins became a proponent of the artistic and creative dimensions of advertising and organized the National Arts Club's first showing of advertising art.

The other discovery was Ralph Holden, who would become his partner when they established their own agency, Calkins and Holden, in January 1902. Dissatisfied with his job in the freight department of the Baltimore and Ohio Railroad, Holden embarked on an advertising career when he joined the Bates agency. Calkins and Holden became close friends despite their divergent personalities. Calkins was shy, timid, introverted; Holden was confident, independent, outgoing. In his autobiography, Calkins described the relationship as a "cross-matched team": "He was a business man with a business mind, accurate, exact, definite, qualified to talk terms, make arrangements, and report clearly and conscientiously, while I, concerned with the creative, imaginative, artistic side of the work, was apt to be vague and impatient of details. To put it briefly, Ralph contributed the brass tacks and I the red fire" (p. 191).

In a 90th birthday interview, Calkins said his partner was "the man who made it possible for me to be a success. . . . Mr. Holden had the business sense and the ability to help me overcome the handicap of being deaf" ("Earnest Calkins," p. 39).

Calkins and Holden has been credited with setting up the first modern advertising agency. The agency has also been credited with helping to change the function of an advertising agency from merely placing advertisements to the creation of displays and entire campaigns. Calkins and Holden established an in-house typographical and art department, then considered an innovation in the industry. At its peak, Calkins and Holden was a large agency, its clients including H. J. Heinz, E. R. Squibb, Beech-Nut, Pierce-Arrow, Thomas A. Edison Industries, and Ingersoll Watch. The agency also handled promotions for *Saturday Evening Post*, *Woman's Home Companion*, *McCall's*, and *McClure's* magazines. According to Roland Marchand's *Advertising the American Dream*, Calkins and Holden was the fourteenth largest advertising agency in the nation in 1927 (p. 33).

The Calkins and Holden agency may best be remembered for two advertising campaigns early in the partnership's history. For the Force breakfast cereal account, Calkins wrote hundreds of jingles for a cartoon character he created, Sunny Jim, who was transformed from Jim Dumps by eating Force. Sunny Jim became a national celebrity, appearing in Force ads on billboards and in streetcars, magazines, and newspapers. One Sunny Jim jingle said:

> Jim Dump's half-sister, pale and slight,
> Had very little appetite.
> She said: "Such dainty-looking food
> Will please the most capricious mood.
> So crisp and light–it takes my whim!"
> "It takes with all," quoth Sunny Jim.

A similar strategy was used for the Delaware, Lackawanna and Western Railroad account. Calkins created a cartoon character, Phoebe Snow, to show that the railroad's cars were cleaner because hard coal was used in locomotives. A jingle said:

> Said Phoebe Snow, about to go
> Upon a trip to Buffalo:
> "My gown keeps white both day and night
> Upon the Road of Anthracite."

Years later, Calkins defended those early advertising campaigns, commenting: "Let no modern, efficient advertising man sniff at this old fashioned humble record. What we did in those days was fresh and new then as any modern development is now" (*"Louder Please!"*, pp. 204–5).

Calkins retired from the advertising business in 1931, five years after the death of his partner in 1926. The advent of radio (which he could not hear) and Holden's death were his reasons. The Calkins and Holden agency later became Fletcher Richards, Calkins and Holden and was merged into the Interpublic group of advertising and public relations organizations in 1963.

Throughout his career and after his retirement from the agency business, Calkins was a prolific writer, defending the advertising business and calling for higher artistic and professional standards. With Holden as coauthor, Calkins published *Modern Advertising* (1905), the first such textbook. In 1925 he was awarded Harvard University's Edward W. Bok medal for his pioneering efforts to raise the standards of advertising. In *Business the Civilizer* Calkins insisted that truth is a powerful advertising technique, arguing that the industry must go beyond the "truth-in-advertising" slogan the Associated Advertising Clubs touted with "the virtuous unction of Sunday-school evangelists" (p. 121). Instead, Calkins called for honesty and humility to make advertising more credible: He wrote: "How seldom do we admit that our product is not the best, the most widely sold. How seldom do we concede merit to a competitor. And how it would strengthen our story if we did! How much we need a little humility in our copy to neutralize the bragging note" (p. 120). Indeed, Calkins credited advertising for improving the overall standards of business: "Advertising brings business out in the open where it can be observed by all. In the limelight of publicity, questionable practices must fade away" (p. 282).

In similar fashion, Calkins often issued impassioned pleas for making advertising hospitable to the world's best artists. The industry had emerged in the 20th century as the great patron of artists, Calkins argued: "In the fifteenth century the great opportunity of the artist was the Church. To-day it is business" (*Business the Civilizer*, p. 136). Modern mass production efficiency did not satisfy consumers' souls, he argued, because consumers demand beauty in the artifacts of everyday life. A beautiful picture in an advertisement was superior to words.

Moreover, advertising had a direct impact in making consumer products and their packages more attractive, Calkins argued. Most products and packages were so commonplace and unattractive that they spoiled the artistic quality of their advertising—"and thus began that steady, unremitting pressure on the manufacturer to make his goods or his packages worthy of being placed in an artistic setting" (*Business the Civilizer*, p. 249). Calkins saw advertising as a major force in a commercial artistic revolution: "[G]ood taste passed from the advertisement to the package, and from the package to the product. . . . Immediately these better-designed goods and packages demanded a better environment in which to be sold, and thus we have a revolution in the furnishing of shops and stores" (p. 253). Advertising's artistic and professional standards were tools to be used to engineer consumption, according to Calkins, who coined the term "consumer engineering"—"shaping a product to fit more exactly consumers' needs or tastes . . . any plan which stimulates the consumption of goods" ("What Consumer Engineering Really Is," p. 1).

Ernest Elmo Calkins died at his Park Avenue home on October 4, 1964, at the age of 96. Four years before his death, the Art Directors Club of New York awarded him its medal for special merit, citing him as an advertising pioneer who "more than any other single man brought dignity and stature to our business." *Advertising Age* ("E. E. Calkins," p. 19) called him a "giant of creative advertising" whose career was "a crusade for truth and good taste in advertising."

FURTHER READING

Works by Calkins

Advertising. Chicago: American Library Association, 1929.
The Advertising Man. New York: Charles Scribner's Sons, 1922.
"And Hearing Not." New York: Charles Scribner's Sons, 1946.
The Business of Advertising. New York: D. Appleton, 1928.
Business the Civilizer. Boston: Little, Brown, 1928.
"Louder Please!": The Autobiography of a Deaf Man. Boston: Atlantic Monthly Press, 1924.
Modern Advertising, with Ralph Holden. New York: D. Appleton, 1905.
"Now Is the Time to Advertise." *The Review of Reviews* (March, 1930): 52–56.
"What Consumer Engineering Really Is." Introduction to Roy Sheldon and Egmont Arens, *Consumer Engineering: A New Technique for Prosperity*. New York: Harper, 1932.

Works about Calkins

"Earnest Calkins, Ad Pioneer, Dead." *New York Times* (October 6, 1964): 39.
"E. E. Calkins, 96, Giant of Creative Advertising, Dies." *Advertising Age* (October 13, 1964): 19.
Foster, G. Allen. *Advertising: Ancient Market Place to Television*. New York: Criterion Books, 1967.
Fox, Stephen. *The Mirror Makers: A History of American Advertising and Its Creators*. New York: William Morrow, 1984.
Marchand, Roland. *Advertising the American Dream: Making Way for Modernity, 1920–1940*. Berkeley: University of California Press, 1985.

NOTABLE CLIENTS/CAMPAIGNS

Delaware, Lackawanna, and Western Railroad (1900s)

Force breakfast cereal (1900s)

Beech-Nut (1920s)

E. R. Squibb (1920s)

H. J. Heinz (1920s)

Ingersoll Watch (1920s)

Pierce-Arrow (1920s)

Thomas A. Edison Industries (1920s)

JOHN CAPLES
(May 1, 1900–June 10, 1990)

Marjorie J. Cooper, Richard W. Easley, and
Leslie Cole

John Caples worked for more than 50 years in advertising. His first job was with Ruthrauff and Ryan, a leading mail-order agency; later, he joined Batten, Barton, Durstine, and Osborn.

A native of Manhattan, John Caples was born on May 1, 1900. His father was a physician from Ohio, reputedly a skilled, concerned, and altruistic general practitioner. His mother, a bright, studious college graduate, was particularly interested in the arts and literature, and she passed these interests on to John.

John learned to read and write at an early age as a result of his parents' relatively high educational levels. In spite of this accomplishment, however, he did not stand out as a student when he attended the exclusive Horace Mann School in New York, nor did he excel as a student at Columbia University, which he later attended.

Caples's freshman year at Columbia was overshadowed by World War I. At Columbia he became an apprentice seaman student but would have remained in school until graduation, when he would have entered the naval reserves, had it not been for a single English assignment. His professor decided that each student would deliver a two-minute speech to the entire class. John, terrified of public speaking, considered any option that might get him out of the assignment, including dropping out of school. On the first day of speeches, Caples was called on first; he explained to the professor that he was not prepared. Subsequently, he began to skip the class in order to avoid giving a speech.

As a result, John eventually dropped out of Columbia altogether and joined the navy for four years as an ordinary seaman. He decided that the navy offered a promising career, so he set his goals on passing the naval academy entrance exam, a feat accomplished by only 100 men a year. Nevertheless, in 1924, John was admitted to the academy, where he began his education in engineering. To satisfy his desire for writing, John wrote for the college magazine, the *Annapolis Log*, and eventually became an associate editor.

At the end of his senior year, John's fear of public speaking came back to haunt him. Each senior was to give a short speech after the graduation dinner. He was so scared that he smuggled a bottle of gin into a shower stall, and he and his roommate alternated taking swigs. After it was all over, John did not even remember giving his speech. A classmate assured him that he did complete the assignment, and he ended up with a passing grade. The navy offered every graduate in his class the chance to relinquish his commission in exchange for a B.S. degree. John gladly did so.

After graduation, he accepted a position with New York Telephone as a student engineer for $27 a week. Soon bored with the job, John sought the help of a vocational guidance counselor, Dr. Katherine Blackford. After considerable testing, Dr. Blackford advised John that he lacked ambition, that his mind was only moderately quick, that he was not industrious, that he was excessively ambitious, and that he craved power and recognition. Her closing remark was, "I would not discourage you in your ambition to develop yourself for a writing career" (Granville, p. 64). At the suggestion of Dr. Alvin Johnson, his mother's former economics professor, he focused his sights on a career in advertising. Dr. Johnson advised that advertising experience would make Caples a better writer than would newspaper reporting; it would also make him more money.

Frustrated with his inability to transfer to the advertising department of the phone company, John quit and accepted a job with Certain Teed as an assistant to the assistant advertising manager. Instead of writing, however, John found himself performing work that was entirely clerical. Upon inquiry, John found that the ads were written by an outside agency. Soon after, he resigned from the company, severely pessimistic about his future.

His next job search was long and frustrating. He obtained a list of advertising agencies from the New York library and began calling them one by one. After repeated failures he signed up for a summer course in advertising copywriting at the Columbia Graduate School of Business. This course was the turning point for John's career and aspirations. The professor, Bill Orchard, was a man with tremendous experience and a reputation for turning out excellent prospects for copywriting jobs. Orchard was a copy editor at the George Batten advertising agency, which later became Batten, Barton, Durstine and Osborn (BBDO).

After the summer at Columbia, John accepted a position with Ruthrauff & Ryan, and so began his advertising career. His initial experience at R&R was described as working in "slave quarters." Writers worked very hard, were given only the bare essentials, and were not permitted to have contact with the client. However, John loved the work and learned very fast. His first advertisement to be printed was for Arthur Murray Dance Studios. Caples said he learned two important lessons from his early work at R&R: First, people want very much to be popular and, second, they are always seeking a quick, easy way to solve their problems ("A Dozen Ways to Develop Advertising Ideas," p. M4).

During his early career John Caples learned that rewording old successful ads was a logical step in designing new successful ones. After all, this approach worked in other professions, such as engineering and medicine. Rather than eliminating creativity, Caples believed this method gives one's imagination a higher platform to spring from and the opportunity to add a personal, imaginative touch. Using this philosophy and experience, Caples went on to write one of the most famous mail-order ads of all time for the U.S. School of Music. The headline read, "They laughed when I sat down at the piano—but when I started to play!", and it was very successful for the client. It also became an overnight success story for John Caples and was the subject of everything from vaudeville acts to cartoon takeoffs. Eventually, this advertisement became noted as one of the 100 greatest advertisements of all time.

After his success at R&R, John Caples began to search for a job that would fulfill his desire to learn more about the advertising industry. He interviewed with Bruce Barton of Barton, Durstine and Osborn, who had been one of his idols while in college, and despite his nervous nature, John secured a job on April 8, 1927, following a very persistent effort. He stayed with BBDO for the remainder of his career in advertising.

Throughout his years at BBDO, John Caples had many significant achievements. He started out working on various mail-order accounts, including Phoenix Mutual and the Alexander Hamilton Institute. Eventually, John's work earned him the respect of not only the staff of BBDO, but the industry as well. Just before the Depression, he had his first article published. It was titled, "Why Mail Order Advertisements Have More Punch" and was printed in *Advertising & Selling*. In 1930 Caples saw several of his articles published in respected trade magazines. This achievement paved the way for his first book, which has seen four editions and many printings. *Tested Advertising Methods* is a compilation of his earlier articles and thoughts from his personal diary, which he kept avidly. Other books were to follow. In 1941, following these achievements, Caples was promoted to vice president at BBDO.

Throughout his career Caples visited classes at the New York Ad School to share his experiences. Then, in 1952, he got the chance to teach at Columbia University. In fact, it was his old teacher Bill Orchard who asked him to take over his classes for a year. John gladly accepted and soon was over his fear of public speaking.

Noted for his research into scientific methods of testing advertising's effectiveness, Caples lectured extensively on these methods. He also supervised advertising research for Du Pont, General Electric, U.S. Steel, Lever Brothers, Goodrich, the U.S. Navy, and many other large organizations. Often ignored or ridiculed, the concept of testing eventually became an accepted part of advertising development. John Caples, more than any other man, was responsible for it.

After his teaching experience, Caples continued working and publishing. From 1972 until his death in 1990 he was a featured columnist in *Direct Marketing* magazine.

For achievements throughout his career, Caples was the recipient of the annual award of the National Association of Direct Mail Writers and the Hundred Million Club Leadership Award. Perhaps his most significant accomplishments were his induction into the Copywriters Hall of Fame in 1973 and the Advertising Hall of Fame in 1977.

Though John Caples projected the image of a hard-nosed businessman and advertising executive, few who knew him would have described him that way. Those who were close to him describe him as having been a very personable man with a knack for understanding human nature.

Throughout his career Caples influenced the minds and work of some of today's greatest advertising executives, including David Ogilvy and Phil Dusenberry. For example, Ogilvy said of Caples that he was "an indomitable analyzer and teacher of advertising" and "a first-rate copywriter—one of the most effective there has ever been" (*Tested Advertising Methods*, p. vii).

As a child, Caples never dreamed that he would become an advertising legend—it just happened. After more than 50 years in the advertising business, the late John Caples is just that, a legend. His creative ads revolutionized mail-order advertising. His insistence on testing raised the consciousness of the entire advertising community to the importance of using sound research in developing successful campaigns.

FURTHER READING

Works by Caples

Advertising for Immediate Sales. New York: Harper, 1936.

Advertising Ideas: A Practical Guide to Methods That Make Advertisements Work. New York: McGraw-Hill, 1938.

"A Dozen Ways to Develop Advertising Ideas." *Advertising Age* (November 14, 1983): M4–M5, M46.

The Effects of Comparative Television Advertisements That Name Competing Brands. New York: Ogilvy and Mather, 1975.

How to Make Your Advertising Make Money. Englewood Cliffs, NJ: Prentice-Hall, 1986.

Making Ads Pay. New York: Dover, 1957.

Tested Advertising Methods. 4th ed. Englewood Cliffs, NJ: Prentice-Hall, 1974.

Works about Caples

Advertising Today/Yesterday/Tomorrow: An Omnibus of Advertising. Editors of *Printer's Ink*. New York: McGraw-Hill, 1963.

Bovee, Courtland L., and William F. Arens. *Contemporary Advertising*. 2d ed. Homewood, IL: Richard D. Irwin, 1986.

Clark, Eric. *The Want Makers. The World of Advertising: How They Make You Buy*. New York: Viking Penguin, 1988.

DeVoe, Merrill. *Effective Advertising Copy*. New York: Macmillan, 1956.

Granville, Loren. "The John Caples Story." *Direct Marketing* (October 1990): 62–66.

Hafer, W. Keith, and Gordon E. White. *Advertising Writing: Putting Creative Strategy to Work*. 2d ed. St. Paul: West Publishing, 1982.
"John Caples Dies." *Retrospectives in Marketing* 4 (December 1990).
Mayer, Martin. *Madison Avenue, U.S.A.* New York: Harper, 1958.
Norins, Hanley. *The Compleat Copywriter*. New York: McGraw-Hill, 1966.
Pope, Daniel. *The Making of Modern Advertising*. New York: Basic Books, 1983.
Santoro, Elaine. "Creative Classics." *Direct Marketing* (May 1988): 69–71.
Schofield, Perry. *100 Top Copy Writers and Their Favorite Ads*. New York: Printer's Ink, 1954.
Watkins, Julian Lewis. *The 100 Greatest Advertisements*. New York: Dover, 1959.
White, Gordon. *John Caples: Adman*. Chicago: Crain Books, 1977.
Wright, John S., and Daniel S. Warner. *Advertising*. New York: McGraw-Hill, 1962.

NOTABLE CLIENTS/CAMPAIGNS

Alexander Hamilton Institute

B. F. Goodrich

Du Pont

General Electric

Lever Brothers

Phoenix Mutual

U.S. Navy

U.S. School of Music

U.S. Steel

BARRON G. COLLIER
(March 23, 1873–March 13, 1939)

Sammy R. Danna

Barron G. Collier dominated the transit advertising industry for approximately 40 years–from 1900 to his death in 1939. He was also famous for many other business enterprises such as hotels, banking, and real estate. In fact, he became the biggest landowner in Florida during the latter part of his life. Although a relatively small amount of information appears in advertising publications, his work in the transit field was significant.

Collier was born on March 23, 1873, in Memphis, Tennessee to Cowles Miles Collier, an artist, and Hannah Shackelford Collier. Upon completion of his public school education, Barron worked in an advertising brokerage firm that specialized in selling streetcar poster space. In 1900 he left for New York.

Collier founded Barron G. Collier, Inc., in 1900, and was its president and a director until his death. The firm became one of the most important and influential advertising operations in America. It claimed to be the first to place ad placards in subway cars and eventually controlled the advertising concessions for street railway and subway cars not only in New York, but in many other cities as well. It also operated 230 newsstands in New York subway stations.

Collier married Juliet Gordon Carnes on November 26, 1907. They had three sons: Barron, Jr., Samuel Carnes, and C. Miles.

Collier established the Collier Service Company of New York as a specialty agency offering advertising services and to sell bus ads. The company employed some of the best writers in America, including F. Scott Fitzgerald and Ogden Nash. In 1910 Collier was contracted by the Wrigley chewing gum company to create a campaign in Buffalo, New York, where gum was quite difficult to sell. Collier began what was probably one of the best known ad campaigns in the world and developed the famed Spear Man symbol, which was displayed on transit cards on buses throughout Buffalo. The Buffalo campaign was so successful that it spread from city to city throughout America.

By 1917 Collier had built such a strong organization that he felt secure enough to deny the customary 15 percent commission for services rendered by advertising agencies. For years he was able to employ such high-handed methods, seemingly without injury to himself or the transit advertising industry. Such actions could be interpreted as the independence of Collier's transit advertising hold, ultimately retarding the overall development of the industry from 1917 to 1929 (Ulanoff, p. 395).

In 1935, in order to combine car advertising in greater New York and Westchester County under one umbrella organization, Collier merged the Manhattan Advertising Agency and Broadway Surface Advertising with the Collier Service Company.

Throughout his career, Collier was often termed a "self-made man," rising from his first position with a Memphis ad brokerage firm, where he learned everything possible about the rudiments of the business. His fame and fortune were made in New York, home of his advertising, real estate, and other profitable enterprises. During four decades there, he became good friends with New York mayors John F. Hylan and James J. Walker. Walker was often a guest aboard Collier's yacht, *Florida*, and Hylan distinguished Collier by appointing him special duty police commissioner, which placed him in charge of the Bureau of Public Safety. He conducted numerous campaigns to make city streets safe by using his advertising experience. One of his posters featured the fictitious character Aunty J. Walker (anti-jaywalker), a stern policewoman who warned pedestrians against jaywalking.

Some of Collier's major business ventures were the Intercounty Telephone and Telegraph Company; Street Railways Advertising Company; Florida Gulf Coast Hotels; Collier Brothers; Collier Service Corporation; Collier Advertising Service; Empire State Development Company; Pacific Railways Advertising Company; Philadelphia Advertising Company; United Brokerage Company; Western Advertising Company; and United Land and Stores Development and Improvement Company. Collier was the president of all these firms. As if this were not enough, he also served on the board of directors of the Baltimore Commercial Bank, Eastern Advertising Company, Gainsborough Studios, and Charles Marchand Company.

Although he was involved in many enterprises, Collier always remained rather personally devoted to activities related to transit advertising. For example, in the 1930s, his own words of wisdom were posted in streetcars under the heading: "Barron Collier Says."

Despite his multiple business ventures, Collier also became intensely interested in law enforcement, holding such public offices as member of the Sheriff's Jury of New York City and deputy sheriff of Westchester County, New York. In addition, he was appointed consul general at-large for the Republic of Georgia and decorated by the governments of Italy, Belgium, Austria, Panama, and Portugal. These awards and honors were bestowed upon Collier for exceptional contributions of service and other assistance to the respective parties involved. In 1931 he received an honorary doctorate from Oglethorpe University in Atlanta.

Collier's real estate empire in Florida made him the largest individual property holder in the state, with a staggering 1,186,000 acres. During a 20-year period, he became a leader in reclaiming and developing a large section of the Everglades for home building. He was instrumental in the completion of the Tamiami Trail from Tampa through Ft. Myers to Miami. In addition, Collier established a chain of Florida hotels and extended his business enterprises to include bus lines, banks, newspapers, a telephone company, a steamship line, and various farming operations. The value of his Florida investments was estimated between $16 and $17 million.

Collier held a myriad of chairmanships and directorships, most notably with the New York and national Boy Scout organizations. He served as acting president of the Boy Scout Foundation of Greater New York, succeeding Franklin D. Roosevelt when he became governor of New York. He was also a member of the executive board and a director of the Boy Scouts of America. In addition, he was actively involved in the New York Southern Society, the Italy-America Society, Tarrytown Hospital (New York), the Travelers Aid Society, and the National Institute of Social Sciences. Not to stray too far from his advertising affiliations, he chaired the publicity committee of the American Transit Association. Collier also found time for recreational pursuits such as traveling and yachting. He was also quite fond of art.

Collier died of a heart attack at Columbia Presbyterian Medical Center on March 13, 1939. He would have been 66 years old in ten days. Although he had been ill for some time, his death was considered untimely.

Upon his death, Collier controlled advertising on almost all city transit lines in the United States, so it is perhaps amazing that shortly after his death the Collier empire collapsed. Some 20 Collier leases in Boston, Philadelphia, Washington, and other cities were combined to form National Transitads.

FURTHER READING

Works about Collier

Bovée, Courtland L., and William F. Arens. *Contemporary Advertising*. 3d ed. Homewood, IL: Richard D. Irwin, 1989.
National Cyclopaedia of American Biography. New York: J. T. White, 1895–1984.
Ulanoff, Stanley M. *Advertising in America*. New York: Hastings House Publishers, Communication Arts Books, 1977.
Who Was Who in America 1897–1942. Chicago: A. N. Marquis, 1943.

NOTABLE CLIENT/CAMPAIGN

Wrigley's chewing gum (1910)

DRAPER (DAN) DANIELS
(August 12, 1913–May 7, 1983)

Thomas A. Bowers

Draper Daniels was a copywriter and executive in advertising agencies in New York and Chicago for more than 40 years. He worked for Young and Rubicam, McCann-Erickson, and Kenyon and Eckhardt in New York and for Leo Burnett, McCann-Erickson, Compton, and his own agency, Draper Daniels, in Chicago. He was also active in Democratic Party politics and served in the U.S. Department of Commerce during the administration of President John F. Kennedy.

Daniels was born on August 12, 1913, and died May 7, 1983. He married Louise Parker Lux Cort on October 9, 1937, and was divorced from her in 1967. They had four children: John, Bruce, Marie, and Curtis. He married Myra Janco on August 18, 1967.

Daniels was born on his grandfather's farm near the small town of Morris, New York. His father, John Albert Daniels, a senior coastal geodetic survey engineer, charted the inland passage to Alaska. His mother, Fanny Martha Daniels, taught English and history at Morris Central Rural School.

Daniels was valedictorian of his class at Morris High School. In 1934 he earned a B.A. in journalism from Syracuse University after only three and one-half years. He was a columnist for the student newspaper, managing editor of the humor magazine, president of Theta Alpha fraternity, and a member of two journalistic honorary societies, Sigma Delta Chi and Pi Delta Epsilon.

In his autobiography, *Giants, Pigmies and Other Advertising People,* Daniels said his journalism degree "turned out to be something less than a certified pass to employment" (p. 2). Unable to find work in journalism, he held a string of odd jobs before he borrowed $400 and returned to Syracuse to work on a master's degree and a teacher's certificate. Officials in Morris had promised to make him principal of the local school for $3,600 a year if he got his master's degree, but his mother told him she would not work for him and threatened to quit her teaching job if he became principal. Local Democratic Party members wanted him to run for public office, but the township was solidly Republican. He also considered a job teaching English and social science for $1,600 a year.

Daniels' dilemma between graduate school and a job was solved when the Vick Chemical Company offered him a position in its training program in New York. He had visited the city when he was 14 and vowed he would never live there if he could help it, but the offer of $100 a month plus expenses and a company car won him over. He arrived in New York with a typewriter, $30, and a trunk and two suitcases and rented a room at the Terminal Hotel on Lexington Avenue (near Grand Central Terminal) for $7 a week.

After spending a month learning about the history of Vick and its sales techniques, Daniels was sent to Greensboro, North Carolina, to work as a traveling salesman. He also spent some time in the Midwest in charge of sampling crews that distributed product samples door to door.

After 13 months in the South, he returned to New York to become assistant to the head of Vick's sales department, handling correspondence and editing a weekly newsletter for the company's traveling salespeople. Some of his philosophy about advertising and promotion was probably formed at Vick, because Daniels called H. Smith Richardson, chairman of the board, the first advertising giant he ever met (*Giants*, p. 18).

While at Vick, Daniels received an unusual and tempting offer to become a full-time free-lance writer. Horatio Locke, a wealthy Vick employee, offered to pay Daniels the equivalent of his annual salary if he would devote his full time to writing. If Daniels sold any of his writing, Locke would get back the salary plus 10 percent of the proceeds; if Daniels did not sell anything, he would owe Locke nothing. Daniels knew he wanted to earn his living as a writer, but he was not sure how to do it. He figured he could sell stories to the *Saturday Evening Post* or *Collier's*, but he was afraid he could not do any better than that. He also realized advertising was his real ambition: "Having a story in the *Post* or *Collier's* would give me no greater sense of creative fulfillment than writing one of the full-page ads in either of those magazines" (*Giants*, p. 22). He turned down Locke's offer—and another offer to become head of the sales department at Vick—and determined to work his way into advertising.

Daniels got that chance when Vick transferred him to its in-house advertising agency, Morse International, as assistant to the director of public relations. He read every book about advertising he could find and said the best two were *Copy* by Kenneth Goode and *My Life in Advertising* by Claude Hopkins. He started a program of sending news releases about Vick employees to their hometown newspapers and launched an employee publication, *Vicks Family News*. He also wrote unsolicited ads for Vick products, and the company began to run them.

Daniels accumulated a portfolio of his published Vick ads and applied for jobs at Young and Rubicam (the agency he most admired) and Lynn Baker. He accepted the first offer (Baker), but the job lasted only five months.

Daniels was offered a position as assistant advertising director at Irving Trust but turned it down because he thought the company was too staid. He also interviewed at the J. Stirling Getchell agency, where Ernest Dichter, who was becoming well known for his ideas about motivational research, had just been hired. In Daniels's interview, he was told how he would work as a copywriter at Getchell: "First, I would think of a picture. Then I would have a photographer make a lot of shots. From those I would select just the right picture. Then I would turn to type, selecting exactly the right face and size to go with the picture. Then I would work out the headline, pruning it until it would fit the type I had selected." He told the interviewer he would be miserable under those conditions and apologized for wasting his time (*Giants*, p. 35).

Daniels was out of work for two and one-half months before being hired as a copywriter by Young and Rubicam in late 1940 at $4,000 per year. Daniels had long aspired to working at Young and Rubicam, the country's largest advertising agency at the time, because of its reputation: "To copy cubs, copywriters of all ages, and youngsters trying to get into the advertising agency business in the early 1940s, Young and Rubicam was heaven, or next door to it, and God's name was Raymond Rubicam. . . . We were Young and Rubicam, and that meant the best there was. It was more of a religion than it was an advertising agency. The reason was Raymond Rubicam and his disciples" (*Giants*, p. 39). Daniels worked on a number of accounts during his four years at Young and Rubicam, including Borden's, Traveler's Insurance, Lipton soup, Pall Mall, and American Can.

Lured by a salary raise of 70 percent and a promise to pay the difference between his military pay and his agency salary if he were drafted, Daniels left Young and Rubicam in 1944 to become the youngest copy group head at McCann-Erickson. Despite the offer, he was unhappy about McCann-Erickson because of dissension he detected among creative people, researchers, and account supervisors: "Young and Rubicam had been a disciplined army. McCann-Erickson was a loose alliance of warring chiefs" (*Giants*, p. 104). Daniels left McCann-Erickson on good terms but later said, "I have always felt that the agency lacked that sense of common purpose which unites people of divergent abilities and inspires them to do better than any of them could do alone" (*Giants*, p. 135). Among Daniels's accounts at McCann-Erickson were Schenley Distillery, National Cash Register, John Hancock Insurance, Vaseline hair tonic, and Bromo-Seltzer.

After only 19 months at McCann-Erickson, Daniels moved to Kenyon and Eckhardt in 1946. On his first day at work, he wrote an ad for the Chesapeake and Ohio railroad that was eventually called one of the 100 best ads of all time (Julian Watkins, *The 100 Greatest Advertisements*, p. 159). In a speech, Robert R. Young, chairman of the board of the C&O, had lamented the fact that hogs could go across the country without changing trains but humans could not. Daniels studied Young's speech and created an ad with an arresting headline: "A hog can cross the country without changing trains, but you can't."

Daniels was not impressed with Kenyon and Eckhardt: "It combined some very good accounts and some very good people to create office morale roughly comparable to what you would expect to find among long-term convicts in a badly run penitentiary" (*Giants*, p. 148). His unhappiness caused him to start thinking immediately about changing jobs, and he returned to Young and Rubicam as copy chief in 1946 for $1,000 a year less than he had been paid at Kenyon and Eckhardt. The aura and lure to return to Young and Rubicam were too strong: "Suddenly I realized that unless I made it at Young and Rubicam, I'd never be happy no matter where else I made it and no matter how big I made it" (*Giants*, p. 154).

In 1947 Young and Rubicam offered Daniels a choice that changed his career: He could become manager of radio commercials in New York or copy director in Chicago. Daniels took the Chicago job for a simple reason—he would have the freedom to write copy, which Young and Rubicam would not allow him to do as a copy director in New York.

It was an era when agency people in New York thought of working in Chicago as being exiled to Siberia. Part of the problem, according to Daniels, was an inferiority complex among advertising people in Chicago: "Chicago has always had a tendency to confuse size and excellence and to assume that because Chicago is the second largest city it is inevitably second rate. The result is an insecure giant with a trifle too loud a voice and a shade too hearty a handshake. But where New York is smug and provincial, Chicago is warm and receptive, more concerned with the worth of an idea than with who has it" (*Giants*, p. 159).

Daniels flourished in that environment and became the agency's youngest vice president in 1948 and chairman of the plans board in 1949. However, the loss of several of the agency's large accounts because of client buyouts and changes in advertising managers led him to resign from Young and Rubicam in 1954 and to join Leo Burnett.

Daniels found his niche at Burnett and became best known for his work there. He moved rapidly up the agency hierarchy: vice president and copy supervisor (1954), vice president in charge of copy and member of the plans board (1956), director and vice president of creative departments (1957), executive vice president for creative services and member of the executive committee (1958), and, at age 48, chairman of the executive committee—while continuing as head of the agency's creative operations (1961). Apart from those titles, Daniels took great pride in his relationship with Leo Burnett: "After the first three months, whatever my title was, I was Leo's personal copywriter and idea man" (*Giants*, p. 236). Daniels's promotion to chairman of the executive committee was designed to give younger executives like himself greater responsibility for agency operations, although Burnett, aged 69 at the time, continued as chairman and chief executive officer.

Daniels was involved with many of the agency's classic campaigns of that era, including Marlboro and Schlitz. He played a key role in the repositioning of Marlboro as a man's cigarette. Daniels, Leo Burnett, and Lee Stanley, the account's art director, met at Burnett's farm one Saturday in 1954 and planned the Marlboro Man creative strategy and the package redesign for one of the most famous advertising campaigns of all time. Although he said the campaign was an exciting one as far as advertising strategy was concerned, he later regretted his involvement in a cigarette campaign: "If I had known in 1954 what I know now [1974], I would have been . . . against soliciting Marlboro. My own agency has never solicited cigarette advertising, and I don't think cigarettes ought to be advertised. . . . Visually and emotionally . . . the most effective cigarette advertising projects the impression that smoking gives you a great sensation" (*Giants*, p. 245).

Daniels got particular satisfaction from the Schlitz campaign. He had worked on Schlitz while he was at Young and Rubicam in Chicago, and the brand bounced from agency to agency and eventually to Burnett after a five-year sales decline. Daniels concluded that beer drinkers wanted "a light beer with guts," but family magazines and television networks of that era would not allow the use of the word "guts" in advertising, so he used "gusto" instead: "Real gusto in a great light beer." Schlitz sales began to improve almost immediately after the campaign started (*Giants*, pp. 246–48).

The strong attraction of government service and politics enticed Daniels to leave Burnett and the advertising industry to become National Export Expansion Coordinator in President John F. Kennedy's administration on July 1, 1962. The appointment was due in part to the fact that Daniels had been active in Democratic Party politics, beginning with a speech he made as a high school student for Al Smith in 1928. That endeared him to local Democratic Party officials, who named him to the county committee on his 21st birthday. He was an organizer of Advertising Men and Women for President Franklin D. Roosevelt in 1944 and creative adviser for Adlai S. Stevenson's Illinois gubernatorial campaign in 1948. In 1952 he was elected a precinct committeeman in Lake Bluff, Illinois, and president of the Men's Democratic Club of Lake County. He was chosen chairman of the Lake County Democratic Central Committee in 1954 and served a two-year term before stepping down because of business obligations. He was a delegate to the 1956 Democratic National Convention and cochairman of Illinois Business and Professional Men for Kennedy-Johnson in 1960. In 1961 he was mentioned as a possible Democratic candidate for the Senate seat later held by Everett Dirksen.

President Kennedy wanted to remedy the nation's balance of payments problem by increasing American exports, and Daniels's job in the Commerce Department was to coordinate export expansion programs in all branches of government. At a conference of American exporters in New York, he suggested that companies follow a slogan of "Sell American" and revive the spirit of the old clippership merchants. Top management, he said, should take a more active role in exporting, recognize the profit opportunities in the export business, and be motivated by profit, not patriotism. Daniels foresaw that the expansion of the European Economic Community (Common Market) and reduction of trade barriers would greatly expand world markets.

He enjoyed the year he spent in Washington, although he was skeptical of government work in general: "It all seemed like a make-believe world to me. The appearance of successful activity was far more important than the actual success of the activity" (*Giants*, p. 251).

Daniels resigned from the Commerce Department in July 1963 and returned to Chicago to become executive vice president in charge of the central region of McCann-Erickson. He resigned in February 1964 and became executive vice president in charge of creative services at Compton. Motivated by a "desire to call all the signals," Daniels formed Draper Daniels in May 1965 by buying controlling interest in Roche, Rickerd, Henri, Hurst. Daniels was named chairman and chief executive, and Myra Janco, who had been executive vice president at RRHH and who later married Daniels, increased her share of ownership and became president and chief operating officer.

The Daniels agency began with 30 clients, billings of $5 million, and a pledge that it would grow by doing good advertising for clients who placed great importance on advertising rather than by merging with other agencies.

Despite his aversion to mergers, Daniels merged with Arthur and Wheeler in 1976, but retained the name Draper Daniels. Arthur and Wheeler had billed $13.9 million in 1975, most of it for Alberto-Culver, which had an equity share in Arthur and Wheeler and continued to have equity in the Daniels agency.

Daniels sold his agency in Chicago and moved to Marco Island, Florida, where he died on May 7, 1983, at the age of 69.

Daniels had strong beliefs about advertising and was not reluctant to express them. His book, *Giants, Pigmies and Other Advertising People*, was autobiographical but consisted primarily of sketches and opinions of people he had worked with. He was mildly critical of only a few, one of whom was Marion Harper, Jr. In *The Mirror Makers*, Stephen Fox said Daniels did not like Harper (pp. 194–96), and Daniels said Harper was very impressive until "he passed the age of 35 and let ego and optimism dim the brilliant clarity of his mind" (*Giants*, pp. 120–21).

Daniels was obviously affected by his experience at the Burnett agency and impressed by Leo Burnett the man. During 1960 *Advertising Age* published several poems that Daniels had written about life and people in an unnamed advertising agency, including the head man, the research man, the copywriter, the plans board, the traffic man, and the media man. Fox claims the verses, particularly one about the plans board, were based on Daniels's Burnett experience (p. 223). While Daniels had great respect for Leo Burnett's genius, he also gave credit to Richard Heath, one of Burnett's top executives: "Leo wrote the gospel, but Dick Heath preached it to the heathen. Together, they did what neither of them could have done alone" (*Giants*, p. 220).

Throughout his career, Daniels wanted to be an advertising copywriter, and that is how he will be remembered. Three of his ads were selected in 1959 as among the 100 greatest advertisements until that time: Elsie the Cow for Borden, the hog ad for Chesapeake and Ohio, and the Marlboro campaign (Watkins).

Copywriting was Daniels's first love, and he concluded his book with a list of his beliefs about advertising, including the following:

The best advertising is a combination of words that make pictures in the mind and pictures that make words in the mind.
Advertising is a relatively simple business made difficult by complicated people.
Many advertisers fail to get good advertising because they strain the work of first-rate agencies through second-rate people.
Blaming advertising for the ills of society is like blaming the mirror for the warts on your nose. (*Giants*, pp. 253–54)

He and Myra Daniels took a double-barreled shot at advertising at a meeting of two advertising women's organizations in Chicago in 1973. He criticized agency plans boards and client approval committees for diluting advertising into blandness. His wife said group-think, the tendency of a group of people to put loyalty to the group ahead of common sense, was also responsible for consumers' declining confidence in advertising. Together, they told the audience that advertisers had an obligation to be honest in making product claims and to avoid implying that other advertisers made false claims (*Chicago Tribune*, March 20, 1973, sec. 3, p. 8).

For their 1962 college text on copywriting, Burton and Kreer asked Daniels and other advertising experts if copywriters were born or made and asked their opinions of the importance of a college education. Daniels said copywriters were both born and made and had to have an ability to write well and have a natural sales sense. The sales sense, he said, could be acquired. A copywriter must also understand people. "Briefly, a copywriter needs to be born with certain natural abilities, but he needs to work hard to develop them to the full in order to become a really good copywriter" (p. 11). A good copywriter needs to be educated, but that education need not necessarily come from college, Daniels said, citing several well-known copywriters who had never attended college. He believed education gave one good taste, and good taste was essential in copywriters (p. 20).

Humor was appropriate in advertising, Daniels believed, as long as copywriters followed four basic rules (Runyon, pp. 246–47):

1. In most cases, humor is better for selling a low-priced product than it is for selling a high-priced one.
2. Humor is an effective way to put new life and memorability into an old story.
3. Humor is effective in telling a simple story in a memorable manner.
4. Humor is effective in driving home the ridiculousness of an outmoded practice which militates against the use of a new product or method.

Daniels had definite beliefs about what advertising agencies should do for clients and how to please them. During a contentious meeting, he told a Young and Rubicam client, "You seem to think we're here to sell you some advertising and that you're here to buy some advertising. As long as you have that idea, you're never going to get anything worthwhile from any agency. Never forget that we're here to help you sell cake and that's what you pay us for" (*Giants*, p. 165). He said the greatest compliment a client ever paid him came from Don Elliot of Purity Bakeries: "I like Dan. He'd as soon tell you to go shit in your hat as to look at you" (*Giants*, p. 166).

In a 1971 speech to the Life Insurance Advertisers Association in Kansas City, Daniels proposed an unusual nationwide contest in which consumers would judge ads. Daniels said the contest would have four benefits: (1) By having a wide spectrum of consumers participating, the contest would provide good evidence about what makes ads effective. (2) It would provide evidence of what consumers really want instead of what some people say consumers want. (3) It would give national recognition to agencies and advertisers that provide advertising that consumers like. (4) It would focus on good advertising.

Daniels was very critical of advertising media on occasion. In a 1961 speech to a magazine promotion group in New York, he blasted magazines that had a preoccupation with circulation statistics and market research data. He also criticized magazines that were founded primarily to sell advertising instead of serving readers. Daniels said they could not be an effective advertising medium because all a magazine has to sell is its editorial integrity. Daniels also lambasted advertising people who were ashamed of their trade, who felt that the criticisms of advertising were unjustified and un-American, and who felt that such criticism could be countered by a public relations program to give the industry a better image.

The last paragraph in his book summarizes what Draper Daniels thought about advertising: "If I had it to do all over again, I probably would. Advertising can be a worrisome sort of business, but the people—the giants, the pigmies, and others in between—make each day a wild, habit-forming combination of agony and ecstasy" (*Giants*, p. 257).

FURTHER READING

Work by Daniels

Giants, Pigmies and Other Advertising People. Chicago: Crain Communications, 1974.

Works about Daniels

Burton, Philip Ward, and G. Bowman Kreer. *Advertising Copywriting*. 2d ed. Englewood Cliffs, NJ: Prentice-Hall, 1962.

Fox, Stephen. *The Mirror Makers: A History of American Advertising and Its Creators*. New York: William Morrow, 1984.

Runyon, Kenneth E. *Advertising and the Practice of Marketing*. Columbus: Charles E. Merrill, 1979.

Watkins, Julian L. *The 100 Greatest Advertisements: Who Wrote Them and What They Did*. New York: Dover, 1959.

Who's Who in Advertising. New York: Haire, 1963.
Who Was Who in America. Chicago: Marquis Who's Who, 1985.
Draper Daniels's career was also widely covered by the *New York Times* and the *Chicago Tribune*, particularly in the 1960s and 1970s.

NOTABLE CLIENTS/CAMPAIGNS

Chesapeake and Ohio Railroad (Kenyon and Eckhardt, 1940s)

John Hancock Insurance (McCann-Erickson, 1940s)

Schenley Distillery (McCann-Erickson, 1940s)

Traveler's Insurance (Young and Rubicam, 1940s)

Schlitz Beer (Young and Rubicam, Chicago, and Leo Burnett, 1940s–50s)

Campbell's Soup (Leo Burnett, 1950s–60s)

Kellogg's (Leo Burnett, 1950s–60s)

Marlboro (Leo Burnett, 1950s–60s)

Pillsbury (Leo Burnett, 1950s–60s)

JERRY DELLA FEMINA
(July 22, 1936–   )

Tommy V. Smith

Jerry Della Femina—an agency principal with an outspoken flair to be different—is an American success story. He has taught cats to meow on cue in television commercials for Purina's Meow Mix, prompted dialogue between comedy couple Jerry Stiller and Anne Meara for Blue Nun Wine, and brought us an Anglo-Saxon named Joe Isuzu hawking Japanese Isuzu cars and trucks.

Jerry Della Femina was born in Brooklyn, New York, in 1936 to Italian immigrant parents. He did not realize it at the time, but being reared in Brooklyn in an Italian-American home during the Depression would later prove to be advantageous in his chosen profession of advertising.

Della Femina started in advertising during the creative revolution of the 1960s. The creative revolution in advertising, much like the cultural revolution that was taking place in America during the same period, was very antiestablishment; it marked the beginning of an era filled with free thinking and free expression. Della Femina, believing that advertising practitioners needed to be antagonistic, was truly one of the early creative revolutionists. Previously, conservatism and a stuffy, businesslike aura had emulated from briefcase-carrying mass communication executives. Vance Packard's book *The Hidden Persuaders* and the movie *The Man in the Gray Flannel Suit*, based on the book by Sloan Wilson, epitomized the mainstream mass communication movement of the 1950s.

During the creative revolution, Della Femina moved in and out of five Manhattan agencies in six years. In 1966 he briefly worked at Ted Bates as a copywriter under the direction of Rosser Reeves. During his tenure at agencies in New York, Della Femina yearned to establish his own agency. Keeping in mind the creative revolutionists' beliefs, he opened his creative boutique agency as a rebellion against the mainstream and establishment-type agencies that he had worked for in the past. However, the creative boutiques had a flaw that few, including Della Femina, recognized at the time: Their owners had to become conformists and gain new accounts in a businesslike atmosphere or go out of business. Della Femina would learn this caveat after years of success with his ever-growing creative boutique agency.

Jerry Della Femina opened his agency in 1967. During this time in the creative revolution, Italian and Jewish street-smart copywriters and art directors were recognized as having great potential in the advertising profession. Della Femina seized the opportunity and opened a shop with partner Ron Travisano. The coowners, in creative revolutionary style, formulated their own rules for advertising business success. Both worked to build an aggressive, mid-sized Madison Avenue shop called Della Femina, Travisano and Partners.

In 1971, while at Della Femina, Travisano and Partners, Della Femina wrote his doctrine on advertising. Much like John E. Kennedy, Claude Hopkins, and Rosser Reeves had done before him but with a different twist, Della Femina brought forth his philosophy on advertising. Della Femina's work was characteristic of the creative revolution movement with dry humor, tongue-in-cheek, and anti–big agency thoughts. His book, *From Those Wonderful Folks Who Gave You Pearl Harbor*, was hailed as a symbol of the creative revolution in advertising that took place during the late 1960s and early 1970s.

In his book, Della Femina told of both the good and bad advertising practices and practitioners. He also wrote of the qualities of individuality and difference inherent to advertising's creative people. Della Femina included himself in the creative lot. The book's title was even associated with Della Femina's creativity. Originally a brainstorm for Panasonic electronics, its title was intended to be a headline for an ad to help the Japanese electronics giant penetrate the American marketplace. After presentation of the campaign with the headline to Panasonic officials, Della Femina was fired because company officials did not perceive his creativity as being humorous.

Della Femina did not let the Panasonic failure deter him from continuing his creative rebellion. Apparently, other clients accepted and agreed with Della Femina's creativity. His agency's billings rose from just under $50 million in 1976 to approximately $75 million in 1978. Along with the new business, the agency had to increase staff members to accommodate and service the new clients. It grew from 90 to 100 people working for the partners in 1976 to 158 in 1978. The agency also had two offices: one in New York, one in Los Angeles.

Della Femina's agency's early success paralleled that of a competing upstart agency, Scali, McCabe, and Sloves. Della Femina said of his agency's good fortune: "An agency starts up and does some good work, so a lot of advertisers sit up and take notice. But the agency is young, and they're not sure how long it's going to last. They can see it's doing terrific creative work, but they don't know how well it's being managed from the business end. But then, if it does prove to have staying power and does manage to stick around for 10 years, then they figure it's going to be around a while longer" (Swisshelm, p. 35). At the time, Della Femina had good reason to believe that his agency philosophy was on target.

In June 1977 Della Femina acquired the Chemical Bank and Aviance fragrance, two $3 million accounts. Other new accounts included a Ralston-Purina brand, High Protein Dog Meal, for $6 million; a Dow Chemical brand, Dowgard engine coolant; new brands from Richardson-Merrell's Vick Chemical Company; several women's magazines from MacFadden Publications; WABC-TV in New York; and Emery Air Freight. Della Femina's Los Angeles office acquired Lloyd's Bank and the Bekins Company (moving specialists).

Della Femina was certainly successful. Some elements of the upstart agency's success formula included attracting good people, delegating responsibility to staff members, giving copywriters and art directors creative leverage, and trusting staff members enough so that the two agency heads could give them a definite yes or no decision when work was presented in informal meetings.

One very important part of Della Femina's philosophy was to have supervisors who did not restrain talent. He believed that frustrating red tape needed to be removed. He wanted staff members he could depend on to come through for the client with their best efforts. Staff members should not have all their work analyzed through a microscope, according to Della Femina.

Della Femina emphasized that "our kind of management works only because each one of our people here is his or her own best manager. So everyone here has to be hand-picked by us. Our agency is put together much like the New York Yankees, only without all the squabbling. They're either people we worked with ourselves at Delehanty, Kurnit & Geller or at Ted Bates, or they've come from other terrific agencies where they may have been overshadowed by other stars and not have had the chance to shine" (Swisshelm, p. 124). Della Femina, keeping in mind his creative revolutionist roots, believed that to have a powerful company, the people at the top (including himself) had to learn how to give power away.

Della Femina believed that only when he gave staff members leverage did he have powerful people who could think for themselves and not be afraid to recommend radical new ideas for clients and prospective clients. What Della Femina had was many small agencies working on their own within the loose agency framework. At Della Femina's agency, little day-by-day direction for each of these small agencies occurred. Della Femina believed that autonomy was an integral part of his creative revolutionist philosophy. The philosophy, said Della Femina, centered around how a commercial or ad should look. Della Femina stated:

This is one of the few constraints that shows up throughout our reel: that everything that comes out of this shop should show respect for the consumer and never talk down to him. Maybe some people think they should be trying to appeal to that mythical "grown-up with a 12-year-old mentality" they like to talk about, but that doesn't apply here. Sure, we use humor in our commercials. But sophisticated humor, not silly giggles. And if it's a gutsy commercial, it's not cheap gutsy, just for shock effect to grab attention. It's gutsy—or humorous—in a way that relates to the product and relates the product to the consumer. (Swisshelm, pp. 124, 126)

Another part of Della Femina's philosophy was: "Wherever we can, we make creative and media work so closely together that it gives the product an impact equal to much more than the sum of the creative or the media, combined with any other creative content or media execution" (Swisshelm, p. 124). One example of creative and media working together was that the media department suggested that Emery Air Freight buy play-by-play broadcasts of New York Yankee baseball games. Emery, being on a tight budget, wanted impact. After creative and media staff members met and discussed the Emery problem, creative formulated a ten-second spot that the media department agreed was affordable. Media then positioned the spots during the action instead of between innings. The spots were done by "the voice of the Yankees," Mel Allen, for impact.

Della Femina also had thoughts on new business pitches. His philosophy was to talk to a prospect in a relaxed, unpretentious way. Keeping with his anti–big agency procedure stance that was characteristic of the creative revolution movement, Della Femina wanted pitches to involve showing prospects what the agency had done for other clients, how they did it, and why they did it that way in very informal presentations and discussions.

Although the other parts of his advertising philosophy were important, probably the most important was that his agency needed to be driven by creativity. Being from a creative background himself, Della Femina believed that an agency's reputation was built by strong creativity.

Della Femina tried to have very few restraining rules in his shop. His philosophy of few rules coincided with thoughts emulating from other creative revolutionists. The one rule he did establish, however, was that all staff members had to work hard.

Della Femina's agency was successful, and he found that new business came easily after a period of time. With success, he started to retreat from his staunch antiestablishment train of thought. Success also meant that Della Femina wanted his agency to be among the major players in the American advertising arena. Here, strong ties to the creative revolution started to break. Della Femina observed: "It's not so difficult now, but when we started out, the main job was to turn around a prospect's suspicion that we might be too wild for them. So if we've erred since, it's been in the direction of staying a bit on the conservative side of the line" (Swisshelm, p. 126).

Della Femina climbed to the top echelons of the advertising world with most of his creative philosophy and rebellious nature still intact. However, that success was soon spoiled. Clients started leaving Della Femina, Travisano and Partners, and two of the partners quit. After the exodus, Della Femina had only $11,000 in the bank and his bills were about $2,000 a week. With this scenario in mind, he reached back into his rebellious creative philosophy bag to help save his business.

Here is what Della Femina did: He took $3,000, sent out over 1,000 invitations, and threw a giant Christmas party. The next day his agency acquired the advertising business for a large insurance company, and the following day another large billing account was secured. Creativity paid off again. By taking a risk and staging an elaborate party with dwindling resources, Della Femina's creative behavior and risky, roll-the-dice business acumen was still in place.

The agency recovered, and in October 1986 Della Femina, Travisano and Partners was sold to the WCRS Group, London. The agency's ranking in the United States, according to *Advertising Age*, was number 52. With the passing of his agency into a large, multinational corporation's hands, Della Femina's antiestablishment, anti–large position ended. However, Della Femina (who maintained an active role in the agency as chairman) still wanted the agency that bore his name to have the creative freedom of the creative boutique he started in 1967.

By 1988 Della Femina, McNamee/WCRS was formed as the result of a merger between HBM Cremer with Della Femina, Travisano and Partners within the WCRS Group. Louise McNamee's name was added to the agency's name, and she held the positions of president and chief operating officer.

In October 1989 Della Femina, McNamee (ranked number 21 in gross billings in the United States by *Advertising Age*) was sold to Paris-based Eurocom. Della Femina, still rebelling against the establishment as chairman, was so disappointed with the buyout decision that he considered leaving the business. However, he decided to continue with the agency as a major player.

In the March 25, 1991, edition of *Advertising Age*, Della Femina, McNamee was ranked 20th in the United States for the year 1990, with gross billings at $782 million and gross income at $94.2 million. The figures represented a 7.3 percent increase over 1989. In June 1991 Della Femina resigned as chairman of Della Femina, McNamee in New York. Still the protester, he had become disillusioned with the business due to agency mergers, consolidations, and buyouts.

Clearly, Jerry Della Femina helped rebuild an advertising agency that was once on the brink of collapse while holding on to most of his rebellious philosophies. Still feisty, he commented on the status of Della Femina, McNamee in the October 15, 1990, edition of *Advertising Age* (p. 72): "Unless this is going to be one of the top five agencies in the country, why would I want to hang around?" Fortunately, Della Femina is still active in advertising, and the discipline is better because of his presence. In November 1992 he returned to Madison Avenue and once again pitched his advertising expertise to potential clients and partners in order to build a new agency.

Today, Jerry Della Femina is still battling the advertising establishment, still speaking with tongue firmly planted in cheek, and has even returned to his rebellious roots. Fortunately for advertising, Della Femina still believes as he did when his book *From Those Wonderful Folks Who Gave You Pearl Harbor* first appeared in 1971: "Advertising is the most fun you can have with your clothes on."

FURTHER READING

Works by Della Femina

"Advertising Just Isn't Fun Anymore." *Advertising Age* (June 29, 1992):16.
From Those Wonderful Folks Who Gave You Pearl Harbor. London: Sir Isaac Pittman
    and Sons, 1971.
An Italian Grows in Brooklyn. New York: Little, Brown, 1978.

Works about Della Femina

Fox, Stephen. *The Mirror Makers: A History of American Advertising and Its Creators*.
    New York: William Morrow, 1984.
Lafayette, J., and L. Wentz. "Della Femina: I'm Out If Eurocom Won't Act." *Advertising
    Age* (October 15, 1992): 1, 72.
Marra, J. *Advertising Creativity*. Englewood Cliffs, NJ: Prentice Hall, 1990.
Meyers, W. *The Image Makers: Power and Persuasion on Madison Avenue*. New York:
    Times Books, 1984.
O'Toole, John. *The Trouble with Advertising: A View from the Inside*. New York: Times
    Books, 1985.
Schudson, Michael. *Advertising, The Uneasy Persuasion: Its Dubious Impact on Amer-
    ican Society*. New York: Basic Books, 1986.
Swisshelm, G. "Della Femina, Travisano Sees $$ Grow with 'Respectability.' " *Tele-
    vision/Radio Age* (March 27, 1978): 35, 117–126.
Wells, M., and S. Donaton. "Della Femina Returns to Build New Agency." *Advertising
    Age* (November 16, 1992): 46.

NOTABLE CLIENTS/CAMPAIGNS

A&W Rootbeer (DFT, 1971)

Mama Celeste Pizza (DFT, 1972)

Max Factor (DFT, 1972)

Blue Nun Wine (DFT, 1978)

Ralston-Purina Meow Mix (DFT, 1978)

Isuzu (DFM, 1988)

ROY SARLES DURSTINE
(December 13, 1886–November 28, 1962)

Robert McGaughey III and William Ray Mofield

Roy Sarles Durstine, whose name survives in one of the world's largest agencies, worked for 50 years in advertising. He first put in four years with the New York *Sun* as a reporter, then spent the summer and fall of 1912 as public relations director for the unsuccessful campaign of Theodore Roosevelt and the Bull Moose Party. After that it was advertising, first with Calkins and Holden, then Berrien and Durstine, then Barton, Durstine and Osborn, which merged with the George Batten Company in 1928. He remained as president of the latter until 1939, when he formed his agency, Roy S. Durstine.

Durstine was born in Jamestown, North Dakota, on December 13, 1886. He was graduated from the Lawrenceville School and in 1908 from Princeton University, where he was chairman of the Princeton *Tiger*, president of the Triangle Club, and a member of the Cap and Gown Society.

Late in 1912 he took a job with Calkins and Holden, where be became secretary and treasurer in 1914, a position he held until 1918. At the end of World War I, he joined forces with Bruce Barton and Alex F. Osborn to form Barton, Durstine and Osborn. Ten years later George Batten merged his company, which he had founded in 1866, with them, and from 1928 until the present the firm name has been Batten, Barton, Durstine and Osborn (BBDO). Although Durstine was named president of that giant firm in 1936, he left the agency three years iater and founded Roy S. Durstine, as mentioned, where he remained for the rest of his life.

Roy S. Durstine had a lively career before going into advertising. Fresh out of Princeton he was rewarded with a coveted reporter's job with the New York *Sun*. Although it had begun to slip following Charles A. Dana's death in 1897, the *Sun* was still a jewel of New York journalism. Besides, Durstine was given the choice assignment of covering President William Howard Taft at his summer home in Beverly, Massachusetts. He left the newspaper in 1912 for another never-to-be-forgotten experience, serving Teddy Roosevelt in the Bull Moose campaign.

Durstine wrote and published constantly. Two early books included *Making Advertisements and Making Them Pay* and *This Advertising Business*, which were published in 1921 and 1928, respectively. He went to Russia, Germany, and Austria in 1934 and then wrote *Red Thunder*, which he described as "the fascinating record of an American businessman's trip through Russia."

Durstine pioneered in many ways, but his early insight into radio and later television would garner much of the national advertising budget and put his agency ahead of most in the early days of national advertising. In 1926, when radio was still a struggling medium and looked upon with something of contempt by the "print men" of the time, Durstine saw its possibilities. His enthusiasm led BDO to establish the first agency radio department, a natural lead-in to BBDO's later dominance in the field of general broadcast advertising. He was called "the father of commercial broadcasting," and the BBDO 75th anniversary newsletter quotes him as saying, "Advertising came into the world when man became too impatient to wait for Mrs. Jones to tell Mrs. Smith that Brown's pickles were good" (p. 58).

Roy Durstine was vice president and general manager of BBDO from 1928 to 1936, then president from 1936 to 1939. He was replaced by Bruce Barton, whom he had met during World War I while they were doing war work on the home front. By this time, Barton's books *The Man Nobody Knows* and *The Book Nobody Knows*, which were about Jesus Christ and the Bible, had made him internationally famous.

Not only did Roy Durstine write books; he published a number of articles in leading magazines and journals of the day and contributed a chapter to help recruit top young people into advertising. Alden James, author of *Careers in Advertising*, which was published in 1932, asked him to write "The Management of an Advertising Agency," one of 61 chapters. Durstine promoted the notion that advertising was ideas. As for preparation, he examined the 196 members of the agency and revealed that 69 employees had worked for newspapers, 57 had worked in sales, 26 had been teachers, and the others had various backgrounds. While admitting the difficulty of naming the best source of advertising recruits, he did mention graduating classes of colleges (p. 86). His concluding lines about his thrills in working with young advertising people were: "They are a new, versatile type in business—people with brains and hearts and imaginations. Helping them to progress is about the most interesting job in the world" (p. 103).

One of his early articles appeared in *Nation's Business* for June 1925. The title declared that "Advertising Works—But Not Magic." His thesis contained in the opening paragraphs declared that advertising should be a basic part of a business and should feature one or two things, not everything in the store.

People worry over whether advertising is a business or a profession. They admit it isn't a science and wonder whether it is an art. They speak of having faith in it as if it were some new and fantastic cult.

The chief trouble is that it is too often considered as something apart, something to be added on to a business or left off; that you can either take it or leave it alone.

Good advertising is really an integral part of a business. It isn't something to please the president like putting his picture on the letterhead. It isn't a rabbit's foot in the pocket of every salesman. It isn't something to provide a job for the boss' nephew. It is a vital force which has a direct effect upon every department of a business. (pp. 18–19)

He concluded by telling about a hat company that made 414 different hats. By offering seven lines in ten colors, the company reduced expenses by half and tripled its revenue (pp. 18–19).

That same month, for the June 20, 1925 issue of *Liberty*, he wrote, "It's a Personal Matter." He advised those who wanted to get a job simply to say so and not hide behind the fiction of "it's a personal matter," an argument for telling the truth in advertising.

Another article that caused national comment appeared in the August 1925 issue of *System: The Magazine of Business* with the title, "Miss Blotz, Get Mr. Pillsbury on the 'Phone." Since being introduced by Alexander Graham Bell at the 1876 World's Fair in Philadelphia, the telephone had become a mainstay of business. Durstine's message was that telephone manners were horrible and needed improvement. His suggestions, as usual, made sense (pp. 158–60).

Business was nearing its pre-Depression peak when Durstine's next article appeared in *Nation's Business* for June 1928. The title tells the story of advertising as Roy Durstine saw it, "The Machine That Creates Desire." He categorized advertising agencies as those that sell advertising in media; those that work for one manufacturer; and those that produce multivaried work. He explained the latter in great detail (pp. 29, 70–71).

Sometimes Durstine was asked to write for scholarly journals. One such offer came from the American Academy of Political and Social Science. Now that he was the leading exponent of radio advertising in America, he was asked to prepare an article for the *Annals* of January 1935, which he did under the title, "The Future of Radio Advertising in the United States." He marveled that 50 million persons could now listen to the same sound at the same time. In explaining the private commercial system of the United States versus the BBC, he predicted the British might some day have commercials, which they now do. His 15-point plan for improving American commercial radio included many items that have been adopted such as self-regulation codes. He believed what he preached and practiced it. He fought for a code for the advertising business and spent much time promoting the American Association of Advertising Agencies (AAAA), a group for which he served as president in 1925–1926 (pp. 1–7).

Roy Durstine was a man with a message. Besides his writing for the popular press, business press, and scholarly journals, he was ever ready to go far and wide to deliver his call for better advertising. In 1921, for instance, in one of his early noted speeches, he took the train to Atlanta and spoke on June 15 to members of the Associated Advertising Clubs of the World. His presentation was entitled, "Better Copy—and More of It." He called upon copywriters to learn the business, the product, and the market inside and out. Otherwise, he claimed, the advertisement would not be effective. This is a lesson that is still being taught. Two paragraphs from the address summarize his devotion to copy and research:

Copy is the flower of advertising. It is the final expression of the whole enterprise. But the man who feels that copy can be discussed by itself and for itself is a florist, not a horticulturist.

Copy runs back too far into the branch and root of advertising to be considered alone. Somewhere down in the subsoil an idea germinates. When it has been discovered and cultivated and allowed to grow and flourish, it may blossom out some day into a piece of copy. But it must have leaves and a stem and it must spring from roots firmly planted not only on but under the ground—or it has no more life in it than the velvet pansies on your wife's Easter hat. (pp. 1–10)

A few years later in the 1930s Roy was still on the "sawdust trail," speaking to the Associated Grocery Manufacturers of America in New York. The manuscript file carries the date of April 1936. He called this presentation, "Advertising: A Vital Tool in Business."

Paying tribute to the master of radio in politics he began with the line, "The greatest single piece of advertising in modern times was the message which Franklin D. Roosevelt sent over the air on the morning of March 4th, 1933. It took a weary, depression-worn nation and lifted it out of the valley of despair, gave it a thump on the back and sent it on its way rejoicing in the proud fact that the United States of America cannot be licked" (p. 1).

He lauded all forms of advertising, and told about the advertiser who sent letters at three cents postage to 120,420 people in San Francisco at a cost of $3,612.60 but then discovered he could have reached the same number of newspaper subscribers by advertising for $627.20. Then he talked about adding an entertaining radio program at an even lower cost per thousand. Many examples of how advertisers could reach prospective consumers for very little money were given, including the classic Campbell Soup campaign that averaged 36/1000 of a cent per can (pp. 1–15).

Durstine's speech was well received; a number of advertising and business papers quoted several lines from it. The final summation was: "Here we come directly up against the very essence of advertising's value as an economic tool. Without the volume, without the mass production, which advertising has helped to create, the unit cost would be increased far beyond the amount of the advertising. . . . Without this mass production, her husband and her friends' husbands would have no jobs" ("Advertising," p. 7).

Roy Durstine received the first Advertising Award for radio advertising in 1936, which was given annually after that date. He was the first person to persuade U.S. Steel to use an advertising campaign.

He took part in many civic, social, and community activities. He was a member of the University Club; the Maidstone Club of East Hampton, Long Island; the Devon Yacht Club; member, trustee, and past chairman of Guild Hall of East Hampton; and a trustee of the East Hampton Historical Society.

Durstine died in New York on November 28, 1962. He was 75. A devout Presbyterian, his memorial services were held at the Madison Avenue Presbyterian Church on November 30, 1962. His second wife, the former Virginia Gardiner, became chairman of his agency. Other survivors included three children by a previous marriage.

FURTHER READING

Works by Durstine

"Advertising: A Vital Tool in Business." BBDO, Personnel Speeches (April 1936), p. 7.
"Advertising Works—But Not Magic." *Nation's Business* (June 1925): 18–19.
"The Future of Radio Advertising in the United States." *The Annals of the American Academy of Political and Social Science.* Philadelphia: American Academy of Political and Social Science. January 1935, pp. 1–7.
"It's a Personal Matter." *Liberty* (June 20, 1925): 27.
"The Machine That Creates Desire." *Nation's Business* (June 1928): 29–30, 70.
Making Advertisements and Making Them Pay. New York and London: Charles Scribner's Sons, 1921.
"The Management of an Advertising Agency." In *Careers in Advertising,* edited by Alden James. New York: Macmillan, 1932, pp. 84–103.
"Miss Blotz, Get Mr. Pillsbury on the 'Phone." *System: The Magazine of Business* (August 1925): 158–160.
Red Thunder. New York and London: Charles Scribner's Sons, 1934.
This Advertising Business. New York and London: Charles Scribner's Sons, 1928.

Works about Durstine

Newsweek (December 10, 1962): 64.
Time (December 7, 1962): 78.

NOTABLE CLIENT/CAMPAIGN

U.S. Steel

BERNICE BOWLES FITZ-GIBBON
(1894 [?]–February 22, 1982)

Kay M. Nagel

Bernice Bowles Fitz-Gibbon, one of the highest-paid advertising women of the 1940s and 1950s, was a retail expert known for her work with the Macy's and Gimbels department stores. While at Macy's, she created the famous slogan, "It's smart to be thrifty." Later, while working for Gimbels, she developed the well-known phrase, "Nobody, but nobody, undersells Gimbels."

Fitz-Gibbon, or "Fitz" as she was known by friends and colleagues, was born in Waunakee, Wisconsin, to William and Nora Fitz-Gibbon. Though she never supplied her actual birth date for reference books, her obituary said she was 87 when she died in 1982.

As a child, Fitz-Gibbon attended Sacred Heart Academy in Madison, Wisconsin. However, her informal education at home on the farm had a more direct effect on her success in advertising. Fitz-Gibbon's father, a teacher and farmer, expected his children to have a command of language and a keen sense of observation. In her book *Macy's, Gimbels, and Me* Fitz-Gibbon tells of discussions over dinner that often sent her to a nearby dictionary. Her father created games that encouraged his family to use long, descriptive, and colorful words in their conversations. He developed their powers of observation by having them describe various rooms in the house, forcing them to see very common and familiar items in a new way. Fitz-Gibbon later demanded these same skills from herself and her staff in creating advertisements.

To earn money for tuition prior to attending college, Fitz-Gibbon taught at a country school near Waunakee. She was graduated with a B.A. degree from the University of Wisconsin in 1918.

After graduating she continued to teach English at a Chippewa Falls, Wisconsin, high school. She moved to Illinois a year later to become a society reporter for the *Rockford Register-Gazette*. Her ultimate goal was to write essays for literary magazines, but she soon learned that the advertising manager for the newspaper was earning more than twice that of the city editor. She asked to be transferred to the advertising department.

Fitz-Gibbon left the newspaper after a year to join Marshall Field and Company in Chicago as part of a retail training program, with hopes of moving into writing advertisements for the store. She spent a year selling ribbons and furniture for $18 a week, but she made little progress in the advertising department. She left to teach advertising and sales in a Chicago high school, then moved to New York in 1922.

Fitz-Gibbon first sought a position in Macy's advertising department, but Macy's was not hiring at the time. She headed to John Wanamaker, and after just six weeks in the home furnishings department and a sample of Wanamaker's furniture ads in her portfolio, she went back to Macy's and became head of home furnishings advertising, a position she held for six years. Later, she became head of fashion advertising.

Her father's home-style education in language and vocabulary came through in every advertisement she created. "It's smart to be thrifty" is a perfect example of her attention to word choice. In her book she describes her thoughts after seeing John D. Rockefeller, Jr.'s car parked in front of Macy's one day in 1928:

> When you come to think about it, today it is the *fashion* to be frugal. Saving money isn't grubby or gritty any more. Saving money has become the chic thing to do. Yes, *it's the fashion to be frugal*. That would be a good slogan for Macy's.
>
> But *frugal, frugal*, I thought. Who says *frugal*? Thrifty is the word. My grandmother used to call her geraniums "thrifty." *Frugal* sounds too penny-pinching, but *thrifty* has a fine fat flourishing sound. *It's the fashion to be thrifty*.
>
> *Fashion, fashion—fashion* sounds so temporary, and Macy's plans on being in business a long long time. But everybody wants to be smart. *"It's smart to be thrifty."* That's it! The perfect slogan for Macy's! (p. 262)

Fitz-Gibbon's slogan summed up a new philosophy that thrift and elegance were not mutually exclusive, a philosophy that Macy's used to its advantage. The store began to appeal to the rich, knowing that shoppers of more modest means would follow. This new approach, along with the slogan, brought Macy's into a profitable era. However, this was also during the Depression. Despite the success of her slogan, Macy's wanted to cut Fitz-Gibbon's salary, which had grown from $4,000 a year to $19,000. The thought of a pay cut caused her to leave Macy's after 12 years. She was wooed back to Wanamaker's in 1936 as advertising director for $25,000 a year.

This new position presented a challenge for Fitz-Gibbon. The Wanamaker image and advertising had to be changed and updated quickly for it to compete successfully with other major department stores. Despite a small advertising budget, Fitz-Gibbon developed creative events, such as fashion shows featuring Arthur Murray dance instructors and guest speakers at the store. She brought attention to the store's restaurant, an area rarely promoted by department stores, through advertisements loaded with copy designed to make the reader's mouth water.

Fitz-Gibbon also developed a creative use for "buildups" or "position protectors," the small space at the top of an eight-column newspaper ad. She used this space, usually reserved for store hours, telephone numbers, and addresses, for tiny editorials to build the image of the store. She claims in her book that an unbiased survey showed these editorials to be the most read items in the newspaper except for front-page news and says she believes this was one of her biggest contributions to retail advertising.

On one occasion, Fitz-Gibbon used this advertising space to state that people were reading Wanamaker's ads for fun. Though she was criticized by advertising experts and her superiors at Wanamaker's, she soon heard from 20 college composition instructors who said they discussed Wanamaker's ads regularly in their classes, a tidbit that Fitz-Gibbon used to her advantage in later advertisements.

Business increased at Wanamaker's while Fitz-Gibbon was advertising director. But after four years of having her ads tampered with by top Wanamaker officials, she left her position in 1940 to become advertising director at Gimbels.

Gimbels gave Fitz-Gibbon the creative freedom she desired. She wrote sensational ads, such as one promoting cow manure as the perfect Christmas gift. She started friendly feuds with Macy's over quality, price, and availability of merchandise. Her ads were filled with carefully chosen words to educate the customers not only about the product, but also its place in their lives.

During Fitz-Gibbon's first five years with the store, sales increased 96 percent, as compared to 47 percent for New York department stores in general and 50.3 percent for Macy's. This increase was at least partially due to a Fitzkrieg, "a blitz of words springing from the rapier-sharp and highly imaginative brain of Miss Fitz-Gibbon" (Bauer, p. 17).

Fitz-Gibbon's creation of the famous slogan "Nobody, but nobody, undersells Gimbels" shows that imaginative brain, along with her father's influence. She developed the slogan in 1945 to impress readers with Gimbels' lower prices, as she relates in her book:

I couldn't say, "No store sells for less," because the newspapers had censorship rules and would not permit the word *store* to be used in that way. "No one" was feeble. "Nobody" was the right word. "Nobody" was a good full-bodied word with a fine dactylic rhythm. "Nobody undersells Gimbels"—that was a little bald and bleak; and besides I needed more words in order to make the eight-column headline the proper size.

I sat there muttering "nobody, nobody, nobody" when suddenly I remembered the last few lines of a poem by A. A. Milne, "The King's Breakfast." . . . "Nobody, nobody, nobody" was emphatic, but a couple of characters too long. "Nobody but nobody" was just right. (pp. 225–26)

Fitz-Gibbon's slogan and phrasing quickly became part of common usage with slight twists in the wording, such as "no place, but no place" and "no man, but no man." Gimbels used the slogan for many years.

As a manager, Fitz-Gibbon was a perfectionist and taskmaster. She hired only Phi Beta Kappas because she believed they were either naturally brilliant or extremely hard-working. Though she encouraged her copywriters to have wild ideas, there were limits to the mistakes she allowed from her staff. She demanded from them the same attention to language and observation that her father had instilled in her.

Reva Korda, who worked as a Gimbels copywriter, remembers Fitz-Gibbon firing another copywriter "because the poor wretch didn't know if the belt on a dress she had written about was a self belt, or a leather belt. It turned out she'd actually written about the dress *without ever having seen it*. To the head-mistress in Fitz, this was grounds for immediate expulsion" (p. M–11).

However, Fitz-Gibbon's staff respected her. Copywriters followed her from Wanamaker's to Gimbels. She never lacked for applicants for her department. And the fact that Gimbels hired only Phi Beta Kappas, even for the most menial tasks, was great publicity for the store.

In January 1954 Fitz-Gibbon decided to use her retail expertise to start her own advertising agency. It was small, relying on free-lance talent from her Gimbels, Wanamaker's, and Macy's trainees. The agency concentrated on retail institutional campaigns, anniversary celebrations, openings of new stores, and similar events. She also used her retail knowledge to help larger advertising agencies.

Fitz-Gibbon accepted invitations to speak to groups and organizations and wrote numerous articles for women's and fashion magazines, including a column, "Fitz and Starts," which appeared in *Good Housekeeping* in 1955 and 1956. Her topics included the advertising world, advice on how to get a job and make money, and women's place in business. She always included entertaining stories and anecdotes from her own career and her early years on the farm.

By the time Fitz-Gibbon retired in 1964, she had received numerous awards. The Association of Press Editors named her Woman of the Year in Business in 1955. In 1957 *Fortune* magazine called her one of the leading business women in the nation, and the University of Wisconsin Alumni Association named her Woman of the Year.

Fitz-Gibbon died on February 22, 1982, at a nursing home in Onalaska, Wisconsin, six years after moving back to Wisconsin and a month before being installed in the American Advertising Federation Hall of Fame. Her husband, Henry Block, a lawyer, died in 1951. They were married in 1925 and had a daughter, Elizabeth, and a son, Peter.

Fitz-Gibbon's career in advertising was certainly lucrative, a point made in almost every article about her and in her book. However, her success was not a mystery to her. She maintained that with knowledge of grammar and vocabulary, a keen sense of observation, and a lot of hard work, anybody, but anybody, can write advertising copy: If you're content with a crust, stay where you are; but if you want butter on your croissant and a bit of wild strawberry jam, you'll read every word. Certainly if *I* made the grade, *you* can" (*Macy's, Gimbels, and Me*, p. 18).

FURTHER READING

Works by Fitz-Gibbon

"Fitz and Starts." *Good Housekeeping* (January 1955–August 1956).
"The Ghoul with the Green Face." *New York Times Magazine* (February 12, 1961): 33–34.
"Machines for Dictators? Hardly." *New York Times Magazine* (December 6, 1959): 82.
Macy's, Gimbels, and Me: How to Earn $90,000 a Year in Retail Advertising. New York: Simon and Schuster, 1967.
"Wanted—More Bounce to the Ounce." *Harper's Bazaar* (August 1951): 148ff.
"Woman in the *Gay* Flannel Suit." *New York Times Magazine* (January 29, 1956): 15ff.
"Women Bosses." *New York Times Magazine* 1956): 16ff.

Works about Fitz-Gibbon

Bauer, Hambla. "That's Not Blasting—That's Bernice." *Saturday Evening Post* (November 30, 1946): 17ff.
"Fitz-Gibbon, Bernice." *National Cyclopaedia of American Biography.* Vol. I (1953–59). New York: James T. White, 1960, p. 300.
Korda, Reva. "Fond Memories of a 'Hall of Famer'." *Advertising Age* (March 29, 1982): sec. 2, p. M–11.

NOTABLE CLIENTS/CAMPAIGNS

Macy's (1924–36)

John Wanamaker (1936–40)

Gimbels (1940–54)

PAUL FOLEY
(March 12, 1914–October 30, 1983)

Edd Applegate

Paul Foley was 69 when he died on October 30, 1983. He had retired about a year earlier from the Interpublic Group of Companies, the largest worldwide advertising and marketing communications organization at that time. He had served as a director and chairman of the finance committee since 1979. Foley had worked in advertising for more than 40 years.

Foley was born in 1914 and reared in Pontiac, Michigan. His father worked as the managing editor of the *Pontiac Daily Press* until he served as the first federal housing administrator in Washington, D.C. Foley attended Catholic schools in Pontiac and later in Grosse Pointe. Upon his graduation from St. Paul's School, he entered the University of Notre Dame. By the end of his first year, the Depression had set in and he was out of money. He left Notre Dame and went to work in Detroit, where he remained for three years.

When he had saved enough money, he returned to Notre Dame and majored in journalism. He was graduated magna cum laude in 1937, then went to work for several Hearst newspapers, including the *Chicago American*. A journalist who worshiped the English language, Foley gave up writing for newspapers two years later when he accepted a copywriting position at MacManus, John and Adams, an advertising agency located in Bloomfield Hills, Michigan. The agency was responsible for creating advertising campaigns for several divisions of General Motors, including Cadillac and Pontiac.

When the United States was drawn into World War II, Foley could not be drafted because he was too old, married, and had a child. However, Jim Linen, whom he had known in Detroit, was with the Office of War Information (OWI) in New York and persuaded Foley to work for it. Linen sent him to a two- or three-month Bretton Woods Monetary Conference, where he learned from British economist John Maynard Keynes, then to Turkey to head the Istanbul bureau. Foley served as chief until the war ended in 1945.

Foley returned to New York and entered the world of journalism for a second time, accepting a job with the Associated Press. This did not last long, however, for within a few months he was again writing advertising copy for MacManus, John and Adams. He was encouraged by Jim Adams, the president, to write radio commercials, which he did. Before he left in the early 1950s to manage the Detroit office of McCann-Erickson, Foley had been promoted to executive vice president and a member of the board.

According to Foley, he joined McCann-Erickson on the day the agency got the Coca-Cola account, one of its biggest at the time. Although he managed the Detroit office, he continued to write copy. After four years he was brought to McCann-Erickson's New York office, primarily to write copy. Three years later, in 1964, he was promoted to chairman upon Emerson Foote's resignation. Foley understood the advertising industry. More important, he understood the premise on which McCann-Erickson was based. As he expressed in a 1981 interview: "The basis of McCann is Esso/Exxon. That's pretty close to automobiles. And they didn't have enough people that knew that, or felt that kind of a relationship. And I think there was a time when Esso wanted somebody in there who knew something about the automobile business" (Cummings, p. 155).

Foley's successful reign lasted until Armando Sarmento of Interpublic, McCann-Erickson's parent company, informed him that Interpublic's chairman, Robert E. Healy, wanted Foley to take over the helm. Healy had saved Interpublic almost singlehandedly by dismantling its organization. Indeed, 24 divisions were cut to 5 and more than 900 employees were dismissed. Marion Harper, who had been chairman before Healy, had built a sprawling empire that circled the world. Unfortunately, the conglomerate, except for a few divisions, had lost millions of dollars. Now, under Healy's guidance, the company was earning a profit. Sarmento also informed Foley that the company had to go public. As Foley recalled, "Sarmento said, 'And if we're going to go public, we've got to have somebody with some visibility in the advertising agency business, some background that people will understand, and you're the guy to do it' " (Cummings, p. 155).

Foley moved to Interpublic in 1971 as president and chief executive officer. Working with Healy, he helped change Interpublic's direction. The company went public; consequently, a board of directors was created. The company hired excellent people with excellent credentials to oversee new accounts such as financial institutions. Foley and Healy realized that Interpublic had to expand to stay afloat. Interpublic was not an advertising agency in the strictest sense; it did not create any advertising per se. Rather, it was an umbrella involved in marketing communications and overseeing its offspring, which included advertising agencies.

In 1973 Foley became chairman when Healy retired. Expansion continued. Interpublic acquired Campbell-Ewald of Detroit, primarily because the advertising agency's chairman at the time, Tom Adams, wanted to enter the European market. Adams realized that through Interpublic he could be successful. Besides, Adams wanted to attract new clients and additional employees. Interpublic also acquired Sullivan, Stauffer, Colwell and Bayles before Foley retired. The reasons for this acquisition differed slightly from the one for the acquisition of Campbell-Ewald. One was SSC and B's 49 percent interest in Unilever's Lintas Worldwide advertising network. Another reason was SSC and B's list of clients, which included manufacturers of packaged goods or shelf items.

Foley brought in Philip Geier, who had been working for McCann-Erickson and who had plenty of experience in Europe. Geier actually helped Foley with the acquisition of SSC and B. When Foley relinquished the title of chairman in 1979, Geier succeeded him. Foley remained with the company as a director and chairman of the finance committee until 1981.

Foley received several awards for various causes, wrote the book, *Fresh Views of the American Revolution*, which was published in 1976, earned several honorary degrees, and was elected to the Advertising Hall of Fame in 1983. Although he served at the helm of one of the largest marketing communications firms in the world when billings surpassed a billion dollars, he remained a writer at heart. In an interoffice memo, he discussed a poster that had been designed for the New York State Thoroughbred Racing Association. The memo, which was two pages, criticized the typeface that the art director had used. According to Philip H. Dougherty, the memo ended: "You may by now have gathered that I feel rather strongly about this—and about type generally—that's because I believe very much that writing is to persuasion what breathing is to health" (*New York Times*, October 31, 1983, sec. 2, p. 15).

FURTHER READING

Work by Foley

Fresh Views of the American Revolution. New York: Rizzoli, 1976.

Work about Foley

Cummings, Barton. *The Benevolent Dictators: Interviews with Advertising Greats*. Chicago: Crain Books, 1984.

NOTABLE CLIENTS/CAMPAIGNS

Cadillac (MacManus, John and Adams, 1930s–40s)
Pontiac (MacManus, John and Adams, 1930s–40s)
Coca-Cola (McCann-Erickson, 1950s)
Esso (McCann-Erickson, 1950s)
Exxon (McCann-Erickson, 1950s)

EMERSON FOOTE
(December 13, 1906–)

Billy I. Ross

Emerson Foote was "The Huckster." During his four decades in advertising, he served as president of two of America's largest advertising agencies, Foote, Cone and Belding and McCann-Erickson. One of his largest accounts was the American Tobacco Company. Many thought that Frederic Wakeman's novel, and later the movie, *The Huckster*, was about Foote and his work with that account.

Emerson A. Foote was born on December 13, 1906, in Sheffield, Alabama, the son of James and Ruth Foote, but he spent most of his youth in California. In 1922 he graduated from Los Angeles High School at the age of 15. His principal thought he should take a postgraduate semester, due to his age, before entering college, and Foote and his mother agreed with the advice.

According to Foote's unpublished biography, he planned to begin college in the winter of 1924, but prior to that time he decided to look for a job to get some experience (p. 2). With the help of a neighbor, he obtained his first job in a fine stationery store in downtown Los Angeles during the Christmas holidays. His first job was as a wrapping clerk, for which he had no experience.

This was a good job for Foote since he did not have to speak very much with customers. From his early boyhood, he had a very bad speech impediment. Vowels were very difficult for him to pronounce. In fact, when reporting for his first job, he had difficulty telling the manager that his name was Emerson. He got stuck on the "E."

Another job that came his way before college was with the Los Angeles Mutual Building and Loan Association. Foote started as a junior teller, handling withdrawals which included opening piggy banks and counting the contents. He did so well that he was promised a position with the company after college and was encouraged to think of this as a lifetime work.

A year later, however, Foote entered the University of Southern California, a school he had always wanted to attend because his two older brothers were alumni. His first semester, however, winter 1924, would also be his last.

College work was not difficult for Foote and he was not bothered as much as he had expected by his speech impediment. One course, mathematics of finance, he found particularly valuable in doing research when he entered the field of advertising.

Although he could have returned to his job with the mutual company during the summer break, he decided to look elsewhere. Midway during the summer, he obtained a job as a junior salesman for the Greer-Robbins Company, a Chrysler distributor. He was to be paid by commission. Just before starting back to college in the fall he was offered $100 a month to stay on as the clerk in the retail sales department. At first he turned the job down, so the sales manager asked to talk with his mother and father. Together they decided that he should take the job and postpone college.

While working for Greer-Robbins Foote helped solve a record-keeping problem that had plagued the company for some time. He completely did away with an intricate card system, replacing it with a large notebook. Foote claimed that this bookkeeping system positively affected his life.

After San Francisco–area jobs with the J. L. Green Company, Pacific Mutual Life Insurance, and the H. O. Harrison Company, Foote became inspired with the field of advertising. A friend of his from Greer-Robbins introduced him to Sabina Fromhold, which led to dinner and dancing at the Palace Hotel Palm Court. Sabina was a copywriter for a Cincinnati agency. During the evening she said to Emerson, "I think you ought to go into advertising. I think you would be a good account executive" (p. 31). Before Sabina left San Francisco in May 1929, she had agreed to become Mrs. Emerson Foote, but the marriage would not take place for nine years.

At the age of 24 in 1931, Foote entered advertising as an employee of the Leon Livingston agency in San Francisco, whose accounts included the Wells Fargo Bank, American Trust Company (which later merged with Wells Fargo), Levi Strauss, and Carta Blanca, a leading Mexican beer. The largest account was the Pacific State Savings and Loan Association, at that time the largest in the United States.

Foote's first job with the agency was in research, although he felt ill-prepared. His first assignment was to do a study for Levi Strauss. From that position he worked as a copywriter and later became an account executive. While with the agency he became good friends with Harry Berk and Leon Livingston. Berk was instrumental in Foote's advertising future. He left Leon Livingston a short time later to join the J. Stirling Getchell agency in New York.

In 1934 Foote quit his job with Livingston and established the Emerson Foote Advertising Agency. He began doing business with $300 capital plus a $2,000 loan from the James McAlister Company, his only account. At the end of the agency's first month of business, the bank statement showed a balance of 33 cents (p. 46).

At the urging of Harry Berk, Foote flew to New York for a meeting with J. Stirling Getchell. The meeting did not end with a job offer, and Foote returned to San Francisco. Two weeks later he received a wire with an offer to report at a salary of $4,800. Foote left his San Francisco agency in the hands of his partner, Lew Yeomans.

Foote's first assignment with the Getchell agency was to help work on a new business proposal for the American Can Company. He drew from his earlier research experience to help with the presentation. The agency did not get the account, but his work led to research on other accounts.

In 1936, a short time after joining the agency, Foote became ill and obtained a three-week leave with pay from his job. He took a cruise through the Panama Canal to San Francisco and at one time became so deeply depressed that he considered suicide (p. 54). The trip to San Francisco took care of much of his homesickness. He returned to New York by train.

His first major account for Getchell was Airtemp, located in Dayton, Ohio. Airtemp was owned by Chrysler and produced a line of air conditioning for cars. Foote convinced Airtemp to invest most of its small budget in *Life*, a new picture-news weekly that had become an overnight success. The concentration of the budget into only one medium was an instant success.

By 1938 Foote's status had changed only to the extent that he was taking on more accounts for the agency. One assignment, though, the new TWA account, led to a change in his life. He had to fly to Chicago often, thereby giving him the opportunity to see Sabina Fromhold again. Their nine-year engagement ended on April 18, 1938, when they were married.

Again through his friend Harry Berk, an opportunity arose to move to the Lord and Thomas agency, to work specifically on the American Tobacco account and with its president, George Washington Hill. Sabina and Emerson discussed the change and decided he should interview for the position.

He got the job with a salary of $11,000 a year. When Foote joined Lord and Thomas the agency was considered one of the largest in the country, with international offices already established. He considered working with Lord and Thomas and George Washington Hill to be a challenge.

Another opportunity for Foote in going with Lord and Thomas was working for Albert Lasker, considered one of the true advertising leaders of the time. Foote began work on the American Tobacco account in December 1938 and met with Hill a short time later. He reported that the first meeting was very pleasant and he found Hill to be anything but a man-eater. Although he was afraid of him at times, the seven-year experience was a pleasant one (p. 72).

Foote began working on the print media side of the American Tobacco account. He took over the entire account when the broadcast media person was removed in 1939. In addition to Hill, Foote also worked with George Washington Hill, Jr., and Sylvester L. (Pat) Weaver, Jr. Years later, Weaver would become president of the National Broadcasting Company. Weaver and Foote also spent some later years together at McCann-Erickson.

While on the American Tobacco account, Foote worked with two top-rated radio programs: "Your Hit Parade" and "Kay Kyser's College of Musical Knowledge." During the war years Hill wanted "Information Please" with Clifton Fadiman added to American Tobacco's radio shows, along with the theme, "Lucky Strike green has gone to war." (The company had changed the color of its cigarette package from green to white since green ink was needed for the war effort.) Hill wanted the theme repeated so often that the agency got complaints from listeners.

Foote's success with Hill and the American Tobacco account moved him up the ladder at Lord and Thomas. In 1942 Lasker appointed him executive vice president in charge of the New York operation. His salary was $37,500 a year, while his predecessor had received $115,000 a year.

Foote told of a conversation that he had with Lasker about his salary. Lasker said, "Mr. Foote, you've never asked me about money for yourself. I want to ask a very direct question; is that because you don't care about money, or because you think it's a smarter way to handle me?" (Cummings, "The Rise and Fall . . . ," p. M-2). He didn't get a raise after the conversation. However, later the same year, he, Don Belding, and Fairfax Cone became the owners of the agency. Belding became vice president in charge of the Pacific Coast operation, Cone was vice president in charge of the Chicago office, and Foote remained in charge of the New York office.

One of the things that may have led to Lasker's bowing out of the agency was when Foote approached him concerning the 1943 budget. Foote said, "Mr. Lasker, I can't make this budget fit operationally. I can't run the office with it. I think that the problem is this: I believe you are tired of the agency business, which is one reason you came up with these low budgets, and I suggest you liquidate Lord and Thomas and close it up." Lasker replied, "By God, I think I will" (Cummings, "The Rise and Fall . . . ," p. M-2).

After long conversations with his wife and various accountants and lawyers, Lasker made the decision to close the agency. He also visited with George Washington Hill about his decision. Hill disagreed and suggested that the agency remain intact and Foote handle the accounts. By this time Lasker was thinking more of letting the three vice presidents take over the accounts that would remain with the agency. He was definite, however, that the name be changed from Lord and Thomas.

Lasker's first thought was that the agency be named Belding, Cone and Foote, but after his visit with Hill he agreed with the name of Foote, Cone and Belding, with Foote as president. Neither of the other two was concerned that the agency's name had Foote listed first.

Lasker then called Belding and Cone to New York to discuss the disposition of the agency. The biggest problem was money. None of the three vice presidents was in any position to pay what the agency was really worth. With some creative financing, they came up with $100,000. Lasker helped arrange for lines of credit that made it possible for the new agency to exist. As Foote would later characterize the agency takeover: "We were all sort of shell-shocked, and they [Belding and Cone] knew as well as I that we had fallen into a bed of clover—and whose name came first didn't seem like a very big consideration" (Foote, p. 98).

RCA was one of few accounts that the new FCB did not retain. American Tobacco remained as the largest single account, and the addition of part of the Campbell Soup account made up for the loss of RCA. Two years later, the agency landed the Postum account for General Foods. Young and Rubicam and Benton and Bowles already handled most of the other General Foods products. Foote, Cone and Belding sat in on the original presentation to General Foods; two weeks after their presentation, they received word that they had the account. Later the agency also added Hallmark Cards, through the efforts of Cone in Chicago.

When George Washington Hill, Sr., died unexpectedly on a fishing trip to Canada, there was speculation about who would succeed him. Many thought it would be his son, George, Jr., but for some unknown reason the board bypassed him for Vincent Riggio. At the time the change did not affect Foote or FCB. Later, however, American Tobacco moved $2 million from FCB to Ruthrauff and Ryan. Much of this was for the Jack Benny radio show that Ruthrauff and Ryan had been handling.

In 1946 General Motors approached FCB with the possibility of working out a program with Bing Crosby. This would have been a big account for the agency, and Foote enjoyed the idea of working with Crosby. Even though it appeared that the agency had an inside track to do the show, it never worked out. Crosby received a better offer from Philco and accepted it.

This did not end Foote's involvement with radio personalities for the agency, however. American Tobacco, which had left with part of its account to work with Ruthrauff and Ryan, asked Foote if he would like to have the Jack Benny show. It did not take long to answer "yes," and FCB had it.

Foote's old friend from the Leon Livingston days in San Francisco, Harry Berk, reentered his life in 1945. Berk thought that his wartime service in Europe could help initiate FCB International, with an office in London. Foote and Belding agreed. (Lord and Thomas had been international before Lasker split the agency up, but the Canadian and London offices had not become part of FCB.)

The international idea was a success from the beginning. Berk obtained accounts in England and Switzerland, and at his insistence, Foote made many trips to Europe. The first he made by himself; he later traveled with his wife.

In 1947 things were running very smoothly for the agency and for Foote. Work for American Tobacco and the Jack Benny show was going well. In reference to Benny, Foote said: "I took care to see that I interfered in no way with the handling of the program but I did get to know Jack Benny fairly well personally, and I must say that in my book he was truly a remarkable person" (Foote, p. 131). He related that some 20 years later he was in Las Vegas and had a call from Benny, who was performing at his hotel. Benny got him a front-row table for the show and invited Foote and his guests back to his dressing room afterward.

All was not perfect in Foote's life, however. In an interview with Barton Cummings, he said:

I could not possibly relate my life story in advertising without telling you that part of it, substantial parts, were marred by what must be called mental illness. I have abandoned the euphemistic and somewhat confusing term "nervous breakdown," which doesn't mean anything.

It's not that you're babbling or raving, or running around in circles, but you're not well. Well, I was a manic depressive. Most of my trouble came from the manic phase.

I struggled on with psychiatrists for a long time, and had a couple of hospital experiences. This series of illnesses is what cost me my position, my stockholding in Foote, Cone & Belding. ("The Rise and Fall . . . ," p. M-2)

One of the occasions on which Foote's mental state caused a decision that he later referred to as his biggest mistake was in re-signing the American Tobacco account. He did not do this, however, without discussing it with Belding, Cone, and Lasker. All agreed with the decision, which was not based on the studies that were beginning to show that cigarettes were bad for a person's health. In fact, at that time Foote thought that cigarettes were good for you. Nor was it because Hill had died. Riggio, the new president of American Tobacco, and Foote worked well together. At the time that FCB resigned the account (1947), billing was more than $11 million.

Foote's mental illness started developing during the period he was considering resigning the American Tobacco account. He spent long hours on the job and basically overextended himself. This led to a collapse and ended in a hospital's mental ward. He was given electroshock treatments plus psychiatric care. After a few days he was back at work.

Even though the New York office of the agency lost its biggest account in 1948, it still showed a slight profit. To replace it, Foote worked hard and obtained the Emerson Radio and Phonograph account. This did not amount to anywhere near the billing of American Tobacco, but it did help.

Foote claimed that it took him years to realize the full impact of resigning such a large account. After resigning it, he said: "I noticed that in many ways, some subtle, I no longer had the same influence in my company as I had before, and I was taught a lesson I should have known. What counts in an advertising agency is not how much stock you own. It is how much billing you control. While the amount of stock I owned at FCB remained the same before and after the American Tobacco resignation, the amount of billing I controlled obviously went way down" (Foote, p. 137).

Harry Berk resigned as head of FCB international operations after a problem arose between him and Belding. Foote took over and started regular flights to Europe, especially to Switzerland, in an effort to keep the clients Berk had obtained. Following one of his trips back, his wife sensed he was so tired that he needed to take off a few days before returning to the office. One of his psychiatrists visited his home and suggested electroshock treatments be administered again. After a short rest, he returned to the office.

Belding and Cone did not press Foote to resign during his illness. In March 1950 they gave him a leave with pay. Staying away from the office was not helpful. His wife, along with his brother and a psychiatrist, advised him to enter the Westchester branch of New York Hospital in White Plains. At this time, Belding and Cone did not want him out of the agency. During this stay in the hospital he was considered an involuntary patient, but was never given any medication.

After three months, representatives from the agency called on Sabina in an attempt to work out some settlement for Foote's share. A financial offer was made that Foote thought was not the true value of his stock, but it was a time in which he needed the money. He and Sabina finally settled for $753,000. When Foote came out of the hospital, he was no longer associated with Foote, Cone and Belding. Foote told Cummings: "I felt that, putting it in military terms, they had left me for dead on the field of battle. They thought I was all washed up in the advertising business" ("The Rise and Fall . . . ," p. M-4).

After getting back on his feet, he decided to try his luck at another job in advertising. He visited with Stanley Resor of J. Walter Thompson and Sigurd Larmon of Young and Rubicam, but no offers came. He also talked to Fred Gamble, president of the American Association of Advertising Agencies, and was told that it would be better not to try to get back in the agency business with his history. Lasker also advised him not to go back into advertising.

With time on his hands, Foote accepted a position as vice-chairman of the American Cancer Society's board of directors. This was a great boost for his morale, and the contacts helped him get reestablished in a business environment. Another service activity came his way when Dr. William C. Menninger asked him to head the New York committee for the Menninger Foundation.

His luck for an advertising position changed, however, at a luncheon sponsored by *Look* magazine when he was seated next to Marion Harper, head of McCann-Erickson. Three weeks later Foote became a vice president and general executive at McCann-Erickson. This was in 1952; he stayed with the agency for 13 years.

At McCann-Erickson he worked on many different accounts—Junket Brand Foods, Esso, Congoleum-Nairn, Gruen, Coca-Cola. During his first year with the agency, the board (at the suggestion of Harper) made him executive vice president, a position that had not been filled for a number of years.

Because of Foote's international experience with FCB, Harper decided to send him to Europe to spend some time with McCann-Erickson offices in Germany, France, Denmark, Norway, and England. Sabina accompanied him on the month-long visit.

Foote's attitude toward McCann-Erickson had always been positive since they hired him after his illness, yet the direction in which Harper was moving the agency became a concern. He was beginning to divide the agency into various components, much like an advertising department store. An advertiser would contract with different parts without using the whole. This was the beginning of what was later to be called Interpublic. Harper knew that Foote did not agree with the concept but continued in this direction nonetheless.

In December 1956 Foote decided to separate from McCann-Erickson. Harper tried to talk him out of his decision but to no avail. His main reason for leaving was his feeling that the division of the agency was not the right thing.

Less than a month after leaving McCann-Erickson, Foote was back in the hospital. This time his stay was about seven months. After getting out, he again wanted to return to advertising. Bertram W. (Pat) Geyer, chairman of the board of Geyer Advertising, invited him to join the agency as chairman of the board, with Geyer moving up to chairman of the executive committee. This was near the end of 1957, and within a very short time after joining the agency, his depression returned. He continued to try to concentrate on his job, even though he did not feel he was effective.

The spring of 1958 brought an unusual happening: Harper wanted him to rejoin McCann-Erickson as a senior vice president. At first he declined the offer, thinking that he owed Geyer for helping him obtain a job, but Harper insisted. He finally accepted the position. Geyer was very disappointed and told Foote that he had done "an immoral thing" (Foote, p. 190).

Two years after his return to McCann-Erickson, Foote was elected president. Much of his early work after returning was in the Chicago office. In fact, Foote said it was like being a commuter. One of the major Chicago accounts was Swift and Company. Ray Weber was the advertising manager who, in Foote's opinion, was one of the most competent he had ever worked with.

Another outstanding ad man Foote worked with was Robert M. Gray, advertising director of Esso, in Houston. Over the years they became good friends, and Foote claimed that "in all the years I spent in advertising I never dealt with anyone whom I respected more highly" (Foote, p. 199).

Working with the National Cash Register Company in Dayton, Ohio, brought Foote in contact with yet another ad man who became a close friend, George Head. Their friendship led to many cracks about "Head and Foote."

December 1962 was a tragic month for McCann-Erickson. Harrison King McCann, founder of the agency, and his wife were killed in a car accident. After McCann's death, Harper proposed that Foote be made chairman of the board in addition to his job as president. In January 1963 Foote was elected to the position, but emphasized that there was no doubt about who was boss—Marion Harper.

In the meantime, Interpublic's growth had continued. In late 1963 Harper acquired Erwin, Wasey, Ruthrauff and Ryan, a large agency that required a complex stock exchange. Because of the timing, Harper asked Foote to replace him as a speaker to the Australian Association of National Advertisers. Foote accepted and made his first trip to Australia.

The acquisition of Erwin, Wasey, Ruthrauff and Ryan and other agency actions began to bother Foote. He and Harper had disagreed on other occasions, but always to his advantage. Foote claimed that "the man for whom I worked was the soul of consideration and courtesy in the way he treated me, but I just didn't believe in the whole thing and the direction it was taking" (Foote, p. 208).

During most of Foote's career in advertising he had worked with the health fields. He was very active in the American Cancer Society and had become increasingly concerned about cigarettes. However, his actions could not be as open as he would have liked due to McCann-Erickson's tobacco accounts, which had billings of almost $20 million. Foote discussed his feelings about the situation, and together they agreed that he would leave the agency in a year. After a generous offer to remain with the agency until he was 65, Foote's resignation became effective in December 1964. It took until spring of the next year to work out an agreement for handling his Interpublic stock. He finally received $349,000 for his 20,000 shares.

A new job and a different type of career began immediately after leaving McCann-Erickson. Foote accepted the chairmanship of the National Interagency Council on Smoking and Health. The council had been organized earlier in 1964 as a combined effort of the American Cancer Society, the American Lung Association, the American Heart Association, and the American Public Health Association. One of the responsibilities of the new job was testifying before congressional hearings on smoking. One committee member asked Foote, "Mr. Foote, would you not say that your conversion from the role of a man who used to advertise cigarettes to your present role against the tobacco industry is about the greatest conversion since Saint Paul was struck down on the road to Damascus?" (Foote, p. 215). Foote replied that it had taken him 17 years to speak out against cigarettes.

Although this position took up a lot of his time and effort, he continued to be involved with other advertising business. At the suggestion of his wife, Foote began to look for a possible return to advertising, a decision he would later regret. He decided to run a full-page ad in *Advertising Age*. Responses came quickly.

The offer that seemed most right at the time was from Kastor, Hilton, Chasley, Clifford and Atherton. Shortly after Foote joined the agency the president (Henry Kahn) died. So much had depended on him that the agency began to lose money rather quickly. Foote again developed another manic period and spent a few weeks in the hospital. He returned to the office but never felt that he was fully effective. One of his contributions was in getting Lee Baer to become president, with Foote remaining as chairman. Baer helped reverse some of the downward trends.

In 1967 the name of the agency had been changed to Emerson Foote, and negotiations were started to sell to Bozell and Jacobs of Omaha. The sale was completed with Foote remaining as a director and consultant for five years.

He did not stay out of advertising completely after selling the Emerson Foote agency. Foote accepted a part-time position to head a campaign to alert the public about the problems of overpopulation. This gave him an opportunity to return to one of his earlier advertising career positions—copywriter. The campaign involved many full-page ads in the *New York Times*.

While traveling to India for the Population Crisis Committee, Foote received some unexpected yet pleasurable information. The Advertising Women of New York (AWNY) had presented him with an ELA award.

Foote's last advertising position came from the National Liberty Corporation in Valley Forge. The company had been very effective in selling insurance by direct mail. His part-time position was as consultant first, later as chairman of the board of one of the subsidiary companies.

On Saint Patrick's Day in 1972, Sabina and Emerson moved from New York to Carmel, New York. Although completely out of advertising, Foote continued to serve on many nonprofit boards. One of his last activities ended in 1977 when he resigned from the board of the Menninger Foundation. The foundation bestowed on him an honorary life trusteeship with a "diploma" that thanked him for a quarter century of service.

As Foote looked back over his years in advertising, there were many people who stood out. He felt that Albert Lasker was the all-time number one advertising person. He considered Marion Harper as one of the most brilliant men with whom he had ever worked. George Washington Hill was one of the most astute advertising clients in his book. In the 1930s C. H. Turner, president of Hastings, was his toughest-to-please client. Robert M. Gray of Exxon and Ray Weber of Swift and Company were very capable advertising persons. And Margo Sherman of McCann-Erickson was the most effective organizer of creative people he had ever known.

In 1985 Foote said, "Looking back, I know I have not accomplished all that I should but I have accomplished all that I could—or nearly so. All in all I have had a very satisfying life for which I am grateful to Providence, and my family, and especially to my wife, Sabina" (Foote, p. 235). Sabina died in October 1985.

FURTHER READING

Work by Foote

Unpublished autobiography. 1985.

Works about Foote

Cone, Fairfax. *With All Its Faults*. Boston: Little, Brown, 1969.
Cummings, Barton. *The Benevolent Dictators: Interviews with Advertising Greats*. Chicago: Crain Books, 1984.
———. "The Rise and Fall—and Rise Again—of an Adman." *Advertising Age* (August 16, 1982): M–2–M–3, M–4.

Gunther, John. *Taken at the Flood*. New York: Harper, 1960.
Knapp, Jeanne M. *Don Belding: A Career of Advertising and Public Service*. Lubbock: Department of Mass Communications, Texas Tech University, 1983.
Wakeman, Frederic. *The Huckster*. New York: Rinehart, 1964.

NOTABLE CLIENTS/CAMPAIGNS

Airtemp

American Tobacco

General Foods

Gruen

New York Central

RCA

TWA

JO FOXWORTH
(?–   )

Elsie S. Hebert

For more than 40 years, Jo Foxworth has been an advertising agency executive, author, columnist, and lecturer. She is president and CEO of her own Manhattan agency, Jo Foxworth, which she founded in 1968. She has also been one of the nation's foremost advocates for improving career opportunities for women within the corporate management structure.

Born in Tylertown, Mississippi, in the pre–World War II period, she became a spokesperson for greater educational and business advantages for women while still in college. Since those days Foxworth has authored three books that address the career interests of women: *Boss Lady*, *Wising Up—The Mistakes Women Make in Business and How to Avoid Them*, and *Boss Lady's Arrival and Survival Plan*. The first, *Boss Lady*, published in 1978, is semi-autobiographical and was a best-seller, with more than 800,000 copies in circulation. It has become something of a "cult book" on college campuses and corporate premises.

For 11 years (1967 to 1978) she wrote a column for *Advertising Age*, giving wry commentary on a wide variety of advertising developments. During this period she was named Advertising Woman of the Year five times by major professional organizations, including the American Advertising Federation and Advertising Women of New York. She served two terms as governor of the American Advertising Federation's Second District, 1966 to 1968, and two terms as president of the Advertising Women of New York, 1963 to 1965.

Additionally, Foxworth was voted the National Headliner Award by Women in Communications in 1982. In the same year her alma mater, the University of Missouri, awarded her its highest honor, the Missouri Medal, for distinguished service in journalism.

A wry sense of humor and a frank delivery, softened by a trace of a Southern accent, have brought wide demand for Foxworth as a lecturer at professional seminars, university forums, and conventions throughout the country, as well as guest appearances on radio and television programs.

Her development as a dynamic public speaker with a unique style has its roots in Jo Foxworth's early youth and education. After graduation from high school in Tylertown, she was sent to the Mississippi State College for Women in Columbus, because her mother felt her daughter was too young to attend a coeducational institution. Foxworth's father died when she was nine years old. It was at MSCW that Foxworth first attracted attention as a public speaker—and was expelled from the college. She made a speech attacking the president of the state-supported school and the Mississippi legislature because she did not like the school's curriculum:

I did not approve of the fact that they wouldn't give us a total education. We were educated mainly to be planters' wives, and I had not met a planter whose wife I wished to be, so I began beating the drum for them to give us some other things, other courses, in addition to the liberal arts, which I believe very strongly in, particularly for an advertising education. But I wanted to learn some other things, too. (Cummings, p. M4)

Foxworth enrolled at the University of Missouri after she left MSCW, receiving a bachelor's degree in journalism in 1941 after just one year and a summer session. She said that she had to finish up quickly because of her family's shortage of money.

Her first job was with a newspaper in McComb, Mississippi, selling advertising for $10 a week. She describes her technique: "I found it was easier to sell an ad than it was to sell blank space. I would write the ad, and lay it out, and it was easier to sell it that way" (Cummings, p. M4). A year later Kennington, a department store in Jackson, wanted to start an advertising department and hired Foxworth to head it. She was also placed in charge of display.

But Foxworth's ambition was to lead eventually to the advertising scene in the East. After nine years with the Jackson store and after her mother moved to Baton Rouge, she accepted a job as ad manager of a department store in Louisville, Kentucky. However, she was unhappy with her employment situation and left after only five months.

Her next move was to Philadelphia, where she spent a year and a half acquiring valuable experience as advertising and sales promotion director of Nan Duskin, a fashion house. Here Foxworth established herself as a fashion commentator by conducting a series of fashion shows featuring top U.S. and European designers. Also during this period she began going to New York, and in an interview with Bart Cummings, chairman emeritus of Compton International, for *Advertising Age*, Foxworth said: "I began to meet people my own age and people in the ad business—copywriters and art directors. And I was interested in what they were doing. I knew they were making about twice as much money as I was. And they weren't better copywriters than I was. So I decided I would come over here and give it a whirl, and I did" (p. M5).

At this point in her life Foxworth's foremost ambition was to work for the legendary advertising great Marion Harper at McCann-Erickson. Her friends at

McCann advised that they could not hire her without agency experience. They told her to get some experience and to come back in about a year. So, in 1954 she joined J. M. Mathes, New York, as associate copy chief. Her speculative work on Crown Cork and Seal, Burlington Industries, and Herman Miller, was credited with landing the accounts.

Ten months later McCann-Erickson acquired the Westinghouse account and began hiring additional personnel to work on it. Even with her limited agency experience, Foxworth was employed as a copywriter. In 1956 she was made copy group supervisor and later became creative group supervisor, responsible for more than $17 million in billings. Other accounts on which she worked included Nabisco, Coca-Cola, Nestlé, Buick, Chesterfield, Owens-Corning, and Hilton Hotels. She also wrote copy for the Barry Goldwater political advertising campaign.

At this time McCann-Erickson was the largest firm within the Interpublic group of companies. In 1962 Foxworth was moved to Johnstone, Interpublic's fashion agency, to head the creative division, and within two years her executive capabilities brought her promotion to vice president and later executive vice president of Calkins and Holden, another Interpublic agency.

In 1968, when the board of directors of Interpublic voted Marion Harper out of leadership, Foxworth decided to open her own agency. "I was very old to be a copywriter, but young to be head of an agency. So I started one up with Steve D'Agostino as my first client" (Cummings, p. M51). She had been working with the D'Agostino supermarket account at Calkins and Holden and had great respect for Steve D'Agostino, then executive vice president and later chairman of D'Agostino Brothers, who joined the Jo Foxworth agency as executive vice president.

The agency's first office was opened in one of the D'Agostino buildings at 130 East 85th Street, on a balcony overlooking the supermarket floor. *Advertising Age* wrote on May 6, 1968, that the new agency would specialize in food, fashions, and home furnishings. "The new shop will be available to work on special creative products for other agencies" ("Jo Foxworth Inc.," p. 3).

Foxworth brought wide recognition to D'Agostino advertising with her unique creative approach. "It's got a light touch and a spirit one doesn't generally associate with that genre of advertising, either in newspapers or on radio," Philip H. Dougherty stated in the *New York Times* on July 7, 1981. For example, a headline of one of the supermarket's print ads might read: "If there's no D'Agostino near you . . . move," or a listener might hear a radio ad, set to music, that began: "Please, Mr. D'Agostino, move closer to me." Foxworth's philosophy is that you shouldn't take yourself too seriously. "Take the business seriously, but not the message" (p. 20).

Since its founding in 1968 the Jo Foxworth advertising agency has grown and made several office moves. In August 1992 it moved to its present location at 155 East 31st Street. The D'Agostino firm is still the agency's major client. Also included on the client list have been a division of J. C. Penney; Lamston's, a New York variety store chain; the U.S. operations of Japan's Shiseido cosmetics; and the food service division of Chiquita Banana.

In addition to her agency work, Foxworth travels throughout the United States, making 15 to 20 speeches a year to executive women's groups. She feels that the best press she ever received for a speech was that which followed her presentation of the "Nine Commandments for Women in Business" at the 1962 convention of the Advertising Federation of America in Boston. It was run by over 600 newspapers.

These commandments, which are still widely reprinted, are:

1. Thou shall try harder; thou need not be only number two.
2. Thou shall know when to zip thy lip and listen quietly.
3. Thou shalt not attempt to hide behind thine own petticoat.
4. Thou shalt speak softly and carry no stick, except lipstick.
5. Thou shalt serve thy lady boss as graciously as thou servest any man.
6. When success cometh, thou shalt not get too big for thy bustle.
7. Thou shalt watch thy language; there may be gentlemen present.
8. Thou shalt not match martinis with the men.
9. Thou shalt save thy sex appeal for after five, even though thy C cup runneth over.

Joan Paganetti, editor of *Retail Ad Week* in New York, asked Foxworth in an interview published in *Advertising Age* about changes in opportunities for women in advertising in the past 20 years. In addition to pointing out that most of the changes have occurred in account services and that there are more women account executives, she also noted that products "no longer have gender." Today women write copy for products that were once considered solely within the male domain. However, Foxworth observed, there still are not many female art directors or women as top executives: "Perhaps the most significant thing is that one thing has not changed at all. There are very few women at the top unless they own their companies. There isn't an ad agency in all of New York where a woman has any real muscle . . . where women decide things, like are we going to expand? Are we going to borrow $200,000? Are we going to take this account or aren't we?'' (p. M16).

Foxworth's personal and professional guideline has been to portray the image of a woman who knows what she is doing, who is capable of listening and speaking—and is *effective*. "In my opinion, being effective is the only way to achieve an identity of your own" (Paganetti, p. M16).

FURTHER READING

Works by Foxworth

Boss Lady: An Executive Woman Talks about Making It. New York: Thomas Y. Crowell, 1978.

Boss Lady's Arrival and Survival Plan. New York: Warner Books, 1986.

"Dentists Beware—Sears Moves into Teeth Care in a Big Way." *Advertising Age* (May 23, 1977): 54.

"Does Business Boom When U.S. Casts Aside Its Chastity Belt?" *Advertising Age* (June 2, 1975): 40.

Wising Up: The Mistakes Women Make in Business and How to Avoid Them. New York: Delacorte Press, 1980.

"You May Be Washing, Spraying Away All Your Sex Appeal." *Advertising Age* (March 7, 1977): 38.

Works about Foxworth

Cummings, Bart. "The Benevolent Dictators—Jo Foxworth: Energetic Creator of Ads, Speeches, Books and 'Nine Commandments.' " *Advertising Age* (February 20, 1984): M4–5, M51.

Dougherty, Philip H. "Advertising: Messages with a Bit of Humor." *New York Times* (July 7, 1981): sec. 4, p. 20.

Foremost Women in Communications. New York: Foremost American Publishing, 1970.

"Jo Foxworth Inc. Opens Its Doors at Point of Sale." *Advertising Age* (May 6, 1968): 3.

"Jo Foxworth Is Named AFA's '66 Adwoman of Year." *Advertising Age* (June 12, 1966): 3.

Paganetti, Joan. "When the 'Boss Lady' Speaks, It's Worth a Listen." *Advertising Age* (April 2, 1984): M12, M16.

Price, Margaret. "An Uphill Battle for Female Managers." *Industry Week* (June 23, 1980): 33, 35–36.

"Supermarketers Tune into Radio Advertising: Changing Lifestyles Broaden the Audience Base for Media Category." *Chain Store Age Executive* 64 (February 1988): 68, 70.

Wakin, Edward. "The Many Faces of Corporate Politics." *Today's Office* 18 (April 1984): 36–45.

Notable Clients/Campaigns

Buick

Chesterfield

Chiquita Banana

Coca-Cola

D'Agostino supermarkets

Hilton Hotels

J. C. Penney

Nestlé

Owens-Corning

Shiseido cosmetics

Westinghouse

J. STIRLING GETCHELL
(July 7, 1899–December 17, 1940)

Arthur J. Kaul

J. Stirling Getchell's flamboyant use of dynamic photos, bold headlines, and personalized copy established an innovative and widely imitated advertising style during his meteoric Great Depression career. The campaigns he created, directed, or influenced for the nation's largest advertisers totaled more than $100 million, including a precedent-setting comparative advertising campaign for Plymouth automobiles.

Getchell was born in New York on July 7, 1899, the son of John Burt Getchell, a silk salesman, and Edna Locke Getchell, a teacher. A childhood bout of rheumatic fever left him with a weakened heart that contributed to his early death. He was a willful and restless youngster who resisted and resented discipline and rules. He attended Peddie Institute, but ran away from home when he was 17 to join General Pershing's pursuit of Pancho Villa in Mexico. He enlisted in the New York National Guard's Machine Gun Troop when the United States entered World War I, later serving in the U.S. Army Air Service.

At war's end, Getchell returned to the United States and joined a small New York advertising agency in 1919 as a $25-a-week copywriter. During the next 12 years, he would work for more than a dozen agencies, his usual term of employment lasting from three months to less than a year before quitting or getting fired. His first major agency job came in 1924 with Lord and Thomas, where he wrote for the Studebaker account. A year later Getchell joined the George Batten Company in time to save the Colgate Rapid Shave account with layouts using microphotographs showing lather softening whiskers (actually fine-tooth combs). Batten account executive Taylor Adams recalled that Getchell left the agency because "he wouldn't stay long on a job . . . where he couldn't be king" (Adams, p. 51).

Getchell joined J. Walter Thompson, flouted company rules, yet became one of the agency's resident stars, according to Stephen Fox (p. 164). For Goodrich tires he created the Silvertown Safety League, a safe-driving crusade that "eventually enrolled over 2.5 million people'' (p. 164). Getchell left J. Walter Thompson for a $50,000-a-year job with Lennen and Mitchell, leaving again in 1931 to establish his own agency, J. Stirling Getchell, with former JWT art director Jack Tarleton.

The J. Stirling Getchell agency, founded on borrowed money and relentless enthusiasm, survived the first year of its life during the Depression on service fees for free-lance work. Getchell and Tarleton created ads for Chesterfield, Vick's, General Tire, and Lydia Pinkham. For a General Tire ad photo, they staged an auto accident, complete with dissheveled clothes and the bewildered expressions of victims of bad tires. For Lydia Pinkham's Vegetable Compound, a patent medicine that promised cures for countless feminine maladies, Getchell produced an ad with a classic headline over a distraught woman, saying to her husband: ''I'm sorry . . . not tonight!''

The Getchell agency's first major breakthrough came after only eight months in business when it won the Chrysler's DeSoto account. With lavish photographs, Getchell created a series of DeSoto ads around the ''Expect to be stared at'' theme, attracting the attention of consumers and the automobile and advertising industries. DeSoto sales climbed, earning Getchell the chance to develop an advertising campaign to introduce the 1932 Plymouth, Chrysler's bottom-of-the-line car. His task was to produce advertising that would create the image of Plymouth as a serious competitive challenger to industry leaders Chevrolet and Ford. The result was a sensational series of ads that violated the industry taboo on comparative advertising with the theme, ''Look at all three.'' Chrysler executives objected to the ads, but Walter Chrysler overruled them and enthusiastically gave his go-ahead to run them.

The ''Look at all three'' ads, first run in April 1932 when Ford and Chevrolet were introducing their new models, showed Walter Chrysler below the headline, with copy quoting Chrysler on reasons to buy Plymouth over the unnamed competition. By June Plymouth sales had jumped 218 percent, and the next campaign—''Plymouth sets the pace for all three''—helped to boost Plymouth's share of the low-priced market from 16 percent in 1932 to 24 percent a year later.

With the DeSoto and Plymouth advertising campaigns, a distinctive Getchell style emerged that emphasized huge, bold headlines and beautiful, flamboyant, and innovative photographs which often broke with precedent. According to King Harris, who began his advertising career in the agency mailroom, his boss possessed a typographic instinct that fused words and pictures into a dramatic presentation. Getchell's style of ''ad-making,'' a term he coined, required copy and illustration to produce a deeply felt emotional impact (p. 59).

Getchell's successful ad campaigns opened the doors to other major accounts. For the Socony-Vacuum Oil Company, he created the ''Friendly service'' theme for Mobil gas and oil filling stations. Other clients included: Airtemp (air conditioning and heating systems), Devoe and Reynolds (paints and varnishes), Kelly-Springfield Tire, Mayflower Stations, Sobol Brothers Service Stations, the Illinois Meat Company, and Schenley Distillers. At its height, the Getchell agency was one of the ten largest in the nation, with branch offices in Detroit, Chicago, Kansas City, and Los Angeles and more than 100 employees.

In the ten years of its existence, J. Stirling Getchell employed some of the nation's greatest advertising people. Getchell had a knack for hiring creative talent; his interviews with job seekers amounted to mental jousts. He would typically ask prospective employees which person, living or dead, they would most want to study if they were given a year to do so with all expenses paid. An unconventional answer often resulted in an on-the-spot hiring. Yet, Getchell's track record for hiring administrators and account executives was dismal. In the three years King Harris spent with Getchell, the agency had 15 to 20 vice presidents, earning it the reputation for having a revolving door.

The Getchell agency put a premium on creativity and enthusiasm. A creative idea session with Getchell in charge could be a harrowing experience, with the staff enduring a barrage of threats and curses alternating with good-natured cajoling. Getchell's enthusiasm and drive kept everyone competing against each other to develop the best idea for an advertising campaign. Good ideas were the key to success, and Getchell was the catalyst that produced them. Writing in the mid–1930s, William E. Berchtold praised Getchell for putting "live, human values into every advertisement. Still no pusher of buttons, Getchell has a hard time keeping his feet off his highly polished desk, deserts his finely furnished office whenever possible in favor of a copywriter's cubbyhole" (p. 33).

A member-at-large of the executive board of the American Association of Advertising Agencies, Getchell presented a paper at the spring meeting in 1935. According to *Advertising Age* ("Flay Critics," p. 27), Getchell recommended "ample diagnosis, simple news technique, dramatic human photos, sincere, honest copy, but above all, enthusiasm for the product." With the exception of enthusiasm and the personal touch, Getchell would offer "no rule for producing advertising, each campaign being an evolutionary process."

In October 1936 Getchell divorced his wife of 17 years, Marjorie Lillian Jeliff Getchell. His second marriage, to Sarah Paschall Davis, a New York debutante and daughter of President Roosevelt's ambassador-at-large in Europe, Norman H. Davis, on December 21, 1936, made headlines. Two sons were born of the marriage, David Paschall Getchell on February 25, 1938, and Michael Stirling Getchell on October 19, 1940.

J. Stirling Getchell's meteoric advertising career ended on December 17, 1940, when he died of a streptococcus infection at Columbia-Presbyterian Medical Center at the age of 41. He had been hospitalized since March, spending his time building a group operation within his agency and training key executives to carry on the business. Two years later, without its dynamic leader to ramrod projects, the Getchell agency went out of business.

FURTHER READING

Works about Getchell

Adams, Taylor. "Close Shave, but Stirling Getchell Charms Colgate with 'Small-Bubble Lather.' " *Advertising Age* (July 22, 1974): 51.
Berchtold, William E. "Men Who Sell You." *New Outlook* (January 1935): 27–33, 55.
"Flay Critics of Advertising at Four A's Meet." *Advertising Age* (April 13, 1935): 27.
Fox, Stephen. *The Mirror Makers: A History of American Advertising and Its Creators*. New York: William Morrow, 1984.
Harris, King. "How Stirling Getchell Chased Walter Chrysler—and Hired a Mail Boy." *Advertising Age* (July 31, 1967): 59–60, 62.
Marchand, Roland. *Advertising the American Dream: Making Way for Modernity, 1920–1940*. Berkeley: University of California Press, 1985.
"Stirling Getchell, Copy Wizard, Dies after Long Illness." *Advertising Age* (December 23, 1940): 1.

NOTABLE CLIENTS/CAMPAIGNS

Airtemp

DeSoto

Devoe and Reynolds

Illinois Meat

Kelly-Springfield Tire

Mayflower Stations

Plymouth

Schenley Distillers

Socony-Vacuum Oil

HOWARD LUCK GOSSAGE
(August 30, 1917–1969)

Kim B. Rotzoll

From the mid–1950s to his death in 1969, Howard Gossage served as advertising's resident gadfly. An honored practitioner through his own unorthodox approach to advertising messages, Gossage above all attempted to raise his colleagues' consciousness in relation to what he saw as advertising's clear abuses—its basic lack of restraint, fueled by the morally corrupt commission system; its disregard of audience sensitivities; and its frequently destructive relationship with the media. His legacy is thus multifaceted, as this posthumous citation attests: "For his distinguished and consistent contributions to the craft of advertising writing and for the strong and positive influence he had on the advertising industry, The Copy Club elects Howard Luck Gossage to the Copywriter's Hall of Fame."

Described variously as "a tall, pale advertising man with one of the great heads of gray hair in the U.S.A., flowing back like John Barrymore's" (*Is There Any Hope*, p. xvii) and "an unforgettable figure about town [San Francisco]: flowing white hair, a perpetually gaunt, drawn and handsome face" (p. xxv), Gossage was born on August 30, 1917, in Chicago, growing up in Queens, New York, Denver, New Orleans, and Kansas City. He was educated at the University of Kansas City, and after time as a World War II navy combat pilot and two years as promotion manager for radio station KLX in San Francisco, he did doctoral work at the universities of Paris and Geneva.

"I got into advertising, actually, because there wasn't anything else I knew how to do. I think a successful ad man has to have something missing in his character, the way an actor does" (p. 155). At 36, Gossage had his first advertising job at San Francisco's Brisacher, Wheeler and Staff, bought within a few years by Cunningham and Walsh, with then vice president Gossage quitting shortly after. "All of the jobs I have had since the navy (and three before) have either resulted in firing or in leaving in dudgeon, save two, I think. . . . I am not a very good boss, but a damn sight better than any other, for me" (p. 155).

His self-employment began in 1957, with a partnership with J. Joseph Weiner in San Francisco's original Firehouse No. 1, where, as columnist Herb Caen would later observe in attempting to depict Gossage's Renaissance style:

You'd find yourself building a pastrami sandwich next to Dr. Benjamin Spock. Or pouring a beer for John Steinbeck. Or listening to Buckminster Fuller. Or laughing at the bad jokes of Marshall McLuhan. (Gossage, more than any other person, was responsible for the launching of McLuhan as a household name—a job he took on, like so many others, just for the hell of it, ''let's see if it works.'') Robert Manning, editor of *Atlantic Monthly*, was a Gossage luncheon regular. And writer Tom Wolfe, who invented a new style of reportage. (p. xxv)

Gossage was, in a word, eclectic, and this intense pleasure in the act of communicating with diverse people about diverse subjects predictably infused his approach to the advertising message. Columnist Alan Cundall noted ''the three Gossage trademarks: the indirect approach using long copy, the frivolous contest, and the reply coupon.'' But these were merely the surface dressings of a deep-seated communication philosophy (*Is There Any Hope*, chs. 16, 17):

(1) That advertising should be involving for the audience. That they should be offered some reward for partaking of the message, be it entertainment, information, or simply the satisfaction of message-producing curiosity.

(2) That to be involving it is better to plan carefully for one or a few truly arresting messages than to fight a war of attrition. ''You don't have to bruise an elephant with 100 BB guns to kill him. One shot in the right place will do.''

(3) That truly involving advertising begins when you can establish a ''conversation'' with the audience via response mechanisms. That, as in any true conversation worthy of the name, the initiator should wait for a response before replying. ''Over the years I suppose I have had the top 10 coupon-drawing ads in the *New Yorker*.''

(4) That the advertiser is more likely to succeed by trying for a hole in one each time, ''particularly if he starts 2 inches from the cup''—that is, if he narrows his objectives for advertising to those best suited to that form of communication.

It is, then, predictably, an audience-oriented philosophy, fueled by the presumed enlightened self-interest of the advertiser. How did it work in practice?

Qantas. Assigned the problem of establishing Qantas as a factor in the Australian airline market, Gossage offered a name-the-kangaroo contest with the headline, ''Be the first on your block to own a kangaroo.'' The winner—7,500 entries later—was the name ''Sam,'' by the seven-month-old daughter of a copywriter for another airline. The follow-up ad announced, ''New York child wins kangaroo, her first!'' The *New York Times* ran a large picture, and ''for the modest expenditure of $15,000 these ads made Qantas an important factor in the travel business overnight'' (ch. 16).

Blitz Brewing. In order to promote the Oregon Centennial, Gossage placed a 1,000-line ad in every Oregon newspaper (as well as in the *New Yorker* and the

Village Voice) offering free Oregon fir trees. The *New Yorker* ad read in part: "KEEP TIMES SQUARE GREEN! A modest reforestation proposal from Oregon's largest and only brewer. . . . Just think what reforestation will do for Times Square! Cool and green, teeming with game, salmon swimming up the Pepsi-Cola sign to spawn."

In total more than 100,000 trees were sent out. "But," Gossage observed, "the tree distribution is beside the point. Blitz hadn't run a newspaper ad in two years. All their competitors advertised heavily. Six weeks later we did some research and asked which beer was the largest newspaper advertiser. Blitz was, said 52 percent" (p. xix).

Paul Masson. Gossage promoted Paul Masson brandy with memorable observations about its major generic competitors: bourbon ("Kentucky is a great place for breeding horses") and vodka ("If you can't see it, taste it, or smell it, why bother?"). Sales allegedly increased 46 percent in two years. Gossage later claimed he resigned the account in a conversation with Masson's president somewhat like this: "I don't like your advertising." "But *you* do it." "That's just it" (p. xix).

Rainier ale. In addition to a 1,000-mile hike to Seattle headed by a 79-year-old retired postman, Gossage's most renowned effort here was spurred by a media buy. He channeled some of Rainier's budget into his favorite good music station (KSFR-FM), then in desperate financial straits. Needing a music-related theme, he offered listeners Brahms, Beethoven, and Bach sweatshirts ("A brewer's idea of culture"). This time the client's well-being was not substantially enhanced, although the Gossage agency grew a new arm (Intrinsics) to handle the first wave of sweatshirt orders, which later exceeded 200,000. The account eventually went elsewhere (pp. 64–65).

Irish whiskey. Many would choose this series as the quintessential Gossage campaign. Hired by the Irish Export Board to promote Irish whiskey in America with the modest budget of $56,000, Gossage and colleagues Weiner and Freeman developed a feeling for Irish culture from the 12th-century *Book of Kells*. What followed was a series of technically exquisite advertisements attempting to capture the Irish "attitude and tone of language" (pp. 169–78). (Here, as elsewhere, were the distinctive contributions of designer Marget Larsen.) This series represents the most explicit example of Gossage's assumption about audience involvement. The first ad, dealing with Irish coffee ("Has Ireland been led false by a baked brazilian berry?"), ended with "It'd be like teaching your grandmother to," and the copy of the next (16 days later) began "suck eggs." He then recapitulated and went on with the saga. Other ads offered "pride" and "profit" badges, promoted the Irish Geophysical Year (which appeared, under special permission, in *Scientific American* and drew seven responses from the South Pole), and other audience-involving items tied to the basic sales story. Sales reportedly moved upward more than 50 percent (pp. 169–78).

Fina. Assuming that people were becoming jaded with gasoline companies' promotion of additives, Gossage whimsically suggested that Fina stations offer pink air for tires. Subsequent ads offered pink valve caps, pink balloons, pink aerial knobs, and more as a way of indicating pink air's presence. The theme continued in other messages attempting to demonstrate the company's versatility. The "pink air pipeline" dealt with Fina's network of refineries, and the award of "15 yards of pink asphalt" was meant to publicize its asphalt-production prowess. Gossage noted that Fina's advertising budget decreased every year, and that the company "had the lowest percentage of advertising cost against gross sales of any firm in the petroleum industry" (pp. 49–62).

Eagle Shirts. The Eagle Shirt Company of Quakertown, Pennsylvania, had not advertised in 40 years. During that time they had built their reputation as a supplier of high-quality men's shirts for retailers. Eagle finally decided that a reputation of their own was a safer bet than the pecuniary whims of retailers. So began the "Dear Miss Afflerbach" ads. The first depicted a man's shirt under the headline: "IS THIS YOUR SHIRT? If so, Miss Afflerbach will send you your Eagle label."

They received 200 responses. The second message became the stuff of legend. Under the headline "Send for your free Eagle shirtkerchief (shirtkin?), (nap-chief?)," Gossage offered a sample of shirting showing the company's quality stitching and "thread-checked" buttonholes. There were 11,342 replies, the all-time record for a *New Yorker* advertisement at that time. A 200-page book of the ads and the correspondence was published by Macmillan under the title *Dear Miss Afflerbach*.

Scientific American's readers fly for business and pleasure, so Gossage conceived the 1st International Paper Airplane Competition on the magazine's behalf. It was promoted through ads in the *New York Times*, the *New Yorker*, *Travel Weekly*, and the *San Francisco Chronicle*, was written by colleague Jerry Mander, and totaled about $40,000 in space costs. It drew 11,000 entries from all over the world, and the "final flyoffs" in New York were attended by more than 150 reporters and photographers (pp. 187–92).

Land Rover. Memorable Gossage efforts here included a poll on readers' opinions about whether Rover should advertise on billboards, a message extolling the virtues of Rover as a getaway (and chase) car, and a series about the car's safety harness: "HOW TO GET YOUR HUSBAND TO FASTEN HIS ROVER 2000 SAFETY HARNESS: Tell him it's a Sam Browne belt and he looks like a World War I aviator."

In addition, the Gossage agency (12 employees at full tide) was responsible for dramatically effective ads on behalf of saving the Grand Canyon from damming, redwood forests from clearing, and the Caribbean island of Anguilla from being submerged under British rule, in addition to various fights on behalf of freedom of the press (i.e., freedom to publish without slavish dependence on advertising revenue) and antiwar causes.

Some indication of the seamlessness of Gossage's business life and personal philosophy can be seen in the termination of his association with highly successful client Fina gasoline. On March 24, 1964, four months after the assassination of

John F. Kennedy, *Look* magazine ran "Memo from a Dallas Citizen," written by Gossage's American Petrofina client J. M. Shea, Jr. In it he criticized Dallas civic leaders for failing to oppose extremist organizations in the city, and generally tolerating a potentially violent climate. Shea was critical of his own inactions and mentioned in passing that he was involved in the oil business.

Some of the resulting wave of indignation touched the company (e.g., 17 credit card holders returned their shredded cards) and the Dallas *Morning News* editorialized against Shea's action. Eventually, the management and directors of Fina demanded that Shea agree not to write anything for public consumption without prior approval.

Shea resigned, and Gossage immediately resigned the Fina account, telling Peter Bart of the *New York Times*, "One of the few things you can do in this business is decide whose money you wish to take" (pp. 178–79). Shea was later added as a partner in the Gossage agency. At the time of the resignation Fina was by far the Gossage agency's largest client.

Advertising as an institution, Gossage contended, could only be marginally justified economically and not at all aesthetically. There was, he felt, simply too much advertising devoted to trivial concerns. In one of his more enduring phrases, he asserted that advertising could be likened to a "multi-billion dollar sledgehammer driving a 40¢ economy-sized thumbtack." Specifically: "With a couple of notable exceptions, the biggest spenders in advertising—the categories which dominate the industry—are economic pipsqueaks. Soap, aspirins, compounds, toothpaste, beverages, tobacco, cosmetics, breakfast food, and so forth, comprise a ridiculously dinky percentage of our gross national product, but they spend most of the advertising money." He reasoned that since these are exactly the types of products that we would normally not get along without anyway ("If Procter and Gamble stopped advertising tomorrow do you suppose anyone would be any dirtier?"), the result is a frenzied attempt to exploit an increasingly jaded audience (ch. 1).

Worse, Gossage felt, the advertising business refused to acknowledge its tendency toward exploitation and its diminished effectiveness. It closed ranks when confronted with what he saw as self-evident truths and stood ready to "defend them to the death."

I can think of a lot of things I don't defend to the death. I won't defend Dristan's right to drain sinuses all over my living room or the right of all those silly, grinning, preposterous hair preparation commercials that make me want to rip the set out of the wall. And I won't defend to the death a station's right to lure me into seeing a movie and then clobbering me all during the last half of it—after I'm hooked—with triple spots every ten minutes, as happened the other night. And I won't defend to the death outdoor advertising's right to stick up a board along the freeway built with my tax money so that I have to look at *it* instead of my beautiful city. (ch. 2)

Advertising's "natural" turf, Gossage held, was propaganda—"the dissemination of instruction and information by an interested party"—but practitioners attempted to compensate for lack of real informational content by repetition, thus entering the domain of exploitation. This resulted in a narcotic-like addiction to ever bigger ad budgets with ever diminishing justification as potentially useful propaganda.

This, Gossage felt, was buttressed by a basic misconception that advertising practitioners hold. They regard the audience incorrectly—as individuals gathered by the media to read or watch something else, the non-advertising content. Thus, advertisers never think of the assembled as their audience and, hence, feel no particular obligation to them—as, for example, does the actor. Given this erroneous premise, Gossage asserted, all sorts of sins are permissible—mind-dulling repetition, vapid messages, every conceivable abuse of taste.

All of this, Gossage felt, could be changed if advertising practitioners could only begin to think of those attracted to the media as their audience as well. But are people interested in the non-advertising content, the ads? Of course, he contended, for "people don't read advertising per se. They read what interests them. *And sometimes it's an ad*" (ch. 3). All it takes, then, he argued, is to make the advertising interesting, useful, entertaining—a message to warrant attention and respect for itself. Thus engaged, Gossage thought, those involved in the advertising process would inevitably do better work for their audience and, hence, for themselves.

Yet, Gossage apparently held little hope for the agency business as basically constituted. The chief—but not the only—culprit was clearly the commission system of agency remuneration: "The agency is given a kick-back of 15 percent for buying, not selling. This would have some justification if, as it was when the system began, the agency really performed a selling function for the advertising medium. But this is no longer true, nor has it been for 50 years" (ch. 1).

This leads, Gossage argued, to a business where one's income is dependent upon the amount of money spent rather than the amount that comes in. Inevitably, he felt, this produces "mutual distrust and enormous psychological barriers" (ch. 1):

It affects advertising budgets in the sense that the agency is constantly put in the position of justifying ever higher budgets.

It affects the agency's sense of integrity in the sense that it is not being paid directly for what it produces—advertisements. An advertisement is a commodity whose price should vary according to its worth comparative to other similar commodities. As it is under the zany commission system, the best ad in the world has no price tag at all; it is sort of tossed in for the privilege of collecting 15 percent on all of the customer's money you spend.

Inherent in this system, Gossage contended, is the consequence that since advertising budgets are inevitably large, there need not be painstaking care devoted to the communication potential of each individual advertisement and its singular exposure. It can always be assumed that enough media weight will be utilized to "drive the message home."

Predictably, then, the Gossage agency operated on a fee system. Noting that their fee was substantially higher than the 15 percent commission would be, Gossage stated: "In the first place we believe our work to be superior to that generally available and therefore worth more. In the second place, we find that our clients can easily afford it because they get more out of it, and also because we tend to spend far less money in total than is usual. So they make out and we make out. In addition, we write contracts with them in which our fee increases each year as their business increases" (ch. 1).

And what of the media in which the advertisements appear? Predictably, Gossage held strong opinions: "In this country we have seen the effective control of our press shift from the public, for whom it presumably exists, to the advertiser, who merely uses it to sell his wares to the public" (ch. 10).

Clearly, Gossage regarded media audiences as individuals to be respected, not as "fish in a barrel" in an advertiser's game preserve. Yet, he felt advertisers regarded the media merely as convenient conduits for their sales messages and thought little—if at all—about the relationship between reader (or to a lesser extent the listener or viewer) and the medium.

He saw the same forces at work in all the advertising media, but he seemed particularly sensitive to the fate of newspapers and magazines. As he saw it, the fateful turn in the road came when the publisher first decided to sell his publication for less than it cost to produce it, with the difference—and the profit—coming from advertisers. Thus, the reader "lost his economic significance and became circulation" (ch. 10). The future of publication was no longer in the hands of its readers: "It seems to me that any publication represents a contractual agreement between the publisher and the readers. He will undertake to publish something to their tastes and they, on their side, will support the publication as long as he does. Now, this is a perfectly just and reasonable arrangement embodying such sturdy traditions as democracy, free enterprise, and freedom of choice. But none of it means a damn as long as the rug can be jerked from under it by a third party" (ch. 10).

Gossage used this thinking to explain the demise of big-city newspapers and large-circulation magazines, which died "not because the readers didn't like them, but because the advertisers don't." This became the subject of an ad he inserted in the *New York Times* after the death of the paper's West Coast edition. Purchasing the space with $1,600 of his own funds, Gossage used it to ask, "What good is freedom of the press if there isn't one?," noting that a paper he cared about had died and no one had asked him—or any other reader—if he would be willing to pay more to keep it afloat. The real measure of the importance of a magazine or newspaper, he thought, should be how much you would pay to keep from being deprived of the next issue (ch. 10). If advertisers and publishers could begin to appreciate that index, the relationship between a medium, its audience, and its advertisers could be substantially improved.

Gossage still regarded television, with all its many abuses, as a "proper advertising medium." For, he contended, "a medium to me is one that communicates something else and *also* communicates advertising. Even a triple-spot of Gardol, Dristan, and Naire has the good grace to bring you a 1933 all-talkie" (ch. 10). But billboards, Gossage repeated endlessly, "intrude themselves on you without your permission" (ch. 12). He raged against them throughout his career, whimsically suggesting billboard parks where aficianados could enjoy them, "away from distracting traffic sounds" (ch. 12).

Gossage learned of his leukemia on Valentine's Day 1968, and he was given six months to live. He made it for a year longer than that, during which, according to his *Ramparts* colleague Warren Hinckle:

he adopted the Caribbean island of Anguilla and helped the natives declare a Quixotic independence, organized a publishing company, launched an environmental organization, developed the theory and structure of a new science for the middle-aged he christened "Mediatrics," agitated to make San Francisco a city-state, wrote a brilliant advertising campaign against the Anti-Ballistic Missile in which he likened the ABM to the fallout shelters of the fifties, planned an academic seminar on the subject of Hell, to be held in Dublin and opened with a Mariachi Mass, coined the phrase "Ear Pollution," for the problem of noise, which he had plans for solving, began compiling a massive "Dictionary of First and Last Lines" of appropriate books and plays, discovered an obscure professor named Leopold Kohr whose recondite wisdoms about the dynamic of bigness in society were such that Gossage handicapped him as the McLuhan of the seventies, worked out a plan to render unnecessary the remaindering and destruction of unsold books, gave dozens of speeches warning advertising men to repent before it was too late for him to save them, got one of his kids out of jail on a marijuana charge, went to Europe several times, arranged for Jessica Milford to handle his funeral so the undertakers wouldn't dare to gouge, and wrote an essay about dying which he titled, "Tell Me, Doctor, Will I Be Active Right Up to the Last?" (*If You Have a Lemon*, pp. 353–54)

Herb Caen, writing the day after Gossage's death in the *San Francisco Chronicle*, entitled his tribute, "A Singular Man." Singular, he was, and so, it can be argued, is his multifaceted legacy to contemporary advertising thought and practice.

FURTHER READING

Works by Gossage

"Advertising Has Tremendous (Unwanted) Economic Power and Here Are Things It Should Do about It." *Advertising Age* (May 5, 1969): 99–102.
"Creativity Comes Best from 'Extra-Environmental Man,' Not Stuck with Past, Says Gossage." *Advertising Age* (March 6, 1967): 95–102.
"The Easy Chair—How to Look at Billboards." *Harper's* (February 1960): 12–16, 21.
"Freedom of the Press . . . Is There Such a Thing?" *Media/Scope* (May 1969): 71–74.
"The Golden Twig—Black, White, and Pango Peach Magic in Advertising." *Harper's* (March 1961): 64–68.

"How to Want to Do Better at Advertising." *Penn State Journalist* (January 1963): 1–4.

"If You're Stuck with a Lemon, Make Lemonade." *Advertising Age* (February 3, 1969): 24.

"Is Advertising a Dinosaur?" Speech to the San Francisco Junior Advertising Club, January 8, 1959.

Is There Any Hope for Advertising? Edited by Kim Rotzoll, Jarlath Graham, and Barrows Mussey. Urbana: University of Illinois Press, 1986.

"Tell Me, Doctor, Will I Be Active Right Up to the Last?" *Atlantic Monthly* (September 1969): 55–57.

"Transition." *Newsweek* (July 21, 1969).

"Understanding Marshall McLuhan." *Ramparts* (April 1966): 34–39.

"Where Are You When the Paper Is Blank?" Speech to the San Francisco Magazine Representatives Club, February 17, 1959.

Works about Gossage

"The Adman Who Plays with Paper Airplanes." *Business Week* (February 11, 1967): 74–76.

"Advertisers Are Killing or Altering Media, Heedless of Public: Gossage." *Advertising Age* (February 3, 1969): 3, 104.

"Advertising—The Kooksters." *Time* (October 26, 1959): 96–97.

Caen, Herb. "A Singular Man." *San Francisco Chronicle* (July 10, 1969): 29–30.

Cundall, A. W. "The Medium Is the Gossage." *Western Advertising* (January 10, 1968).

"Gossage Forms New Agency for Placement of Ads." *Advertising Age* (July 10, 1967): 10.

"Gossage Memory Honored in Copy Hall of Fame." *Advertising Age* (March 30, 1970): 74.

"Gossage on Media." *Media/Scope* (May 1969): 71–75.

"Gossagisms: Sometimes Funny, Sometimes Poignant—Always Disturbingly Trenchant." *Advertising Age* (July 14, 1969): 10.

Hinckle, Warren. "The Adman Who Hated Advertising." *Atlantic Monthly* (March 1974): 67–72.

———. *If You Have a Lemon, Make Lemonade.* New York: Putnam, 1973.

"Mavericks on Madison Avenue." *Saturday Review* (December 14, 1963): 60, 65.

"Scientific American Paper Plane Contest Lampoons Super-Jet." *Advertising Age* (December 19, 1966): 10.

Stermer, Dugald. "Advertising Is No Business for a Grown Man." *Ramparts* (September 1969): 21.

"They Write Ad Conversations." *Printer's Ink* (August 5, 1960): 45–49.

"Who 'Understands Media'? Gossage Does; Explains All." *Advertising Age* (May 9, 1966): 40.

NOTABLE CLIENTS/CAMPAIGNS

Blitz Brewing

Eagle Shirts

Fina gasoline
Irish Export Board
Land Rover
Paul Masson
Qantas
Rainier ale
Scientific American

PAULA GREEN
(September 18, 1927–   )

J. Nicholas De Bonis

In December 1969 Paul Green launched her own advertising agency, one of the first major Madison Avenue agencies to be headed by a woman. The decision meant abandoning a stellar 13-year career at Doyle Dane Bernbach in New York, where she had worked her way up to become DDB's first woman creative management supervisor. But the risk she took has paid dividends for numerous clients for whom Paula Green, Inc., has designed successful, award-winning campaigns and advertisements—and for at least two dozen women whose lives were saved by an American Cancer Society campaign Green created. After four decades as an advertising professional, Green is still setting goals and enjoying the career she all but stumbled into.

Paula Green was born on September 18, 1927, in Hollywood, California, to Myron and Elizabeth Grobstein Green, who were major influences in her early life. Their work ethic was instilled in their daughter at a young age. Her father had emigrated from Russia as a young boy. As a young man, he worked days and studied civil engineering at night at tuition-free Cooper Union in New York. When her father could not find an engineering job in Depression-era Hollywood, he dug ditches to support his family. "My parents always said, 'I don't care what kind of work you do, even if you scrub floors. Do it well. There's no dishonor in any kind of work,' " recalled Green during a series of 1991 interviews with the author.

Her mother "was the most brilliant woman I ever knew," according to Green, a vital, lively individual. Elizabeth Green had disregarded societal convention by continuing to work as an executive secretary after her marriage. But when Paula was born, her mother became a homemaker, raising Green and her younger brother. The two most important things Green's mother did for her were to send her away to school at Berkeley and then to New York. "Mother was a very unselfish woman," Green said with honest affection.

As a high school student, Green worked Saturdays to earn lunch money at a

5-and-10-cent store and in the basement of the May Company, a Los Angeles department store, selling clothes. Learning to wait on people and to be interested in them contributed to her ability years later to communicate through advertising, Green believes.

Going to college was not a given in the mid 1940s. Few families could afford private colleges, and admission to the state school, UCLA, was based on high school grades and a rigorous entrance exam. "You took the test, held your breath and hoped," remembered Green, who was a commuter student during her freshman year. With her mother's encouragement, she transferred to the University of California at Berkeley after taking a year off to earn money on which to live. Living away from home for the first time and being at Berkeley was an enormous change, but Green loved it. She lived in a co-op where the residents shared the housework, which was less expensive than a dormitory or apartment. Her first job was cleaning the bathrooms—"the new girl's job," laughed Green, which is why she doesn't ask others to do her "dirty work" even today. Green was graduated summa cum laude with a general major in English, speech, and drama.

At her mother's urging, Green visited New York shortly after graduation, and when she decided to stay, her mother was not surprised. "Mother felt going away was very important for me, because I root very quickly. I sit down and roots go right around the chair," smiled Green. "She saw what I needed and didn't think I'd get it in Los Angeles." Green loved New York. Being away from where she was raised, where she knew everybody and everybody knew her, was liberating and gave her an important sense of unencumbered freedom. "Not uninhibited," she explained carefully. "But nobody knew what my personal baggage was. They saw me as they saw me."

She arrived in New York with her B.A. and the ability to type 65 words a minute and take Gregg shorthand, and began to search for a job. In college she had thought about becoming a teacher or a reporter and she yearned for the stage, but she believed she would never make it as an actress. One day a friend suggested she try advertising, to which Green replied, "What's advertising?" Ultimately, to land a job as a secretary for the sales promotion manager at Fawcett magazines, Green told "a little white lie"—that she had worked as a secretary at an advertising agency for three months. It was her introduction to the advertising profession and her big break.

"I had the luck to meet up with a man who knew his business and generously shared what he knew with me," Green said in tribute to her mentor at Fawcett, Hunter Snead. A "prodigiously talented man," Snead opened the advertising career door for her. "Thank goodness I was able to go through it, because I got a lot of experience very early." Snead taught Green how to write promotional copy, merchandising tips, and how to create layouts. What he did not teach her directly she learned by observing. One day she was assigned two merchandising memos to do over the weekend at home for extra pay. "I was going to see my own words, my own ideas in print. And I tell you, when that happens, you're hooked'' (''Tips,'' p. S2). By the time Green left Fawcett, she had become sales promotion manager.

Green moved to Grey Advertising as a sales promotion copywriter, but the birth of her son, Joel, interrupted her career. Several years later she returned to work so that her husband, John Glucksman, could finish his engineering degree. ''I didn't choose to go back to work, though I might have eventually done that,'' she admitted with typical candor. ''Necessity said I should try to find a job.'' She raced Joel to a day-care center in the morning before work, and her husband came home from school in the afternoon to take care of their son. They also had neighbors who helped out, and her mother-in-law sent a woman who ultimately became Joel's surrogate mother. ''She was a black woman of the greatest dignity. Joel always said he had two mothers,'' reflected Green. ''Things worked out very well. We were lucky''—despite the fact that many people in the early 1950s were unsympathetic to a working woman with a young child, and there were no support groups.

Green returned to work as a copywriter in the promotion department of *Seventeen* magazine. One of her early campaigns helped boost the magazine's image among advertisers by showing that young women in the 1950s did things besides spend money. ''Their perception was that girls at 17 are devoted to clothes,'' Green explained. ''My campaign was about how the young woman of the house did the shopping and then made dinner. That she helped a lot around the house and did a lot of the cooking.'' Advertisers responded favorably.

After two years, having worked her way up to become *Seventeen*'s promotion director, Green left to join the L. C. Gumbinner agency as a copy contact. Gumbinner, according to Green, was a small, old-fashioned agency headed by ''a very smart man.'' She learned more about business there than she did about copywriting. Her first exposure to how a client's products were made came when Gumbinner took her to a factory. And the agency gave her a lot of responsibility, treated her like an adult. ''I did a lot of trade ads that didn't look anything like the trade ads Gumbinner usually did,'' said Green. ''I did totally different things, but they didn't step on me.'' Copy chief Milton Goodman liked her writing, but thought there was too much of it, so he taught her how to edit. She also helped write the music for a number of radio campaigns, her first foray into writing for that medium.

While at Gumbinner, Green began to notice the ads being done by Doyle Dane Bernbach. ''I loved their ads and knew I could do them, too,'' she related. ''I wanted desperately to go to DDB.'' Most of DDB's staff were people Green had known at Grey Advertising, but she could not ask for a job until she knew that ''if they didn't take me, I wouldn't die,'' she commented, bemused even today at her insecurity. A position opened at DDB; Green applied and was hired as a copywriter. Later she became a group head for the agency, then DDB's first woman creative management supervisor.

During Green's early days at Doyle Dane Bernbach, the agency was formulating what has been characterized as a creative revolution in advertising. "We recognized that people aren't dumb, that good, intellectually sound, witty advertising would sell," she recounted. As a result, the creative people at DDB became more important, more visible. The agency's creative culture also demanded that people not only turn out volume, but each advertisement was supposed to be good. When the client did not like something, whatever was done next had to be better. "You were held to very high standards Or you held yourself to high standards because you knew this was DDB. You couldn't sluff off," Green declared.

Bill Bernbach's influence helped shape Green's creative philosophy. He allowed the staff to do creative things that were completely different from his own creative style and could recognize a good idea even when it was not his, according to Green. Before ideas or copy went to Bill, she learned to "hunt for the holes," something she does even today. "You didn't want to create anything you'd be embarrassed for him to see."

Perhaps the most famous of the campaigns Green created at DDB was for a then little-known rental car company named Avis, whose "Avis is only no. 2— we try harder" slogan has become part of the American vernacular. Hubert Humphrey wore an Avis button while campaigning for the presidency, referring to his status as Lyndon Johnson's vice president. Not coincidentally, Green worked as a speech writer for Humphrey prior to the 1968 Democratic convention. She also convinced Quaker Oats to market a new product as Instant Quaker Oats, instead of Quaker Instant Oats, to capitalize on the company's established name. The Burlington Mills crisscross weaving pattern used for a number of years as the corporate logo in TV ads was another Green concept. And her campaign for S&W green beans won the first CLIO advertising award for writing.

By the end of 1969, Green had decided she had reached a point where there was no place higher for her to go at DDB. "They already had a president, Bill Bernbach," Green laughed. "I'd gone pretty far, but that was going to be it." A friend, Murray Dolmatch, was leaving his job at another advertising agency and suggested the two start their own. Green Dolmatch lasted eight years and evolved into Paula Green, Inc., when the partnership dissolved.

Much of Green's success in advertising has come from campaigns in which she has done things "that have never been done or that I don't know I can't do." To be successful "you have to find something that nobody's explored before or explored it a different way or didn't know it was there to do." She approaches an advertising campaign from both an engineering and problem-solving perspective. The former is what she calls "cantilever" creativity; a cantilever is a beam or structure supported at only one end, like houses on hillsides in her native California. "It looks like they have no support, but it's there." The same is true for creative ads. "The idea is based solidly in something. Even if it's way out, it's supported. For example, who would think of union members singing to you on TV?" challenged Green, alluding to the famous award-winning campaign she created for the International Ladies Garment Workers Union (ILGWU). Singing was part of the union's tradition; it sang at conventions or whenever members gathered. Green pulled the union's own tradition into TV with the song she wrote for them. "Look for the Union Label" is a much sung, often parodied tune inexorably tied to the image of American labor.

Music is another of Green's loves. As a young girl, she studied piano with a teacher who encouraged her, who was "another one of those people who made you hate yourself if you weren't prepared," Green remembered, "like Bill Bernbach." She has written a number of successful musical pieces for advertising. "The words and music usually occur to me at the same time."

Creating a successful campaign also requires problem definition, according to Green. "You take the problem at hand—not the one you like better or the one that's prettier or easier—and you come to grips with it, manage it. And when you've defined the problem, you've really arrived at the ad." She believes in directness and simplicity in an advertising message, but that does not mean dull. The acid test? "If I can read the copy aloud without wincing, it's okay. I have to feel that I would be pleased if anyone else read it."

Another of Green's passions is cooking, and a number of her clients over the years have been from the food and wine industries. One of her own agency's first clients was Seagram's Leilani Hawaiian rum. "I'd always known women were a good target for a lot more than traditional women's products," said Green, an insight which resulted in a successful, low-budget campaign for Leilani. Because rum is used primarily as a mixer, Green created a theme campaign that asked, "Why shouldn't a woman make a good daiquiri?" It was the first national advertisement placed with *Ms.* magazine, which later asked Green to be its agency. She created a campaign for *Ms.* that promoted the magazine as a viable advertising vehicle for businesses: "Don't you wish there was someplace besides the FTC where they take your advertising seriously? There is. *Ms.*"

In the early 1980s she pitched a campaign to Goya, the no. 1 Hispanic food company in America. "I thought it was time that they should come into the marketing mainstream," Green explained. "They have a great line of beans— red beans, dried beans, all kinds of beans. I told them that everybody eats beans, that non-Hispanics in New York would like their beans, that it wouldn't be any problem to translate their products to the general market." The campaign's highly recognizable slogan, "Goya, oh boy-a!", was eminently successful.

Green also launched Subaru into the U.S. market as a competitor to Volkswagen with the headline, "The Subaru is *not* a Japanese beetle." Green's husband taught her a lot about cars "that I turned into copy. We had a wonderful line for Subaru—'At 70 mph, it doesn't even breathe hard'—which compared the powerful little Subaru engine with the VW." She also wrote and did the voice-over for a Subaru campaign targeted at women and created a magazine ad for the Subaru station wagon that was the first car advertisement to be run by *Family Circle* in a number of years.

A brush with cancer prompted Green to offer her services to the American Cancer Society, which resulted in one of her most professionally fulfilling campaigns, a breakthrough TV spot about breast cancer. "I thought perhaps I could be useful," she said about the motivation work with the ACS. "I thought it was very important to get the attention of women. I think one of my main talents is that I can reach people so that they're moved. When I feel something deeply, I want to communicate that to someone else so they get the same kind of feeling." Green's commercial about breast self-examination in early 1970 broke through broadcast taboos. "Who'd dare say 'examine your breasts' on TV 20 years ago?" she asked. The advertisement was run as a public service announcement on New York stations. After six weeks the local ACS office could not handle any more exam requests and had to close its switchboard. The ACS subsequently documented that at least 24 women's lives were saved as a direct result of the campaign. "That's no small gift," Green said humbly. "You think your life isn't totally misspent when you can be responsible for something like that."

During the 1991 Persian Gulf War, the State of Israel asked Green to write a radio campaign for its bonds. She wrote and recorded it in 24 hours. "Israel had defense dollars, so these were peace bonds, not war bonds. The message was that, when you buy State of Israel bonds, your dollars do the work of peace—peace dollars for school and resettling." It was, in Green's words, "an interesting experience in terms of copy and for myself." The campaign was so successful that the drive's goal was surpassed and Green was awarded Israel's Gates of Jerusalem medal.

As one of the first women to head her own advertising agency, Green has at times been called an advertising pioneer, a role she shrugs off. "I don't think I've ever been a political feminist; I've not been on the barricades. However, I've always valued what feminists were doing. I've always known what women can do, are doing." She hates being labelled as "a woman" in a male-dominated profession, arguing that it is nicer to be recognized for one's work than for gender. Green was thrilled when the daughter of a client once told her that she had read about Green in her advertising text. "They didn't read about me as a woman. They read about me as an advertising person. That was kind of nifty."

Green was part of a talented pool of women who were at DDB in the late 1950s and early 1960s which included Mary Wells, Judith Protas, Lore Parker, Rita Selden, and Phyllis Robinson, who supervised the group. But Green downplays the significance of gender at DDB. "Practically everybody there was good. There wasn't a thing about women. You were a writer or you weren't. You went to meetings as a copywriter, not as a woman copywriter. Nobody ever apologized for being a woman."

When Green opened Green Dolmatch "it never occurred to me that the advertising industry was male-dominated. I didn't think, 'There are so many men. Am I ever going to make it?' " Nor had she been raised to believe that there would be career roadblocks because she was a woman. "My family never said, 'Because you're a woman, you've got to watch out.' Or, 'Don't expect to be able to do this or that.' Never. Women today sort of take a lot of things for granted," adds Green as an afterthought. While there are more women in important advertising positions in the 1990s, virtually all of the women heads of advertising agencies have the job because they started the agency, observes Green. "As long as business is mainly run by men, I think it's much harder for women. Businessmen don't mingle with women. I think younger men have learned to some degree to look at women not just as women, but as people to do business with. As people of stature, of substance, who have good ideas, who operate well."

Green's gender was an issue in two situations she recalls. One was during a client meeting about a campaign for a new laundry detergent on which Green was the copywriter supervisor. "I kept trying to discuss doing laundry and the men wouldn't listen. I finally said, 'I don't understand you guys. I'm the only one here who's ever done a wash and you won't listen to me.'" The brand manager snarled at me and said, 'You sound like my wife,'" related Green with relish.

The second was when an early Green Dolmatch client told Murray Dolmatch that he was not going to have Green on his account because she was a woman. "We didn't take the account," said Green. "Nobody was going to tell me I couldn't go to a client meeting. Not in my own agency. That was intolerable. That's not the same thing as a client who doesn't like your ideas. I wouldn't throw a client out for that." Any agency's client list is ultimately self-selective. "When people come to you, they know you're a woman. That doesn't throw them," explained Green. "If they have anti-woman feelings, they won't come in the first place. They come because of your work. The people who wanted to do business with me accepted me." Green's clients, in her words, have always been "first-rate clients, people who made first-rate products. Clients you didn't have to be ashamed of working for. I've been quite fortunate to have the kind of clients that I respect."

Green admits that she has always "had strong views. That's sometimes harder for people to deal with than my being a woman." But she believes in treating people with honesty and fairness and dignity. "I respond to people. I have a wonderful rapport with the women of the ILGWU, for example. They're good people. They work in factories, I don't. But we see each other as people." Green's agency reflects this philosophy; it is small and personal, which has been, in her estimation, an important benefit for her clients.

And she's proud of the important social ramifications of some of her work. "If we can talk about cancer on TV today with a little more respect and I had a hand in it . . . if unions are talked about and viewed today with a little more respect and I had a hand in it . . . if women today are regarded as intelligent, capable, creative people and I've had a hand in it . . . then it's been enormously rewarding. It's nice being known by your work, that you did this terrific thing. Not that you were terrific, though that's nice to know," Green laughed. "But that you did something that people responded to." While Green uses the terms "break," "luck," and "good fortune" to describe her "solid, enduring, and lasting" career, she also "worked my ass off," she emphasized. "That's how

I do it—very hard work. I like to work. Work is very important. As long as my head's busy, I'm wonderful.''

Any self-assessment automatically gravitates to Green's parents and to her own family. ''I had terrific parents. I was very secure. Independent. And John and I have a good family life. John's a great husband, because he's always been really supportive of me, always—and it was more than window dressing. Together we have a very wonderful son. He's a decent, honorable young man of great compassion. And wisdom. When you've raised an individual you feel is a worthy person, that's really an achievement.''

Green sees herself as ''a little country girl from Hollywood'' who ended up in New York hobnobbing with ''masters of industry, the greatest photographers and filmmakers, people who wrote music, movie stars, and even important politicians.'' She stopped. ''Wow. I didn't think that would happen to me,'' she said with unassuming awe. ''How could you possibly conceive of something like that when you're growing up? I couldn't. You don't know enough to even imagine it. And I keep going on to new things and new excitements,'' she added with characteristic enthusiasm, ''which is terrific.''

FURTHER READING

Works about Green

Buxton, Edward. *Creative People at Work*. New York: Executive Communications, 1975.
Dobrow, Larry. *When Advertising Tried Harder*. New York: Friendly Press, 1984.
''Executives: Four Who Made It.'' *Time* (March 20, 1972): 83.
Fox, Stephen. *The Mirror Makers: A History of American Advertising and Its Creators*. New York: William Morrow, 1984.
Hishio, Tadahisa. *Great American Copywriters*. Tokyo, 1969.
Meyers, William. *The Image-Makers*. London: Orbis, 1984.
''On American Woman Creators.'' *Sen Den Kaigi* magazine, special issue (1984).
''Tips on Job Hunting: Paula Green.'' *Advertising Age* (February 23, 1981): S 2.
Who's Who in America, 1990–91. Wilmette, IL: Macmillan Directory Division, 1990.
Who's Who in American Jewry. Los Angeles: Standard Who's Who, 1980.

NOTABLE CLIENTS/CAMPAIGNS

At Doyle Dane Bernbach

Avis

Burlington Industries

General Foods

Heinz

Polaroid

Quaker Oats
S&W fine foods

At Paula Green, Inc.

American Cancer Society
Goya foods
Hathaway shirts
International Ladies Garment Workers Union
Ms.
New York Times
Paramount poultry
Seagram Leilani Hawaiian rum
Sterling National Bank, New York
Subaru
U.S. Public Health Service

GEORGE HOMER GRIBBIN
(1907–August 26, 1981)

Charles S. Madden, Marjorie J. Cooper, and
Leslie Cole

George Homer Gribbin spent over 50 years in the advertising business—first in retail advertising for a variety of department stores and later as a copywriter and executive for Young and Rubicam.

Gribbin was born in 1907 in Nashville, Michigan, and graduated Phi Beta Kappa from Stanford University in 1929. He then worked as a copywriter for several department stores, including J. L. Hudson in Detroit, Bamberger's in Newark, and Macy's in New York. In 1935 Gribbin joined Young and Rubicam as a copywriter and rose to the rank of copy supervisor in 1942. His rapid rise through the ranks of Young and Rubicam from copywriter to chairman and chief executive officer parallels the years of the development of the advertising industry in the United States.

From the time he began in the 1930s, Gribbin's only time away from Young and Rubicam was while he served in the army from 1942 until 1945. He joined the service as a private and rose to the rank of captain. After the war he became a vice president for radio and television copy in 1951; in 1954 he became the agency copy director for print and television. He was named a senior vice president in 1956, president in 1958, chief executive officer in 1962, and chairman in 1963. He retired in 1965 and returned to school to study for a master's degree in the humanities at Manhattanville College.

From the time of his retirement, Gribbin continued as a consultant to Young and Rubicam. In 1977 he accepted a position as dean of the agency's creative workshop and traveled to its offices across the United States and around the world to conduct seminars. Some say his boldest contribution was in pioneering Young and Rubicam's expansion abroad as a consultant in the later years. His visits to and research into the markets of Argentina, Brazil, and Japan led to the opening of offices in each of those countries.

At a time when print advertisements were becoming more graphic and contained fewer words, Gribbin set the pace for small "essays" on his product. He is best remembered for some ads that, while they may appear dated today, were attention-grabbing, clever, and well crafted. Gribbin's writing was packed with homely little details that made the copy believable and his subjects very personal. He was a master at creating empathy between the reader and his advertising characters. He also enjoyed using humor, the wilder and more whimsical the better; yet his humor never detracted from the essential advertising message.

Gribbin suggested this simple formula for writing magazine copy (Norins, p. 181):

1. With the help of your art-director create a picture that will make a prospect look at the headline.
2. Write a headline that you are sure will make the prospect read the first sentence of copy.
3. Write a first sentence of copy that you are sure will make the prospect read the second sentence.
4. Continue this process until you are sure that the prospect will read the final word of the ad.
5. Make sure that the picture and all these words add up to a story that will make the prospect's mouth water for the product.

While many copywriters find the concept of a formula objectionable, they still find it difficult to disagree with the elements in Gribbin's prescription.

Gribbin revealed, in a speech presented at a meeting of the American Association of Advertising Agencies, another method he used for successful copywriting. He said, "I make it a point to compare ads to people. I say to myself, would I like a man or woman to act the way this ad does? Would I choose this ad—if it were alive—for a friend?" Surely Gribbin's observation, at the very least, previewed the theory of "brand personality" that was to become a Madison Avenue buzzword.

Among the clients for which he wrote his special ads were Travelers Insurance, Borden's milk, and Arrow shirts. Some of Gribbin's more notable copy included the following:

• A homely man declared, "Even I look good in an Arrow shirt!"
• A man smartly dressed sitting with a beautiful woman kneeling at his feet says, "I expect other girls to propose to me, too." He goes on to recount that the way he became so popular was due to his mother. One night while playing cards she said, "Chauncey, the trouble with you is your shirts—they look funny. If you had a shirt like the fellow I saw in the Arrow ad, you may get a girl. And you are old enough to have one." Chauncey explains that he went out and bought an Arrow shirt. Now all the girls want to marry him, and he expects more proposals followed by happily married life (Schofield, p. 38).
• A man is pictured talking to a horse hitched to a milk wagon. The unusual headline reads, "My friend, Joe Holmes, is now a horse." Joe, who had died, had always

wanted to be a horse. Now he has returned as the animal of his choice. "I am now wearing a comfortable collar for the first time in my life," said the horse (alias Joe). "My shirt collars always use to shrink and murder me." Gee, his friends think, I should have told him about Arrow shirts, which never shrink (Watkins, pp. 132–33).

Gribbin also was legendary in his philosophy of how creative people should work, and he himself set the tone of creativity at Young and Rubicam. When asked once why so many outstanding companies came to Young and Rubicam through the 1940s and 1950s, he replied, "One of the greatest assets of this agency is that a man here feels he can express himself as a writer" (Mayer, p. 68).

Gribbin's commitment to individual writing style can likely be traced to an incident that occurred early in his career. He told the story of how when he first came to Young and Rubicam, he was assigned to the Packard automobile account and was told to write the way his predecessor, Jack Rosebrook, had been writing. "I got lost in the minutiae of phrasing, imitating Rosebrook. In six weeks they took me off the Packard ads. I said to myself, 'Well, maybe I can't write the Packard account. I don't know. But what I do know is that I can't write like Rosebrook. I've got to write like Gribbin.' Over the years I've learned that if we have a writer and we tell him, 'Do it in this particular style,' we'll get less good advertising" (Mayer, p. 68).

Not surprisingly, under Gribbin's creative leadership, Young and Rubicam was known as a team. By the time Gribbin became president in 1958, Young and Rubicam had about 60 companies as clients, would not accept clients for which billing was less than $300,000, and was billing a total of more than $230 million. At this time Y&R was the third largest agency in the United States.

Gribbin's work in retail advertising in the early years made him a "craftsman of words" and led to his commitment toward the end of his career to the preservation of dignity in the industry. His commitment to well-written ads was noted by all in the industry during his career as a copywriter. For example, while president of Young and Rubicam, Gribbin led an industry-wide debate concerning the misuse and ultimate corruption of English by practicing advertising people. He spoke before the advertising writers association of New York and made his case by saying, "I believe that one of the main causes of the disrespect in which advertising and the people in it are so frequently held is our own disrespect for the basic tool of our trade—language." He went on to add, "If advertising is fundamentally based on the power of words, why is it that our business is so eternally disrespectful of them? Do we gain from that? I think we lose" (Bart, "Advertising: 'Trade Lingo,' " p. 29).

"A lot of educated consumers live in this country and a lot of clients who not only went to college but often read things of higher literary value than sales figures or each other's annual reports. . . . I don't have to tell professionals like you how easily contempt for the writer can lead to distrust of what he writes" (Bart 1963, p. 53).

That speech was the opening salvo of what became a passion for Gribbin in later years to call for constraint by advertising people. He argued against hard sell, legal puffery, and what he later called "hermaphroditic copy" (the kind that shouts so loudly that it creates the headache its product is designed to relieve) (Norins, p. 4). His commitment to professionalism and restraint triggered a discussion that lasted for several years.

Gribbin's commitment to word crafting followed him throughout his career. Draper Daniels, author of *Giants, Pigmies and Other Advertising People*, shared what he believed to be Gribbin's style by saying that Gribbin was "the best teacher I ever met in advertising. He was one of the few top writers I ever knew who could break writing down and show you why he did what he did. He would follow a long sentence with a short explosive one that either drove a point deep into the reader's consciousness or made one want to keep on reading" (p. 67).

Other stories about George Gribbin reflect on his management style with employees. When Gribbin had to fire people, he would try to do it as quickly and as painlessly as possible. Bill Casey, who was a copywriter at Young and Rubicam, told the story that he was called out of a Saturday night bath by Gribbin to be fired. "You're too late," Bill replied, "I quit last Friday. I'm all packed up" (Buxton, p. 188).

Daniels shared another insight when he explained how Gribbin had taught him to ask for a raise: "Don't ask for one," he advised. "They won't give it to you. Get an offer from another agency, but don't make the mistake of going in and asking Sid to match it. It won't work. Turn the offer down and then tell me about it. I'll tell Sid. Watch and see what happens." (Daniels, p. 32). Daniels followed the direction and the raise came through shortly.

During the time when he was president of Young and Rubicam, Gribbin stated to a newspaper reporter who was looking at the growth of several major agencies: "Billings are important, but Young and Rubicam's goal is to sell the maximum goods for the clients we serve."

George H. Gribbin died in 1981 while vacationing with his wife in Portugal. At that time he resided in Greenwich, Connecticut, and was 74 years old.

FURTHER READING

Works about Gribbin

Advertising Today/Yesterday/Tomorrow. New York: McGraw-Hill, 1963.

Bart, Peter. "Advertising: New Sunday Supplement." *New York Times* (March 13, 1963): 16.

———. "Advertising: 'Trade Lingo' Now under Fire." *New York Times* (April 12, 1962): 57.

———. " 'Shouting' Ad Men Called Obsolescent." *New York Times* (April 28, 1962): 29.

Buxton, Edward. *Creative People at Work.* New York: Executive Communications, 1975.

———. *Promise Them Anything.* New York: Stein and Day, 1972.

Daniels, Draper. *Giants, Pigmies and Other Advertising People*. Chicago: Crain Communications, 1974.

Fox, Stephen. *The Mirror Makers: A History of American Advertising and Its Creators*. New York: William Morrow, 1984.

"The Mammoth Mirror." *Time* (October 12, 1962): 85–90.

Mayer, Martin. *Madison Avenue, U.S.A.* New York: Harper, 1958.

Norins, Hanley. *The Compleat Copywriter*. New York: McGraw-Hill, 1966.

Schofield, Perry. *100 Top Copy Writers and Their Favorite Ads*. New York: Printers' Ink, 1954.

Schuyler, Philip N. "Gribbin Marks 25 Anniversary at Y&R." *Editor & Publisher* (September 3, 1960): 17, 24.

Spielvogel, Carl. "Advertising: Case for Plainer Language." *New York Times* (October 28, 1955): 57.

———. "Advertising: Top Shifts at Young & Rubicam." *New York Times* (October 21, 1958): 43.

"Young and Rubicam Officer Retires." *New York Times* (August 2, 1965): 34.

Watkins, Julian Lewis. *The 100 Greatest Advertisements*. New York: Dover, 1959.

NOTABLE CLIENTS/CAMPAIGNS

Arrow shirts (1930s and 1940s)

Borden's milk (1940s and 1950s)

Travelers Insurance (1940s and 1950s)

MARION HARPER, JR.
(May 14, 1916–October 25, 1989)

Carolyn Stringer

Marion Harper, Jr., is best known as the man who built the Interpublic conglomerate and changed the way that advertising agencies do business.

He was born on May 14, 1916, in Oklahoma City. His father was advertising
director of the *Daily Oklahoman*, and his mother wrote a column for the newspaper. When he was five, Marion's parents divorced.

The young Harper lived with his mother in Oklahoma City until he left to
attend prep school. His father, who had become a vice president of General
Foods, persuaded his former wife that their son should go to school in the East.
Marion attended Andover and later Yale, from which he was graduated in the
top 10 percent of his class in 1938.

After working for a year as a door-to-door salesman, Harper joined the
McCann-Erickson advertising agency in New York as a trainee in the mail room
at a salary of $14 per week. While delivering the mail, he learned the names,
titles, and job functions of agency executives and other employees. While sorting
mail, he learned their interests by noting the type each received. He spent a
great deal of time in the creative and research departments, where he became
intrigued with the question of what makes an ad effective.

He began comparing ads that had achieved high scores in Starch studies.
(Starch measured readership of ads by interviewing magazine subscribers and
asking them which ads they noticed and which copy points they remembered.)
While studying the tested ads, Harper found that some creative techniques seemed
to produce higher scores than others. He proposed that McCann-Erickson attempt
to isolate elements in ads that contributed to higher and lower readership scores.
If such elements could be determined, they could be used to predict readership,
he reasoned. His project was approved, and Harper was moved to the research
department, where he was named manager of copy research.

While working in research, he met Virginia Epes, a young woman from
Virginia, and they were married in 1942. Together, they worked on the magazine

readership project, and not only isolated elements that contributed to effective ads, but also developed a formula by which they could rate effectiveness before publication. McCann-Erickson used their formula for many years to pretest ads.

Two years after joining the research department, Harper was promoted to associate director. In 1945 he was named head of research; he was 29. In *Giants, Pygmies and Other Advertising People*, Draper Daniels, who joined the agency during that time, describes Harper: "Although he was over six feet tall and had a big frame, he carried extra pounds that made him look flabby. There was nothing flabby about his mind" (p. 114).

As research director, Harper continued to study the ingredients that go into effective advertising. When he learned of a system that rated radio program content, he gained exclusive rights to it for the McCann agency. Called the radio program analyzer, it entailed playing radio programs for respondents and asking them to register positive and negative reactions to different parts by pressing buttons. Afterward, each respondent was asked why he registered positive or negative reactions, thus giving valuable information for determining program content. Harper reasoned that the technique could be used to test the effectiveness of radio commercials as well as programs, and he adapted it for his agency's use. The radio analyzer and the magazine readership study became powerful tools used by Harper and other McCann executives to secure new business for the agency.

Under Harper's leadership, the research department became the driving force of the agency. He attracted bright young people to his department, many of whom later became successful executives at McCann and other agencies. Harper's talents and leadership abilities attracted the attention of McCann-Erickson president Harrison McCann, who was then in his 60s and considering retirement. McCann chose Harper as his assistant. A year later McCann became chairman of the board, and Harper was named president. He made it from the mail room to the president's office in nine years; he was 32.

As president, Harper concentrated on making the advertising produced by his agency more effective. He applied the science of psychology and researched consumer attitudes and opinions as he tried to determine what motivated them to buy. To acquaint his executives with his ideas and methods, he initiated training sessions, then organized retreats. He developed still more new techniques for testing ads. His "relative sales conviction" was a method of testing copy by placing two or more ads in dummy issues of magazines along with other ads. Interviewers would then show the ads to readers and carefully document their reactions. This method of testing, although time-consuming, enabled the agency to select the more effective creative approaches.

Because so many people were involved in the planning and preparation of advertising, Harper became concerned about the quality of agency work. To maintain quality control, he set up various review boards of top executives, who checked the work as it progressed through the agency to the final product. The review boards ensured that the work was done properly, that it accurately reflected the agency's findings about the product, and that it carried out its advertising objectives.

Harper also experimented with eye-pupil dilation, which measures the degree of interest a person has to certain stimuli. The theory was that when people looked at pictures that interested them, their pupils dilated. Harper saw that this research could be applied to advertising and that people's interests in the visuals shown in ads could be measured, so he adapted the technique for his agency's use.

During the 1950s Harper concentrated on reorganizing the agency and increasing its billings. By 1953 McCann's billings had risen to $100 million, double those of 1948 when he had become president. Harper added impressive new clients and new agency personnel during this time. Emerson Foote, founder of Foote, Cone and Belding, joined McCann-Erickson, later to become its president.

By 1956 McCann's billings again doubled, reaching $200 million, as the agency added one of its biggest clients, Coca-Cola. Harper won the account over such competitions as Young and Rubicam by concentrating on the product as one with worldwide appeal that needed a global marketing and advertising strategy. The Coke account was the largest that had ever switched from one agency to another as of that time.

The Coca-Cola victory illustrates Harper's expertise in making new business presentations. He thought that an agency should concentrate more on the client's problems and opportunities and less on the agency, so he and his staff often poured hours of work into new business preparations, burrowing through exhaustive research. They spared no effort in their preparations, accumulating large amounts of charts, graphs, slides, and other visual materials. Harper usually let his associates make the presentation, but when asked to comment at the conclusion, he would amaze those present with detailed statistics and other facts. He could commit a great deal of information to memory in a short time, then speak for an hour or more without notes. He gave clients the impression that he was an authority on their businesses, and he assured them that he could produce results because his advertising would be based on research.

As Harper perfected his presentation techniques, McCann-Erickson's client list grew. According to an article in the March 30, 1964, issue of *Newsweek*, he landed thirteen new accounts (including Coca-Cola and Westinghouse appliances) worth over $45 million in one year ("What Makes Marion Harper Run?", p. 63).

In 1958 Harper shocked the advertising world by resigning the larger Chrysler account to take on Buick, hoping that it would lead to more business from General Motors. Such practices were criticized by some of his peers, but Harper's agency continued to grow. By 1960 McCann's billings had risen to more than $300 million, and the agency counted as its clients Bulova, Esso, Nestlé, Westinghouse, Coca-Cola, Buick, and Standard Oil.

McCann-Erickson had been retained by Standard Oil overseas since the 1920s.

Harper continued and expanded the overseas operations, acquiring agencies and forming partnerships in such countries as Australia, England, New Zealand, Japan, and France for clients such as Bristol-Myers, Goodyear, Westinghouse, and Coca-Cola. Overseas billings approached $100 million by 1960.

While expanding his operations, Harper pondered the problem of agencies servicing competing accounts. He was often unable to approach a new client because McCann handled one of its competitors. He reasoned that competing accounts could be serviced under one corporate umbrella if they were handled by completely separate agencies. In 1954 he had purchased the Marschalk and Pratt agency and expanded its client base. By retaining its separate identity, he was able to service accounts through Marschalk and Pratt that would have been considered in conflict with other accounts in the McCann stable. The success of Marschalk and Pratt fortified Harper's belief that he could own more than one agency. He reasoned that a large holding company could be formed to which parallel agencies would belong, with each agency acting independently. Because no client information would be exchanged among them, these agencies could service a variety of clients, including those in competition with each other. The creative independence of each agency would be important to the plan. They would operate separately except for submitting projections of anticipated billings and reports of their progress in meeting their goals. Each agency would pay a fee to the holding company for legal, personnel, and other services.

Harper continued to buy agencies, and in 1961 he folded them all into the Interpublic Group of Companies, a new conglomerate whose name he had taken from a German research firm owned by McCann. Harper viewed Interpublic as a marketing communications organization, offering diverse services to fulfill a variety of client needs.

He formed a centralized planning and marketing organization to promote Interpublic services and acquire new accounts. He took three departments from McCann-Erickson and formed new companies to specialize in public relations, sales promotion, and market research. By lifting the status of these functions, he was able to attract many bright people who produced high-quality work. The companies' separate corporate structures and distinctive names also made it easier to persuade clients to pay for these separate services.

To experiment with what he called cocreativity, a high-powered version of brainstorming, Harper founded Jack Tinker and Partners. He believed that a group of extremely bright people could solve problems and produce better creative work. The group was composed of Tinker, who had been head of creative services at McCann; Dr. Herta Herzog, a psychologist and authority on motivational research; Mary Wells, who later founded the Wells, Rich, Greene agency; and others. Tinker and Partners produced outstanding campaigns for such products as the Bulova Accutron watch and the Buick Riviera automobile.

In addition to his innovations at Interpublic, Harper engaged in other pursuits during the early 1960s. He owned a resort hotel on Long Island, a roadside candy factory and store in Maryland, a Washington, D.C., publishing company, and a herd of Black Angus cattle in Virginia. He was an avid reader, and often was portrayed in magazine articles as reading a book while pedaling an exercise bicycle. He and his first wife, Virginia, the mother of his four children, divorced. He remarried in 1963, this time to Valerie Feit, a former Paris fashion consultant.

As Harper continued to buy agencies in the 1960s, the huge Interpublic complex grew at a rapid pace. In his biography *Marion Harper*, Russ Johnston noted that "in 1965 and up to July of 1966, Harper added new companies at the rate of one a month. The parent company could boast of 200 offices in 100 cities in 48 countries. The world-wide staff, serving 1,900 clients, numbered 8,700 people—5,500 outside the United States" (p. 261).

Harper's goal was to make Interpublic a $1 billion business by 1970, and he was relentless in his pursuit of new clients. Many of his moves were controversial and provoked criticism from the advertising industry. He continued to add new people to the Interpublic organization, and some agencies accused him of raiding them. Many executives he hired left Interpublic after a short stay, perhaps suggesting that Harper might have been a genius at organization and at getting business but lacking in his ability to deal with people.

The acquisition of agencies and the hiring of many high-priced executives resulted in enormous overhead for this affiliate system. Adding to the high cost of doing business were the corporate life-styles of Harper and his associates. Some examples were the housing of Tinker and Partners in an expensive New York hotel suite and Harper's purchase of aircraft for Interpublic use. In *The Mirror Makers*, Stephen Fox said, "The Interpublic fleet of five airplanes, known as the Harper Air Force, included a DC–7 for the boss, furnished in French provincial. His suite boasted a king-size bed, private library, and a sunken bath" (p. 266).

Although Interpublic had grown into a huge advertising empire, Harper, as president and chief executive officer, still ran everything himself, approving all major decisions. The giant complex simply became too large for one man to manage in such detail. A series of unprofitable ventures, the huge overhead, and a downturn in business caused a severe profit squeeze. During this time some clients moved to other agencies because they became worried about Interpublic agencies servicing not only their accounts, but those of competitors. Although Interpublic's agencies were to operate separately, the clients gradually became concerned that leaks of confidential information might occur.

By 1967 billings were $700 million, but losses were estimated at $2 million to $3 million, and Interpublic was in difficulty with several major banks on loan agreements. Harper brought Robert E. Healy, a former Interpublic executive with extensive account management experience, back from semi-retirement to correct the financial woes. Healy instituted many cost-cutting measures, but the banks were not satisfied. They forced Harper's removal in order to protect their heavy loans. On November 7, 1967, in an Interpublic board meeting, the motion was made to remove the 51-year-old leader from office. Harper called for the vote, and all six board members voted for his removal. It was recommended that he stay in a position that focused on getting new business, but he would have no authority in the management and operation of the huge complex. After a few months Harper left Interpublic. Healy was able to turn the huge conglomerate around, and within one year, the company was again making a profit.

Harper worked as a management consultant, joined a small agency for approximately five months, then disappeared for almost 12 years. He surfaced again in 1979 at his mother's home in Oklahoma City, and talked informally with a reporter from *Advertising Age* about publishing a work that would include "new theories and views of marketing as well as other aspects of company operations Mr. Harper believes must be looked at in new ways" (August 27, 1979, p. 1). Harper died of a heart attack on October 25, 1989, in Oklahoma City, where he had lived for the previous 20 years. He was 73.

Harper's ideas and accomplishments are reflected in today's agencies that have merged to form huge, multibillion-dollar corporations offering a variety of services to clients. The merging of many functions such as advertising, public relations, and sales promotion under a single corporate umbrella has enabled firms to offer integrated marketing communications, a concept that is strongly reminiscent of Harper's plans for Interpublic.

FURTHER READING

Work by Harper

"The Decade of Incentive." A series of annual marketing forecasts based on studies by the Market Planning Corporation. New York: McCann-Erickson, 1960–69.

Works about Harper

"Changing the Format." *Business Week* (December 2, 1967): 42.

Daniels, Draper. *Giants, Pygmies and Other Advertising People*. Chicago: Crain Communications, 1974.

Danzig, Fred. "Interpublic's Marion Harper Dead at 73." *Advertising Age* (October 30, 1989): 1, 74.

Fox, Stephen. *The Mirror Makers: A History of American Advertising and Its Creators*. New York: William Morrow, 1984.

"Harper Hits Ad World's Misuse of 'Creativity.' " *Advertising Age* (October 31, 1960): 1, 12.

Johnston, Russ. *Marion Harper: An Unauthorized Biography*. Chicago: Crain Books, 1982.

Klaw, Spencer. "What Is Marion Harper Saying?" *Fortune* (January, 1961): 122–26, 128, 132, 134, 137–38.

"What Makes Marion Harper Run?" *Newsweek* (March 30, 1964): 63–66.

NOTABLE CLIENTS/CAMPAIGNS

Alka Seltzer
Buick
Bulova
Coca-Cola
Exxon
Miller Brewing
Nabisco
Nestlé
Swift
Westinghouse

MARGARET HOCKADAY
(January 8, 1907–December 18, 1992)

Roxanne E. Neuberger-Lucchesi

Margaret Hockaday founded one of the largest small agencies in New York in 1949. For the next two decades her agency created some of the most notable and quotable advertising on Madison Avenue. Hockaday advertisements were offbeat, whimsical, and saucy. They evoked surprise, puzzlement, delight, and curiosity from Madison Avenue, the general press, and consumers alike.

Hockaday was born on January 8, 1907, in Wichita, Kansas, to I. Newton and Bird (Bohart) Hockaday. Her grandmother was Abraham Lincoln's cousin, which made Hockaday a collateral descendant of the president. When she was four, her father, a paint manufacturer, left and eventually moved to California. He left his wife with three small children: Margaret and her brothers, Lincoln and Newton. The family moved from Kansas to Oak Park, Illinois. Hockaday's father visited once or twice, but she never saw him after the age of seven. He died in 1928.

Hockaday's mother found employment as a publisher's representative. The children were surrounded with books and magazines, a literary environment that might have influenced the career choices of all three. Newton worked for Henry Luce at *Time*, and Lincoln became the chief aide to Joseph Pulitzer, Jr., publisher of the *St. Louis Post Dispatch*. Margaret started her career as a copywriter for Marshall Field in Chicago.

Oak Park was the home of Frank Lloyd Wright, and growing up there may have influenced Hockaday's lifelong interest in architecture. "It contains all the arts of living," she said. An admirer of Wright's houses, Hockaday and a friend visited his school in Taliesin, Wisconsin, in the hopes of someday studying there. She fondly remembered staying at Wright's first house, which he built in 1911 for his mother. Because there were no scholarships available, Hockaday instead went to Vassar College to study English and history. She graduated in 1929 and started working at Marshall Field for $25 a week. Her interest in architecture and design never faded. In fact, her appreciation for design and furnishings influenced many of her most famous campaigns.

. After five years with Marshall Field, Hockaday moved to New York. She spent two years as fashion editor at *Vogue*, then moved to *Harper's Bazaar* in 1936. She also worked at J. Walter Thompson for a short time. As a fashion coordinator in charge of photographic sittings, she canvassed the city in search of special props. Assignments ranged from locating an organ grinder with a monkey in the middle of winter to finding a special plate for a mustard advertisement. The experience was invaluable, as it gave her background on the operations within an advertising agency. "I looked back and wished I would have asked about how they handled billings of the agency" (Hockaday, interview with the author, 1992).

In 1941 Montgomery Ward challenged her to help it incorporate fashion into its mail-order catalog. She was awed by the ability of the mail-order house to sell products to consumers sight unseen, and she learned one of the most important lessons in advertising while working for Sewell Avery. She credited him with teaching her that "there are no hicks left in the country" (Bowen, p. 33).

During World War II Hockaday decided "selling fashion didn't seem quite right," so she started teaching social studies at Columbia University's Lincoln School. She also took courses at Columbia and earned a master's degree in education in 1947. However, it is not surprising that she returned to the publishing industry after the war. During high school and college she encouraged friends to write stories. She would type them up, create a layout, and print little booklets. One of her more notable was written while she was at Columbia. She wrote the *WAF—A Handbook for Air Force Women*, published in 1954.

After the war Curtis Publishing introduced *Holiday*, an experimental leisure magazine. Hockaday was hired as fashion editor. Her interest in architecture carried over—she filled the fashion pages with newly built contemporary houses. Upon locating an intriguing house, she would uncover the owner's name and write a letter requesting permission to use it in a fashion photograph. She delighted in exploring and said, "I think you can go anywhere if you have an idea" (Hockaday, 1992).

She felt the advertising industry was the right place to combine her skills in retailing, publishing, and merchandising, so she and Alvin Chereskin, a friend just back from the military, opened Hockaday Associates. They took over a one-chair barbershop at 58th Street and Second Avenue. With a few geraniums in the window and handmade office furniture, the agency opened in 1949. It later moved to 575 Madison Avenue.

At first things were relatively quiet because the agency did not have any clients. While waiting to sign on their first, she pursued publication of *What to Wear Where*, a handbook for travellers in the United States, the Caribbean, and Mexico. The concept of the pocket guide came about while she was at *Holiday* but was rejected by management. Her intuition told her it was a good idea, so she sent a fund-raising proposal, including a magazine mock-up, to top department stores. Once the handbook was in circulation, *Holiday* realized its appeal and leased it as a reader's service publication.

Hockaday felt that "advertising is not a message applied to the company body just to make it feel good. Advertising is more of a sauna. A combination of the shock of the hot box followed by a deep freeze plunge." Her agency's campaigns were far-reaching and evoked many responses, from letters to complaints to wagers. Unusual responses were welcomed, as Hockaday felt they were a measure of each campaign's success.

Capezio, the footwear manufacturer that billed itself as "the dancer's cobbler since 1887," signed on as Hockaday Associates' first client. However, the agency did not produce a Capezio advertisement for six years. Instead, it created "delightfully mad" mailing pieces and displays to position Capezio as a "state of mind."

The hero of the Capezio campaign was Polka Dotta, a playful character created by art director John Ward Emerson. Hockaday sent Emerson to finger-painting school for six-year-olds, and there he created the red, orange, and yellow character to illustrate the happy state of Capezio.

In 1956 Capezio ran its first advertising campaign. Polka Dotta asked consumers, "Are you mad enough for Capezio?" Even though the ads did not show the product, they inspired women to write in, exclaiming, "Yes, I'm mad enough for Capezio! Where do I buy them?" (Johnson, p. 50).

The company introduced new Capezio stockings with Polka Dotta dancing atop stems representing them. Here he inquired, "Are you mad enough to pick Capezio stemwear?" Buyers signed a pledge vowing never to use the word "stocking" in reference to Capezio ever again ("Capezio Extends 'Madness,' " p. 3). The campaign continued with a patriotic headline in 1961. Polka Dotta, in an Uncle Sam's hat, proclaimed "Hail Capezio! With liberty from conformity for all."

Hockaday's love for poetry, verse, and literature were evident in many of her campaigns, including Capezio. Polka Dotta introduced himself with a musical message: "Yippe-Yi, Yippe-Yo, I'm Polka Dotta of Capezio. Cobbler to dancer and necromancer keeper of the made and merriest feet."

Many in the advertising industry were less than enthusiastic about the productless ads. When criticized for producing Capezio's unusual ad campaign, Gertrude Koehring, copy chief at Hockaday Associates, responded, "But would Lord & Taylor have slathered 750 dressing rooms with a mundane ad? Would shoe stores across the country have plastered the poster on buses moving down Main St.? And would Capezio have become the No. 1 seller of shoes of this ilk?" (Koehring, p. 92).

Hockaday proclaimed, "We certainly owe [offbeat advertising] to our public. They have a right to expect some entertainment and excitement for their loyalties. [Nonconformist advertising] leads to the best selling climate of all—the state of mind" ("Offbeat Ad," p. 1). Her analysis of the offbeat approach was threefold:

"Is it beautiful, will it grow, and does it sell" (Hockaday, "Offbeat Copy," p. 148).

Hockaday cautioned advertisers not to expect a consumer to buy their products "just because you patterned her on the noodle machine." She said the consumer "is going to express her outrageous, provocative, irrational prerogative. Her privilege. She is going to make her own emotional connection between herself and your product" (Hockaday, "Consumer's Irrational Prerogative").

"Irrational prerogative" was Hockaday's term for a consumer's whim, her emotional excuse to buy. She said the secret to channeling this unpredictable intuitive impulse with advertising was to be human with "just enough imagination to want to do the unpredictable" (Hockaday, "Man's Marvelous").

Because of her insights into the consumer's psyche, visual bent, and ability to get straight to the point, Hockaday was dubbed a "copywriter extraordinaire." A copywriter remarked, "She begins a copy block at a point most of us never reach." One case in point was a letter to a grass seed grower that started with, "Goodness! I couldn't sleep this morning for hearing the grass growing" (Bowen, p. 30).

Instead of a warm fuzzy friend like Capezio's Polka Dotta, Hockaday gave Fuller fabrics, its second client, a chauffeur. He drew crowds seeking autographs as he drove the "richest fabric in town" around. He never needed to search for for an available automobile; corporate presidents offered the use of their treasured Stanley Steamers and Dusenbergs (Johnson, p. 50).

An early riser, Hockaday was known to work a 16-hour day, with lunch at her desk. She built her agency from a staff of 3 to about 40 people. Billings had increased to approximately $5 million when she retired in 1968. Because the agency was small, staff members pitched in on every account. Many agencies on Madison Avenue marvelled at how they worked together "almost as a ballet team—each one being violently individual" (Bowen, p. 38). Hockaday's niece Susan Hockaday Jones said, "I often felt that the whole agency spoke with her voice. Yet part of her ability as a director and manager was that she would draw out of people wonderful things" (interview with the author, 1993).

Connecticut was Hockaday's weekend destination. She entertained frequently at her little 1755 saltbox house in New Milford. "You were liable to meet anybody at her New Milford dinner parties," a friend recently remarked, "from a lady preacher to a gentleman farmer, from a local carpenter to a New Yorker writer." Hockaday loved to cook. The little house had a one-room addition "containing what could pass as the most modern and expensive kitchen in the United States" (Bowen, p. 30). She would awaken surprised weekend guests with magnificently prepared breakfast trays. For dinner parties, she carefully searched her vast collection of cookbooks for recipes that could be prepared early so as to be free to entertain.

Walking was a favorite activity because "it takes you out of the manufactured world, into the inspirational world of nature." She took long walks through the fields and woods at New Milford, developing what she referred to as "mushroom eyes'' (Schuyler, p. 19). ''The first time you look in the woods for mushrooms all you see are twigs and fallen leaves; after a while, though, you see all sorts of tiny mushrooms you never knew were there'' (Duhé, p. 38).

Several pieces of furniture manufactured by a Hockaday account, Dunbar, made the 90-mile trip to her retreat as well. A Dunbar sofa, covered in golden fabric, was the first piece taken to New Milford. Hockaday, her art director, and a photographer carried the piece across a pasture to a grassy hillside behind her house, watching every step for fresh manure. The resulting advertisement proclaimed, ''The long green hill of our desire.'' Outside the traditional living room setting, the sofa ''stood alone in the whole outdoors. To a land-hungry, house-hungry America, this picture looked good'' (Hockaday, ''Offbeat Copy,'' p. 49). ''It was the association of a dream and a hope with that product that would give you an emotional reward. We sold everything that way'' (Hockaday, 1992).

After the Hockaday campaign was launched in 1953, Dunbar chairs would turn up in the most unusual places—at the bus stop, perched in a tree, at a sewing circle, on the steel bars at a construction site. The Dunbar chair serving on the witness stand in a New Milford courtroom evoked an alarming response. Rumor had it that Hockaday was to be declared in contempt of court (Bowen, p. 30). The ads were placed in the *New Yorker*, the *New York Times*, *House Beautiful*, and *House and Garden*. This unconventional collection of furniture ads is also preserved in *The Dunbar Book of Contemporary Furniture*, a coffee table book published in 1956.

Hockaday's Dunbar ads created immediate response from the trade press, dealers, and consumers. An ad featuring four little girls playing musical Dunbar chairs created renewed interest in the regular dining room line. Within the first three years, sales for the entire line doubled.

The vast success of the Dunbar campaign inspired the rest of Madison Avenue to follow Hockaday outdoors. Central Park, the Bronx, and Greenwich became popular locations for photo shoots. One photographer, tired of hauling around heavy equipment, considered going on strike to encourage a move back to the studio. Another complained, ''It's gotten so that you can't even photograph a ham hock indoors'' (Bowen, p. 30).

Hockaday made headlines in 1959 when her agency won the women's sports-wear division of Jantzen in an agency competition including McCann-Erickson and Batten, Barton, Durstine and Osborn. The $1 million budget was significant for the agency that previously billed an annual total of $2.5 to $3 million. Copywriter Zimi Koehring and art director Alvin Chereskin created the ''Just wear a smile and a Jantzen'' campaign to position the swimwear line as fashionable among the beach crowd (Tyler, p. 37). In Hockaday fashion, the campaign theme was extended to include a color movie, ''Once Upon a Smile,'' for the sales drive and a giveaway record of Hockaday's ''Jantzen Smile Song'' (Russell, 1963). The company later introduced a bathing shoe with a spinoff of the successful slogan, ''Smile little shoe, you're a Jantzen.''

Hockaday said her agency attracted companies ready to take a leap. Success is "being on the edge of change and willing to grab it" (Hockaday, 1992). She encouraged moving decisions from bureaucracies to the "vigorous, perilous climate of a small performing group . . . the responsible connection between client and agency, product and people is crystal clear. No one is boxed in" (Hockaday, "Let's Put the Risk Back"). Clients who did not appreciate her unconventional style were resigned by the agency because rapport was a needed ingredient for success. She said, "If they don't believe in what you're trying, you really can't do much for them" (Johnson, p. 51).

When Austin, Nichols and Co. Inc. was ready to update the image of Grant's 8 Scotch whisky, it hired Hockaday Associates. Hockaday suggested that "Scotch, perhaps like an auto, was essentially a 'fashion' item that's 'in,' what the people in the know prefer, what they buy" (Russell, 1963). To position Grant's as the fashionable scotch, a handsome young writer sitting with his Olivetti typewriter asked, "As long as you're up, get me a Grant's." The Hockaday influence could be found in the choice of chairs used in the print advertisements. The young gentleman and his Olivetti moved from chair to chair, including an Eames chair, an old British officers' campaign chair, Edward Wormley's cane-back, Bruno Mathsson's laminated wood and canvas webbing chair, a Margherita chair, and Marcel Breuer's Vassily chair (McQuade, p. 68).

The Grant's slogans inspired many writers, cartoonists, TV commentators, columnists, government officials, comedians, and showmen. The slogan "invaded even the grave and stately editorial pages of the *New York Times*" (Lee, p. 27). The free publicity was worth well over a million dollars. Even after the Grant's campaign was retired, catch phrases remained. A 1980 *New York Times* headline stated, "As Long as Carter's Up He'll Get You a Grant" (Clark, p. A19).

Hockaday positioned B. H. Wragge dresses to the elite by suggesting that the wife of "J.P." an infamous banker robber baron, wore them. After the image was established, advertisements piqued interest by changing the initials in the ads. Consumers began to send guesses as to whose names were being featured.

A 1960 campaign for Crane stationery prompted people who never wrote letters to pick up a pen to complain, to commiserate, to defy, to heckle, and to gossip. One ad in particular elicited a protest in the *New Yorker* magazine. The ad featured a lonely brownstone sitting amid rubble. Agatha Winthrop, a fictional character created by copywriter Jean A. Zuver, wrote a letter with the following text: " . . . so you see, my dear sir, how much the brownstone means to me. Surely, your impending skyscraper might fit in quite nicely elsewhere. Cordially, Agatha Winthrop." The owner of the brownstone wrote that the house featured in the ad was his. He did not know who Agatha was, and she did not write a letter on "Crane's Greylawn paper with a tissue-lined envelope" at his house (Alden, p. L64).

Hockaday attributed her agency's success to "connecting the product with the idea of the product, the symbol of it." Many times the symbols were characters that personified the brand or the user of the product. Presented with the challenge to sell Adler socks during an era when sockless sneakers were fashionable. Hockaday hoped the "adorable but sort of terrible Clean White Sock" Adler girl conjured up the secretive "femmes fatales" images teenagers had of themselves ("Campaign with Sock," p. 18). A cartoon-like storyboard told of the "Life and High Times of the Arkin Girls." The dynamic duo wore Arkin's fashions on every adventure, whether it was buying a new car or table-hopping in New York's best restaurants. Expressive Theodora sold Tycora yarn to the trade, and a rascally little mouse sold Tycora men's hose.

Within an industry dominated by men, Hockaday felt that clients who could not work with women were missing out. She was "convinced that women have the edge on mere man in finding the extra plus that makes the ordinary extraordinary in advertising" (Schuyler, p. 17).

Stafford P. Osborn, the advertising manager of Reed and Barton's silver, once described his company's relationship with Hockaday as "somewhat like George Apley trotting off with Ethel Merman." The conservative Boston client appreciated the "tremendously spirited, bright, creative being in Hockaday Associates." Hockaday met the challenge of getting sterling silver noticed in an era of stainless steel and glass with, "You're just camping out till you come home to sterling," and "Don't let Daddy give you away till he gives you your sterling."

In 1962 Hockaday married L. Bancel LaFarge, keeping her maiden name professionally. LaFarge was a prominent architect who shared her love for the arts and structural design. He was the grandson of John LaFarge, the famous painter. After World War II he was decorated by numerous countries for supervising the return of artworks looted by the Nazis. Later, as an architect, he designed homes in the Beaux Arts, modified contemporary, and English country manor styles. Together they remodeled the Manhattan brownstone in the East 60s where they lived.

The couple retired in 1968. Reflecting upon her career, Hockaday said, "I really hit it at a very good time. We were doing original, way out things and it was the beginning of that era" (Hockaday, 1992). D. James DeWolfe, president of Hockaday Associates, and Joseph F. Giordano, executive vice president and creative director, purchased the agency and it became Hockaday DeWolfe Giordano. The Hockaday name was retired after the transition period.

Within the next two years, the couple moved to Nantucket, where they spent much of their time building and remodeling. They built a winter house out of the guest house for their summer home. "She was constantly renovating and building and constructing and adding on. All that energy that used to go into the advertising agency went into this environment," said her niece Susan Jones. "She was in love with architecture. She loved the way in which space, furnishings, activities, and light mixed together."

Later they moved to Pennswood Village in New Town, Pennsylvania. Never far from publishing, Hockaday wrote a clever booklet commemorating their first five years at the retirement community. Gardening and the design of gardens also captured Hockaday's attention, and she designed the communal gardens at Pennswood. LaFarge died in 1989, and Hockaday returned to Manhattan. Her one criterion for finding an apartment was that it be close to the New School for Social Research. She was writing a play and the concept evolved into a film, so she enrolled in several scriptwriting classes. She had hoped to direct the film she had been working on about retirement communities when she died on December 18, 1992.

Hockaday's approach to advertising was inventive and offbeat. Her saucy ad campaigns moved people to a "happy state [where] the consumer feels more chic, prouder, younger, more secure with the product, for no tangible reason that he or she can name" (Hockaday, "Offbeat Copy," p. 158).

FURTHER READING

Works by Hockaday

"The Consumer's Irrational Prerogative." Unpublished manuscript, 1964.
"Let's Put the Risk Back into Advertising." Speech presented at the AAAA western region's 28th annual meeting, November 1, 1965.
"Man's Marvelous Confounding Machine." Speech given to the Houston Advertising Club, February 21, 1964.
"Offbeat Copy." In *The Copywriter's Guide*, edited by Elbrun Rochford French. New York: Harper, 1958.

Works about Hockaday

Alden, Robert. "Advertising: Wraith's Plaint Brings Repercussions." *New York Times* (October 5, 1960): L64.
"Arkin Startles Fashion Ad Circles with Novel Cartoon Strip Campaign." *Advertising Age* (September 3, 1956): 27, 79.
"Campaign with Sock." *Printer's Ink* (May 25, 1962): 18–19.
"Capezio Extends 'Madness' with Stemwear Push." *Advertising Age* (December 9, 1957): 3, 36.
Clark, Timothy B. "As Long as Carter's Up He'll Get You a Grant." *New York Times* (April 21, 1980): A19.
Duhé, Camille. "Cultivate a Pair of 'Mushroom Eyes.' " *New York Herald Tribune* (May 26, 1963): 38.
Flint, Peter B. "L. B. LaFarge, 89, an Architect." *New York Times* (July 4, 1989): 2.
Johnson, Phylliss. "Some People Can't—Hockaday People Can—Create 'Mad,' Informal Ads." *Advertising Age* (March 11, 1957): 50–51.
Koehring, Gertrude. " 'Twice Slapped' by Woolf, Copy Chief Reports Loyal Following for Both Clients." *Advertising Age* (June 24, 1957): 92.
Lee, Henry. "Hockaday Associates—Margaret Hockaday." *Madison Avenue* (December 1963): 26–28, 32, 50.
McQuade, Walter. "So Long as You're Up, Pour Me Some Nostalgia." *Architectural Forum* (October 1965): 68.

"New Capezio Ads Hail 'Liberty from Conformity for All.' " *Advertising Age* (February 27, 1961): 1B.

"Offbeat Ad Can't Be Beat—If You Dig It: Hockaday." *Advertising Age* (November 25, 1957): 1, 8.

Russell, Alfred. "Margaret Hockaday Has Got the Creative Touch That Sells." *New York World Telegram* (April 8, 1963): 31.

Schuyler, Philip N. "When 2 + 2 = 5, Then Hockaday Is Adding." *Editor & Publisher* (October 6, 1962): 17, 19.

Tyler, William D. "Creativity May Raise Its Lovely Head." *Advertising Age* (December 28, 1959): 37.

NOTABLE CLIENTS/CAMPAIGNS

Adler socks

American Cancer Society

Arkin fashions

B. H. Wragge dresses

Capezio

Crane stationery

Dunbar furniture

Fuller fabrics

Grant's whisky

Health-Tex

Jantzen

Reed and Barton silver

Tycora yarn

CLAUDE C. HOPKINS
(August 27, 1866–September 21, 1932)

Tommy V. Smith

"C. C.," Claude Hopkins, the famous advertising man who merchandised automobiles, tires, foods, and patent medicines, rose from a copywriter's position to serve as both president and chairman of the board of Lord and Thomas in New York. He was the first advertising practitioner to put coupons in ads offering a free sample of the product advertised.

Claude C. Hopkins was born in 1866 in Spring Lake, Michigan. At age 17 he was a lay preacher, and by age 18 he was preaching in Chicago. However, Hopkins rebelled against his family's strict Baptist and Scotch Presbyterian brands of religion and entered Swenburg's Business College to study bookkeeping. His first job after school was with the Grand Rapids Felt Boot Company for $4.50 a week.

In the late 1890s Hopkins joined the Bissell Carpet Sweeper Company, and invented selling strategies that gave Bissell a virtual monopoly in the home carpet-cleaning business. He wrote advertising copy and sales promotional materials such as pamphlets and booklets. While at Bissell, Hopkins was supposedly the first advertising writer to promote a household appliance as a Christmas gift.

Hopkins then went to work as advertising manager for Swift at the Union Stockyards in Chicago. After successfully promoting Swift products, he decided to leave the meat packer because "about all my conceptions of selling in print were taboo." He believed that he "had to escape those restrictions to accomplish my ambitions" (Hopkins, *My Life*, p. 75). Seeking new challenges, he moved on to the agency side of advertising.

Hopkins did advertising for Dr. Shoop's Restorative patent medicine company while he was employed by the J. L. Stack advertising agency. Hopkins said of patent medicine later: "It's a class of advertising of which I no longer approve" (p. 76). While at Stack, he persuaded his agency to let him write the advertising copy not only for Dr. Shoop's, but for Montgomery Ward and Schlitz beer.

Hopkins had great success with Schlitz, which was fifth in the American market when he took on the account. First, he went to school to learn the science of brewing. This practice of learning about the client's business practices firsthand is still used today as a preliminary to writing advertising copy. He created a strong "reason-why" campaign. In one ad, Hopkins wrote that Schlitz cleaned its bottles with "live steam." Other brewers did the same, but Hopkins was the first to use the claim. In another ad, Hopkins stressed that Schlitz tapped 4,000-feet-deep artesian wells for its water, rather than Lake Michigan. Another ad stressed that the beer was aged for six months. Still another told consumers of the 1,200 experiments with the original mother yeast cell (all Schlitz beer was developed from the original cell) used to bring out the beer's utmost flavor.

For the campaign, Hopkins wrote the noted signature line, "The beer that made Milwaukee famous" (a slogan that is still used today, even though Stroh's bought Schlitz in 1981). In a few months, with the help of Hopkins's campaign, Schlitz moved from fifth in sales to a neck-and-neck battle with Budweiser for first. This campaign was also important because it gave Hopkins the basis for other campaigns to come. The campaign was based on Hopkins's style and research, which were much like the latter-day techniques Rosser Reeves called the "unique selling proposition" (Reeves, p. 47).

Hopkins furthered his advertising career by developing ads for Liquizone germicide. He helped sell it with the sampling method, a technique he applied to products ranging from tires to toothpaste.

At the age of 41, Hopkins was hired by Albert Lasker to write copy for Lord and Thomas in New York for $185,000 a year. Despite the huge salary, Hopkins was notoriously stingy, and he was said to have never paid more than $6 for a pair of shoes. His second wife, however, persuaded him to buy a yacht, employ gardeners on their estate, and purchase Louis XVI furniture.

Lasker, noted for his ability to recognize talent (he had hired John E. Kennedy earlier), was at times weary of creative talent like Hopkins. He once told a group of copywriters, "You think managing copywriters is a snap? You have taken some hairs out of me. I had a breakdown that kept me out five and one-half months. I couldn't talk for five minutes without starting to weep" (Lasker, 1963, p. 51). Hopkins did, however, help Lasker build Lord and Thomas. By 1927 it was just behind total billings leader J. Walter Thompson in the United States.

Under Lasker, Hopkins conceived the famous tag line, "The cereal shot from guns," for Quaker Oats' puffed wheat and puffed rice. Hopkins also created the copy and concepts that made many other products famous, including Palmolive, Goodyear, and six different automobiles (Chalmers, Hudson, Overland, Willys, Reo, and Studebaker).

Hopkins perceived the importance of brand images. He helped establish Pepsodent from its inception with a strong awareness appeal. This included using the following copy platform: "The natural idea in respect to a tooth paste is to make it a preventive. I resolved to advertise this tooth paste as a creator of beauty." He stressed, "Every advertising campaign depends on its psychology.

Success or failure is determined by the right or wrong appeal'' (Hopkins, *My Life*, p. 156).

Hopkins was a hard worker, seldom leaving his office before the early morning hours. Sunday was thought to be his favorite day of the week because he could work without interruption. The hard work did, however, take its toll, because Hopkins suffered from mental breakdowns and bouts with neurosis.

For clients, Hopkins invented ways to distribute new products such as test marketing and sampling by coupon. He is also credited with inventing copy research and being a practitioner of the experimental method of testing new ideas in search of better results.

Hopkins climbed the corporate ladder and served as president and then chairman of Lord and Thomas despite his demeanor and speech impediment. He was a shy, bespectacled, mustached, meek little man who spoke with a strong lisp. His nickname was "Thee-Thee," because that was how he pronounced his initials, "C. C." Hopkins stayed at Lord and Thomas for 18 years, retiring in 1922.

Hopkins's tenure at Lord and Thomas made him into a noted advertising practitioner, and his ideas were saved for posterity when he penned *Scientific Advertising* in 1923. According to David Ogilvy, quoted on its front cover, "Nobody should be allowed to have anything to do with advertising until he has read this book seven times. It changed the course of my life." In 1927 Hopkins wrote *My Life in Advertising*.

In *Scientific Advertising* Hopkins formed a basic doctrine for creativity in advertising which applies today. The following are some of his most enduring tenets:

1. The only purpose of advertising is to make sales (p. 220).
2. Ad writers abandon their parts. They forget they are salesmen and try to be performers. Instead of sales, they seek applause (p. 223).
3. Don't think of people in the mass (p. 224).
4. The advertising man studies the consumer. He tries to place himself in the position of the buyer (p. 225).
5. The purpose of a headline is to pick out people you can interest (p. 236).
6. Advertising without [strategy] preparation is like a waterfall going to waste (p. 281).
7. Almost any question can be answered, cheaply, quickly and finally, by a test campaign (p. 294).
8. Platitudes and generalities roll off the human understanding like water from a duck. They have no impression whatever. To say, "Best in the world, Lowest prices in existence," etc. are at best simply claiming the expected. But superlatives of that sort are usually damaging. They suggest looseness of expression, a tendency to exaggerate a carelessness of truth. They lead readers to discount all the statements that you make (p. 249).

Like John Powers before him, Hopkins was an advocate of straightforward, simple, brief copy with little or no illustrations. He used a direct, no-nonsense style, and he also believed that "frivolity has no place in advertising. Nor has humor" (Hopkins, *Scientific Advertising*, p. 182).

Hopkins did have his critics, however. For example, Raymond Rubicam believed that Hopkins had devoted his life to cheating the public. Theodore MacManus, father of the second school of creative thought in advertising, believed that Hopkins wrote down to people. In contrast, other advertising practitioners have been favorably compared and shown allegiance to him. Rosser Reeves even credited the creation of his "unique selling proposition" to ideas purported by Hopkins in *Scientific Advertising*.

Claude Hopkins was devoted to making advertising truthful and informative to consumers. To stress this point he prefaced *My Life in Advertising* in this way:

Naturally I learned more from experience than those who had a lesser chance. Now I want that experience, so far as possible, to help others avoid the same difficult climb. I set down these findings solely for the purpose of aiding others to start far up the heights I scaled. There is nothing to be gained for myself save that satisfaction. Had someone set down a record like this when I began I would have blessed him for it. Then, with the efforts I here describe, I might have attained some peaks in advertising beyond any of us now. May I live to see others do that. (p. 2)

Hopkins died in 1932 in Spring Lake, Michigan. He is a member of the Copywriters Hall of Fame, and in the April 19, 1976, commemorative edition of *Advertising Age*, he was named as one of the greats of advertising.

FURTHER READING

Works by Hopkins

My Life in Advertising. 1927. Reprint. Lincolnwood, IL: National Textbook, 1987.
Scientific Advertising. 1923. Reprint. Lincolnwood, IL: National Textbook, 1987.

Works about Hopkins

"Claude Hopkins, Former Lord and Thomas Head, Dies." *Advertising Age* (September 24, 1932): 1–2.
Fox, Stephen. *The Mirror Makers*. New York: Vintage, 1985.
Lasker, Albert D. *The Lasker Story as He Told It*. Chicago: Advertising Publications, 1963.
Reeves, R. *Reality in Advertising*. New York: Knopf, 1961.

NOTABLE CLIENTS/CAMPAIGNS

Bissell carpet sweepers
Goodyear

Liquizone germizide

Palmolive

Pepsodent

Quaker Oats

Schlitz beer

Studebaker

Van Camp's pork and beans

JOHN E. KENNEDY
(July 7, 1864–January 8, 1928)

Tommy V. Smith

John E. Kennedy was a highly creative individual with a flair for salesmanship. Using his "salesmanship in print" technique for writing copy, he helped clients sell goods to targeted people during a period in American history when the Industrial Revolution was occurring.

Kennedy was born in Canada on July 7, 1864. The tall, strapping, handsome ex-member of the Royal Canadian Mounted Police started his career in advertising as ad manager of the Hudson's Bay department store in Winnipeg in the 1890s. While at Hudson's Bay, he first wrote copy that was unspecific, literary, general, and lacking definite information. In other words, Kennedy first wrote image-style advertising.

After his stint at Hudson's Bay, Kennedy, like ad men who followed including David Ogilvy, passed through a series of jobs. Some of his adventures included serving as business manager for a Montreal newspaper, writing ads for the Regal Shoe Company in Boston, promoting his own clothing and shoe inventions, and writing copy for Postum. In 1903, shortly before Claude Hopkins helped create ads for Dr. Shoop in Racine, Wisconsin, Kennedy also wrote for the patent medicine manufacturer. However, his position among the elite of advertising was established when he traveled to Chicago.

In the spring of 1904, at the Chicago office of Lord and Thomas, Kennedy appeared seeking a position. Upon his arrival, a note was sent upstairs to upper management. Kennedy, who was waiting downstairs, had included in his note the following statement: "I can tell you what advertising is. I know you don't know. It will mean much to me to have you know what it is and it will mean much to you. If you wish to know what advertising is, send the word 'yes' down by the bell boy" (Lasker, p. 19). A junior member of the agency, Albert Lasker, received the caller. Lasker, who would be noted later for recognizing great creative talent, had been seeking a creative stance that he could incorporate into his agency's philosophy. When he and Kennedy finished talking hours later,

Lasker finally believed he had his definition. Kennedy was hired for $28,000 a year; within six months he was making $75,000.

Advertising, Kennedy told Lasker, is "salesmanship on paper" (p. 19). This idea was not new, but Kennedy was the first to make the principle work in an agency setting. He also did not take full credit for the radical idea. Charles Austin Bates, who wrote an advertising column in *Printer's Ink*, had promoted the idea in 1886. Bates wrote in the September 6, 1905, issue of *Printer's Ink* that "advertisements are printed salesmen."

Kennedy's primary stance in advertising was to write copy that, instead of merely attracting customers, would show in print the basics that a good salesman would say face to face. He did not want to employ general claims, puffery, or the image style in his writing.

Kennedy's secondary position in advertising was to apply salesmanship in print with "reason-why" copy (pp. 19–20). He believed that an ad should offer consumers a concrete reason why the product was worth purchasing. To Kennedy, a good ad was a rational, unadorned instrument of selling. True "reason-why" copy was logical, persuasive, easy to understand, and sought conviction from the average mind (Fox, p. 50).

To Kennedy's credit, like the incident in which he gave credit for the salesmanship-in-print idea to Bates, he did not claim to have invented the "reason-why" copy style also associated with his name. Kennedy, who wrote patent medicine ads, said that the truthful manufacturers used good "reason-why" principles in their advertisements.

Kennedy also knew how to target his client's consumers with language that could be understood. He warned, like Bates before him, against writing copy over the consumer's head. The average person, Kennedy believed, was not stupid but instead shrewd and open to appeals made by sensible arguments in advertisements (p. 50). The appropriate language premise is still used today by advertising copywriters.

Lasker, recognizing Kennedy's talent, hired him as Lord and Thomas's chief copywriter. Kennedy wrote ads using his salesmanship-in-print and "reason-why" copy style in a visually distinctive way with heavy italic type, frequent underlining, and capital letters in the headlines. He noted that advertising is more than simply keeping the product's or company's name before the people; instead, advertising should be like a salesman who provides information to help make the sale (p. 50). To Kennedy's credit, his "reason-why" style was soon imitated by other agencies. Lasker and Kennedy, however, did not mind the imitation.

To help bolster Lord and Thomas business, Kennedy's creative philosophy, entitled "You Must Do the Sum to Prove It," was put into a 1905 booklet penned by him, *The Book of Advertising Tests*. Lord and Thomas spent thousands of dollars to publicize Kennedy's thoughts in the work. Over 7,000 copies of Kennedy's doctrine were distributed, and hundreds of letters a week from inquiring manufacturers were received by the agency. The booklet, which was used by Lord and Thomas as the foundation of the agency's position and stance on advertising practices, was the forerunner of materials used by agencies today when they pitch new accounts.

The Lord and Thomas booklet also contained information that was the forerunner to copy testing methods. "Test your usual copy in one city against Lord and Thomas copy in another and compare the results" the pamphlet encouraged. This early method was expanded when Claude C. Hopkins later worked for Lord and Thomas.

Kennedy's salesmanship-in-print and "reason-why" copy was hard-hitting, serious, and businesslike. The technique was much like the "hit the mule over the head" technique espoused by Rosser Reeves with his "unique selling proposition" (Reeves, pp. 47–49, 54–59). With Kennedy's style guiding the agency, Lord and Thomas challenged J. Walter Thompson for the leading advertising agency position in America.

Kennedy did not accept authority well and wrote at his own whim, sometimes with deadlines quickly approaching. As with many creative people, he was highly protective of his work. Often, he would insist that his copy run exactly as written. He also worked into the late hours, sometimes at home. As is often the case even today, management was cautious and critical when working with a highly creative person like Kennedy. Lasker considered him a problem employee, despite the new business, fame, and agency position he helped bring to Lord and Thomas. Lasker said, "He could have been something; something was wrong that Kennedy didn't become one of the great men of the world—I mean of the commercial world" (Lasker, p. 21).

Kennedy did, however, study clients in depth. He would study the market, look at the manufacturing process, imagine the potential customers, interview customers (the forerunner to today's focus groups and individual intercept interviews), list negatives and positives associated with the product, and list selling points.

While at Lord and Thomas in late 1904, Kennedy wrote mail-order copy for the "1900" Washer Company of Binghamton, New York. In one famous ad, Kennedy used his salesmanship-in-print and "reason-why" techniques. To further Kennedy's creative style and to help prove that it worked for customers, Lord and Thomas ran Kennedy and non-Kennedy ads in an early testing experiment to prove that his copy was more effective. According to *Judicious Advertising*, an organ produced by Lord and Thomas and sent to clients and prospective clients, the Kennedy ad with the personalized "reason-why headline," "Let this machine do your washing free," was compared to the non-Kennedy ad with the headline, "Those chapped hands." The non-Kennedy ad measured 350 lines, cost $1,680, and produced 1,498 inquiries at a cost of $1.12 per inquiry. In contrast, the Kennedy ad in the same magazine occupied only 149 lines, cost $715, and in the first seven days pulled 1,547 inquiries at a cost of 47 cents each. "It will ultimately produce 3,000 inquiries at a cost of 24 cents each," the publication also noted.

In the copy block, Kennedy "sold" the customers on the idea of owning a washer. As was the case with many expensive products in 1904, the "1900" washing machine was sold on the installment plan: $2 down and $2 a week, for a total of $12. In his copy, Kennedy explained that a woman's time was worth at least $1.20 a day, because that was what she had to pay a laundress for the work. Because the machine did a day's work in half a day, it would save her 60 cents per day, according to Kennedy's copy.

After approximately two years, which was longer than his tenure at other jobs, Kennedy left Lord and Thomas. He briefly wrote copy for a Baltimore department store, returned to Lord and Thomas in 1911 for a shorter stay than his first, free-lanced, and sold real estate in Los Angeles.

Kennedy also became wealthy after his departure from Lord and Thomas. B. F. Goodrich tires paid him $20,000 a year for half his time to create advertising. In spite of his free-lancing, though, he began to lose contact with the advertising establishment. Albert Lasker, Kennedy's old boss, said that he even lost track of Kennedy. Kennedy died on January 8, 1928, in Michigan.

Kennedy, along with his successor at Lord and Thomas, Claude C. Hopkins, would together become known as the fathers of the first school of creative thought in advertising. They formulated basic beliefs still used today. A fitting tribute to Kennedy's importance comes from Lasker: "The history of advertising could never be written without first place in it being given to John E. Kennedy, for every copywriter and every advertiser throughout the length and breadth of this land is today being guided by the principles he laid down" (Lasker, p. 38).

After his death, Kennedy was elected to the Copywriters Hall of Fame.

FURTHER READING

Work by Kennedy

The Book of Advertising Tests. New York: Lord and Thomas, 1905.

Works about Kennedy

Fox, Stephen. *The Mirror Makers: A History of American Advertising and Its Creators.* New York: William Morrow, 1984.
Lasker, Albert D. *The Lasker Story . . . As He Told It.* Chicago: Advertising Publications, 1963.
Reeves, Rosser. *Reality in Advertising.* New York: Alfred A. Knopf, 1961.

NOTABLE CLIENTS/CAMPAIGNS

Armour Star ham

B. F. Goodrich

Dr. Shoop's patent medicine

Fairy soap
Force breakfast food
"1900" washers
Postum
Quaker Oats

ALBERT D. LASKER
(May 1, 1880–May 30, 1952)

Edd Applegate

Stephen Fox wrote, "If the early twentieth century in advertising history can be described in a phrase, it would be: The Age of Lasker" (p. 40). Indeed, Lasker worked for, then owned the Lord and Thomas agency for more than 40 years.

Albert D. Lasker was born on May 1, 1880, in Freiburg, Germany, to parents who were from Galveston, Texas. When Lasker was old enough to travel, his parents returned home.

Lasker's father, who was from Germany, moved to the United States when he was 16, and eventually settled in Galveston, where he became a successful businessman and president of several banks. Although he loved his children, he was not demonstrative, and Lasker grew up feeling that he had to prove himself to his father. This sense of insecurity plagued him for most of his life.

In elementary school Lasker was not a very good student, primarily because he was interested in other things—like earning money. At 12, he founded a four-page weekly newspaper, which he wrote, edited, and published. Titled the *Galveston Free Press*, the paper earned a profit of $15 a week for over a year. The paper contained aphorisms, a column on the theater, jokes, announcements, and a column by the editor. It also contained advertisements. Lasker sold the space, then created the advertisements for the various merchants.

In high school he edited the school magazine—one of the first in the country—and managed the football team. In addition, he worked as a bookkeeper for his father and as a journalist for the Galveston *Morning News*, for which he covered sports, politics, business, crime, and the theater. Upon his graduation in 1896, he worked full time for the paper. He left the *News* when he turned in a review of a play that he had not seen but knew by heart. The play had not been performed because the theater burned. Lasker realized he had made a serious mistake. Credibility was important to him. He moved to New Orleans and worked for the *Times-Democrat*. Then he moved to Dallas, where he worked for the Dallas *News*. When he returned to Galveston, his father suggested that he go into advertising. Lasker did not like advertising; he wanted to edit and publish a small newspaper in Texas. His father agreed to buy a small newspaper for Lasker on one condition: that he work in advertising for a brief period. Lasker agreed, but he never worked in journalism again.

Lasker's father knew D. M. Lord of the Lord and Thomas advertising agency in Chicago and asked him to give his son a job. Lasker left Texas in 1898; he was 18. He was given a salary of $10 a week and within a month lost $500 to a gambler. Of course, he did not have $500. He went to see Ambrose L. Thomas, another partner of the agency, and explained what had happened. According to Lasker,

I had never before sold anything to anybody, but I did a salesmanship job that day. I talked Mr. Thomas into advancing me $500—which was a fortune in those days. He went with me, and we settled with the gambler. Both he and I were sure that the gambler had cheated me, but the gambler had the due bill, and so we settled with him for $500. (Gunther, p. 39)

Lasker could not leave advertising as he had planned: He owed Thomas too much money. He worked first as an office boy. A year later, when a salesman quit, Lasker asked Thomas if he could take over the territory until a replacement was found. Thomas agreed. Lasker worked hard and within months had proved that he could interest clients. One, the Wilson Ear Drum Company, had been with the agency for several years. Lasker learned that the company's advertisements were considerably small and that the "common sense ear drums" were sold by mail. The agency received a 10 percent commission.

Lasker knew that he could improve the client's sales by improving the advertisements. He went to see George Wilson, the owner of the firm, and said:

Suppose Lord & Thomas could multiply your sales. That would be very good for you, and it would multiply our volume of business with you, because you would spend more money. We will write a new kind of copy for you, but you must pay us fifteen per cent commission on all ads that contain the new copy. If at the end of ninety days the results haven't increased, we'll give you back the money, and your account will still be on a ten per cent basis. But as an earnest that you are interested, you will have to pay me a fee of $500. (Lasker, "Personal Reminiscences," p. 78)

Lasker hired a friend, Eugene Katz, to write copy for several advertisements and had a photograph taken of the firm's artist cupping his ear. He showed the "Deafest deaf man you ever saw" advertisement to Wilson, who used it, and sales increased. The company had been spending $36,000 a year with Lord and Thomas. Within a year the company spent $240,000. Lord and Thomas earned $36,000 from this account instead of the usual $3,600. Lasker had succeeded. He employed this technique on several clients. Sometimes it worked, sometimes it failed.

Lasker studied copywriting and wondered what caused some advertisements to work and others to fail. He would learn part of the answer later.

In 1901 Lasker met Flora Warner. He was 21 and she was 22. Although he had paid his debt to Thomas and was earning $60 a week, he realized that he could not support two people. He met with Thomas and informed him that he wanted $5,000 a year. Thomas asked if he wanted more, but Lasker refused. He told Thomas that he eventually wanted to become a partner.

Lasker married Flora a year later. Their marriage brought them three children. However, Flora contracted typhoid fever and later phlebitis, becoming a semi-invalid who needed medical attention for most of her life.

Lasker's salary had doubled by 1903, when Lord retired. Lasker purchased Lord's share of the agency and was made a partner. He then had time to concentrate on copy.

In 1904, John E. Kennedy sent a note to Thomas claiming that if he desired to learn what advertising was he would tell him. Kennedy was waiting downstairs in a saloon. Thomas dismissed the note, but Lasker was curious. He met with Kennedy. Kennedy informed Lasker that advertising was "salesmanship in print." Whether Kennedy got this idea from Charles Austin Bates is anyone's guess, but Bates had said eight years earlier that "advertisements are printed salesmen" (Fox, p. 50). Lasker desired to learn more from Kennedy, so he hired him to write copy. From Kennedy, he learned that consumers needed a reason to buy something. If a reason could be given, and it was sound, consumers would react positively toward the product. Through Kennedy, Lord and Thomas pioneered "reason-why" advertising, which other agencies adopted.

Using this form of advertising, Kennedy and Lasker created a speculative campaign for a firm that manufactured washing machines. The company's most popular advertisement showed a woman chained to a washtub; the headline read, "Don't be chained to the washtub." Kennedy knew that the advertisement was negative and consequently would not work as well as an advertisement that was positive. He created one that showed a woman sitting in a chair, reading a book, and effortlessly turning the handle of a washtub. The headline read, "Let this machine do your washing free" (Gunther, p. 60). Lord and Thomas got the account.

Lasker helped publicize Kennedy's discovery in the agency's house organ, *Judicious Advertising*, and in other publications. As a result, Lord and Thomas acquired more clients, until it became the largest advertising agency in the United States. According to a writer for the trade journal *Advertising & Selling*, Kennedy's discovery became "the foundation stone of successful advertising" (Fox, p. 51). However, Kennedy owed much to Lasker. After all, he hired him.

Kennedy left Lord and Thomas within two years. According to Lasker, "Kennedy left us, for what reason I do not know, and I went on as best I could with the momentum of what I had learned from him and of what the others had learned. We were also learning lessons from the results we were getting" (Lasker, "Reminiscences," p. 79). Lasker was now in charge of editing all copy that was written for clients, even though he did not write any himself. He also introduced ideas used in campaigns.

Thomas died in 1906, and Lasker, together with Charles R. Erwin, purchased his share of the business. Erwin remained a partner until 1912, when he sold his share of the agency to Lasker.

Claude C. Hopkins, one of the best copywriters of his (or any) day, was hired by Lasker in 1908. Hopkins employed Kennedy's style but, unlike Kennedy, who worked slowly and methodically, he worked fast. As he put it, he put in two years' worth of work each year he worked. Lasker paid Hopkins well— more than he had paid Kennedy, which was $75,000 a year. Lasker knew that Hopkins was worth every penny. Hopkins enjoyed visiting clients to see how products were manufactured. He visited Quaker Oats and saw how the company produced rice and wheat cereal. From this visit, he changed the name of one of the company's products from Wheat Berries to Puffed Wheat, and employed the line, "Foods shot from guns." He liked mail-order advertising, in which he eventually specialized, and he was intrigued by testing. He employed testing with the use of coupons and samples in numerous campaigns. For another product, a toothpaste, he learned what plaque meant. The advertisement played up beautiful teeth and how the consumer could have them; in addition, the advertisement offered a sample of the product. By using coupons and samples he traced who responded, and this information benefited the client.

Lasker learned a great deal from Hopkins and vice versa. Indeed, Lasker was responsible for Americans' purchasing orange juice. Lord and Thomas got the Sunkist account, and Lasker learned that citrus growers in California produced so many oranges that they cut down orange trees to limit the supply. Lasker, primarily to stop the destruction of the trees, had campaigns created to encourage consumers not only to eat oranges but drink orange juice. Consumption of the product increased so much that trees were spared.

Lord and Thomas acquired the B. P. Johnson account in 1911. The company manufactured soap products, including Palmolive, which at the time enjoyed only modest sales. When Lasker and Hopkins learned that the product was colored green because of two ingredients, palm and olive oils, they realized an opportunity. They would play up its beauty instead of its power to clean. The campaign was tested, and within several years Palmolive was the leading brand.

Another client was the Van Camp Packing Company of Indianapolis, which manufactured canned foods, including pork and beans. Lasker and Hopkins employed tasting demonstrations, then created advertisements that asked consumers to compare Van Camp's pork and beans to other brands. Consumers reacted positively to the advertisements and purchased Van Camp's. For other Van Camp products, they used the power of suggestion and coupons.

Although Lasker preferred that the agency handle clients that manufactured convenience goods, the agency was also successful with automobiles and tires. For each client, Lasker relied on the "reason-why" style of copy. For Goodyear, Hopkins created the phrase, "No-rim-cut tires," which informed consumers that

Goodyear's straight-side tire, if punctured, would not cut the rim. Each campaign was successful because Hopkins focused on changes that occurred in the industry.

Lasker made mistakes, however. He loaned money to one automobile manufacturer and invested in another. The latter cost him almost $1 million. Perhaps he had been naive—after all, he was not that old—or he was merely caught up in the times. Industries were changing or growing, and new products were being produced by the hundreds. Lasker learned quickly from his mistakes.

Lord and Thomas continued to prosper. Indeed, billings rose from $3 million in 1906 to $6 million in 1912, the year Lasker became sole owner of the agency. It had branch offices in New York, Toronto, Paris, London, San Francisco, and Los Angeles, and Lasker made sure that each paid for itself. As Don Belding pointed out, "He demanded maximum results from his men . . . and he did not let the agency stray into extracurricular activity and gather a lot of appendages, or barnacles as he called them" (p. 67). In fact, Lasker fired a certain number of employees about every four years. Those who produced, however, like Hopkins, stayed with the agency until they left to pursue other opportunities or retired.

Before he became intrigued with politics in 1918, Lasker had contributed much to advertising. He had been partly responsible for the salesmanship-in-print and "reason-why" styles of copy. He had been partly responsible for "scientific" advertising. He helped train personnel, some of whom moved to other agencies or founded their own. He promoted ethical principles and was vehemently opposed to questionable or dishonest advertising.

For the next several years, Lasker worked first for the Republican Party, then for the presidential campaign of Warren G. Harding, and finally for the United States Shipping Board, which he directed. He did not like working for the government, though, so in 1923 he returned to Lord and Thomas, which Hopkins was directing. Lasker immediately learned that the agency was no longer the largest in the country. This bothered him. It had lost some clients because of internal problems. Personnel in certain offices argued over which style of advertising to employ. Other agencies, such as J. Walter Thompson, were filling advertisements with colorful art, different typefaces, and borders. Headlines, to Lasker, seemed to play a secondary instead of a primary role in these advertisements, and body copy was not necessarily "reason-why." Hopkins had created an art department, which Lasker opposed because of costs. Hopkins, who for years had gotten along well with Lasker, suddenly realized that there were too many differences between them. He retired from the agency in 1924 and started a copywriting service.

Lasker hired Ralph Sollitt, who had worked for the Shipping Board. Then he fired every employee in the New York office. In order to make Lord and Thomas the largest agency in the country, he had to take drastic steps. First, he talked at great length to his subordinates; he explained how Lord and Thomas was founded as well as what he had accomplished. In short, he presented his life to them and expressed the style of advertising Lord and Thomas should create.

Second, advertisements to attract new clients were created and published in trade journals. These were subtle compared to the advertisements for other agencies, but Lasker's style of advertising paid off.

One new account in the 1920s was the Kimberly-Clark product Kotex. The product had been on the market for some time, but sales were slow. Lasker believed that Kotex could be sold successfully if the correct strategy was implemented. The agency created factual advertisements, which were eventually accepted by certain magazines. A newspaper campaign was created to inform women that Kotex would be available in plain packages in certain stores. Another campaign was created to inform organizations, including school boards, how girls could be taught feminine hygiene. The campaigns worked, and sales increased dramatically.

In 1924 the agency got another Kimberly-Clark product, Kleenex. Lasker was not as interested in this product as he was in Kotex, however, because he believed it would never replace a handkerchief. Ernst Mahler, inventor of the product, made Lasker realize the importance of the product when he asked, "A. D., do you enjoy putting germs in your pocket?" (Gunther, p. 155). Lasker persuaded Mahler to increase the size of the product, and the agency staff created a different box. The advertisements sold Kleenex as the "handkerchief you can throw away."

Lord and Thomas earned millions from Kimberly-Clark. By the end of the 1920s, however, almost 60 percent of the agency's billings came from the American Tobacco account, Lucky Strike. As Lasker recalled,

The big cigarette companies had started some time between 1912 and 1923 to make the present type of cigarettes, domestic Virginia and Turkish tobaccos mixed. I think the first two to make it were Camels and Chesterfields. The American Tobacco Company was late in starting. Up to 1923, or even 1925, the American Tobacco Company must have had over fifty brands, and those fifty brands would be pushed and advertised—each with a little appropriation. (Lasker, "Personal Reminiscences," p. 82)

Lasker got the Lucky Strike account from George Washington Hill, the president of the company, and persuaded him to invest more money in advertising the Lucky Strike brand. By doing so the agency could conduct a national campaign. One day Lasker and Flora were eating at the Tip Top Inn. Because Flora had gained weight, she had been advised by her doctor to light a cigarette before each meal. When she did on this occasion, the proprietor informed Lasker that he could not allow a woman to smoke in public because it would offend others. This incident opened Lasker's eyes. Women were treated like second-class citizens. He realized that if he could change the public's attitude toward women smoking in public, he could capture another market. Lasker thought of women who lived in Europe; they smoked in public. Lasker thought of women who would capture the public's attention. He recalled,

It was very natural that my mind went to the opera stars, because at that time there were only one or two American stars, and the rest were foreign.

Then we developed what we called our "precious voice" campaign. As they were singers, they said, "My living is dependent on my being able to sing, and I protect my precious voice by smoking Lucky Strike." (p. 84)

The advertisements ran colorful photographs of stars in their costumes. The stars accepted the assignments without pay; to them, the publicity was more important.

Almost overnight women began to smoke in public. The taboo had been broken. Several months later several companies that manufactured candies placed advertisements informing consumers that smoking was not good for their health. Lasker reacted by seeing Hill and, together, they came up with the line, "Reach for a Lucky instead of a sweet," which was added to the "precious voice" advertisements.

Within a few years, Lucky Strike was America's best-selling cigarette, and Lord and Thomas earned millions from the account.

In 1926 Lord and Thomas became Lord and Thomas and Logan when Lasker asked Thomas F. Logan, who owned the Logan agency, to consolidate with Lord and Thomas. Through him Lord and Thomas acquired some excellent accounts, including the Radio Corporation of America (RCA), which was headed by David Sarnoff, whom Lasker had met. Sarnoff had been instrumental in creating the National Broadcasting Company (NBC) in 1926. As radio became popular, programs were created and eventually sponsored by advertisers. Lasker had an hour-long program created for one of his accounts, Palmolive. When this proved successful, he had programs created for other sponsors. By 1928, the year Logan died, Lord and Thomas was responsible for about 50 percent of the advertising placed with NBC. Other programs were created for other advertisers, including "Amos 'n' Andy" for Pepsodent, "The Story of Mary Marlin" for Kleenex, and "Information Please" for Lucky Strike. With the help of radio, Lasker's Lord and Thomas agency became the largest in the world in the 1930s.

While the country faced the Depression, Lord and Thomas continued, but at a slower pace. In 1931 Lasker cut salaries by 25 percent. Two years later he fired more than 50 employees. Was the Depression taking its toll on Lasker? Or was it age? Or was it worry?

In 1936 Flora died, and Albert Lasker was distraught. The love of his life had left him alone. Lasker was 56. What would he do? Advertising was no longer interesting to him. By 1938 he retired from Lord and Thomas, and Don Francisco succeeded him as president. Lasker resumed the position when Francisco left the agency to go to work for the government. Pearl Harbor had been bombed by the Japanese, and the country faced another world war.

During his brief retirement, however, Lasker met an actress, Doris Kenyon, in California, and, after a few weeks, married her. The marriage ended in divorce within a year.

In 1939 he met Mary Woodard Reinhardt in New York. They dated for over a year, then married. Lasker realized that Mary had interests similar to his, including politics, business, and religious beliefs. He realized, too, that Mary's love saved him from losing his mind. Two years later he informed her that he was going to retire from the agency. According to John Gunther, there were several reasons:

First, he was . . . tired. Second, he was bored. Third, the new generation of executives with whom he had to deal seemed far beneath his standards. Fourth, he wanted to devote himself to public service. Fifth, he felt that shortages induced by the war effort were bound to curtail sales of consumer goods, on which his business largely depended. Sixth, . . . Edward [his son] had made it clear that he did not wish to succeed his father in the business, and would not return to advertising after the war. (p. 269)

Lasker met with his three senior executives, Emerson Foote, Fairfax Cone, and Don Belding, and the Lord and Thomas agency soon became Foote, Cone, and Belding. Lasker, of course, informed the agency's major clients of his decision and persuaded most to stay with the new company.

Lord and Thomas as an agency died on December 30, 1942. Albert Lasker, who believed that a good advertisement must have a central idea, news, and enough creativity to make the central idea sing, died of cancer ten years later. He was 72.

FURTHER READING

Works by Lasker

The Lasker Story . . . As He Told It. Chicago: Advertising Publications, 1963.
"The Personal Reminiscences of Albert Lasker." *American Heritage* (December 1954): 74–84.
"Reminiscences." Columbia Oral History Collection, 1949–1950.

Works about Lasker

Belding, Don. "End of an Era in Advertising." *Advertising Agency and Advertising & Selling* (July 1952): 66–67, 116–18.
Cone, Fairfax M. *With All Its Faults.* Boston: Little, Brown, 1969.
Fox, Stephen. *The Mirror Makers: A History of American Advertising and Its Creators.* New York: William Morrow, 1984.
Gunther, John. *Taken at the Flood: The Story of Albert D. Lasker.* New York: Harper, 1960.
Hopkins, Claude C. *My Life in Advertising.* 1927. Reprint. Lincolnwood, IL: National Textbook Company, 1987.
"Indelible Mark on Advertising Left by Lasker, Agency Pioneer." *Advertising Age* (June 9, 1952): 1, 67, 70–71.

NOTABLE CLIENTS/CAMPAIGNS

"1900" washers (1900s)

Wilson ear drums (1900s)

B. P. Johnson soap (1910s)

Goodyear (1910s)

Pepsodent (1910s)

Quaker Oats (1910s)

Sunkist (1910s)

Van Camp Packing (1910s)

American Tobacco (1920s)

Kimberly-Clark (1920s)

RCA (1920s)

MARY GEORGENE BERG WELLS LAWRENCE
(May 25, 1928–   )

Deborah K. Morrison

Born to a generation of women who eventually sought to change the landscape of American culture, Mary Wells came of age at a time and place when she could also reshape the world of American advertising. Though her talent for conceptualizing and articulating new ideas brought her fame and subsequent fortune, she was most often described by virtue of her gender: a woman playing in a man's world, a knockout with a celebrity attraction for publicity and magazine photographers, "that little blonde bomber" who pioneered a new spirit for the industry. The agency she founded in 1966—Wells, Rich, Greene—continues to be savvy, much the way its founder was described during her heyday in the 1960s and 1970s, even though she relinquished her role as president in 1990. Controversy over her paradoxical role as a powerful woman who failed to hire other women for top management in her agency had some effect on her legacy as the brains behind the hottest shop of the creative revolution.

Mary Georgene Berg was born in Youngstown, Ohio, in 1928, the only child of Waldemar and Violet Berg. Her early years were full of dancing, drama, and theatrical elocution lessons, a remedy for the extreme shyness her mother saw in the girl and as an escape route from the routine steelworker marriages set for young women of that region in that era. The plan worked well; at 17 she left for New York with its promise of show business and the theater. She enrolled in the Neighborhood Playhouse School of the Theater, where she counted among her classmates the actors Richard Boone and Darren McGavin. After two years she left for Pittsburgh to attend the Carnegie Institute of Technology, where she met and married Bert Wells, an industrial design student. She was 17 with short brown hair, nicknamed "Bunny," and possessed a strong sense of the dramatic to guide her future.

Wells's writing career began in 1951 as an advertising writer for McCelvey's department store in Youngstown. In 1952 she was back in New York and, for a year, was the fashion advertising manager of Macy's. The next year she was offered a position as writer and copy group head at McCann-Erickson, where she remained for three years. During that time she worked with Phyllis Robinson (later a member of the Copywriter's Hall of Fame), who, Wells said, "is the most open minded, is the most fair and good. I would buy a used car from Phyllis Robinson" (*Advertising Age*, June 2, 1969), p. 74.

Wells's leap into the limelight began with her move to Doyle Dane Bernbach, as associate copy chief and head of new-products development during the years Bill Bernbach and his creative vision began to change the world of advertising. "A fantastic education," she said of that period. "Everyone cared only about how effective an ad was. No one drank. There were no aspiring novelists hiding out. No one did anything but work" (*Advertising Age*, April 5, 1971, pp. 57, 58). For seven years Wells worked on the DDB accounts (the resulting work still shows up in advertising awards annuals as being representative of the best advertising has to offer); Volkswagen and Avis Rent-a-Car campaigns both bore her mark. These years offered her a chance at honing skills for creating break-through work, and refined her instinct for understanding maximum creative drive as a key to great advertising. Bill Bernbach told her, "You're not much of a writer, but your thinking's pretty good." Ned Doyle on Mary Wells: "You're not much of a thinker, but your writing's pretty good" (*Advertising Age*, June 2, 1969, p. 74). No matter the perspective, Wells had the instincts of an aggressive and highly creative advertiser.

As a result of working with these creative leaders, she said, she learned to listen. Yet there was not much to teach Mary Wells. In 1964 she was 35 years old, now dramatically blond (and called Mary by her colleagues), with a flair for clothes and a personal style that made stuffy client meetings come to a halt. She was also the lauded copy chief and vice president of an agency making its mark for intelligent and aggressive work, earning $40,000 a year at a time when the average salary in the United States for men was less than $10,000. Mary Wells had arrived.

In 1964 Jack Tinker was hired by Marion Harper's Interpublic agency to form an advertising think tank, an idea factory of bright creatives who would conceptualize strategy and execution, then pass the ideas on to a larger shop for traditional production. Jack Tinker and Partners, housed in a penthouse off Madison Avenue, hired Mary Wells for a salary of $60,000, where she and a handful of other people made this new concept in advertising productivity come to life. Their first client was a small product from Miles Laboratories with a reputation for advertising featuring a pubescent spokescharacter. Wells, along with Richard Rich and Stewart Greene, offered the country the "No matter what shape your stomach's in" television vignettes that gave Alka-Seltzer a personality and direction. The work was praised with industry creative awards and popular recognition; the TV jingle became a hit record on the *Billboard* charts. The concept of a highly creative message as highly effective advertising was born.

The second client for Tinker's shop was Braniff International, a small, relatively unknown airline with a lackluster reputation, but with the financial backing to make a mark in the aviation industry. With Rich and Greene working again as her creative partners, Wells reinforced the idea of this new fully conceptual approach to advertising being the answer to Braniff's needs. Not only was there a new style of communication in store for the airline, but the agency submitted a new style of operation for corporate consideration. The advertising would coincide with restyled interiors in all the planes, new nontraditional uniforms for stewardesses, and a retooled image that suggested a fun, sexy, modern approach to air travel. Harding Lawrence, president of Braniff, agreed to the radical ideas, and later gave credit to the repositioning of the company's image and amazing success, citing "The end of the plain plane" concept and its accompanying sexy "air strip" philosophy of stewardesses changing their Pucci uniforms in flight as the basis for revitalization.

In 1966, with two major advertising successes to her credit, Wells was given a raise to $80,000 (she once said that Tinker created an atmosphere where people worked their hearts out, not their guts, and got paid well to do it) and a request that she sign a long-term contract with Tinker. Explaining that the overnight success of Tinker and Partners and the subsequent pressure to perform the next time in equal measure constricted her ability to experiment in suitably creative fashion, Wells resigned her position. Other explanations for her resignation show a power struggle: When Tinker fell ill with a heart attack, Wells expected to become president of the shop. Two partners, Herta Herzog and Myron Mc-Donald, threatened to resign rather than work for Wells; McDonald was named president. After Wells's resignation, Richard Rich and Stewart Greene quit also, stating that their partnership with Wells was what created the magic of their successful campaigns. After deliberation on the many lucrative offers from other agencies, the three ventured into what most advertising creatives dream of doing to assure the creative fires will be full flame; they opted to open their own agency. On April 4, 1966, Wells, Rich, Greene (WRG) opened in temporary offices in the Gotham Hotel on Fifth Avenue, with Mary Wells's mother answering the telephone and new clients ready for partnership with the upstart agency.

The first client to rally around Wells and her staff was the successful Braniff International, with Harding Lawrence leading the foray of investors eager to support a bound-for-glory new venture. Quick to follow on the client roster were Benson and Hedges 100s, Persona razor blades, the Burma line of men's toiletries, Utica Club beer, and La Rosa spaghetti. After six months in business, WRG was billing $30 million and received much comment in trade publications and trendy New York magazines.

The advertising became almost secondary to the celebrity Mary Wells had become, the brainy blond with the tough-as-nails professionalism making her mark among the males of advertising's finest agencies. *Fortune* saw her as a "striking well-turned-out blonde who combines the cool sophistication envied by other women as 'the New York look' with the subtle allure men find difficult to describe without allusions to sports cars" ("On Lovable Madison Avenue,"

p. 143). A detached, confident, and aggressive air—the velvet glove style of management, it was said—gave support to her reputation as a formidable leader, and led more clients to the doors of the most phenomenally successful young agency in history.

Her personal life changed as well as a result of her rise in professional status. In 1965 she was divorced from Bert Wells, then an art director at Ogilvy and Mather, and, in November 1967, married the man whose company she had turned around, Harding Lawrence of Braniff. The news of Mary Wells's marriage became fodder for gossip columns as well as the pages of trade magazines. The hype was heavy: a fairy-tale fantasy with an edge, since the princess in this story was not only blond and sexy, she could slay the dragon as well—if not better—than any man in the advertising kingdom.

Indeed, in a front page article, *Advertising Age* (July 1, 1968) suggested the saga of Mary Wells mixed with music and high-kicking dancers might well make a Broadway play, calling her the "phenomenon of Madison Avenue" and the "white goddess of advertising." The direction of her leadership caused some of this comment; WRG was investing 50 percent of its money on creative talent at a time when most agencies were spending 20 to 30 percent, a tactic she saw as making a statement about the type of advertising she wanted to create. "We invested in a number of really superior creative people in the beginning, when we really didn't need them, and we were criticized for elevating the scale of creative salaries but it's what we believe in." A greater part of her legacy than the personal style and "golden girl" rhetoric, her emphasis on the creative function as the lifeblood of the "hot shop" began a trend that lasted over the next 25 years for smaller shops to open with cutting-edge writing and art direction and make their mark. Her clients respected, even flocked to this philosophy, and her reputation for commanding the client/agency relationship was shown in part by her aggressive nature with those people for whom she worked. "There are two things we want to know from a perspective client. Will he allow us to do great advertising? Is the product a good one? It doesn't have to be superior, but hopefully, it will be unique. And we want to know management's attitudes about things in general and about us in particular (*Advertising Age*, July 1, 1968, p. 47).

Wells's long tenure as chairman and president of WRG proved to be lucrative both financially and as symbol of her power in the industry. In 1969 she was making $225,000 a year, the highest paid woman in the world. That year, she was inducted into the Copywriters Hall of Fame and lauded as advertising's most widely publicized "symbol of glamor—success—wealth—brains—and—beauty" (*Advertising Age*, June 2, 1969, p. 1). At 40, she was the youngest member ever of the Hall of Fame and quite possibly the inductee with the most presence at the podium. "I'm in excellent health," she told the audience, "and I've got impact you haven't felt yet. So don't relax" (*Advertising Age*, June 2, 1969, p. 1). It was a whirlwind of public recognition during this time: She was named one of the Ten Most Successful Women in American Business, Marketing Stateswoman of the Year, one of the Ten Women with the Most Charm in America, and, in 1971, Advertising Woman of the Year. She was also granted an honorary doctor of law degree from Carnegie-Mellon University in Pittsburgh.

By 1971, five years after its opening, WRG had massed billings of $100 million, with clients including TWA (the Braniff account was resigned a year after WRG's start-up), Alka-Seltzer, Benson and Hedges 100s, Philip Morris, Procter and Gamble, and American Motors. When the American Motors account was wrested away from neighboring agency Geyer Morey Ballard after a 28-year history, a banner was hung outside the GMB office: "Hello Mary. The Now Car has the Now Agency." Even her rivals agreed that Mary Wells's agency was the most exciting in town.

In the late 1960s and early 1970s, as the women's movement grew and filtered into the advertising agency culture, Wells became the center of some controversy. At WRG she surrounded herself with men, excepting those secretaries and personal assistants on whom she counted for organizing her life and social schedule, and moved no women into upper management positions. She expressed her no-nonsense philosophy concerning women in the workplace in strong terms: "The idea about American men trying to keep women down in business is hogwash. I've never been discriminated against in my life, and I think the women who have would have experienced it anyway—no matter if they were men or cows or what have you" (*Advertising Age*, April 17, 1967, p. 86).

Yet others, especially women in the industry, began to take issue with her stance. Writer Amelia Bassin, accepting an award in 1970 as Advertising Woman of the Year from the American Advertising Federation, called Wells to task. Mary Wells, according to Bassin, was "the perfect example of the kind of woman who should be leading women," yet she offered few opinions on the women's movement or the advertising industry's treatment of women. "I can well believe Miss Mary never got discriminated against. There is no privileged class in the world to compare with beautiful women. . . . It's difficult to tell if success has spoiled Mary Wells; but, boy, is she ever spoiling success!" (*Advertising Age*, December 7, 1970, pp. 48, 50).

Wells relied upon her reputation as a "brainy blond bombshell" to work in her favor, saying, "It was more fun when they [the clients] thought I was a sexy blond" (*Advertising Age*, May 3, 1976, p. 24). She continued in paradoxical manner, arming herself with the strength of a woman who had been in command for years and who was herself responsible for that climb. "I'm not a feminist, not in the serious activist sense, but I have very strong feminist feelings about things like the Equal Rights Amendment and salaries. I feel strongly about the unfairness that exists. A lot is changing, though; a lot more women are coming into this business and they are very good, very useful." Yet, at her agency, she promoted no women to the board of directors or to top management and associated mainly with men away from work as well.

During the 1970s she was appointed to some political committees—Vice

President Rockefeller's Commission on Critical Choices in America and President Ford's Council on Inflation—and served on corporate boards for some of her agency's clients, such as Ralston-Purina. She continued her involvement with presenting ideas to clients, and was still considered the front person for her agency's success and image. In the 1980s Wells began to spend more time at her expensive homes spread across the world—Arizona, Dallas, Acapulco, and the French Riviera—but still managed daily contact with her office and freely offered her opinion on the state of creative work. "How puny our courage," she said of advertising as a whole, "and how poor our spirit. What a bore advertising is becoming" (*Advertising Age*, March 22, 1976, p. 17). What she wanted for her agency and for her industry were hot, fresh ideas that people would notice. Conservative times, conservative ideas were not for Mary Wells.

In 1990, as she announced her retirement as president of WRG at the age of 62, Wells finished her tenure as leader of the then 15th largest United States–based agency. She was making over $500,000 per year and owned approximately 85 percent of the company. (The agency went public in 1967—"a big waste of time," said Wells—and then went private again in 1977.) Much of her time is now spent at her home on the French Riviera, though she retains the title of chairman and founder of the company she forged.

Author's Note: After her marriage to Harding Lawrence in 1967, Wells began using his name professionally as well as personally. "Mary Wells" is used throughout this chapter for continuity and because biographers, industry insiders, and some reference materials continue to refer to her in that manner.

FURTHER READING

Works about Wells

"The Best Paid Woman in America: Mary Wells Lawrence." *Vogue* (February 1972): 42.

Della Femina, Jerry. *From Those Wonderful Folks Who Brought You Pearl Harbor*. New York: Simon and Schuster, 1970.

Fox, Stephen. *The Image Makers: A History of American Advertising and Its Creators*. New York: William Morrow, 1984.

"The Girl Who Painted the Planes." *Business Week* (January 21, 1967): 106.

"Guard Changes at Era's Hot Shop: Mary Wells Starred in the Golden Years of U.S. Advertising." *Advertising Age* (April 23, 1990): 61.

Lois, George. *George, Be Careful*. New York: Saturday Review Press, 1972.

"On Lovable Madison Avenue with Mary, Dick, and Stew." *Fortune* (August 1966): 142.

"Sledgehammer Sell." *Life* (October 27, 1967): 101–102, 104, 106.

Many articles about Wells appeared in *Advertising Age, Business Week, Newsweek*, the *New York Times, and Time* from 1965 to 1990.

NOTABLE CLIENTS/CAMPAIGNS

Alka-Seltzer
American Motors
Benson and Hedges
Braniff International
Philip Morris
TWA

THEODORE F. MACMANUS
(November 29, 1872–September 12, 1940)

Tommy V. Smith

Theodore MacManus, a prime mover in the success of many products during his long advertising career, came to be well-known for his expertise in automotive merchandising, first as the advertising manager for the Yale automobile, thereafter for leading manufacturers including Ford, Packard, General Motors, and Chrysler.

Theodore Francis MacManus was born in Buffalo, New York, in 1872. Early in his childhood, his working-class Irish-Catholic family moved to Toledo, Ohio. While in Toledo, MacManus became bored with formal education and left school to become an office boy at Standard Oil in Cleveland. Soon dissatisfied at Standard Oil because of the "Teapot Dome" scandal, at age 16 he became a reporter for and then managing editor of a Toledo newspaper.

After leaving the editor's position, MacManus entered advertising for the first time, with a department store in Pittsburgh. Bored with retail, MacManus did sales management for coffee and wholesale grocery firms. It is interesting to note that MacManus, like other advertising practitioners of the day and many to follow, held a wide array of jobs. Anxious to return to advertising, he left the sales profession to write advertising copy for the automobile industry in Detroit, for such makes as Chrysler, Hupmobile, Dodge, Packard, Apperson, and Stearns-Knight.

It was, however, his work for General Motors that propelled him into copywriting stardom. As the star copywriter, MacManus produced ads for products specifically targeted to a particular kind of audience. He was assigned to write for high-ticket luxury cars such as Buick and Cadillac. Buick and especially Cadillac were then targeted to elite customers. The cars were expensive, top-of-the line items that wealthy consumers bought after careful planning and comparison. MacManus did not try to persuade the consumers to buy the product on impulse with hard-sell, heavy-handed tactics. Instead, he wrote copy to build a durable image of reliability and quality in hopes that the consumer could be finessed into buying. Thus, soft-sell and image-style advertising was Mac-Manus's forte.

MacManus disliked campaigns and advertising aimed at fast sales. He said in 1910 that companies, through advertising claims prepared and placed by hard-sell agencies, were purporting lofty reputations intended to increase sales on a short-term-only basis (Fox, p. 71). He believed that advertising should be used to build long-term relationships a step at a time.

MacManus's image-style advertising copy relied on a slow accumulation of favorable impressions built by truthful, meaningful, sensory-driven, esoteric, and mentally stimulating statements. He said that his copy was both suggestive and honest in tone. MacManus also believed that sensory persuasion techniques were very appropriate (p. 73). With these thoughts in mind, MacManus became the father of the second school of creative thought in advertising.

This second school was in direct contrast to John E. Kennedy's and Claude C. Hopkins's first school of creative thought in advertising. Instead of using "reason-why" and "scientific" tactics, MacManus believed that advertising was more effective when a copywriter's imagination was used (Hopkins, p. 1). In turn, he believed that the consumer's imagination could be stimulated by reading and digesting long copy blocks and provocative headlines. According to Fox, "Hopkins wrote down to the public, MacManus up to it" (p. 73).

MacManus did not believe in testing advertising on consumers as Kennedy and Hopkins did. Instead, he believed he knew what consumers intuitively wanted and then wrote what he himself would like to read in ads for his products.

MacManus was the first advertising practitioner to believe that appeals are tools that should be used in all creative copy. A behaviorist/psychologist and pioneer advertising researcher named John Watson, who worked for J. Walter Thompson, would later confirm that psychological appeals are useful in copy-writing. MacManus stated that appeals aimed toward the virtuous character of the consumer were needed in advertising. He also stated that all consumers were searching for truth and goodness in advertising (p. 73).

MacManus's second school of creative thought in advertising, with image and soft-sell techniques, was best applied to large, expensive, durable items with prestige associations. The items suited for soft sell were bought infrequently and not on impulse. MacManus believed that his copy gave consumers friendly, favorable, long-term impressions (p. 73). In other words, with the help of MacManus's long copy advertising being recalled by the consumer, the product would sell itself in the long term. David Ogilvy would also later believe that long copy was an appropriate tool.

The most famous MacManus ad was for Cadillac. The thought-provoking, black-and-white print ad carried the headline, "The penalty of leadership." It appeared nationally only one time, in the January 2, 1915, issue of the *Saturday Evening Post*. This technique of using the impact of one-time national exposure was pioneered by MacManus. Since 1915 this technique has been used by others.

For example, Apple introduced its Macintosh computer with one TV commercial during the 1984 Super Bowl game.

The "Penalty" ad was formal, dignified, and boastful, and had snob appeal. The copy alluded to the fact that Cadillac had used research and development to help establish its superiority to all other motorcars. With the help of MacManus's ads, Cadillac acquired a reputation for reliability and high quality. Cadillac then, as now, was General Motors' flagship brand. General Motors used Cadillac then, as it still does today, to introduce innovations that usually filter down to its other divisions.

At the time, Cadillac had built its prestige and high-quality reputation on a four-cylinder engine. Packard, Cadillac's main rival, introduced a model with six cylinders. Cadillac was thus trailing Packard in innovation, and consumers left for its main competitor. In the fall of 1914, however, Cadillac introduced a revolutionary V–8, but it had mechanical problems. In response, Packard announced that Cadillac was having safety problems and again trailing in quality. With this in mind, MacManus had to help alleviate the crisis situation facing Cadillac with an ad. The following is that copy block that appeared in the January 2, 1915, issue of the *Saturday Evening Post*:

In every field of human endeavor, he that is first must perpetually live in the white light of publicity. Whether the leadership be vested in a man or in a manufactured product, emulation and envy are ever at work. In art, in literature, in music, in industry, the reward and the punishment are always the same. The reward is widespread recognition; the punishment, fierce denial and detraction. When a man's work becomes a standard for the whole world, it also becomes a target for the shafts of the envious few. If his work be merely mediocre, he will be left severely alone—if he achieves a masterpiece, it will set a million tongues a-wagging. Jealousy does not protrude its forked tongue at the artist who produces a commonplace painting. Whatsoever you write, or paint, or play, or sing, or build, no one will strive to surpass or to slander you unless your work be stamped with the seal of genius. Long, long after a great work or a good work has been done, those who are disappointed or envious, continue to cry out that it cannot be done. Spiteful little voices in the domain of art were raised against our own Whistler as a mountebank, long after the big would had acclaimed him its greatest artistic genius. Multitudes flocked to Bayreuth to worship at the musical shrine of Wagner, while the little group of those whom he had dethroned and displaced argued angrily that he was no musician at all. The little world continued to protest that Fulton could never build a steamboat, while the big world flocked to the river banks to see his boat steam by. The leader is assailed because he is a leader, and the effort to equal him is merely added proof of that leadership. Failing to equal or to excel, the follower seeks to depreciate and to destroy—but only confirms once more the superiority of that which he strives to supplant. There is nothing new in this. It is as old as the world and as old as the human passions—envy, fear, greed, ambition, and the desire to surpass. And it all avails nothing. If the leader truly leads, he remains—the leader. Master-poet, master-painter, master-workman, each in his turn is assailed, and each holds his laurels through the ages. That which is good or great makes itself known, no matter how loud the clamor of denial. That which deserves to live—lives.

Cadillac's wealthy, well-read consumers admired, digested, and identified with the "Penalty" ad, even though the product was not mentioned in the copy. In fact, the only association with Cadillac in the ad was the logo in a circle in the upper right-hand corner. No illustration was present and plenty of white space was used. A slogan under the Cadillac name but still within the circle read, "Standard of the world."

After the ad ran, MacManus was criticized by his colleagues for writing fluff. However, in spite of the criticism, the ad was a success. Cadillac received requests for reprints, and salesmen used copies to give to buyers. Along with the requests for the ad, Cadillac's sales rebounded. Reprints of the ad were tacked on walls, included in sales manuals, and often cited in sales meetings. Cadillac even used the ad again years later, and parts were used in local newspaper campaigns.

MacManus commented that the ad was successful because the readers considered themselves leaders and that they secretly suspected that they were the victims of enmity and injustice (Fox, p. 74). Thirty years after the ad first appeared, *Printer's Ink* asked its readers: What is the greatest advertisement of all time? The "Penalty" ad won overwhelmingly.

Riding the success of the "Penalty" ad, MacManus continued to climb in the advertising profession. After many years with General Motors, he entered the agency side of the business. By 1927 he was head of the ninth largest agency in the United States, Theodore F. MacManus, later renamed D'Arcy, MacManus and Masius.

MacManus was not fond of the advertising profession. He believed that many advertisers and advertising agents were unscrupulous. Hard-sell advertising, MacManus said, assumed that consumers were rapidly lapsing into a state of imbecility (p. 74). The Depression brought exaggerated claims by some manufacturers and advertising agents, just when advertising was trying to distance itself from the untruthful patent medicine advertising of the late 1800s. MacManus at times wanted to leave advertising but felt he could not escape its iron hold (p. 74).

MacManus's creative platform relied on earnest, solid, dignified, reputation-building techniques. In other words, he produced an image style of advertising resembling that of Elmo Calkens. To MacManus, image was paramount in advertising, and the only way to penetrate the subconscious of the reader was through a slow accumulation of positive images. MacManus, who died in 1940 near Sudbury, Ontario, was the leading advocate of advertising by suggestion during his career, and his second school of creative thought in advertising lives on today.

FURTHER READING

Works by MacManus

Men, Money and Motors. New York: Harper, 1929.
The Sword-Arm of Business. New York: Devin-Adair, 1927.

Works about MacManus

Fox, Stephen. *The Mirror Makers: A History of American Advertising and Its Creators*.
     New York: William Morrow, 1984.
Hopkins, Claude C. *Scientific Advertising*. 1923. Reprint. Lincolnwood, IL: National
     Textbook, 1987.
"Theodore MacManus Dies Suddenly in Summer Home." *Advertising Age* (September
     16, 1940): 41.

NOTABLE CLIENTS/CAMPAIGNS

Apperson

Cadillac

Chrysler

Dodge

Hupmobile

Packard

HARRISON KING MCCANN
(November 4, 1880–December 31, 1962)

Leslie Cole, Charles S. Madden, and
Richard W. Easley

Pop culture in America has been shaped by advertising. Ads have told us what to eat, what to wear, where to buy products, and basically how to live. Looking back at the evolution of advertising, it is necessary to inquire about the early pioneers. One such early pioneer was Harrison King McCann. Sometimes referred to as Harry, he was a man who moved behind the scenes of advertising. Other writers and colleagues have described him as quiet, competent, and intensely loyal. His important contributions to the world of advertising were not in the areas of great copy or slogans, but rather in the development of the business of advertising.

McCann was born in Westbrook, Maryland, in 1880. He was graduated from Bowdoin College in 1902, after which he went to work on Wall Street. His education had not been geared toward advertising. As fate would have it, though, near the office of his firm was an advertising agency. Occasionally, McCann would find his way to the agency and talk with the agent. At times, he would even get involved in the business of the agency. He found that he enjoyed advertising and decided to pursue a career in the field.

Before plunging into the agency business itself, McCann held a number of positions with companies such as Poland Springs Water, where he worked as a sales representative, and New York Telephone, where he was an early advocate of public service advertising. This work on the client side of the business would obviously influence his later agency work.

It was his position at Standard Oil, however, that would catapult him into the agency business. McCann went to work for Standard Oil in 1921 in the advertising department. Due to the implementation of antitrust legislation, the Standard Oil trust was being dissolved. In an effort to retain some centralization in the promotion efforts, McCann volunteered to form his own agency to keep the various portions of the dissolved Standard Oil relatively intact. This decision was supported by Standard Oil personnel. It is easy to see the benefits of this decision to all parties. The Standard Oil people were able to retain some synergy from their previous efforts. McCann also promised that the advertising department employees of Standard Oil would be employed by his new agency. But the biggest benefit went to McCann. He was finally in the advertising agency business. The H. K. McCann Company was formed.

This move immediately placed the agency on a national level. The various parts of Standard Oil were divided into different companies throughout the United States. Shops needed to be accessible to clients in all areas. Unlike many others, which needed time to grow nationally, the new agency opened shops across the country to serve the needs of its clients.

Service to clients was something that was extremely important to Harry McCann. He not only followed the Standard Oil companies across the United States, but also around the world. Their advertising needs overseas were no less important than their domestic needs. In 1927 offices were opened in London, Paris, and Berlin.

The beliefs held by McCann about service to clients extended beyond the accessibility factor. By the time of his retirement from the agency that bears his name, McCann-Erickson was serving clients in many ways. For example, under H. K. McCann's care, it developed a strong interest in providing research services for its clients. During the 1950s it placed a great deal of emphasis on what motivates consumers to act. The need to understand the marketplace may have reflected McCann's early career on the client side. Additionally, the agency provided a full-service library in order to answer questions and meet the needs of clients.

In the early days of the agency, client needs were limited. McCann noted that as the clients' needs and demands grew, so was it necessary for the agency's services to grow. This position is still reflected by the agency's perception that it is a "total marketing" shop; advertising is just a portion of its services.

By 1927 H. K. McCann was approximately number five in a listing of the country's largest advertising agencies. However, as the Depression approached, McCann's business savvy was once again employed. As clients began to cut back on their usage of agencies, McCann merged with A. W. Erickson in 1930. This was a good match. Sadly, Albert Erickson and Harry McCann would work together for only another six years. After the death of Erickson, Harrison McCann became sole owner of the agency.

The agency grew under McCann's leadership. During this time, he acted as a mentor to many different names in advertising. One such person was Marion Harper, Jr. From McCann, Harper learned the business of advertising, and he learned early. Harper was made president of the company at the age of 29. Much of what McCann-Erickson is today can be credited to the joint efforts of McCann and Harper. McCann took the lead in client relationships, while Harper learned the business. Over time, however, McCann slowly turned the reins over to Harper. Harper has noted that it was McCann's hands-off approach that led to the easy transfer of leadership in the late 1940s and 1950s.

Another aspect of McCann's management style involved his relationship with employees. He was not comfortable firing employees, nor did he outwardly give orders to subordinates. In looking at his career, his most active work on behalf of the agency was using his ability to interact with the heads of corporations, convincing them of the need for advertising.

It was this management style that allowed McCann-Erickson to take strides in the area of employee relations. McCann believed that "the people who work in the agency should have the profits from it" ("Half a Century," p. 56). McCann-Erickson had an employee benefit plan by 1943, allowed employees to purchase stock in 1946, and also allowed them to purchase voting stock through the benefit plan in 1956. At his retirement in 1958 from the position of chairman of the board, McCann sold his equity stock in the company, paving the way for the employee benefit plan to hold the majority of voting stock.

These efforts demonstrate the type of man Harrison McCann was. As noted earlier, he was not often in the limelight. In fact, he appeared to shun recognition. He was not comfortable with public speaking, preferring to share his knowledge with his staff. Yet, he was an integral part of advertising through his service to the industry. For example, he had been chairman of the board of the American Association of Advertising Agencies. He devoted time as a director of the National Outdoor Advertising Bureau, as well as a number of other institutions.

In cataloging Harrison McCann's attributes, in addition to his quiet leadership style, there are several characteristics to note. His interests were in the business of advertising. He acted as the liaison in developing accounts, rather than being the creative mind behind them. He had good business judgment. When he discovered that the agency commission on outdoor advertising was 17.65 percent, while other forms earned a commission of only 15 percent, he was determined to make outdoor ads a primary part of the McCann-Erickson business.

Another important McCann attribute was his ability to choose employees wisely, as demonstrated by his choice of Marion Harper. He also looked into the future of advertising by realizing the importance of marketing research. His choice of Bowdoin alumnus Dr. L.D.H. Weld to develop the research end of McCann-Erickson earned the agency accolades for estimates of total advertising volume.

One of McCann's strongest characteristics, shown time and again, was his intense loyalty. Going back to the Standard Oil days, when dissolution appeared imminent, McCann promised to take care of the advertising employees. It was noted at his retirement that he had had the same secretary, Kitty Kelly, since his time at Standard Oil. Looking to fire an employee who appeared to be unprofitable, another employee approached McCann on the issue. McCann refused, saying that while the unprofitable employee might not be getting the job done, to fire him would probably leave him jobless. Another example is seen in his devotion to fellow Bowdoin graduates. Many of the top managers at

McCann-Erickson earned their degrees at Bowdoin. This fierce loyalty did not stop with the hiring of Bowdoin grads; he also served the college in later years. Additionally, his loyalty to his clients, beginning with Standard Oil, was quite evident.

In an example that displays McCann's sense of loyalty, Draper Daniels, in *Giants, Pygmies and Other Advertising People*, tells the story of the endless road to find an adequate department head for the radio department at McCann-Erickson. Department heads would come, size up the situation, and often find themselves out of a job. It soon became clear that a particular individual was responsible for causing these employees' problems. Her name was Dorothy Barstow. The new department head would target her as the problem, report his findings, and pursue her dismissal. It would not be forthcoming. Dorothy Barstow also held the title of Mrs. H. K. McCann (p. 110).

Another characteristic of McCann was his ability to stay calm above the turmoil of everyday events. He took the loss of one client quite calmly when he said: "Every business suffers a percentage of losses. Ours has been surprisingly low" ("Half a Century," p. 56).

McCann's contributions to the world of advertising were important and represent his personality. First, he pursued a marketing research focus. As the agency grew, it developed subsidiaries, one of which was Marplan. Marplan provided research support not only for the clients of the parent company, but for other agencies as well. These subsidiaries, as well as the McCann-Erickson agency, operated under a parent umbrella, Interpublic.

Second, McCann is considered one of the pioneers of the branch operation of advertising agencies. While New York is where H. K. McCann started, it quickly grew beyond its boundaries. The need to be accessible to clients was foremost.

Third, McCann was one of the first advertising men to develop an international network of agencies. Not only did he open McCann-Erickson shops around the world, but he purchased agencies already in business. By 1962 McCann-Erickson had operations in 22 countries.

Harrison McCann led a full life. Upon his retirement in December 1958, he recognized and appreciated the field he had chosen. He had been in advertising for nearly 46 years. He described the work as being "so stimulating that you never get bored" ("Half a Century," p. 56). Sadly, it was just four years later, on December 21, 1962, that McCann and his wife were killed in a car accident on Long Island. An early pioneer in the development of advertising and the agency business, he died at the age of 82, but his legacy lives on.

FURTHER READING

Works about McCann

Daniels, Draper. *Giants, Pygmies and Other Advertising People*. Chicago: Crain Communications, 1974.

"Half a Century in Ad Business—46 Heading Own Ship—McCann Found It 'Never Boring.' " *Advertising Age* (December 22, 1958): 56.

"Harper Becomes Board Chairman; McCann Retires." *Advertising Age* (December 22, 1958): 1, 56.

NOTABLE CLIENT/CAMPAIGN

Standard Oil

DAVID OGILVY
(June 23, 1911–   )

Danal Terry

Founder and chief executive officer of Ogilvy and Mather Worldwide, David Ogilvy was born on June 23, 1911, in Horsley, near London, the son of an Irish mother and Scottish father. His father's business failed when David was three. David lost his beloved nanny, and the family moved to London to live with his maternal grandmother. He relates in his autobiography that at the age of six his father decided that his diet should include raw blood and calves' brains washed down with beer, for strength and intelligence. This "noble experiment" became the title of his autobiography, *Blood, Brains and Beer*.

Grandfather Ogilvy was to influence young David, and his advice was remembered. As Ogilvy relates in his autobiography, his grandfather advised him to study J. P. Morgan's philosophy. He did. He noted that Morgan referred to his partners as "gentlemen with brains." Ogilvy built his empire by following that philosophy.

Ogilvy was not a good academic student. A rebel who questioned dogma and authority, he resisted learning. Nonetheless, after years in boarding schools, he earned a scholarship to Christ Church, Oxford, but poor grades in chemistry and a lack of enthusiasm led to expulsion after two years.

After being expelled from Oxford, he escaped to France and got a job in the "hot-as-the hinges of hell" kitchens of the Hotel Majestic in Paris. As the newest apprentice chef, his job entailed shaving down the meat-carving table twice a day and preparing meals for customers' dogs. Although terrified by the head chef, Pitard, he was promoted to making hors d'oeuvres. His experience in the hotel provided him with a wealth of anecdotes with which he later peppered his writings. And the personality of Monsieur Pitard provided a model of what a manager of a great establishment probably must be—a captain in ruthless pursuit of perfection, with no tolerance for ineptitude. Pitard's influence would serve him well in the development of the Ogilvy and Mather empire twenty years later.

The Aga Cooker was a coal-fired constant-temperature stove developed by

Gustaf Dalén, the Nobel Prize-winning Swedish physicist. Ogilvy's elder brother, Francis, was involved with the marketing of the Aga Cooker, and this offered the young Ogilvy an opportunity to sell the stove in Scotland. He returned to Britain and found his Majestic experience useful in persuading prospects of the value and quality of the Aga. He discovered he was capable of convincing the owners of stately homes to purchase the expensive appliance. "I learned to *sell*, which means listening more than you talk, knowing your product inside out, having a sense of humor, and telling the truth" ("Keeping Up," p. 17). His success at selling the cooker earned him a commission to write a manual outlining the secrets of his winning method. The manual, which he titled "The Theory and Practice of Selling the Aga Cooker," landed him a position at the Mather and Crowther advertising agency in London. At the age of 25 David began a three-year stint in London writing copy, much of which was influenced by the styles of the best New York agencies, which the young David followed with a subscription to a clipping service. His longing for adventure—fired by *Huckleberry Finn*—drove him to seek his fortune in America.

Armed with letters of introduction to Dr. Libman, of the Rockefeller Institute of Medical Research, and Alexander Woollcott, the drama critic, he headed for the States. There he met the likes of Harpo Marx, George Kaufman, Ruth Gordon, Tom Lamont (a partner in J. P. Morgan's bank), Rosser Reeves (then a copywriter at Blackett-Sample-Hummert), Tim Finletter (later Secretary of the Air Force), and Secretary of Labor Francis Perkins, who gave him a work permit. He became a disciple of Reeves's, and over lunches with the one-year-older copywriter was indoctrinated into the Claude Hopkins style of advertising, based on dedication to salesmanship and "reason-why" copy. He met Reeves's sister-in-law and shortly afterward married her. During this time he met another strong influence on his life, Dr. George Gallup.

By correctly predicting the outcome of the 1936 presidential election, Gallup had gained wide renown. David joined Gallup at Princeton. For the next few years he learned Gallup's polling methods and the value of consumer research. His skill as a salesman was put to good use by Gallup, who had been unable to sell the merits of his research to dynastic studio heads like David Selznick, Walt Disney, and Samuel Goldwyn.

David measured the popularity of movie stars, pretested the audience acceptance of films, tested the selling power of titles, and measured the awareness levels of moviegoers prior to a film's release—what David called the "Index of Publicity Penetration." One of his surveys for RKO Radio Pictures resulted in a secret list of "box office poison" and catapulted famous stars into oblivion by showing how low in esteem they were held by the public. In evaluating a star's popularity in terms of contribution to film receipts, David discovered that future President Ronald Reagan was worth only a fourth of the likes of Clark Gable or Spencer Tracy.

His experience under Gallup instilled a profound respect for the value of research, which became deeply integrated into his advertising philosophy. Near the end of their Princeton stay, the Ogilvy family added a new member. In 1942, David Fairfield Ogilvy was born. He would be their only child.

During World War II David left the Gallup organization to work for the British Secret Service under Sir William Stephenson, who was one of the primary liaisons between President Roosevelt and Winston Churchill. David was charged with collecting economic intelligence on Latin America. Later he became second secretary on the staff of the British Embassy in Washington, where his writing skill was honed by drafting diplomatic telegraphs that could survive the multilevel bureaucracy before being sent.

While working in Washington during the war, Ogilvy and his wife spent frequent weekends in Lancaster Company, Pennsylvania, getting to know the Amish descendants of German immigrants. He came to respect the hardworking and jovial people who shunned modern conveniences. In 1946 he purchased an Amish farm near Intercourse, Pennsylvania. For three years David tried unsuccessfully to make a go of farming, but his dislike for backbreaking labor and frustration at being at the mercy of nature for his income drove him into the business world. At the age of 38, David moved to Madison Avenue.

With $6,000 of his own and $80,000 start-up capital supplied by Mather and Crowther (his former employer) and another British agency, Ogilvy and Mather was born in September 1948. Although he put himself in charge of research, his creative genius could not be subdued. One of his first big successes was with the Hathaway Shirt Company. He wrote the copy for the client's ads and insisted that art director Vincent DeGiacomo shoot the photographs of the model with a patch over one eye. Andy Byrne has said that the real reason for the success of the campaign was that it "had the best damned shirt copy written before or since" (p. 26).

Ogilvy approached the creative process with a unique vision. Although in his own later writings he pledged allegiance to the "reason-why" approach, his work showed influences that went beyond straightforward salesmanship in print. To reconcile these divergent approaches, he sought the wisdom of another advertising guru, the retired Raymond Rubicam. He made a pilgrimage to Rubicam's retirement home in Maine and kept in touch with him through a series of letters. Rubicam found in his ambitious disciple a spokesman for his own philosophy, which was never published. David, as good a listener as he was a speaker and writer, absorbed Rubicam's advice and incorporated it into his own campaigns.

The impact of Rubicam on David created a chasm in his relationship with Reeves that took years to mend. Reeves saw the Rubicam influence as a rejection of the hard-sell approach.

The success of the Hathaway campaign and the one David created for Schweppes, convincing the bearded client to become the symbol of his company in their ads, brought rapid recognition to the Ogilvy organization. It attracted other clients, including Rolls-Royce, Dove soap, Sears Roebuck, Guinness, Shell Oil, and the governments of Puerto Rico, Great Britain, France, and the United

States. The headline that David wrote for Rolls-Royce has gone down in advertising history as one of the most memorable ever written.

Although his ability to write copy that *sold* was becoming legendary, he always submitted his work to colleagues for editing. Of the 26 headlines he wrote for Rolls-Royce, his team selected, "At 60 miles an hour the loudest noise in this new Rolls-Royce comes from the electric clock." He followed it with a two-line subhead and 13 paragraphs of solid "reason-why" copy. Rolls-Royce sales jumped 50 percent.

With proclamations from *Advertising Age* and *Time* recognizing David as "one of the greatest creative minds in the advertising business" and "the most sought-after wizard in the advertising business," the Ogilvy organization grew rapidly. Its reputation for unique creative approaches attracted package goods clients and larger budgets. By 1964 the agency had surpassed $75 million in billings, following the publication of David's best-seller, *Confessions of an Advertising Man*. In the same year Mather and Crowther in London and David's New York office merged. The merged expanded operations into Europe and brought total billings to $130 million. In 1989 Ogilvy and Mather was acquired by WPP, a holding company which also owns J. Walter Thompson. David became chairman of WPP, the biggest advertising company in the world.

In 1991 Ogilvy and Mather had 246 offices in 52 countries, with 7,000 employees and billings of $5 billion. In February 1989 Ogilvy and Mather had become the first international advertising agency to be granted the right to operate in the former Soviet Union.

In his autobiographical notes prepared for *Who's Who in Advertising*, he lists himself as "copywriter," rather than as chairman of the board. But his abilities as a manager cannot be denied. His influence on his staff was inspiring. He wrote thousands of memos and policy papers to be distributed to his staff, spelling out his philosophy for every aspect of the business. *Confessions of an Advertising Man* and his later books were compiled to a great degree from those papers. But despite his success at leading the massive organization, it became an unpleasant chore, providing little personal satisfaction. "I have developed an almost uncontrollable distaste for my job: the paper, the unappreciative clients, the perpetual firefighting, the humbug" (Fox, p. 261). As CEO he found it difficult to relinquish the job of copywriting to his staff, but recognized that by continuing to write he pitted himself against his own team to the detriment of their morale. It was a sacrifice that he dutifully swallowed like the castor oil served him by his childhood nanny. He later recalled, "If you're good at creating, for goodness sake don't waste your time in top management. I made that mistake" (Higgins, p. 76).

The success of Ogilvy and Mather was not merely the product of good advertising and inspiring management. David approached the marketing of his agency with cunning and persistence. He made remarkable speeches, and they carried his name far beyond the confines of the rooms in which he spoke. His wit allowed him to criticize his audiences. He denounced billboards and creativity at the expense of salesmanship. He attacked the commission system, and his was the first major agency to change to compensation by fee. He promoted his agency by getting involved with organizations that also provided opportunities to meet potential clients. He became a director of the New York Philharmonic in 1960. At the request of John D. Rockefeller III, he became chairman of the Public Participation Committee of Lincoln Center. And in 1962 he became a trustee of Colby College. But his fame spread fastest and furthest upon publication of his first book, *Confessions of an Advertising Man*. Published in 1963, the book presented David's theories on what constitutes good advertising. An entertaining and readable "how-to" book for account executives, advertisers, creatives, and anyone else involved in the advertising process, it rapidly became one of the industry's classic texts. And it brought David widespread renown. Over a million copies have been sold, and it is available in 15 languages. In 1978 his autobiography, *Blood, Brains and Beer*, was published and in 1983, *Ogilvy on Advertising*. In his 75th year, his partners presented David with a privately published compilation of his memos, *The Unpublished David Ogilvy*.

David was elected to the Copywriters Hall of Fame in 1963. In 1967 Queen Elizabeth II made David a Commander of the British Empire. The same year, David bought a 12th century castle in France, and in 1973 went to live there. In 1991 the French Government made him an Officer of the Order of Arts and Letters. Although officially retired, he remains on the board of directors and continues to bombard his partners with memos." In 1991 at an Association of National Advertisers meeting, he was still speaking his mind on his philosophy of advertising as expressed in Ogilvy and Mather's slogan, "We Sell. Or Else" (Dagnoli, p. 1).

In the preface to the 1988 edition of *Confessions of an Advertising Man*, David sums up his philosophy. One of the overriding principles that influenced most of his work was that advertising, no matter how creative, must never lose sight of its primary reason for existence—that of selling. And although he has been one of advertising's most influential practitioners, he has also been a stern critic of the industry at times. "Advertising should not be abolished. But it must be reformed" (p. 164). When told at the ANA convention that he is "known as perhaps the last great figure in the advertising world," he replied, "If it is, it's a pity" (Dagnoli, p. 54). Through his writings and public speeches he has made sure that others can reach his stature by standing on his shoulders.

FURTHER READING

Works by Ogilvy

Blood, Brains and Beer, The Autobiography of David Ogilvy. New York: Atheneum, 1978.

Confessions of an Advertising Man. New York: Atheneum, 1963.

Ogilvy on Advertising. New York: Crown, 1983.

"Principles of Management." In-house folio. Chicago: Ogilvy and Mather, 1968.
The Unpublished David Ogilvy. New York: Crown, 1986.
"What We Believe and How We Behave, the Corporate Culture of Ogilvy and Mather as Set Down by David Ogilvy." *Viewpoint* (September-October 1990): 14–15.

Works about Ogilvy

Blount, Steve. "Page One: One Man Who Changed the Way We Do Our Business." *Madison Avenue* (July 1983): 1.
Byrne, Andy. "Stupid Bastards, Aren't They?" *Direct* (October 1991): 25–27.
Dagnoli, Judann. "Ogilvy at 80, Grand Old Adman Holds Forth on Compensation, Mergers." *Advertising Age* (November 1991): 1, 53.
Fox, Stephen. *The Mirror Makers: A History of American Advertising and Its Creators.* New York: William Morrow, 1984.
Higgins, Denis. *The Art of Writing Advertising, Conversations with Masters of the Craft.* Lincolnwood, IL: National Textbook Company, 1965.
Jacobsen, Kenneth. "David Ogilvy." *Adweek* (January 28, 1991): 16–17; (February 4, 1991): 24, 29; (February 11, 1991): 30–31.
"Keeping Up with David Ogilvy." *Viewpoint* (August 1989): 17.
Leiss, William, Stephen Kline, and Sut Jhally. *Social Communication in Advertising.* 2d ed. Ontario: Nelson Canada, 1990.
Mayer, Martin. *Madison Avenue, U.S.A.* New York: Harper, 1958.
Mehlman, Barbara. "David Ogilvy." *Madison Avenue* (July 1983): 85–91.
Wentz, Laurel. "On the Record; David Ogilvy: 'I Feel Very Sad.' " *Advertising Age* (May 8, 1989): 1, 74.
Winski, Joseph M. "A Giant Bows to 'Jackasses.' " *Advertising Age* (May 22, 1989): 70.

NOTABLE CLIENTS/CAMPAIGNS

Hathaway shirts (1950–1970s)

Dove soap (1952–present)

Schweppes (1953–present)

Government of Puerto Rico Industrial Development Campaign (1954–late 1950s)

Rolls-Royce (1957–1961)

Maxwell House coffee (1958–present)

Shell Oil (1960–present)

Sears (1961–present)

ALEX F. OSBORN
(May 24, 1888–May 5, 1966)

Donald E. Parente and John R. Osborn

Alex Osborn was the quintessential adman. Although he thought of himself primarily as a creative person, he was very much a pragmatic businessman. He is best known as the father of "brainstorming" and as one of the founders of Batten, Barton, Durstine and Osborn (BBDO). He began his work in advertising in 1915 as the manager of the E. P. Remington agency in Buffalo, New York. In 1960 he retired from active involvement with the advertising industry when he resigned from BBDO.

Advertising was an emerging field in the early 1900s, and Osborn had the drive, discipline, and imagination to do well in it. Along with Bruce Barton and Ben Duffy, he was most responsible for the character and growth of BBDO. From its inception on January 1, 1919, to well into the 1980s, BBDO consistently ranked among the top five U.S. agencies in terms of total billings.

Alexander Faickney Osborn was born on May 24, 1888, in New York to John and Kate Osborn in the year of the "big blizzard." Osborn always claimed that although he was Bronx-born it was not in poverty. His father was an accountant of somewhat modest means. The family lived in a house 25 feet wide, but they had a bathroom—and "even a furnace." Compared to some of the neighbors, they lived "in luxury." From the young boy's perspective, his father "always made ends meet but could build no nest egg. Since his job depended on politics, we were continually fraught with fear lest he be ousted. The possibility of the poorhouse was seldom out of our minds."

The sense of insecurity no doubt left an indelible impression on the young Osborn. Well over 50 years later, in a book he wrote on creativity, *Your Creative Power*, he was able to recall something that had happened when he was six years old. Apparently, he was awakened one night by his mother and father talking in another room. It seems his father was about to lose his job and had not saved enough money to live on for more than a few months. His father told his mother he was worried about her and the kids.

. Eventually, the parents went to sleep, but the boy stayed awake, until about four in the morning. Little Alex then went to his mom and dad's bedroom, woke them up, and in a confident voice said, "I heard you and Mama talking, and I couldn't get back to sleep. Don't worry about money. Remember that box of pencils you gave me last Christmas? I still have them, and I'll go down on the corner and sell them for five cents apiece—so we will be all right" (Osborn, J., p. 48).

Osborn attended elementary and high school in the Bronx. He went on to Hamilton College, a small liberal arts school in Clinton, New York, where he was graduated with a bachelor's degree in psychology. Osborn showed early on the kind of determination and vision that would serve him well in his later years. A week before he started college, he confided to a friend that there were three things that he wanted to do there: "belong to a dramatic organization, edit the weekly college newspaper, *Hamilton Life*, and manage the football team" ("Idea Man of Buffalo," *Advertising and Selling*, p. 1). He managed the football team and worked for the school newspaper, but the college did not have any dramatic organizations. So, along with a couple of friends, he organized a drama club, or a dramatic "clique," as he put it, since they were pretty snobbish about whom they would let belong.

As was common with a number of advertising pioneers, Osborn started out in the newspaper business, working first as a cub reporter for the *Buffalo Times* and later as a police reporter for the *Buffalo Express*. He lost his first job because the newspaper was having financial problems, but he lost the job at the *Express* because his supervisor, a crack editor, did not think that he had the aptitude (Osborn, J., p. 14).

Osborn left the newspaper business somewhat hardened and perhaps forever apprehensive about job security. He took on various jobs, including statistician for a milling company, publicity man for the Buffalo Chamber of Commerce, and bed salesman for the Hard Manufacturing Company in Buffalo.

Though he was no longer working with news copy or releases, he stayed close to his writing, issuing poems and essays under the pen name "Ted Scott." He made friends at the bed company but took some ribbing about his fascination with ideas. A program for a 1913 sales convention offers the following verse:

> Osborn be of dreamy eye
> who dreams a lot of pipes
> His only ideas that succeed
> Are the paltry few he swipes. (Osborn, J., p. 20)

Alex stayed with Hard Manufacturing for three years.

Osborn loved to tell people why he left the company. One day his employer took him aside and said, "You will have to let up a bit. Do you realize that if sales keep up like this, we will have to enlarge our factory?" (Alan Ward, speech to the Buffalo Advertising Club, January 19, 1978). The advice prompted Osborn to quit and join the E. P. Remington agency in Buffalo. This was a house agency for a patent medicine maker, where he proceeded to bring in new business that soon dwarfed the patent medicine side of the enterprise.

About this time, he was running an applied psychology course for 250 staff members of the Ford Motor Company, lecturing nights on advertising at the YMCA, and teaching Sunday school. He was also active in the New York National Guard. He explained his busy life this way: "Well, I was engaged, and promised myself that I would marry when I had acquired $1,000. This seemed like a good way to get it." He and Helen Coatsworth, daughter of a renowned Buffalo lawyer, were married on September 5, 1916. After the wedding, Osborn felt the need to improve his financial status in a manner that would be more compatible with family life.

The $37-a-month flat was more than he could afford, but he had an idea for a client, the General Baking Company. It included a baking contest to get women to tell the company what kind of bread they wanted. The morning of October 14, 1916, was "zero hour." The pre-contest ads had been run. The rest was in the "lap of the gods."

Alex started for downtown Buffalo at 7:30 to be there when the contest doors opened at 8. On the way, he wondered what would happen if only a handful of women brought their bread to the Y.W.C.A. A few blocks from the "Y", just before 8 o'clock, he had a sinking sensation. The contest would be a fizzle. So he walked around and around another block. Then decided to face the music. And there on West Mohawk Street in front of the Y.W.C.A. was a noisy mob. Over 1,000 women. Each with her own freshly baked loaf, fighting to get in.

More than 2,000 contestants showed up that day. The $37-a-month flat was safe. And other contests all over the country resulted in a Bond bread slogan, "Made as 43,040 housewives showed us" (Personal papers, p. 7).

The origin of BBDO stemmed from work Osborn did for Bruce Barton on the United War Work Campaign during World War I. This work was a money-raising project for the YWCA, the YMCA, the Salvation Army, and four other national drives. The group was dubbed "The Seven Sobbing Sisters" and raised $200 million.

Bruce Barton had enlisted another volunteer, whose assignment was to go to France and secure front-line material for publicity back home. His name was Roy Durstine. He had been in the advertising agency business with a man named Berrien. Osborn had never met Durstine, but they had several mutual friends.

Meanwhile, Durstine had returned from Europe and had taken an office next to Osborn, who by this time had moved to New York. Late in November 1919, when Osborn was preparing to go back to Buffalo for good, he invited Bruce Barton to lunch with him at the Oyster Bar in Grand Central Station. Sitting at the counter, Barton said to Osborn: "What do you think I ought to do, now that this job is over?"

"I should think you would go back to editing some magazine," said Osborn.

"That's the last thing I want to do," Barton replied.

"Well," said Osborn, "why not go into the advertising agency business? You are a natural for it."

"No," said Barton, "I wouldn't think of doing that. I'd hate to have to hire and fire and to keep track of money and all that."

"Well, get somebody in with you who has that capacity and who likes the business end."

Barton asked, "Who?"

"Roy Durstine," said Osborn.

After lunch Osborn went into Durstine's office. He said to him: "I just changed the name of your firm from Berrien and Durstine to Barton, Berrien and Durstine."

To which Durstine replied: "How about making it Barton, Durstine and Osborn?" (Personal papers, p. 7).

Osborn explained that he wanted to continue to live in Buffalo. So, on January 1, 1919, the firm of Barton and Durstine was started, without Osborn. A few days later, however, Osborn received a letter from Barton and Durstine offering him an equal interest in the company if he would join them within six months.

During that period, Barton and Durstine agreed that Osborn would never be asked to come to New York, but could continue to live in Buffalo and run the office there. That was how Barton, Durstine and Osborn got started on August 1, 1919 (Personal papers, p. 3). The name Batten would be added much later.

In 1920 BD&O operated out of two offices: one in New York and the other in Buffalo. The client list at that time included accounts such as McGraw-Hill, General Baking, Condé Nast Publications, *Scribner's* magazine, the New York *Tribune*, the Wildroot Company, and less known businesses such as the Buffalo Housewrecking and Salvage Company.

Osborn was a frequent contributor to trade publications such as *Printer's Ink*. Some of his articles in the 1920s included "Can Barney Google Sell Bananas at the Follies? . . . publicity that derides the product may be of no value to the advertiser" and "Dick, the Salesman, Teaches Me Three Things . . . an advertising man's personal experience as to lessons to be gleaned from a day's work with a wide-awake salesman." Though the titles lacked brevity, they were apparently regarded with great interest among members of the burgeoning advertising community (Osborn, J., p. 28).

In these early years, Osborn made many key decisions that would mold the future of the agency. One seemingly insignificant decision was to hire an office boy by the name of Ben Duffy. He was unlike many of the other people who rose to prominence in the field of advertising, including those at BD&O. He was not from one of the Ivy League schools, as was so typical at other major agencies. In fact, he had dropped out of high school and had grown up in a tenement. In contrast, BD&O was conservative and very Republican. Still, Duffy would eventually rise to become president of the agency and lead it through its most expansive period before retiring in 1957.

Another decision would involve a move in 1928 of the Manhattan office to a building already occupied by another agency, the George Batten Company. This agency had been in business since 1891, but George Batten, the founder, had died in 1918, and the agency was not keeping pace with other shops in acquiring new business. William H. Johns was the president and apparently approached Roy Durstine about combining the two companies. There is no evidence to suggest that George Batten ever met Barton, Durstine, or Osborn. In 1928 BD&O merged with the older George Batten Company, and the name became Batten, Barton, Durstine and Osborn. The name, once likened to the sound of a trunk falling down some stairs and later shortened to the bouncy cadence of BBDO, became a source of endless joy to Jack Benny, Fred Allen, and other comedians, and entered into the folklore of America.

In 1924 Osborn was appointed to the board of directors of one of his smaller clients, the Wildroot Company. This sign of appreciation for his involvement and input foreshadowed one of his most significant business contributions. Wildroot was producing an alcohol-based hair tonic in a shed on Jefferson Avenue in Buffalo. The company's annual advertising expenditure was a meager $70,000. Osborn suggested that they make a nonalcoholic cream type of hair tonic, similar to Brill Creme, which was successful in England. This suggestion produced cries of outrage. "What man would put salad dressing on his hair! Impossible!" Osborn persisted. Finally, Wildroot Oil was launched. Within a few years it was the best-selling hair tonic in the United States. The annual advertising appropriation grew to over $4 million.

BBDO made it through the stock market crash of 1929, and in the early 1930s Alex Osborn expanded his involvement into issues beyond advertising. He worked with President Herbert Hoover on a plan to stabilize prices and continued his civic involvement in Buffalo, working with the mayor to reduce unemployment.

Meanwhile, back on the advertising front, the Madison Avenue end of BBDO was gaining momentum as a leading advertising agency, with a heavy involvement in the development of the medium of radio, under the firm, decisive rule of Roy Durstine. By the mid–1930s, the company boasted five branch offices, ever-increasing billings, and a satisfied client list. Bruce Barton had begun an involvement in politics, having been elected to Congress.

Alex was extremely content. He was home with his family of five children, involved in the civic vitality of his beloved Buffalo, and had a stable and profitable business to provide security. Thoughts of early retirement even crept into his plans for the future. Then, in 1939, almost without warning, distress signals began coming from Madison Avenue. The company's profits were plummeting. Key personnel were threatening to leave. Rumors spread about the potential loss of clients. The problems would eventually culminate in Durstine's leaving to establish his own agency. The call went out from New York to Osborn to come down and set things straight. The promise that he would never have to leave Buffalo was forgotten. Osborn's increasing preference to focus on creative matters would have to be set aside.

One day, Osborn bustled down from Buffalo, perhaps not fully realizing that he was embarking on a trip that he would replicate almost every weekend for the next ten years.

His first task upon arriving in New York was to evaluate the situation. This he did by producing a mammoth document, "BBDO's Business Problem: an adman's study, done mainly after hours, without the benefit of accountants, lawyers or engineers." Having been named general manager of the operation at that time, he started to tackle the rebuilding task. He described the process as follows:

I quickly concluded that much of our trouble was due to inadequacy of creative effort. So my main task was to serve as a creative coach—to induce people to put their imaginations to greater use—to get them to produce more and better ideas for our clients. So evening after evening, groups of about a dozen would gather and jointly think up ideas and help solve specific problems. These sessions were exclusively creative. Criticism of ideas was tabooed. Evaluation was postponed until the next day.

In 1939, these pow-wows first became known as "brainstorm" sessions. Since then the word "brainstorming" has evolved until it now denotes a principle—a principle of creative thinking which calls for suspension of judgment during ideative effort—a principle which scientific research has recently found to be even more productive in individual effort than in group collaboration. (Personal papers, pp. 3, 4)

So it seemed there was a way to meld the demands of BBDO as a suffering business entity and the notions of applied creativity with which Osborn had been dabbling.

But major problems remained as 1940 came around: among them, the potential loss of clients and key personnel. Osborn was proud of what took place in 1940— proud of his associates and, in a human way, proud of himself.

Osborn had cut his compensation to less than one-third of the pay he received in 1926. He was also working almost "twice as hard" as he had in 1926. He lost weight and was put on "nerve-allaying dope morning and night" by his doctor. Once again, as he had much earlier in life, he had to deal with the prospect of losing a job. Only this time, it was not so much his job personally as it was the "500 families who depended on BBDO for their livelihood" ("Scriblets," p. 2).

On a lonely train ride back to Buffalo, Osborn wrote in a family newsletter he periodically sent out, "It was I who started this institution in 1919. It has become one of the three greatest businesses of its kind in the world. If you don't accept the challenge to carry it on, you are a coward, AFO . . . you're yellow!" ("Scriblets," p. 2).

Alex Osborn had gone into the fray either to fail (as was his expectation) or to carry BBDO through to a point where, if it failed, the fault would not be his. To this latter end, these things had to be achieved:

1. The shaky finances had to be strengthened.

2. The desertions of key people had to be averted.

3. The volume of business had to be held intact.

4. There had to be proof that new business could be obtained despite the absence of Durstine, on whom this function had solely depended.

In 1939 BBDO's profit went to over $350,000, against a loss of $180,000 in 1938. The threats of creditors were withdrawn. Bank balances were again adequate.

In order to encourage key management people to stay on with a floundering firm, Osborn worked out a plan that made BBDO not only a viable, but an attractive place to work. He once told a group of BBDO'ers that he would like this epitaph on his tombstone: "He thought up the BBDO stock plan" (Osborn, J., p. 39).

Desertions ceased. Ben Duffy was offered $25,000 but decided to stay at $15,000. Frank Mahoney, a senior manager, was offered $25,000 but preferred to stay at $14,000. Jack Cornelius, head of the Minneapolis office, was tempted by Getchell at $60,000, by Lord and Thomas at $40,000, by Blackett Sample and Hummert at $50,000, and by General Mills at $30,000. He decided to stay with BBDO at $17,000. At least six other men on whom the life of BBDO depended were likewise tempted, but they decided to stay with BBDO. In no case did Osborn try to meet the larger offers others held out.

In April 1939 over $5 million of BBDO volume was supposed to be in the vest pocket of Durstine, who had headed the firm and who had set himself up to take this business away. Not one dollar of this volume did BBDO lose to him.

The advertising world had expected BBDO to crack up. Outsiders could not believe that BBDO had been turned from dangerous deficits into safe profits. They could not believe that 1940 was the greatest year in BBDO's history since 1929, with $3 million more volume and $600,000 more earnings than in 1938. But they (with many at BBDO) still had their fingers crossed. Osborn was a nice fellow, but BBDO had no spark plug. BBDO was still doomed to fall apart.

It happened. In the summer of 1940, the General Baking Company left BBDO. This event was thought to be the beginning of the end. Here was the account that Osborn had built from nothing in 1918 to well over a $1 million a year. Osborn had held this account for 22 years, the longest any man had held an account in the history of the advertising agency business. He assumed people realized that BBDO had failed to land a single important new client since he had come down "from the sticks."

All of Osborn's heroics were to fall flat unless he could prove that, under his administration, BBDO could land a big new account. This was the challenge of the hottest month in many years, July 1940. Osborn started on his chase for the Goodrich tire account. July, August, September, October, Osborn added to his other chores the task of thinking up something new to do, each and every day, to land Goodrich.

By mid-October, it seemed a lost cause. On October 24, the Goodrich president phoned Alex Osborn. "One of our boys just told me you have lost the General Baking Company account." He sounded hurt, as if he meant to say: "You let me down. I was for you. But my associates were not. I might have swung them over. But they have now proved to me that your outfit must be slipping or otherwise you would not have been let out by General Baking ("Scriblets," p. 5).

The next morning Osborn went to see George Morrison, the new president of General Baking. He had been hired by a major stockholder who had given but one command: to get rid of BBDO.

That Friday morning, sitting at Morrison's desk, Osborn told him about the phone call from the Goodrich president. Before he had finished, Morrison reached for his phone and called the head of Goodrich (a man he had never met). "I understand you are thinking of taking on BBDO. It might help you to know that in the last six months I have looked into 32 agencies and, *if I had my own way*, there is only one agency I would select for my company, and that agency is BBDO" ("Scriblets," p. 5).

Osborn signed the Goodrich account. For him, it meant a lot more than mere money. In the family newsletter, he explained:

Until he was 50, AFO was fairly successful in his business. But how did he know he wasn't just lucky . . . carried along on another guy's back? That fear has always haunted AFO . . . the fear that he was a false-alarm. It is somewhat of a triumph for a man to prove at last that, after all he MAY not have been a false-alarm throughout his first 30 years of business-life. ("Scriblets," p. 6)

In 1942 McGraw-Hill published Osborn's *How to "Think Up,"* a slim volume that discussed the creative process. This was followed in 1948 by *Your Creative Power*.

Osborn's unique commuting habits and his routine of getting up every morning long before dawn to think up ideas for his books could only have been kept up with the bottomless understanding of his wife, Helen, gave. He never hesitated to acknowledge how much it meant.

Alex Osborn began working on his next book, *Wake Up Your Mind*, in 1952, and then, on the realization that only one college course on creative thinking was offered in the United States and there were no textbooks, he wrote *Applied Imagination: The Principles and Procedures of Creative Thinking* in 1953. On June 2, 1954, the Creative Education Foundation was founded on the royalties from the book, and the first seminar on creative problem solving was conducted.

In 1960 the Creative Education Foundation was gaining momentum, and Osborn resigned from BBDO's board of directors after 40 years. His goal was to have more time for the foundation and his family. His most recent work, *The Goldmine between Your Ears*, had become popular, and he began work on *How to Become More Creative*, which would be published in 1964.

"Alex Osborn spent his entire life being creative and curious. It was typical of him that he permitted researchers at Buffalo's Roswell Park Memorial Institute to give him experimental drugs in their quest for a cure for the rare ailment which claimed him on May 5th, just short of his 78th birthday" (BBDO Newsletter, May–July 1966).

Author's Note: The authors gratefully acknowledge they had access to the personal papers of Alex F. Osborn. In addition, John Osborn is the grandson of Alex Osborn and retains many vivid memories of his grandfather. In some instances, the words in this article were used by Alex Osborn verbally or in his papers, even though there may not be an accompanying citation.

FURTHER READING

Works by Osborn

Applied Imagination: The Principles and Procedures of Creative Thinking. New York: Charles Scribner's Sons, 1953.
The Goldmine Between Your Ears. New York: Charles Scribner's Sons, 1955.
How to Become More Creative. New York: Charles Scribner's Sons, 1964.
How to "Think Up." New York: McGraw-Hill, 1942.
"Scriblets." Unpublished. November 1, 1940.
Short Course in Advertising. New York: Charles Scribner's Sons, 1921.
Wake Up Your Mind. New York: Charles Scribner's Sons, 1952.
Your Creative Power. New York: Charles Scribner's Sons, 1948.

Works about Osborn

Alex F. Osborn: Biography. BBDO Public Relations Files, 1953.
Fox, Stephen. *The Mirror Makers: A History of American Advertising and Its Creators*. New York: William Morrow, 1984.
"Idea Man of Buffalo." *Advertising & Selling* (September 9, 1937): 12.
Osborn, John R. *Alex F. Osborn*. Unpublished. March 1984.

NOTABLE CLIENTS/CAMPAIGNS

American Tobacco

Armstrong Cork

B. F. Goodrich

Chrysler
Du Pont
General Baking
General Electric
Royal Crown Cola
Wildroot hair tonic

VOLNEY B. PALMER
(1799–July 29, 1864)

Bonnie Vannatta

Volney B. Palmer was the nation's first adman and father of today's advertising agency. During 27 years, from 1837 to 1864, he lifted advertising to a higher plane. He made it part of the marketing mix, and introduced the concept of advertising media planning. He was the first to sell the idea that advertising can detonate sales and profits. Later, his agency became part of the powerhouse N. W. Ayer and Son, the oldest advertising agency in the country.

Palmer was born near Wilkes-Barre, Pennsylvania, in 1799. His father was a lawyer and active in politics. In 1818, when Palmer was 19, the family moved to Mount Holly, New Jersey, and started a newspaper. The entire family worked at the paper. *The New Jersey Mirror* ran advertisements typical of the period— rewards for lost horses and runaway apprentices, cures for strange-sounding maladies, and stagecoach schedules. The remaining hole was devoted to six-week-old news from Europe, clippings from other newspapers, poems, essays, local news, and an editorial.

Running a newspaper in the 1800s had some similarities to running a newspaper today. Publishers had trouble obtaining a steady supply of newsprint at reasonable prices. In addition, they had trouble circulating their newspapers regularly to subscribers, as well as convincing loyal subscribers to pay—preferably in advance. During hard times, subscribers in arrears were urged to pay in cash, if they could, or in hay, wood, oats, cheese, or other commodities.

When Volney Palmer's father died in 1842, his mother, Jerusha, took over as publisher of the newspaper. She was very successful. When she died in 1856, Volney Palmer's sister, Eliza, took the reins of publisher. Volney Palmer and his brother, Strange, however, had nothing to do with the newspaper after 1830. They moved to Pottsville, Pennsylvania, where Volney was active in the real estate business. Unfortunately, there is little known as to what Palmer's other activities were during this period.

In 1841 Palmer, with his wife, Eliza, and family, moved to Philadelphia, where he proved to be upper management timber. He opened a real estate business. The entire country, however, was in a depression sparked by the panic of 1837. Philadelphia was nearly brought to a standstill. To help eke out a living, Palmer also opened a coal office and at the same time became an agent for advertising and subscriptions for a few nearby newspapers. This eventually grew into the first advertising agency in the United States.

According to Donald R. Holland, the idea for an advertising agency was a result of Palmer's long stint in the newspaper business. Holland says that Palmer, "under the pressures of making a living when a living was hard to make" (p. 10), began an advertising agency partly out of desperation, to augment his other business interests. Later, his agency became a profit center in its own right.

Palmer sold space in newspapers to advertisers; in return for his services, he deducted a commission before he paid the publishers. He floated the notion of a "system of advertising." This phrase appeared frequently in all of Palmer's writings. He urged business people to advertise on a regular basis, to use ads to develop new markets, and to take advantage of the flexibility of advertising to target markets in specific regions or in specific seasons. This setup was the forerunner of today's advertising agency.

As early as 1846, Palmer had branch offices in New York, Boston, and Baltimore. He preached the doctrine of a systematic program of advertising, created the commission system, and positioned the advertising agency between client and publisher.

The term "advertising agency" was not used by Palmer until he included it in an advertising insert in *M'Elroy's Philadelphia Directory* in 1849. He published a list of the advantages of advertising through the Palmer agency in his *V. B. Palmer's Business-Man's Almanac*.

In 1849 Palmer claimed to be the sole representative of 1,300 of the estimated 2,000 U.S. newspapers published that year. A manufacturer or retailer considering an advertising program would walk into one of Palmer's offices, look over a list of newspapers available, examine specific newspapers from the racks of publications, indicate the market area that interested him, describe the seasonal preference, and reveal the amount of money that could be spent. Palmer then prepared a speculative presentation, which included space rates for each newspaper and the total proposed expenditure. To renumerate his agency for this work and for the hands-on preparation of the advertisements (including copywriting and layout), Palmer deducted a commission (historians believe it was 25 percent) from the publisher's bill before payment. Palmer did not charge the client for his estimates or for setting up the advertisement. No obligation was required of the merchant. This was the first time anything like this had been done. Business people were aware of advertising, but not of advertising in an organized, systematic way. The publisher of the *Baltimore Sun* testified in 1843 that "Mr. Palmer is, we believe, entitled to the credit for originating and establishing upon a general scale in this country, this new and important public convenience" (Holland, p. 12).

Palmer was a man ahead of his times. He called on business people and urged them to spend money on advertising, as mentioned. One pitch that he made contained the following:

A capitalist who freely spends one hundred thousand dollars to build and furnish a grand hotel . . . would stare if you suggest the outlay of $5,000 in letting everybody know that such a hotel had been opened; and so he spends ten thousand dollars in rent, for servants, superintendence, etc., while waiting for his house to become known . . . which a judicious outlay of $5,000 for advertising at the outset, would have saved and transmuted into profit. (*Supra*, p. 60, note 8)

To those merchants skeptical of investing in advertising, Palmer launched another broadside:

As a general rule, an advertisement in a paper now will meet the eyes of four to 10 times as many persons as a like announcement would have done twenty years ago. It is easy to place one where it will meet the eyes of one hundred thousand persons within two days, or by using half a dozen newspapers to challenge the attention of half a million people. (*Supra*, p. 61, note 8)

According to Holland, Palmer helped accelerate the Industrial Revolution:

In the 1840s, the pieces were beginning to fit together: production, distribution, market, transportation and the means of communication by way of newspapers. All had advanced to the point where Palmer was able to assemble them into a whole and call it a "System of Advertising." (p. 19)

S. M. Pettengill, in an article entitled "Reminiscences of the Advertising Business," which appeared in the December 24, 1890, issue of *Printer's Ink*, said that each day at about 10 A.M., Palmer would sally out in the narrow Philadelphia streets to find new clients. Signing on a new client was a cakewalk for Palmer. He would march into the counting room of the merchant, announce himself confidently, and hand out his card. Then, if they were willing to listen, he gave his pitch (p. 686).

Palmer presented a strong argument for the "billiard ball principle," which says that advertising can be likened to the opening break shot in pool or billiards. That is the moment events take place. The scope of the reaction is related to the force of the shot.

Palmer would tell advertising success stories, then show the merchant how he could easily double business and profits by doing the same thing. The next day Palmer would return with an estimate and a list of newspapers he advised. He usually walked out with a contract.

Pettengill, an employee at the agency, described Palmer in the following manner:

A short, thick-set gentleman of good address, genial and pleasant in manner, and had a good command of language, full of wise saws and modern instances. He was a capital story-teller, wore gold spectacles and carried a gold-headed cane, and was a first-rate canvasser. He had more self-possession and assurance than any man I ever knew. (p. 687)

No one knows whether Palmer attended college, but his writings, according to Holland, reveal a man at home among the classics (p. 33). He understood the power of the written word and was a skilled copywriter. He stressed the importance of advertising first and the services of the Palmer agency second. Service both to the publisher and the advertiser was the distinguishing mark of the Palmer agency.

Palmer's final days are shrouded in mystery. An article in the advertising journal *Fame* said that he became violently insane and that Horace Greeley hired a man to take care of him. There is no evidence, however, to support this claim, according to Holland (p. 35).

In the late 1850s Palmer formed a partnership with three men who worked for him as managers of his offices, John E. Joy, J. E. Coe, and W. W. Sharpe. The agency's name was V. B. Palmer and Company. Upon Palmer's retirement, Joy and Coe came to control the Philadelphia and New York offices, and Palmer's name was removed. Later, Sharpe became manager and then owner of the New York office. By the turn of the century the agency, which went by Sharpe's name, became one of the best known in New York.

The office in Boston was taken over by S. R. Niles, who had been hired when Pettengill left. Niles, who knew advertising well, became a successful advertising agent in Boston.

Upon Palmer's death in 1864, the Philadelphia office became known as Coe, Wetherill and Smith. The name was changed to Coe, Wetherill and Company upon Smith's death. Francis W. Ayer purchased this agency in October 1877 and incorporated it into his own, N. W. Ayer and Son. In this way, Palmer was the progenitor of one of the world's largest advertising agencies.

What Palmer's agency did—assist with budget planning, evaluate and select media, prepare advertisements, produce advertising copy, interject promotion and public relations, service accounts, proof, deliver, and bill—are all functions of today's advertising agency. His marketing of the concept of a regular, planned, strategic program anchors him as one of the major players in the history of advertising.

FURTHER READING

Works by Palmer

Supra. Pamphlet. 1855.

V. B. *Palmer's Business-Man's Almanac*. New York: 1849, 1850, 1851 (only three issues are known to exist).

V. B. Palmer's American Newspaper Subscription and Advertising Agency. New York: 1855. (Only two copies exist: one in the Library Company of Philadelphia, a private library founded by Benjamin Franklin, the other in the British Museum, London.)

Works about Palmer

Fox, Stephen. *The Mirror Makers: A History of American Advertising and Its Creators.* New York: William Morrow, 1984.

Holland, Donald R. *Volney B. Palmer (1799–1864): The Nation's First Advertising Agency Man.* Lexington, KY: Association for Education in Journalism (now the Association for Education in Journalism and Mass Communication), 1976.

Hower, Ralph M. *The History of an Advertising Agency: N. W. Ayer and Son at Work, 1869–1949.* Rev. ed. Cambridge: Harvard University Press, 1949.

Marchand, Roland. *Advertising the American Dream: Making Way for Modernity, 1920–1940.* Berkeley: University of California Press, 1985.

Pettengill, S. M. "Reminiscences of the Advertising Business." *Printer's Ink* (December 24, 1890): 686–90.

Wood, James Playsted. *The Story of Advertising.* New York: Ronald Press, 1958.

NOTABLE CLIENTS/CAMPAIGNS

1,300 newspapers

JOHN E. POWERS
(1837[?]–April 20, 1919)

Ted Curtis Smythe

John E. Powers was a single-minded man whose emphasis on simple, direct writing and truth in advertising had an important impact on the advertising of his day and on those copywriters who emulated him, because they also had learned that truth had its advantages in the marketplace.

Powers deliberately—it appears—obscured the facts of his background, so we are not even sure he was born in 1837 on a central New York State farm (Fox, p. 26). Perhaps it is just as well. We pick him up as he is traveling to England in 1868 to promote the Willcox and Gibbs sewing machine. On the ship, his son John O. later reported, Powers had plenty of time to consider methods of selling and advertising. He decided, his son claimed, on the policy of "let the seller beware of betraying his customers." This was a concept only a few others had put into practice. Fortunately for Powers, one of those who believed the customer should be treated fairly would be John Wanamaker of department store fame. Even Marshall Field of Chicago had not yet developed or expressed his famous "the customer is always right" (Appel, pp. 85–86).

Powers arrived in England and immediately began practicing "spare" American-style advertising, using fiction and jingles to attract British readers. He also created new marketing devices. He used all forms of communication to reach potential buyers, even including a free Christmas pantomime at Drury Lane Theatre. Costumed actors, using a story form, showed how the sewing machine worked. The advertising itself sometimes used odd type displays to attract attention, somewhat along the lines of Robert Bonner's ads a couple of decades earlier. Powers also experimented successfully with a free trial use of the machine before one was committed to buy it. He linked this concept with an easy payment plan. In an advertisement Frank Presbrey reprints from a British publication, Powers wrote: "Machines of other makes in exchange at their market value. Easy terms of payment, without extra charge, for those who cannot pay the full price at once. Illustrated book (96 pages) free.'' These innovations would become very popular in the United States (pp. 304–5).

Upon his return to America, after successfully creating a market for the sewing machine, Powers became business manager and publisher of the *Nation*. He had once sold subscriptions to the weekly; now he attracted advertisers to it by emphasizing the need for each field or industry to prepare copy distinctive to it. In booklets he prepared for advertisers, he warned against slavishly following a style that was not appropriate to the advertiser. In an advertisement Presbrey reprints, Powers wrote: ''A good bargain in advertising, i.e., a low rate, is always of less account than to say the right things to the right people in an acceptable way.'' As Presbrey points out, this was a foundation principle with Powers. This concept, as applied by Powers, meant he had to understand the product and the audience in order to write a proper advertisement (p. 306). He was not the only advertiser to espouse this view, but he certainly had few comrades in the 1870s.

Powers began writing ads for the Lord & Taylor department store in New York, applying principles he had gleaned from his own experiences as well as his analysis of contemporary retail advertising. He followed the same general practice he had pursued earlier: use of a narrative, copy-oriented style without adornment or illustration. This became a hallmark of Powers advertising. He emphasized short, one- to three-word headlines. For Lord & Taylor he limited himself to 100 words, but the ads attracted readers, including John Wanamaker of Philadelphia.

Wanamaker, who already shared Powers's viewpoint on candor in advertising, recognized the style of the Lord & Taylor ads as being similar to ads that earlier had appeared in English newspapers and magazines. He queried the company and found that Powers was willing to become an ''advertising counselor'' to Wanamaker, starting in May 1880. For much of the next decade the Wanamaker style was very much a Powers style.

Powers changed the display type used in Wanamaker ads, but he pursued the same lines of thought Wanamaker had followed before: candor, truth, and fairness to the customer. Even more than Wanamaker, Powers focused on direct, simple English to catch the reader's full attention. He used body type that was much more readable than most used in the newspapers of the day, whether in news columns or advertising, and his ads stood out.

Joseph H. Appel, who later headed advertising for Wanamaker stores, wrote extensively about Powers's contributions to the Wanamaker style in *Growing Up with Advertising*. Appel was at pains to show that Powers added to, but did not create, the Wanamaker style of candor and simplicity, full disclosure, and honest copy. Yet, even Appel was bemused by Powers's candor:

Powers carried frankness to such a degree that if a fashionable fabric was frail and would not give good wear *he advertised the fact.* . . .

There is a tale of a Wanamaker rubber goods buyer who stopped Powers on the floor of the store.

"Won't you mention our department in the next ad?" he asked.

"Anything particular?" said Powers.

"Well, between you and me," was the buyer's reply, "we have a lot of rotten gossamers that we wish to get rid of."

Powers took notes. The next day, the buyer's unbelieving eyes beheld an ad reading "we have a lot of rotten gossamers and things we want to get rid of." But by noon the lot was snapped up by shoppers appreciating the honesty. (pp. 88–89)

Powers was never an easy man to get along with. He was independent in his views, and when his boss did not share those views, Powers would not back down. There is some discrepancy as to what happened to end Powers's career with Wanamaker. Different sources provide contrary information. Both Appel (p. 89) and Presbrey (p. 308) say Powers resigned in 1886 to begin a free-lance career as a copywriter for various national advertisers. Stephen Fox says he was fired in 1883, hired back in 1884, then fired for good in 1886 (p. 27). Wherever the truth lies, Powers began a new career, writing copy for Scott's emulsion and Beecham's pills (both patent medicines), Murphy Varnish, Vacuum oil, and Macbeth's lamp chimneys. His distinctive style was soon seen wherever those ads appeared.

One contemporary claimed Powers was "never an advertising agent or copy writer, for he was content with nothing less than being the advertiser wherever he bestowed his labor." This may well have been hyperbole, yet Powers himself expressed the same thing when he wrote: "Whatever a manufacturer can do better than anyone else, and has time to do, let him do it himself, or let it be done immediately under his supervision. Whatever parts of his process he cannot do himself, let him get it done by the person or concern that can do it honestly, capably and thoroughly." That meant advertising (Presbrey, p. 308).

While Powers's early contributions to honesty in advertising cannot be denied, he also had a profound impact on raising the role of the copywriter in agency work. Few agencies had their own copywriters during the eighties and nineties. Advertisers sought out Powers because of his skill. This was not lost on other agents and prospective agents; a corps of writers followed in his footsteps. Charles Austin Bates, Nathaniel C. Fowler, Wolstan Dixey, and E. A. Wheatley were four copywriters who gained prominence during the end of the 19th century and into the 20th. Bates said the four had "definitely and publicly follow[ed] Powers as professional copy writers" (p. 309). Just as importantly, they emulated his emphasis on truth in advertising.

Powers died on April 20, 1919. During the last years of his life, his son, John O. Powers, had created a successful advertising agency in his own name.

FURTHER READING

Works by Powers

Unlike many copywriters who followed him, Powers wrote no "how-to" books; his outside writing was confined to a couple of pieces in *Printer's Ink*.

Works about Powers

Appel, Joseph H. *Growing Up with Advertising*. New York: Business Bourse, 1940.
Fox, Stephen. *The Mirror Makers: A History of American Advertising and Its Creators*. New York: William Morrow, 1984.
Presbrey, Frank. *The History and Development of Advertising*. 1929. Reprint. New York: Greenwood Press, 1968.

NOTABLE CLIENTS/CAMPAIGNS

Beecham's pills

John Wanamaker

Lord & Taylor

Macbeth's lamp chimneys

Murphy varnish

Nation magazine

Scott's emulsion

Vacuum oil

Willcox and Gibbs sewing machines

ROSSER REEVES
(September 10, 1910–January 24, 1984)

Tommy V. Smith

Rosser Reeves, father of the "unique selling proposition," was a strong advocate of "reason-why" and hard-sell advertising techniques. He worked his way up through the ranks of Ted Bates Advertising to assume the position of president in the 1950s. Reeves is well-known for his high-pressure, no-nonsense advertising.

Born in 1910 in Danville, Rosser Reeves launched his advertising career in his native Virginia after a chemistry paper he had written came to the attention of a Richmond banker. The paper, entitled "Chemistry and Its Relation to the Enrichment of Life," won a $500 award, and Reeves's name appeared on the front pages of the *Richmond News Leader* and the *Richmond Times-Dispatch*. The banker who read the paper, Thomas C. Bouschall, hired Reeves for $14 a week to work on the advertising department's house publication in 1929. After proving himself as a copywriter, Reeves eventually rose to ad manager of the Morris Plan Bank of Virginia after only six months.

In 1933, three and a half years after starting at Morris Plan, Reeves arrived in New York with $7 in his pocket and two suits in hopes of landing a job with an advertising agency. With the $60,000 Morris Plan advertising account as a bargaining chip, he secured a job with the Cecil, Warwick and Cecil agency, starting at $34.50 a week.

Reeves's early goal in the advertising profession was to become a multimillionaire within 20 years. By 1939 Reeves was earning $35,000 a year at Cecil, Warwick and Cecil and living in a mansion in Westchester, New York. He was 29 years of age.

From Cecil, Warwick and Cecil, Reeves moved to a major hard-sell agency in New York, Ruthrauff and Ryan. He changed jobs in hopes that Ruthrauff and Ryan's advertising philosophy would more closely mirror his own. After three years he joined Blackett, Sample and Hummert as copy chief. Again, Reeves moved in hopes of finding a home with a philosophy that coincided with his hard-sell principles.

In 1940 Reeves was afforded an opportunity in which he could help formulate an agency's philosophy. Happily, he accepted the offer. With the formation of Ted Bates Advertising, Bates and Reeves collaborated to shape the foundation of the premier hard-sell advertising agency in the United States.

An early success for Reeves and Ted Bates was Viceroy cigarettes. In 1945 Reeves noticed a pack of Viceroys on the desk of the president of Brown and Williamson Tobacco and asked him who had the account. The client replied, "Nobody. It's a sleeper—a filter cigarette" (Higgins, p. 106). After talking with Reeves about his hard-sell philosophy, the president allowed him to do a campaign for Viceroy on the $41,000 left over from Kool's production budget (Ted Bates had the Kool account). One ad formulated for Viceroy is classic hard-sell Reeves:

Headline: What *do* Viceroys do for you that *no other* filter tip can do?

Subhead A: ONLY VICEROY GIVES YOU 20,000 FILTER TRAPS IN EVERY FILTER TIP

Subhead B: TO *FILTER-FILTER-FILTER* YOUR SMOKE WHILE THE RICH-RICH FLAVOR COMES THROUGH

Copy: "Those 20,000 filter traps sure give me better flavor than I ever got from cigarettes without filters!"

"Yes, Viceroy's filtered smoke is so much better and I get no tobacco bits in my mouth."

ONLY A PENNY OR TWO MORE THAN CIGARETTES WITHOUT FILTERS

Slogan: World's Largest-Selling Filter Tip Cigarette

Reeves underlined key words, which was much like the technique used by John E. Kennedy earlier. The ad's visuals, which prominently showed a cutaway view of the product's filter, also had drawings of a man and a woman, conversing about the filter. The Viceroy pack and a penny were also shown.

For Reeves's efforts, Viceroy enjoyed success. Reeves recalled that the campaign helped increase sales and the advertising budget given to Ted Bates. Six or seven years later, Viceroy was spending $18 million a year on advertising (Higgins, p. 106).

In 1952 Reeves was a controversial figure because of his use of 10- and 30-second hard-sell television spots for presidential candidate Dwight Eisenhower. Although the spots drew criticism from the news media for containing little information about the candidate's position on critical issues, they helped elect Eisenhower. The famous "spots for Eisenhower" started a trend in political advertising still in use and still criticized today. The Reeves approach revolutionized political advertising and campaigning. Reeves also organized a group that raised $1.5 million to run Eisenhower's saturation campaign in critical states.

Another one of Reeves great successes in hard-sell advertising came with the Anacin campaign in the late 1950s. Reeves recalled that Anacin sales jumped from $17 million to $54 million in six months with the help of his copy. Whitehall Labs, makers of Anacin, were so impressed with Reeves's creativity that the budget was set at $86 million. Included in the campaign was the famous black-and-white television ad with three drawn panels depicting pain in a person's head: static, clanging bell, and electric charge. Along with the visuals, sound effects were used as attention-getting devices. The commercial was action-packed with relief from the irritating noises and visuals coming from the taking of Anacin. Reeves's "reason-why" tag line in the commercial stated that "Anacin gives you fast, fast, fast relief." Reeves commented on the ad: "You can come to me with all the subjective judgements you want, and . . . the artsy-crafty crowd; I have other criteria. . . . A big drug company doesn't spend $86,400,000 unless they're making money on it. That money was spent on one television commercial. It cost $8,200 to produce and it made more money than 'Gone with the Wind' " (Higgins, p. 97).

Reeves also had success in the late 1950s and early 1960s with M&Ms. He recalled his first meeting with John MacNamara, the company president:

As I found out after ten minutes' conversation, the advertising idea was inherent in the product. It was the only candy in America that had chocolate surrounded by a sugar shell. . . . I put the two hands on the screen and said, "Which hand has the M&M chocolate candy in it? Not this hand that's messy, but this hand because M&M candies melt in your mouth, not in your hand." That phrase . . . is a technique. But the idea of the campaign, that these candies do not melt because of the sugar shell, was the easiest thing in the world because it was inherent in the product. (Higgins, pp. 102–3)

Reeves' campaign helped bolster the sale of M&Ms. In fact, sales were so good that the company had to build two factories to handle the increased sales volume.

Reeves helped many consumer package goods companies increase sales. In addition to Viceroy, Anacin, and M&Ms, he also had successes with such notable clients as Colgate toothpaste ("Cleans your breath while it cleans your teeth"), Listerine, and Carter's Little Liver Pills.

Reeves, because of his hard-sell and "reason-why" tactics, was a controversial figure in advertising in the early 1960s. In 1961 he wrote *Reality in Advertising*, which became an international best-seller.

In the book he wrote about the Bates/Reeves hard-sell theories on advertising creativity and effectiveness. Reeves's book drew criticism, especially from those who were the forefathers of the creative revolution that was to come into vogue later in the 1960s. To counter one argument, Reeves maintained that an ad strategy must have a sales base. In contrast, Reeves's critics wanted advertising to amuse, entertain, and soft sell consumers in a free-form, free-thinking, creative way without the client worrying about sales.

In *Reality in Advertising* Reeves stated that advertising copy should be no-

nonsense, hard-selling, and unrelenting. His critics said that he lacked style and finesse. In other words, there were many critical of Reeves's "hit the consumer over the head" style of advertising. One of the attackers, former comedian and then ad practitioner Stan Freberg, called Reeves "the dean of the Gastro-Intestinal School of Advertising" (*Ad Pioneer*, p. 4). In spite of the criticism from "creative types" like Freberg, many of Reeves's clients enjoyed sales successes with the help of his campaigns. He and Ted Bates even acquired new business. After reading advance galleys of the book, Mobil Oil advertising manager J. D. Elgin had the $6 million Mobil account moved to Bates from Compton Advertising.

Included in Reeves's doctrine was his concept of the "unique selling proposition" (USP). Acknowledging a legacy from Claude Hopkins and Kennedy, he adhered to their first school of creative thought with his USP. Reeves thought that copy may make several selling points about a product, but one needs to be highlighted. That one point in every product that should be highlighted is tied to the USP, according to Reeves (pp. 46–62). However, it may be hard for a copywriter to recognize the USP easily, and some research may be needed.

At times a usable USP may be difficult to pinpoint and originality may suffer. With this Reeves thought in mind, the free-thinking creative critics again assailed Reeves as being uncreative. However, Reeves countered and raised warning signals about the preoccupation with originality that can lead copywriters to absurd extremes. Reeves said:

In searching after the different, the clever and the unusual, or in attempting to imitate some truly original approach, writers can forget that an advertising campaign is not designed to express their individual ego or talent for entertaining. Rather, it is a functional tool (reason-why) whose purpose is to fully inform the public via maximum projection of the message. Bring the brick and mortar of the basic claim to life with ideas, information, and specific visual interpretations that speak convincingly about why your product is better. (Burton, p. 302)

If the USP is not easily identified, as the one Reeves identified for M&Ms, a copywriter has to search for perceived value. This perceived value is much like what Hopkins identified for Schlitz beer when he wrote of steam-cleaned bottles. To help identify the USP, copywriters, according to Herb Ahrend, president of Ahrend Associates, should ask, What is the nature and background of the product? What feature(s) and benefit(s) make the product different? And, if the product is not different (like a parity product), what attribute and benefit can be highlighted that have never been highlighted by the competition? (Bly, p. 65)

Once the USP is decided upon, it must be repeated in ad after ad, regardless of how much the repetition annoys, according to Reeves. In other words, continuity and simplicity in advertising are very important.

The USP describes the major advantage of your product over the competition's, according to Reeves. Reeves believed that if your client's product is not somehow different and better than other products of the same type, there is no reason for the consumer to choose your product instead of the competition's. To be promoted effectively and to give your consumer a reason why to buy, your product must have a USP. Reeves stipulated that an ad using the product's USP must convey three things: 1) inform the consumers to buy our product and you will receive this specific benefit, 2) make a proposition to the consumers that the competition cannot and/or does not offer, and 3) make a proposition so vital to your consumers it will pull to your product your competitor's customers. Reeves believed that the USP was not so much something the copywriter put into the advertisement as something the consumer took out ("Ad Pioneer," p. 4).

Reeves believed that the USP is used effectively when the major benefit is featured in the headline. It can also be used as the major theme of the ad.

Critics said that Reeves's book and his USP were nothing more than a new-business pitch. The book did help bolster the Ted Bates client list, however, as Kennedy and Hopkins had done before with their written advertising doctrines.

After many years as the creative director of Bates, Reeves moved from vice-chairman to head of the agency in August 1955, following the death of Thomas F. Harrington. He remained as chairman until his retirement in 1965, the same year he was inducted into the Copywriters Hall of Fame. In retirement, Reeves formed real estate ventures, served as a business and marketing consultant, remained an avid reader, helped launch unknown writers, and was a licensed pilot, avid racing sailor, art and jewelry collector, and chess enthusiast.

In 1976 he and his son, Rosser Reeves III, founded Rosser Reeves, Inc., after the elder Reeves resigned as a consultant to Carter-Wallace. In 1977 Brown and Williamson assigned them a new menthol cigarette, Arctic Lights. The brand failed with smokers and was withdrawn from the market. Shortly after that, Reeves ended his advertising comeback. He died in 1984 at the age of 73 at his home in Chapel Hill, North Carolina.

FURTHER READING

Work by Reeves

Reality in Advertising. New York: Knopf, 1961.

Works about Reeves

"Ad Pioneer Reeves, 73, Dies." *Advertising Age* (January 30, 1984): 4, 85.
Bly, R. *The Copywriter's Handbook*. New York: Dodd, Mead, 1985.
Burton, P. *Advertising Copywriting*. 3d ed. Columbus, OH: Grid, 1974.
Higgins, Denis. *The Art of Writing Advertising: Conversations with Masters of the Craft*. Lincolnwood, IL: National Textbook Company, 1965.

NOTABLE CLIENTS/CAMPAIGNS

Anacin

Bic pens

Carter's Little Liver Pills

Colgate toothpaste

Eisenhower for President

Listerine

M&M candies

Mobil Oil

Viceroy cigarettes

HELEN LANSDOWNE RESOR
(February 20, 1886–January 2, 1964)

Ann Maxwell Keding

Helen Lansdowne began her career as a copywriter in Covington, Kentucky, at the age of 17 and became one of the most significant influences in the advertising industry. She was one of the main architects of the J. Walter Thompson company's growth. Working alongside her husband, Stanley Resor, she served the company for more than four decades as a vice president and director. Together, they built J. Walter Thompson into the largest single integrated advertising agency in the world.

Helen Lansdowne was born in Grayson, Kentucky, on February 20, 1886, to George and Helen Bayleff Lansdowne. Her mother was the daughter of a Presbyterian minister who had graduated from college and then studied for three years at Princeton Theological Seminary. For that time and region, Helen Bayleff came from a background of culture and aspiration. When she was four years old, the second youngest of nine children, her mother left her husband and took her children to Covington, where her two brothers lived. Having no trade and no apparent means to earn a living, she went to work for one brother as a clerk. The other brother helped by furnishing food money, while the oldest girl took charge of the household. Helen's mother eventually became a librarian and sold real estate. While they never lived in dire poverty, this early lesson in feminism and independence sheds light on Helen's later focus on a career (*The Mirror Makers*, p. 94).

In 1903, at the age of 17, Helen Lansdowne graduated high school as class valedictorian in Covington, Kentucky. That same year she began working for the World Manufacturing Company, manufacturers of toilet preparations sold exclusively by mail. In one of the only documents in which she wrote about her career and accomplishments, a stockholder's affidavit filed in the New York County Clerk's office, March 20th, 1924, she stated that she remained there less than a year, leaving for Procter and Collier, a Cincinnati advertising agency located across the Ohio River from Covington which functioned mainly as the house agency for Procter and Gamble. After a year or more as a bill auditor, she moved to the *Commercial Tribune*, a morning newspaper in Cincinnati, where she wrote advertisements for retailers.

A few years later, in 1906, Helen Lansdowne moved to the Cincinnati office of the Street Railways Advertising Company, an organization that controlled most of the streetcar advertising in the United States. About the time that she was offered a position in the company's main office in New York, Stanley Resor asked her to return to Procter and Collier. This was in 1907. In *The Mirror Makers*, Stephen Fox noted that when Stanley Resor asked her to come to work for him, her family warned her not to take the offer, saying, ''He'll work you to death'' (p. 81).

In the 1924 stockholder's affidavit, she wrote that she went to Procter and Collier a second time and, under the direction of Stanley Resor, wrote advertising for Red Cross shoes, Brenlin window shades, and Higgin all-metal screens. According to Fox, Stanley coined the brand name for Brenlin shades and took the unusual step of selling metal screens to the middle class, encouraging them to imitate the habits of wealthier people (p. 81).

A year later, in 1908, Stanley Resor and his brother Walter opened a branch of J. Walter Thompson in Cincinnati. At this point, Lansdowne left Procter and Collier to go along with the Resors as the only copywriter in the Thompson Cincinnati office. She remained there until January 1911, when she was promoted and moved to J. Walter Thompson in New York as a writer (p. 80).

Upon her departure, Helen Lansdowne recommended James Webb Young to Stanley Resor. Young was a schoolmate from Covington, Kentucky, who had quit school in the sixth grade. Stanley hired Young as a copywriter, and Young eventually succeeded him as head of the Cincinnati office (p. 82). Six years later, on March 6, 1917, when she was 31, Helen Lansdowne married Stanley Resor, age 37.

According to her own testimony in the 1924 stockholder's affidavit, Helen Lansdowne was the first woman to be successful in writing and planning national, as opposed to retail, advertising. Most of the J. Walter Thompson Company's clients made products used by women. For these, she supplied the feminine point of view. She watched the advertising to see that the ideas, words, and illustrations were effective for women.

As an example, in 1911, Procter and Gamble introduced Crisco, a vegetable shortening. They broke a 20-year rule and paid an outside agency, JWT, to prepare the opening campaign. On five occasions, Helen Lansdowne traveled to Cincinnati to appear before the P&G board of directors to explain the advertising. This was the first time Procter and Gamble had opened their board meetings to a woman.

Her affidavit further confirms that she wrote the original advertisements for Woodbury's facial soap, Yuban coffee, Lux, and Cutex. During the years she worked on these accounts, she also addressed the sales conventions of the clients, in order to explain why the advertising was prepared as it was. She wrote that her advertising differed so widely from all other advertising appearing at that time in American magazines that such an explanation was needed. She refers to issues of the *Ladies' Home Journal* for this period for examples of her innovations in advertising.

In 1917, when the firm of Libby, McNeill and Libby threatened to take their advertising to another agency, she was asked to come to Chicago and prepare an original campaign for them, even though she was to be married within a month. She went and worked until two days before she was to be married in New York.

As one of advertising's most prominent husband-and-wife teams, Stanley and Helen Resor divided the work load. Stanley tended to the administration, and Helen concentrated on the preparation of ads. It was known that on an informal level, they discussed all aspects of the business—over dinner or on the commuter train to their home in Greenwich, Connecticut. Decisions typically emerged with no clear line of accountability to either.

During 1916, 1917, and 1918, she was one of a committee of three that passed decisions on all policies of J. Walter Thompson, including the payroll and practically all personnel.

She attributes the success of J. Walter Thompson in large measure to the fact that they concentrated and specialized on products sold to women. Aware that a large proportion of retail purchases in grocery stores, department stores, and drug stores were made by women, she and others at JWT focused on women as a target.

She believed that advertising appeals for products bought by women must be made with knowledge of the habits of women, their methods of reasoning, and their prejudices. She claimed that her work for JWT was based on these conditions and principles and stated, "I believe that it is conceded in the advertising industry that our agency is pre-eminent when it comes to advertising articles for women" (stockholder's affidavit, March 20, 1924). She further disclosed that in 1918 and prior years, it was her responsibility to originate key advertisements— advertisements that indicated the appeal to be made and set the style which assistants could follow under her direction or that of Mr. Resor.

Woodbury's facial soap came to J. Walter Thompson as a client in 1910. According to Fox (p. 81), Helen's ads increased sales by 1,000 percent in eight years.

In the 1920s, JWT moved into first place in total agency billings and stayed there for the next five decades.

The Cincinnati team that moved to J. Walter Thompson, New York, included Helen Lansdowne, Stanley Resor, Gilbert Kinney (a classmate of Stanley's from Yale), James W. Young, and Henry Stanton. After only one year, Young and Stanton moved to Chicago to take over the western operation. Kinney remained with the Resors in New York, where he was business head of the agency for the next 35 years.

According to the *J. Walter Thompson Company News* of January 10, 1964, a confidential bulletin for employees, Helen Lansdowne Resor not only exercised a wide influence on the advertising industry but also influenced the field of modern art. Specifically, within the advertising industry, she developed concepts that made advertising an effective sales producer and opened the field to women. In the art field, it was well known that she was a patron, always looking for and encouraging new artists and photographers. James M. Woolf, one of the great JWT copywriters, described her contributions:

Mrs. Resor deserves immense credit for the quality of thinking she has contributed to making advertising copy an instrument of effective salesmanship. In an earlier day, when advertising as a science and an art of persuasion was still cutting its baby teeth, Mrs. Resor pioneered conceptions that to this day are the source of inspiration of many successful campaigns. The advertising agency is in debt to Mrs. Resor—not because she is a woman but because she is the fortunate possessor of a fine mind. (*J. Walter Thompson Company News*, January 10, 1964)

Helen Lansdowne Resor's contributions to the advertising industry begin with a style of advertising that made her one of the most celebrated copywriters of her generation, a style that became the hallmark of J. Walter Thompson's creative work. Her style was intuitive and aesthetic and she trusted her imagination. As Stephen Fox notes in *The Mirror Makers*, she developed an "editorial style" of advertising that imitated the look and layout of the Curtis flagships, her favorite media, the *Ladies' Home Journal* and *Saturday Evening Post* (p. 86). The ads resembled nearby reading matter and typically included a pretty painting, gently pointed selling copy, and an offer of a free or inexpensive sample by mail.

Her most famous ad, for Woodbury's facial soap, established this style with a painting by Alonzo Kimball. The subject of the painting is a handsome couple in evening dress, the man embracing the woman from the side, the woman smiling and winsomely looking away. Beneath the painting is the headline, "A skin you love to touch," followed by seven paragraphs of copy. Albert Lasker of Lord and Thomas declared the three great landmarks in advertising history to be Ayer's introduction of the open contract, his own development of "reason-why" advertising, and JWT's use of sex appeal in the Woodbury's ad (p. 87).

Helen Resor and J. Walter Thompson have been given credit for inventing endorsement advertising. While endorsement advertising had been used for many years, Resor changed the tone of it by persuading society leaders, people of rank, and even members of European royalty to endorse Pond's cold cream. According to the *J. Walter Thompson Company News*, January 10, 1964, central to her approach to endorsement advertising or any other kind of advertising was the concept that copy must be believable. "This concept is her great legacy to JWT and advertising" (p. 9).

Helen Resor's aesthetic contributions ranged beyond advertising. Her interest in architecture and interiors was initially displayed in the decor of the JWT offices, particularly the New York office. In 1927, when the New York office moved from 244 Madison Avenue to the Graybar Building, she took this opportunity to create a showcase in Thompson's new corporate headquarters. Believing that people work better in tasteful, comfortable surroundings, she chose furnishings not as client-pleasers, but to please the occupants. To complete this project, she commissioned Norman Bel Geddes to design a lecture hall; hired numerous interior designers, among them Elsie de Wolfe, to decorate specific offices; commissioned Samuel Yellin to create iron grillwork for the executive wing; and moved an entire colonial kitchen brick by brick to serve as the private dining room (Fox, p. 90).

With an eye for new art trends, she commissioned work by talented artists and undoubtedly contributed to the prominence they attained. She sought out Richard Lippold as one of the outstanding modern sculptors, just as she did Edward Steichen, already recognized as one of the greatest photographers of his time. She is credited with bringing Steichen into advertising at a time when photography was little used in advertisements.

Steichen's notable work in advertising was for Jergen's Lotion, Eastman Kodak, and several charities to which Helen Resor devoted time and attention. These included the Federation of Jewish Philanthropies of New York, the Manhattan Eye, Ear, and Throat Hospital, and the Traveler's Aid Society. It is fair to say that Steichen's work for JWT paved the way for a far-reaching change in the entire appearance of advertising.

Steichen did his first work for JWT in 1923. Up to that time, advertising art was dominated by illustrators. Photographs that were used were ordinary and poorly executed. Looking for ways to make advertising more readable, Helen Resor approached him because of his work for *Vogue* and *Vanity Fair*.

Steichen was interested in bringing realism to advertising. In his autobiography, *A Life in Photography*, he acknowledges that he had noticed and was disturbed by the poor quality of advertising photography. When approached with an offer for Jergen's Lotion, he took the job. The idea was to photograph the hands of a woman who did her own housework, and among the tasks to choose from, he preferred the task of peeling potatoes. He wrote, "Mrs. Stanley Resor, wife of the president of J. Walter Thompson, posed for the hands, and I could tell by the way she cut the potatoes that this wasn't the first time she had done it" (Steichen, pp. 9, 10). Steichen was eventually persuaded to take advertising photographs exclusively for JWT clients.

Revolutionary for its time, Steichen's work helped change the entire appearance of modern advertising. Other famous photographers who did their first advertising work for JWT were Cecil Beaton and Youseff Karsh. Norman Rockwell was also first used by JWT.

Helen Resor was introduced to Mrs. Cornelius Sullivan, a founder of the Museum of Modern Art in New York, then introduced to the board of trustees, and soon thereafter elected to the board. She served as a trustee from May 1935 until February 1940. Through her activities, her interests in modern art and architecture developed. Her collection of paintings and her readings in architecture were also strongly influenced by Alfred Barr. Most likely at his urging, she contacted Ludwig Mies van der Rohe in Berlin in late 1936 or early 1937. After meeting him in Paris during the summer of 1937, the Resors invited him to come to America as their guest. This gave him a reason to leave Germany. He returned with the Resor family to New York, visited them at their ranch in Jackson Hole, Wyoming, and agreed to design a house spanning the bridge, to attach to the existing service building. This marked the end of his European phase and the beginning of his work in America.

Helen Resor wished to improve not only the aesthetic surroundings of the JWT offices but the intellectual and cultural environment. Herself an avid reader, she commissioned historian Lewis Mumford to compile a list of 3,000 books to be purchased for the use of company employees. Fanny Bell of the research library was given the task of supplying the volumes as quickly and cheaply as possible. She began to collect them in February 1927 and ended, without completion, in March 1933. By 1930 books had already begun to disappear from the collection. The last survey, taken on October 23, 1967, listed 44 remaining titles.

Helen Lansdowne Resor was also responsible for recognizing the talent of and supporting the following women writers: Aminta Casseres, Ruth Waldo, Peggy King, Nancy Stephenson, and others. By committing to women writers as she did at JWT, she was credited with influencing the industry so that other talented women writers were able to find opportunities in advertising.

On page 43 of the July 1920 issue of the *Ladies' Home Journal*, an article appears entitled, "Doctor? Lawyer? Merchant? Chief?—Which Shall She Be? Woman's New Leadership in Business." The byline is Harriet Abbott, but anyone familiar with J. Walter Thompson and its history will quickly link Abbott's words with Helen Lansdowne Resor. In this article Abbott writes about an unidentified advertising woman's success, which is attributed to her belief in women's power, honesty, and implicit response to a direct appeal. This woman also prided herself on being able to look into "the heart of a stammering college girl applying for a job and recognize a flicker of genius that could be developed until she and her genius become part of the corporate genius."

Abbott further wrote:

. . . a young woman who claims she can write advertising based upon her ability to write clever place cards is given no place in the organization. She is told that advertising today is not based on cleverness, but on research and statistics, on long months of study of manufacturing, production, previous advertising campaigns, not only of the clients' products but of all competitors' products; that advertising today is concerned with art and the successful advertiser is allied with the art museum of his city, bulletins its lectures and exhibits for his employees and makes copy artistic as well as commercial.

Abbott also wrote that the agency (of the successful advertising woman) searched back into a young woman's interests in college.

Was she attracted by economics, psychology, sociology, history? Was she a real student? Did she really dig out the causes of things, think for herself, enjoy thinking for herself? Or did she learn texts and lectures by rote, pass "exams" with amazing A-plusses, bury her nose constantly in the alcoves of the college library or keep an eye forever over a scope? What was her mother like? Was she a constructively minded woman, seeing a big future dawning for women over the horizon, even though she herself stayed at the grindstone to put her daughter through college? Did she breathe this faith of hers into her daughter, filling her young mind with the vision of a new day for women when they should stand squarely beside men on the platform of achievement?

To have been hired by this "successful advertising woman," a young woman had to answer these questions satisfactorily and provide personal references. If she passed this test, she was hired for a minimum salary of $25 a week, the same as a man.

New York was the first state to make changes in its constitution, and New York City was the central stronghold of the movement. Helen Resor organized a group of JWT women who marched in the suffragette parade in New York following President Wilson's support of women's suffrage in 1915 or 1916.

According to Agnes Court, her secretary for 46 years, "Mrs. Resor got us all big campaign hats to wear of various colors—green, purple, white. We marched from 42nd Street to 59th Street, and after the parade, J. Walter Thompson gave us a big dinner at the Savoy Hotel."

J. Walter Thompson was the first agency to engage women for major positions, and it became known for this. Helen Resor made it the only big agency with a feminist near the top (Fox, p. 288).

Copywriter Peggy King credits Helen Resor with fostering her growth and independence. She wrote that when she was a beginning writer, Resor sent her on a coast-to-coast trip with a photographer. She then sent her to Sands Point, Long Island, to interview Mrs. O.H.P. Belmont and assigned her the first Pond's "great lady" advertisement. She took her to Washington to work on the wartime revisions of government booklets. Taking an even greater interest in her personal development, Resor encouraged her to rent paintings and sculpture from the Museum of Modern Art, to have very good clothes, to work with top decorators at home and in the office. She mentored women writers, knowing they "needed a friend in court" (*J. Walter Thompson Company News*, January 10, 1964).

Peggy King commented further that "she had a dozen ideas to the minute and kept them coming so fast you couldn't possibly keep up and had to sit down afterward with a pencil and paper and try to sort them out." King related that Mrs. Resor had such faith in those who worked for her that they were motivated to put forth more effort.

Nancy Stephenson once asked Helen Resor the best way for a woman to succeed in advertising. Mrs Resor replied, "I really shouldn't answer that. I cheated. I married the boss." But Stephenson noted that anyone who knew her as Helen Lansdowne could tell you that Mrs. Resor was recognized as an outstanding advertising strategist years before she married Stanley Resor.

It was generally agreed upon by those who knew her that she had a brilliant feminine mind that darted and dipped and swooped with terrifying speed and accuracy. She demanded rigor and preparing for a meeting with her required digging for supporting facts and figures weeks in advance. Tiny, easy-to-come-by ideas stood little or no chance with her. She was a creator and executor of grand and daring ideas. To her, nothing was impossible. No thinking was too ambitious, no effort too great if it brought a great idea to life.

Women in advertising, and particularly women in the Thompson offices around the world, owe Mrs. Resor a great deal for the inspiring standards she set for us to follow. (*J. Walter Thompson Company News*, January 10, 1964)

Once, when addressing two apprentice groups, Mrs. Resor spoke on a number of topics including: the value of a general knowledge of the agency, indicating that even with that knowledge, an individual's progress depended on his ability to do the job at hand; and whether or not there was anything new under the sun in advertising, commenting that she did not expect one would recognize advertising in 20 years (*J.W.T. Junior News Letter*, March, 1936).

When asked about the J. Walter Thompson's contributions to advertising, Mrs. Resor indicated that its activities in certain cases led to the widespread use of such forms as editorial copy, photography, and the testimonial. She also commented that the company had always recognized new methods in advertising and used them while they were still news.

Of the most important changes in advertising methods at that time, Mrs. Resor listed the filing of data for agency information by the American Association of Advertising Agencies, the development of radio, and the move toward a 15 percent commission versus cut rate prices. In defense of advertising, she said that the legitimate answer to a critic's attack was the fact that advertising made mass production economical by creating an increased turnover of goods.

Throughout her talk, Mrs. Resor clearly indicated the necessity for discretion on the part of agency members in talking of matters that concerned only the client and those with whom he worked. She also stressed the value of knowing what one was talking about in dealing with businessmen. Authority speaks through figures, and opinions through experience, she said.

Helen Lansdowne Resor was described by those who knew and worked with her as a retiring woman who never took personal credit for her accomplishments. She was rarely photographed, she seldom attended industry meetings, and she authored no books. In the 1924 stockholder's affidavit, she wrote, "I have been asked for articles on myself, on my work, by many of the women's magazines and by the following newspaper syndicates: Doubleday Page Service, McClure Syndicate Service, North American Newspaper Alliance and Hearst's International Service. As publicity of this kind does not appeal to me, I have refused these requests." However, in July 1924, when Stanley Resor was president of the American Association of Advertising Agencies, he and Helen visited London, where they attended a dinner given for overseas advertising agents. The July 23, 1924, issue of *Punch* carried a sketch of Mrs. Resor along with this comment:

The President of the American Association of Advertising Agencies looks like a senator. The wife of the President of the American Association of Advertising Agencies looks like a Rosetti. How frightfully fit and well most of these ladies and gentlemen seem to be! That's through practising what they preach, you know. They keep that schoolgirl complexion. Truth in advertising. . . .

Helen Lansdowne Resor had a long history of public service involvement through advertising. In 1917 and 1918 she was invited by President Hoover to create a campaign for the conservation of food. In addition to this public service campaign, she also created advertisements used during World War I for the Red Cross and the YMCA.

According to the August 5, 1918, *J. Walter Thompson Company News*, ''Mrs. Resor will hereafter direct and supervise all of our war work. For this patriotic work on behalf of the company, she is refusing to accept even the customary honorarium of one dollar a year.'' According to the January 11, 1943, issue, ''Those lights burning in Mrs. Resor's office Christmas Eve weren't candles. Just a huddle on a knockout graphic arts training presentation ordered by the War Department.'' A few months later the full story of JWT and its government client, the War Manpower Commission, was revealed. Helen Resor, Jim Young, and Bill Berchtold, with the support of their complete creative department, created a campaign to get three million women into war factories and related civilian activities by the end of the year. The national magazine and radio campaign, with an emphasis on local advertising, broke the first week of April with the theme, ''Women must work to win this war.'' Local advertising consisted of car cards, posters, newspaper ads, radio spots, publicity releases, and speeches presented by local chairmen in over 100 cities.

A press release from the J. Walter Thompson Company at the time of her death stated that Helen Resor actively supported many other organizations and causes, including: Radcliffe College, the Planned Parenthood Association, the Babies Ward of the New York Post-Graduate Hospital, and the Travelers Aid Society, a shelter for homeless women during the Depression. At the New York Post-Graduate Hospital, she was responsible for improvements the hospital had been trying to make for years without success. After World War II she gave special commissions to artists in England to help them reestablish themselves.

In 1961, when Stanley Resor retired, the J. Walter Thompson Company's billings were over $370 million, and a staff of 6,225 was employed in 55 offices in the United States and abroad. JWT was the first American advertising agency to branch out to worldwide dimensions, beginning its overseas operations with an office in London in 1927. Stanley Resor died on October 29, 1963. Helen Lansdowne Resor died two months later on January 2, 1964. They were survived by their three children: Stanley, Helen, and Ann. By this time J. Walter Thompson had become the largest single integrated advertising agency in the world.

Mrs. Stanley B. Resor was elected into the Advertising Hall of Fame three years after her death. In the *Index*, it is written that ''she will be remembered particularly in two capacities—her own work as a copywriter (she was described by the *New York Herald Tribune* as the greatest copywriter of her generation) and her work as Vice-President and the president's wife of the J. Walter Thompson Co.''

Her Hall of Fame citation acknowledges that she was the first woman to be successful in writing and planning national, as opposed to retail, advertising; that she opened the advertising agency field to women, training many who later became famous in their own right; that she was a constant source of ideas for the staff and for clients; that she brought the feminine point of view to advertising; that she addressed clients' conventions and advised management; and that she supervised two-thirds of the business handled by the New York and Boston offices. It further states:

Her creative, racing mind was constantly suggesting new approaches to advertising of products. She was a coiner of slogans, a promoter of graphics and photography, a genius of the ''key writing'' on many accounts. She revolutionized endorsement advertising by persuading society leaders and even royalty to appear in Pond's Cold Cream advertisements.

FURTHER READING

Work by Resor

''Doctor? Lawyer? Merchant? Chief?—Which Shall She Be? Woman's New Leadership in Business.'' *Ladies' Home Journal* (July 1920): 43 (byline: Harriet Abbott).

Works about Resor

Fox, Stephen. *The Mirror Makers: A History of American Advertising and Its Creators.* New York: William Morrow, 1984.
''In First 100 Years, Thompson Spurs Rise of Magazines, Agency Concept, Ad Role in Sales Strategy.'' *Advertising Age* (December 7, 1964): 31–32, 36.
Steichen, Edward. *A Life in Photography.* Garden City, NY: Doubleday, 1963.

NOTABLE CLIENTS/CAMPAIGNS

Aunt Jemima

Carter's underwear

Charles Williams stores

Cutex nail polish

Kayser underwear and gloves

Lever Brothers

Maxwell House coffee

Nonatuck Silk Company

Pictorial Review

Pond's cold cream and vanishing cream

Pyrex glass

R. F. Simmons jewelry

Schweizer Importers

Silk Association of America

Stork rubber sheeting and pants for babies

Tintex dyes

Woodbury's facial soap

Yuban coffee

PHYLLIS K. ROBINSON
(October 22, 1921–   )

Roxanne E. Neuberger-Lucchesi

Phyllis K. Robinson made history when she joined Doyle Dane Bernbach in 1949. Not only was she the first copy chief at the agency, she was the first female copy chief in all of advertising. She helped mold the creative philosophy of this pioneering agency, and her influence as a supervisor was widespread.

Born October 22, 1921, to Irving and Teresa (Goldschneider) Kenner, Robinson's interest in the advertising business started with a love for writing poetic verses. At age seven she proclaimed her desire to become a poet, then changed her career focus to advertising a few years later. During a 1968 interview for *Advertising Age*, she commented, "I can remember that as a kid I was influenced just by the vitality of some of the retail store advertising that was going on. I can remember telling one of my favorite teachers in school that I wanted to be an advertising writer" (Revett, p. 47).

"When other little girls in P.S. 50 were dreaming of growing up to be Ginger Rogers, I wanted to be Dorothy Parker, and I looked constantly for excuses to write jingles" ("Listen to Angry Young Voices," p. 16).

World War II was starting as she entered college, and the conflicts around the world aroused her interest in political and social issues. Robinson felt it was important to do something to help in these areas, so she enrolled at Barnard College as a sociology major. She pursued her interest in advertising as advertising manager of the school newspaper, the *Barnard Bulletin*. Her career started as many advertising careers have started: She sold and wrote advertisements for local retailers.

While in college Robinson hesitated to enroll in writing courses. "I had this cockeyed notion that I was some kind of writer and I didn't want anybody to touch it. It was like it was something very precious and I didn't want anybody to twist my wrist or make me go in a certain direction" (Revett, p. 47).

Robinson learned to appreciate editors one summer while writing for a society publication called *Park East*. When asked by *Advertising Age* who most influenced her writing career, Robinson mentioned, among others, the man who ran this news magazine, Bob Altshuler. He told her to "cut out the pretentiousness and get to the point. I think it was just the shock of somebody saying that to me that helped me a lot, right away, very fast. I don't think anybody had ever criticized my writing before" (p. 47).

After graduating from Barnard in 1942, she became a statistician for the Federal Public Housing Authority in New York. Two years later she married Richard G. Robinson, a student at Harvard. Soon after he was drafted, and his college career and her work with public housing were interrupted. As the coupled traveled from post to post, Robinson worked at a variety of jobs, and her interest in advertising and promotion reemerged.

The experience she gained at *Park East* was helpful in landing a job at the Methodist Publishing House in Nashville. The second job Robinson held during this period was one with Fairchild Publications, as a reporter for *Women's Wear Daily*. She went from writing ads for religious calendars and "snappy sermons" to covering fashion in Miami (French, p. 410).

In 1945 Robinson and her husband returned to New York. She started a new job as executive editor of the *Tobé Fashion Report* for the Tobé Colburn School for Fashion Careers. The job lasted only a year, because the couple moved when her husband returned to Harvard to finish his senior year. Robinson landed her first agency job; she was hired as a copywriter for women's fashion advertisements at Bresnick and Solomont in Boston.

After her husband graduated in 1946, the couple returned to New York and Robinson went to work for Grey Advertising. She was working in the promotion department when the agency's creative director, Bill Bernbach, spotted her talents and transferred her to the advertising department as a copywriter. Three years later he opened his own agency, Doyle Dane Bernbach, and invited her to join the new company. As copy chief of the 12-person agency she did all of the copywriting.

"My earliest feeling, as Bill Bernbach whisked Bob Gage and me away from a traditional agency setting, was of playing hooky. Holy cow, we thought, we can do all this good stuff and get paid for it" (Robinson, "One of the DDB Originals," p. 6).

Bernbach and Ned Doyle, employees of Grey Advertising, and Maxwell Dane, with a small agency of his own, founded Doyle Dane Bernbach. The agency's client list included a few Dane clients and Ohrbach's department store, taken along from Grey.

According to Robert Glatzer in *The New Advertising*, the agency discovered that an art director and copywriter working as a team produced exciting results. The teams were typically formed by Bernbach or the agency's art director, Gage (p. 18). The art director and the copywriter were considered equals and worked as one. "The emphasis must always be on the excellence of the end product, not on whether you contribute 5 percent or 95 percent of an idea" (Robinson, "Creative Challenge Papers," p. 36).

Doyle Dane Bernbach (DDB) employees appeared to love their work, and visitors to the agency routinely commented on the highly charged atmosphere. That excitement came from the top and filtered down. Robinson said, "Bill was far from a classic father-figure. He wanted you to do your best, but he was highly competitive" (Robinson, "One of the DDB Originals," p. 6). "The rough times for us are not when we're with the client, but when we're with each other. We're very demanding in the creative department—some people say we could run another agency out of our wastebaskets—and we keep asking, 'Is it good enough?' " ("Big Billings," p. 108).

Robinson wrote copy for the very first Ohrbach's ads created at DDB. These well-known institutional ads, positioning Ohrbach's as a high-fashion department store offering low prices, made a splash during the early 1950s. Levy's, a little Jewish bakery in Brooklyn, hired the agency in 1949 to promote its packaged ryes, pumpernickel, and raisin breads. The account went from "nearly bankrupt" status to one of the leading Jewish rye breads in and around New York. DDB took a new approach and targeted the masses, "New York's army of Wonder Bread eaters":

Sales improved, but the largest grocery chains would not stock Levy's until, a few years later, Mrs. Robinson wrote a radio campaign featuring the voice of a little boy asking for "Wevy's Cimminum Waisin Bwead," while his mother tries to correct his pronunciation. People all over New York walked around saying, "I Wuv Wevy's." It was one of the first radio campaigns to use the sounds of speech effectively and humorously and, together with a print ad showing a grocer cowering in the corner of his store against a barrage of packages thrown by irate customers, and saying, "All right, already. I'll stock Levy's," finally cracked the big chain-store market for the company. (Glatzer, p. 54)

"I may be single-handedly responsible for lowering the level of radio advertising by writing one of the first 'funny' spots in recent radio history, for Wevy's cimminum waisin bwead," said Robinson during her acceptance speech into the Copywriter's Hall of Fame.

In the late 1950s Robinson helped DDB earn a reputation for solid television commercials. She was developing award-winning commercials for Chemstrand, Acrilan, and Polaroid. Polaroid moved its account to DDB in 1954. The agency's challenge was to overcome the camera's "gimmicky" image and convince consumers to accept and use the product. Robinson commented in *The New Advertising*, "We told the story in one line: 'How to take a picture one minute and see it the next.' That line said everything" (p. 31).

According to Glatzer, the camera continued to gain acceptance among consumers during the late 1950s. DDB used a series of successful ads, including the introduction of new high-quality black-and-white film with Polaroid photographs taken by professional photographer Bert Stern. The campaign extended to television, with live demonstration commercials on Steve Allen's *Tonight Show*.

In 1961, the campaign moved from demonstration to life-style ads focusing on the pictures themselves. Glatzer reports that one of the most famous Polaroid commercials, created by Robinson and Gage, was a sentimental one featuring the parents of a bride looking at Polaroid pictures at the end of their daughter's wedding day.

"People say that commercial is so moving," says Mrs. Robinson. "What is it? Well, a lot of it wouldn't be possible if Bob Gage and I couldn't say we're human, and we're touched by things, and we put our feelings on the screen. Not to use the tender feelings between people, not to use people's hopes and cares, is abdicating your responsibility. That commercial is an example of this expression of feeling. We had to have the conviction not only that we could get across the feeling of the wedding, but that we could go beyond the triteness of the situation. We felt it was possible to use the tenderer human emotions in advertising without getting icky; and it's a hell of a selling tool." (p. 38)

Other successful commercials included vignettes of friends and families in emotional situations at the zoo and on a train. The smiles and tears developed instantly, as did the popularity of the Polaroid camera. A 1958 magazine ad, featuring a "nerd at the beach" getting attention with his Polaroid camera, confirmed that copy and headlines were not necessary to sell the camera (Fox, p. 254).

One of Robinson's favorite television ads was the Chemstrand hosiery commercial. It took her a mere hour to write the lyrics for the ad, stating, "A lady's not dressed unless her legs are too." It won top honors at the International Advertising Film Festival in Venice and at an *Advertising Age* creative workshop.

Robinson worked with Mitch Leigh, head of Music Makers, on the Chemstrand jingles. This presented the opportunity for her to collaborate with him on a Broadway musical in 1970, *Cry for Us All*. She said the reason she never did anything else on Broadway is that her agency work was always gratifying ("Big Billings," p. 108).

On May 20, 1968, an article in the *New York Times* announced that Robinson would be inducted into the Advertising Writers Association of New York Copywriters Hall of Fame at the Eighth Annual Gold Key Awards dinner. Robinson joined Leo Burnett, George Gribbin, David Ogilvy, Bill Bernbach, Rosser Reeves, Julian Koenig, and Bernice Fitz-Gibbon in the Hall of Fame. At the banquet, Bernbach said that Robinson "evoked from advertisers a new appreciation of advertising creativity. She helped make it possible for Doyle Dane Bernbach to have the courage of its convictions, to know the difference between good creative work and mere creative acrobatics." He also said that Robinson helped to "turn advertising from a business into a profession" ("Listen to Angry Young Voices," p. 16).

Robinson admitted she was tough and had the reputation of being an "iron fist in the velvet glove.'' While she maintained a cordial relationship with her writers, she was not afraid to ask for revisions 20 times (Revett, p. 48).

Among agency founders who first worked at DDB are Julian Koenig, George Lois, and Mary Wells. Robinson supervised both men and women, but she especially helped numerous women get started in the advertising business. Along with Wells, she supervised Paula Green, Judith Protas, Lore Parker, and Rita Selden. Robinson remarked, ''Oh I feel like an old grandmother, I've got all these offspring all over the place. There are a lot of talented people in the business now, but an awful lot of them started [at DDB] and they're clearly under our influence, and acknowledge it'' (Revett, p. 48).

Bernbach was very sentimental and shared this family instinct, but they did not try to create copies of themselves. She attributes the agency success to incorporating fresh strains of talent and encouraging originality with respect and breathing space (Robinson, ''Phyllis Robinson,'' p. 3).

Writing has always been easy for Robinson. ''When I'm ready, I write very quickly. It comes out in a real spurt—as if it has a life of its own'' (''Big Billings,'' p. 108). She has always started each assignment by learning as much as possible about the product. She then lets the words and ideas flow through free association; it does not matter if she is at home, at work, or in between.

Many of Robinson's brainstorming sessions included her most frequent partner, Gage. In her Hall of Fame acceptance speech, she thanked him ''for being the best and most talented partner a writer could have.'' She noted that one should have a deep respect for one's partner's ''idiosyncrasies and work habits. . . . You sometimes have to sit through long embarrassing silences, listening to each other's stomach growl. And sometimes you have to wade through a lot of irrelevant talk. In a really free creative atmosphere, you have to have a profound respect for each other's free associations, no matter how preposterous or tiresome or irritating they are. Because out of this bubbling and babbling might come a great idea.''

Robinson felt quite fulfilled with her work as copy chief. In her Hall of Fame speech, she joked that the big news was that she was not planning to open her own agency. ''To start an agency you've got to have personal ambition, which I have, but a lot of that has been satisfied for me. You have to want to really build something from scratch, and I participated in so much and so thoroughly that I've had that'' (Revett, p. 48).

Robinson stayed at DDB for 33 years. She was promoted to vice president in 1956 and worked in that capacity until 1962, when the Robinson's only daughter, Nancy, was born. At that time she decided to work only three days each week and gave up her job as copy chief. She continued to write part-time for DDB until 1982, when she retired from the agency to open a consulting firm. Robinson also has been involved in public service campaigns. She is a member of the creative review board of the Media-Advertising Partnership for a Drug-Free America and a founding member of Ads against AIDS.

FURTHER READING

Works by Robinson

The Creative Challenge Papers from the 1959 Regional Conventions: How Do We Do It? New York: American Association of Advertising Agencies, 1960.

"One of the DDB Originals Recalls How It All Began with Bill Bernbach." *Adweek* (October 11, 1982): 6.

"Phyllis Robinson: New Face in the Copywriter's Hall of Fame." *DDB News* (July 1968): 1–3.

Works about Robinson

"Big Billings Don't Necessarily Constrict Creativity, Doyle Dane's Robinson Declares." *Advertising Age* (October 20, 1958): 2, 108.

Dougherty, Philip H. "Advertising: Lady Writer Carves a Niche." *New York Times* (May 20, 1968): 74.

Fox, Stephen. *The Mirror Makers: A History of American Advertising and Its Creators.* New York: William Morrow, 1984.

French, Elbrun Rochford. *The Copywriter's Guide.* New York: Harper, 1958.

Glatzer, Robert. *The New Advertising.* New York: Citadel Press, 1970.

"It's More Vital for Adman to Know Ads Than Client's Business: Bernbach." *Advertising Age* (August 14, 1961): 3, 88.

"Listen to Angry Young Voices in Ad Field, DDB's Phyllis Robinson Says." *Advertising Age* (June 3, 1968): 1, 16.

Revett, John. "Comments of a Copy Chief." *Advertising Age* (July 15, 1968): 47–48.

NOTABLE CLIENTS/CAMPAIGNS

Chemstrand

Clairol

Levy's bread

Ohrbach's department store

Polaroid

GEORGE PRESBURY ROWELL
(July 4, 1838–August 28, 1908)

Ted Curtis Smythe

George P. Rowell worked for nearly 40 years in advertising, first with his own agency in Boston and then with his own agency in New York. During this time he became one of the best known agents in the country, pioneering in several areas of advertising. Many of his innovations shaped the field as we know it today.

Born on July 4, 1838, in Concord, Vermont, to Samuel and Caroline E. (Page) Rowell, George lived his preteen years in Manchester, New Hampshire, and metropolitan Boston. He attended the academy in Lancaster, New Hampshire, for four years and spent one semester at the academy in St. Johnsbury, Vermont. He taught in district schools in New Hampshire when he was 16. He then left for Boston, where he became an errand boy, rising to bookkeeper, but in the Panic of 1857 he lost his position and returned to New Hampshire to teach school. That spring he got a job with the *Boston Post* in its counting room. He was associated with newspapers and advertising for the remainder of his life.

When the *Post* sent Rowell to New York to collect on bills owed by advertisers, he was so successful that he began to solicit advertising. He soon learned that advertising rates on newspapers were a flexible commodity; he arranged for the house in which he was boarding to advertise in the paper; he cut his expenses to the bone in the process. He became successful, after a fashion, at selling advertising in the *Post*, earning $14 weekly in 1862, which enabled him to marry his childhood sweetheart, Sarah Burnside Eastman.

After seven years with the *Post* Rowell was earning $18 a week. Nevertheless, he branched out into independent work while he continued to sell advertising for the paper. He produced a daily program for theaters during the three-week holiday season in 1864, an idea he had picked up while visiting New York. He netted $600, a striking sum for the day (he earned less than $1,000 during a good year with the *Post*). His success gave him the confidence to leave the paper in 1865 to launch an advertising agency with close friend Horace Dodd. They rented an office on Congress Street in Boston and invested $6 in circulars. He had much to learn about the business since he came into it as a relative outsider.

A request for a bid on placing advertising in New Brunswick and Nova Scotia caused Rowell to investigate the newspaper situation in those provinces. There was no directory of American and Canadian newspapers available, so he visited itinerate compositors and printers to get a feel for the newspaper situation there. He then bid to publish the ads. After he received the order, he found many of the newspapers no longer existed. Instead, he substituted other papers to the satisfaction of the Hartford publishing house that had placed the order. He was successful, but in the process of placing the order, he recognized how the business was done. He quickly built a proprietary list of newspapers since all advertising agents built such lists. They offered to advertisers something the advertiser could not know: what newspapers existed, what they charged for advertising, and what their ''mechanical'' requirements were (such as width of column, how long the ad could remain unchanged, and so on).

The practice of the time was for advertising agents to bid for an advertiser's campaign; many advertisers produced several campaigns during the year. The advertiser produced the copy and would present it to the agent, noting how large the ad should be and when and for how long it should run. He might include a list of newspapers (if he had previously published advertising), but usually was open for information about other newspapers in the field. The agent with the lowest bid handled the campaign. The very next campaign, the same procedure would take place. In truth, as Rowell said, advertisers who were satisfied with an agent's work tended to stay with that agent year after year, but advertisers were uneasy with this arrangement. They felt they paid more than they had to for space—and they were right.

Rowell did what all other agents did—he bid for campaigns—but he also innovated an alternative access to newspapers, one that made him a highly successful agent for several decades. Since most of the population still lived in rural areas, he built lists of 100 country newspapers which he then sold to advertisers for $100 a month for a one-inch ad in each. This was a cheaper rate than advertisers could get anywhere else, so many began to patronize the George P. Rowell agency in Boston.

Others had tried the same scheme before Rowell, but he required that the advertiser buy the *entire* list. In order to succeed with this innovation, he had to work hard to fill the space he contracted for with each paper. He agreed to place a column of advertising (on the average) in each issue for an entire year. He guaranteed at least one quarter of a column in each issue and never more than two columns without approval of the publisher. Weekly editors, who stared at large, blank sheets of newsprint that had to be filled each week, gave Rowell's agency extraordinary discounts for his guarantee to fill so much space during the year. Rowell then offered cash—for a further discount. He risked losing a great deal of money, but his risk was well rewarded so long as he could fill those yawning advertising columns each month. The low rates enabled him to secure a large number of advertisers (Rowell, *Forty Years*, pp. 173–92). At the end of that first year the two partners had a profit of $10,000 on an investment of $1,000 each. Rowell knew for sure this was to be his life's work.

In 1865 Rowell moved to New York, where the action was. New Yorkers did not take as long as New Englanders to make up their minds, and most of the advertising agencies had already located there. He sold his interest in the *Dial* (a small magazine he and Dodd had bought) to his partner. Rowell took the name of the agency and the lists and accounts outstanding with him to New York, arranging promissory notes for Dodd's share of notes yet to be paid. Dodd's uncle, worried that Rowell would fail, suggested sharp discounts in the notes if Rowell would pay cash. Getting a loan from his father, who had recently sold real estate worth about $8,000—his entire fortune—Rowell paid off Dodd and within a year paid back his father. George P. Rowell never forgot his father's willingness to risk everything he owned on his son's ability (Rowell, *Forty Years*, pp. 116–17).

Soon after getting established in New York, Rowell decided to take his secret information on newspapers, editors and publishers, places, and circulation and issue it in the form of a directory. *George P. Rowell and Company American Newspaper Directory* first appeared in 1869. It was not the first newspaper directory to be published in the United States, but it was the first successful one to be issued in consecutive years. It soon was widely, if poorly, imitated. Only one later directory could begin to compare with it: *N. W. Ayer and Son's American Newspaper Annual*. The latter finally absorbed Rowell's directory in 1908.

Rowell insisted on publishing circulation figures, though other agents did not do so in their directories. When a publisher swore to the circulation figures and offered some form of proof, the directory said "claims." When there was no estimate given by the publisher, Rowell guessed and said "about." This began in the 1869 directory and continued until he shifted to a symbol system. In 1880 an A1 represented a circulation exceeding 100,000 and a K1 represented a circulation exceeding 500. The codes changed over the years. In 1888 Rowell guaranteed a $100 reward for anyone who could prove a certified circulation was incorrect (he based the certification on the publisher's statement and documentation). He did this for nine years, finally discontinuing it in 1897, announcing in that year's directory that he had paid out somewhere "between three and four thousand dollars . . . in forfeits, because nine years of experiment had made it plain that newspaper publishers were not disposed to countenance the Directory in its efforts and were positively opposed to them."

Beginning in 1900 he renewed the practice, only this time publishers had to send $100 in cash to be held by the publisher of the directory until the newspapers wished to remove the guarantees. It would be another 14 years before the Audit Bureau of Circulations would be formed, an industry-supported agency to audit newspaper and magazine circulation. Few could look back at the end of Rowell's career and not recognize that he, probably more than any other person, had legitimized and promoted circulation as a measure of a newspaper. With tongue in cheek, Rowell wrote in 1900 that several publishers had written supporting the directory's efforts:

These responses . . . indicate a change of attitude on the part of some of the leading papers of the country. It is gratifying to note that, after thirty-two years effort to aid honest newspapers and discourage the circulation liar, the Directory publishers are, in the fourth decade of their work, actually receiving some substantial encouragement and aid from men who conduct the best class of newspapers and make a practice of letting their actual issues be known. (*American Newspaper Directory*, June 1900, pp. 6–7)

Many times publishers condemned the directory's circulation figures for their papers, claiming Rowell had no right to publish such figures. In one sense they were right. Rowell did not know what the circulation was of a specific newspaper. His was a guesstimate, and he could make an error as easily as anyone. Every publisher was given an opportunity to state his circulation; most did not take Rowell up on it, at least before 1900.

Once the Harper brothers complained of his figures for *Harper's Weekly*. When he said they had to sign a statement, as would any other publisher, the second-generation members of the firm "looked at each other and one quietly said to the others, 'It seems to me that if Mr. Rowell talks that way we don't want to continue to do business with him'; and the others, in a rather indifferent way, appeared to coincide with that view." The next order from Rowell's agency was refused, so he simply sent the ad through another agency. But since he was not getting the commission he "became less urgent" in recommending the magazine. The Rowell agency had been sending $5,000 in orders monthly; in the future that figure sometimes dropped to $5,000 in five years (Rowell, *Forty Years*, pp. 410–11).

Upon his move to New York, Rowell continued a small quarterly house organ he had started in Boston called the *Advertisers' Gazette*, eventually converting it to the weekly *American Newspaper Reporter*, but using "Advertisers' Gazette" as a subtitle. This publication culled information from newspapers and trade magazines about advertising and newspapers, and it allowed Rowell and his editors to express pungent comments on newspaper publishers' handling of circulation and rates (p. 355).

Rowell's advertising philosophy was simple: Use small advertisements in newspapers. He once wrote: "I am a believer in the newspaper as the best advertising medium. It is the only one I ever recommend" (p. 436). Over the years his emphasis shifted from weekly and small dailies to all dailies, but he still focused on newspapers alone. Because he was wedded to newspapers for his entire advertising career, competitors such as J. Walter Thompson could explore and capture the magazine advertising field in the 1880s and 1890s (p. 445).

From 1871 on Rowell always took at least a four-week vacation, which meant he had to rely upon the talents of his partners and staff. Among those people were Charles N. Kent, a childhood friend who was a lawyer. Rowell persuaded him to come to New York the second year as a partner. His solicitor was John A. Moore, a New Yorker who could not calculate figures but who could charm the advertising from clients. Nelson Chesman, a schoolmate from Rowell's New Hampshire days, also followed him to New York. He was responsible for the list system and was the first editor of the directory. Chesman later opened his own advertising agency, first in St. Louis and then in Chicago and New York (pp. 86–87, 134). With such talent around him, Rowell had time to enjoy the fruits of the business. He even dropped out of the agency entirely in 1880, the start of a seven-year hiatus during which he formed and published a small newspaper in Vermont. He was the quintessential gentleman farmer and gentleman publisher: He failed at both. His seven-year vacation from advertising allowed the agency to decline in influence so that he had to return and reinvigorate it (pp. 290–96).

In 1873 Rowell used his house organ, the *American Newspaper Reporter*, to promote an association of advertising agents whose primary purpose was to provide publishers with a list of ''accredited agents'' deserving of commissions. Anyone not on the list was not considered accredited. S. M. Pettingill was voted president of the two-day convention and received a good deal of attention from outsiders, but Rowell was chairman of the resolutions committee and defended the several resolutions before the convention (reprinted in *Printer's Ink*, August 31, 1911, p. 34). His agency was also represented by Kent, who was temporary secretary. Despite claiming the convention a success in the *Reporter*, the association was short-lived, and he was unable to establish criteria for accrediting agents. Nevertheless, this was a forerunner to the American Association of Advertising Agencies, which was not established until 1917.

The Centennial Exhibition in Philadelphia in 1876 most likely would have proceeded without representation by newspapers had Rowell not become interested in the enterprise. He promoted among American publishers the idea of donating a six-month subscription to the Centennial Newspaper Exhibition. Rowell erected the Newspaper Pavilion, a separate building on the grounds to house the country's papers. Oscar G. Moses, an employee and eventually one-sixth owner of the Rowell agency, built and organized the exhibition. The two-story building was open to the ceiling in the center with tables to display the leading dailies. Pigeonholes surrounded the walls downstairs and up, where a balcony ran around the building with tables and chairs for those pausing to refresh themselves or to read a hometown paper. All 8,129 newspapers were pigeonholed; as copies continued to arrive during the entire period of the exhibition, they were placed in the numbered slots. A special catalog listed all of the papers by number, starting with those of Alabama. Rowell recounted a humorous incident when one Rhode Island publisher, proud of having a circulation over

8,000, became angry when he saw the "number 7,777, or something like that," in the catalog. He thought Rowell had listed his circulation and denounced "the error as an outrage" (Rowell, *Forty Years*, pp. 225–29).

Publishers generally covered the cost of the building by paying for special articles about themselves in the catalog, but it had taken Rowell's efforts and financial support to get the project off the ground. The building cost about $10,000, the total cost for the enterprise just under $20,000. Rowell claimed he could never trace one advertising contract to the exhibition, though he averred the profits that year were larger than in any year from 1871 to 1881. He made three complete collections of the newspapers issued that year. One was sold to the Vatican, he was told, and another to Tasmania. He gave the third set to the Library of Congress (pp. 232–35).

Not everyone was happy with the situation, of course. Philadelphia advertising agents and media seemed miffed that a New York advertising agent would get the exclusive right to create and operate the newspaper pavilion. The editor of the *Printers' Circular* of Philadelphia complained, before the exhibition had taken place, about Rowell's having the "exclusive" use of the building to make money. He concluded: It is "far better to be forever unrepresented than that the press of the United States should be chaperoned before the peoples of the world by grasping advertising agents of smirched reputation" (March 1876, p. 10). We can be sure that if Rowell had not undertaken the enterprise, it would not have been undertaken by anyone.

The *American Newspaper Reporter* was sold, in 1878, along with Rowell's ink business and printers' supplies, to the man who had managed Rowell's warehouse. The magazine changed its focus to news of interest to printers but lasted only a few years before closing (Rowell, *Forty Years*, pp. 279–80). Rowell started another magazine in 1888, one that defined the advertising field for the next several decades: *Printer's Ink*. It was a trade magazine, not a house organ. This small publication soon attracted wide distribution among advertisers, advertising agents, and newspaper and magazine publishers. Its columns contained news, views, and "how-to" articles. It became separated in later years, along with the directory, from the Rowell advertising agency as Rowell grew tired of the business. He sold the agency in 1892, although he remained president of the reorganized corporation without participating in it. This gave the "younger men" a chance to redo the agency, to change its focus. Yet, a few years later Rowell had to regain control in order to keep the agency from going under. As he said, it still carried his name. He had always followed the rule of paying bills as soon as they were proffered; the new "owners" had gotten away from that practice and had incurred debts. He took it over, restored it to health but never to the prominence it once had had, and sold it in 1905.

Divorced in 1890, having sired one daughter, Persis E. Rowell, he married again in 1891 to Jeannette Rigney Hallock. She had been born in Canada, but her family had lived in New York for many years. Rowell died on August 28, 1908.

Rowell had shaped in no small measure the American advertising agency business. He had done this first through the development of the very successful list system. This was eventually superseded by the cooperative system of patent insides and outsides, although it was not done away with entirely during his lifetime. Rowell continued to emphasize the importance of the newspaper, versus the magazine, as a vehicle for advertising, thus missing one of the significant developments in national advertising. He lost interest in the advertising agency business over the years, shifting his attention and time to the *American Newspaper Directory*, still one of the great innovations in advertising, and to the development of *Printer's Ink* as a vehicle for expressing his views on advertising. He marketed a relatively successful patent medicine, Ripans, and sold printers' ink and printers' supplies, including type, for many years. His directory emphasized the circulation of newspapers and magazines from the beginning. Though vilified by some publishers during his career, he was praised, upon his retirement from the field, for his efforts at ridding the industry of circulation liars. He had made a valiant effort, but he certainly had not succeeded in driving out the liars by 1908, the year of his death. A product of his own time, early in his career he made little effort to prove the accuracy of the advertising he promoted, yet his *Printer's Ink* became a leader in the drive for truth in advertising. Rowell's legacy had a long life.

FURTHER READING

Works by Rowell

Forty Years an Advertising Agent, 1865–1905. 1906. Reprint. New York: Franklin Publishing, 1926.
The editorials in *Advertisers' Gazette* and the *American Newspaper Reporter*, until taken over by Valentine, were often written by Rowell. The same was true of early issues of *Printer's Ink*.

Works about Rowell

Dictionary of American Biography. New York: Charles Scribner's Sons, 1935.
Hower, Ralph M. *The History of an Advertising Agency: N. W. Ayer and Son at Work, 1869–1939*. Rev. ed. Cambridge: Harvard University Press, 1949.
The National Cyclopaedia of American Biography. New York: James T. White, 1916.
Pope, Daniel. *The Making of Modern Advertising*. New York: Basic Books, 1983.
Presbrey, Frank. *The History and Development of Advertising*. 1929. Reprint. New York: Greenwood Press, 1968.
Rowell, Roland. *Biographical Sketch of Samuel Rowell*. Manchester, NH: William E. Moore, 1898.

RAYMOND RUBICAM
(June 16, 1892–May 8, 1978)

Elsie S. Hebert

Raymond Rubicam, regarded as "advertising's statesman," cofounded Young and Rubicam, one of the world's largest advertising agencies, in 1923. He is credited with pioneering advertising's "creative revolution" in the 1920s, gaining legendary stature both for innovative operations and creative copywriting. He brought recognition to the work of copywriters and artists at a time when agencies were being directed and controlled by businessmen. His concept that the contents of the advertisement—copy and art elements—are the most important factors in the business has influenced generations of practitioners and the nature of advertising communications. Rubicam believed that advertisements should "mirror the reader to himself" (*Advertising Age*, May 15, 1978, p. 118), then show him how the product serves his needs. He felt that the way to sell was to get the ad read first, and the way to get the ad read was to say more about the reader and less about the advertiser and the product.

Raymond Rubicam was born in Brooklyn on June 16, 1892, the youngest of eight children born to Joseph and Sarah Maria (Bodine) Rubicam, whose ancestors had settled in Germantown, Pennsylvania, in 1725. The original spelling of the family name was "Rubencamm." After losing an inherited family import and manufacturing business, Raymond's father became a trade journalist, and his mother contributed poetry to *Godey's Lady's Book*. When Joseph Rubicam died of tuberculosis in 1897, Raymond was sent to live with various sisters and brothers. He went to school in New Jersey, Pennsylvania, Ohio, and finally Colorado. "These uprootings and diverse surrogate parents produced an unruly boy, restless and constantly in trouble at school. He ran away at least twice" (Fox, p. 128).

Rubicam's formal education ended when he took a full-time job at the age of 15 as a shipping clerk's helper for $5 a week. Although he was unable to attend college and study law, as he had hoped, he turned his talents toward writing, using O. Henry as exemplar. After trying unsuccessfully to get a reporter's job with the Denver papers, he decided to work his way east to Germantown and Philadelphia. During this year-long effort, getting to know the people of America in the style of O. Henry, he worked as a bellhop, usher, movie machine operator, door-to-door salesman of colored enlargements of family portraits, and "chaperone" in cattle cars.

He received a friendly reception from relatives in Philadelphia and shortly was able to use his free-lance feature stories to land a reporter's job with the *Philadelphia Inquirer* at $12 a week. Still holding fast to his ambition to be a short-story writer, 21-year-old Raymond succeeded in getting Gouverneur Morris and Richard Harding Davis to analyze two of his stories. They agreed that he had talent and potential to be a successful writer, but they advised that he defer writing until he was more mature. Morris, however, guided Rubicam in a course of reading and writing for the next year, assistance which Raymond regarded as one of the most "generous things a man could do for a complete stranger" (*Current Biography 1943*, p. 638).

When Rubicam wanted to marry, he felt he needed more money, so he left his newspaper job to sell automobiles. Although he was a successful salesman, his commissions provided a risky income. It was at this point that advertising came to his attention. Writing advertising copy would provide a creative outlet and at the same time sufficient income to launch married life. He began to study advertisements and wrote sample ads for two products made in Philadelphia— one for a plug tobacco, using a slangy Ring Lardner style, and one for a truck company in a "reason-why" style. He tried unsuccessfully to show his creative efforts to the presidents of the companies, but the tobacco company did refer him to its F. Wallis Armstrong advertising agency.

After leaving his ads at the Armstrong office, Rubicam returned each day for nine days, punctually at eight o'clock, as directed, only to sit all day without getting the desired interview. He recalled the incident: "At the end of the ninth day, I exploded. After rehearsing for the receptionist, I went home and wrote a letter calculated to produce an immediate interview or a couple of black eyes for the writer" (pp. 638–39).

The letter, delivered the next day in person, brought results. Armstrong waved the letter at young Rubicam and told him that the ads he wrote did not amount to much, but "this letter has some stuff in it" (p. 639). He was hired as an apprentice copywriter at $20 a week and stayed with F. Wallis Armstrong for three years, from 1916 to 1919. He married Regina McCloskey on November 30, 1916.

In those days with the Armstrong agency, Raymond Rubicam cut his advertising "eyeteeth" under almost sweatshop conditions. Armstrong thought copywriting was a necessary evil in the preparation of ads and was a tyrant to his employees. Nevertheless, Rubicam learned his craft with the help of his fellow copywriters and by studying advertisements created by the J. Walter Thompson agency. He wrote copy for Girard cigars, Blabon linoleum, and Victor Talking Machines, which brought him bonuses and raises and built a portfolio impressive enough to secure advancement.

In 1919 he accepted a better position at N. W. Ayer and Son, the largest advertising agency in Philadelphia, at $125 a week. During the next four years he wrote historic Steinway, Squibb, and Rolls-Royce ads and became one of advertising's leading copywriters. Rubicam followed his own dictum in writing some of the best-known advertising slogans, such as "The instrument of the immortals" for Steinway and "No Rolls-Royce has ever worn out." Still being used today for Squibb products is a slogan Rubicam wrote more than 70 years ago: "The priceless ingredient of every product is the honor and integrity of the maker." He also produced significant campaigns for International Correspondence Schools and for the agency itself.

During this period Raymond was instrumental in bringing to Ayer John Orr Young, a former colleague and account man at Armstrong, with whom he had shared an office. Young had entered advertising as a copywriter under Claude Hopkins at Lord and Thomas in Chicago after completing two years of college. He had an expansive, gregarious personality, and the two men and their families became close friends (Fox, p. 132).

When Wayland Ayer died in 1922, advertising was still much as it was when Rubicam entered the field in 1916: the era of super salesmanship, larger ads, and larger circulation. Large-scale competition developed between advertised brands, and success was measured by "dominant space" (*Current Biography 1943*, p. 639). Account men led and ruled the agency business.

This fact was painfully brought home to Rubicam who, although he was a major factor in his agency's growing success and had been given an overnight 50 percent raise to $12,000 a year, was passed over for promotion to copy chief after Ayer's death. No one from the creative departments had ever been elevated to a partnership at N. W. Ayer, because the agency apparently had not yet come to full recognition of the importance of art and copy. Rubicam's experiences at Ayer and at Armstrong helped him formulate ideas about how an agency should run.

In the spring of 1923 Raymond Rubicam and John Orr Young decided to start their own agency, Young and Rubicam (Y&R), in Philadelphia. Their cash assets were small, but their talents and capabilities were great. Young, 37, had his own philosophy of salesmanship: "I never felt that bird-of-prey instinct which has motivated some salesmen to outstanding success. . . . I tried to let the prospect sell himself" (Fox, p. 133). Rubicam, 30, with his own recognized creative ability, resolved to give more credit to the creative artist. His agency's advertising would put more emphasis on skill and less on bulk. He felt that the trouble with advertising was that it read too much like advertising.

The partners agreed, at the outset, that at Y&R the creative people—the writer and the artist—and those who supported and made their work effective—the merchandising specialists, researchers, and production experts—were to be on a par with the account men.

With only $5,000 capital and one secretarial employee, Young and Rubicam launched their agency literally on a shoestring—the Quick Tipper account, which sold devices for capping shoe laces. After doing some trade and consumer research themselves, Rubicam renamed the product "Presto, the Instant Shoelace Maker" (Young, p. 35). Within about six months the agency landed its first major client. Young was successful in securing one of the General Foods products, Postum.

During negotiations, the General Foods man asked: "If we give you a chance, what product of ours would you want?" Typical of Rubicam was the answer: "Your toughest one" (*Current Biography 1943*, p. 639). His theory was that if the agency could turn a losing product into a big profit-winning one, other business would quickly find its way to the agency. And he was right!

Before thinking about the advertisements themselves, the founders first conducted research to find out why people used the product—a then-unusual step that has continued to serve the agency well. Rubicam wrote a campaign stressing not only the taste, but the soothing effect drinking Postum had on nervous, sleepless people. Ads urged a 30-day trial, with the first week's supply free, and Rubicam wrote different copy for different types of users—another unusual step. As a result, Postum sales sharply increased; Young and Rubicam won the 1925 Harvard-Bok Award for the most distinguished campaign of the year; and General Foods awarded the agency with other accounts: Grape-Nuts, Jell-O, Sanka, Calumet Baking Powder, and others.

In applying his indirect copy approach theory of "mirroring the reader," Raymond Rubicam felt that it was essential to know more, as well as say more, about the customer. To achieve this end, he pioneered in new methods of consumer and media research to ascertain people's preferences, prejudices, newspaper and magazine reading, and radio listening habits. To accomplish this research for the expanding agency, Y&R hired Dr. George H. Gallup, a professor of journalism and advertising at Northwestern University, in July 1932 as research director, initiating an association that lasted the next 17 years. Gallup, who felt that Rubicam was one of the ablest men in advertising and admired him because of his "absolutely rugged sense of honesty" ("Creative Pioneer," p. 118), made this observation: "Rubicam knows he cannot turn the art of advertising into an exact science, but he works hard and spends money freely to get some of the exactness of science into it" (*Current Biography 1943*, p. 639). A few years later Rubicam and Gallup hired David Ogilvy to run the Audience Research Institute at Princeton. Rubicam was its chairman.

Acquisition of additional General Foods accounts helped persuade Y&R to move in 1926 to its present location at 285 Madison Avenue in New York. But Rubicam had no intention of allowing the firm to become a one-client agency. He invested profits into expansion, hiring extra copy talent and a leading art director. Additionally, he invited a merchandising expert, Samuel Cher of the *New York American*, to join the organization to head his own group of specialists.

Ogilvy later wrote that "Raymond Rubicam assembled the best team of copywriters and art directors in the history of advertising. . . . Under Rubicam's inspiration they created advertisements which were read by more people than any other agency's" (Ogilvy, *Ogilvy on Advertising*, p. 194).

As an agency operation, Y&R maintained an open, friendly, informal atmosphere, with no one but the secretaries arriving before 9:30. Substantive conversations frequently took place in the halls or on the run. Former employees recall that Rubicam gave the normally temperamental artists and copywriters special leeway and would ignore details so long as the work was completed on deadline. When there was pressure to get a certain job done, Rubicam called "gang-ups" at four in the afternoon, in which everyone available would join and work into the night. Raymond himself seldom left the office before 7:30 (Fox, p. 135).

During Rubicam's career, Y&R handled advertising for many of America's leading corporations: Packard, Gulf Oil, Parke-Davis, General Electric, Arrow shirts, Travelers Insurance, International Silver, Borden's, Johnson and Johnson, Swan soap, Four Roses whiskey, Metropolitan Life, *Fortune, Life*, and others.

Another advertising innovation with which Rubicam is credited is the development of "sequence-picture copy," an adaptation of both dramatic and comic-strip techniques. He was the first to use Sunday comics as a medium of advertising, creating "Mr. Coffee Nerves" for Postum and "Little Albie" for Grape-Nuts in early ads.

During the "golden age" of radio, most of America listened to programs produced by Y&R and to many created by the agency. Radio personalities featured on Y&R programs were Jack Benny for Jell-O, Fred Allen for Sal Hepatica and Ipana, and Arthur Godfrey for Lipton tea. Dinah Shore, Kenny Baker, and Dennis Day were among those given their first network radio exposure on Y&R shows.

Recognizing early that competition for public interest in radio would put a premium on resourcefulness and creativity, Rubicam staffed the agency liberally to discover and originate shows and improve production. Most of the other agencies at the time were depending on the networks or outside sources for programming and production services. Some of the successful Young and Rubicam productions were the "Kate Smith Hour," "We, the People," "Duffy's," "Bulldog Drummond," "Sherlock Holmes," "Burns and Allen," "Eddie Cantor," "The March of Time," and "The Aldrich Family."

Utilizing the research talents of George Gallup, Y&R was the first agency to measure national radio listening audiences by scientific telephone sampling. It was the first to measure the percentage of listeners who could identify the product's advertising and was a leader in the use of test audiences. The agency was also among the first to create commercials in a dramatic form integrated into the program. Rubicam made extensive use of research to learn what people liked and did not like to hear on the air, including commercials.

John Orr Young, who had been president of Young and Rubicam since its founding, retired from the agency in 1927. Rubicam became president, a title he held until 1934, when he became chairman of the board. From 1927 to 1944, when he retired, he was always chief executive officer.

Rubicam won the respect of his employees because he shared credits and profits generously. Y&R was one of the first agencies to restrict ownership to active employees; absentee ownership was not permitted. At the time of Rubicam's retirement, 38 associates owned 82 percent of the common stock, entirely acquired without direct out-of-pocket investment. A bonus plan and a trust fund helped to "provide for the future" of all employees after three years of service (*Current Biography 1943*, p. 640). The agency was also one of the first companies to adopt a profit-sharing trust under the federal law of 1942.

In addition to his advertising copywriting, Rubicam was an occasional writer on advertising and public affairs for magazines and trade papers. He purchased *Tide*, a promotional periodical, from Time, Inc., in 1930 and turned it into an advertising and marketing journal. In 1932 he helped launch Bride's House, publisher of *Bride's* magazine and *Bride's Reference Book*, and was an owner and director of the firm for many years.

An article Rubicam wrote in 1942 entitled "James Russell—In Memoriam" has been called a wartime masterpiece. It was a tribute to a former Y&R office boy killed on the day of his graduation as an officer in the United States Air Force. The article was included in a school textbook on war subjects, *They Told Their Story*.

Rubicam was chairman of the American Association of Advertising Agencies in 1935 and in 1937 was presented the Advertising Awards Gold Medal for "Distinguished Service to Advertising." In 1974 he was elected to the American Advertising Federation's Hall of Fame, to be followed the next year by election to the Copywriters Hall of Fame.

He was awarded an honorary degree of doctor of laws by Colgate University in 1947 and a doctor of letters by Boston University in 1948.

During World War II Rubicam and his agency were active on many fronts, supporting the war effort. Rubicam was a special assistant to the War Manpower Commission and a director of United China Relief. His agency donated its services to the War Advertising Council, to the Treasury Department on War Loan Drives, to campaigns for Department of Agriculture farm labor recruitment, and for the War Production Board on salvage. Y&R was the official agency of the War Department on WAC recruiting.

After his retirement Rubicam continued to live in New York until 1948. He was active in the affairs of the Committee for Economic Development (CED), a national organization of businessmen, economists, and educators, which had been organized to promote full employment after World War II and the national policies that would support this endeavor. During his chairmanship of the organization's Research and Policy Committee, the CED issued "An American Program of European Economic Cooperation," regarded as a major influence in getting congressional approval of the Marshal Plan. He also served as a director of the New York Life Insurance Company and Bates Manufacturing. Even after he moved to Scottsdale, Arizona, in 1948, he continued to serve as marketing and advertising consultant for Campbell Soup.

Rubicam took an active part in the business and community life of the Scottsdale area, becoming a director of the Valley National Bank and Arizona Bancorporation, a founder and part owner of the Paradise Valley Water Company, a founder of the Tower Plaza Shopping Center, and an officer in a number of other organizations.

Three children were born to Raymond Rubicam and his first wife, Regina McCloskey: one son and two daughters. Their marriage ended in divorce in 1939. In 1940 he married Bettina Hall in San Francisco, and the couple had two children, a son and a daughter.

Raymond Rubicam died at his home in Scottsdale on May 8, 1978, at the age of 85. A lasting tribute was made to this legendary advertising giant by David Ogilvy, who has achieved this stature himself: "The two best agencies in the world are the lengthened shadows of Raymond Rubicam. He was my conscience for 40 years, teaching me that advertising has a responsibility to behave" (Ogilvy, *Ogilvy on Advertising*, p. 194). Typically, he did not leave a legacy of a list of advertising rules; he challenged the future generations at Y&R to "resist the usual."

FURTHER READING

Works by Rubicam

"Johnny Russell—In Memoriam." In *They Told Their Story*. New York: Harcourt, Brace, n.d.
"The Lost Moment." *McCall's* (January 1946).

Works about Rubicam

Bernstein, Sidney R. "Why Ray Rubicam Never Wrote His Own Story." *Advertising Age* (May 15, 1978): 118.
"Creative Pioneer Raymond Rubicam Dead at 85." *Advertising Age* (May 15, 1978): 3, 118.
Fox, Stephen. *The Mirror Makers: A History of American Advertising and Its Creators*. New York: William Morrow, 1984.
Kingman, Merle. "Long-delayed Reminiscences of Ray Rubicam." *Advertising Age* (May 29, 1978): 29, 35.
Ogilvy, David. *Confessions of an Advertising Man*. New York: Atheneum, 1963.
———. *Ogilvy on Advertising*. New York: Crown, 1983.

"Raymond Rubicam." In *Current Biography 1943*. New York: H. W. Wilson, 1944.
"Raymond Rubicam." In *Current Biography 1978*. New York: H. W. Wilson, 1978.
"Raymond Rubicam, 85, Co-Founder of Largest U.S. Ad Agency, Dies." *New York Times Biographical Service* 9 (May 1978): 661–62.
"Tributes and Memories for Raymond Rubicam." *Advertising Age* (July 23, 1977): 46, 49.
Who's Who in America, 1978–79. 40th ed. Chicago: Marquis Who's Who, 1977.
Who's Who in Finance and Industry, 1974–75. 18th ed. Chicago: Marquis Who's Who, 1973.
Who's Who in the West, 1976–77. 15th ed. Chicago: Marquis Who's Who, 1976.
Young, John Orr. *Adventures in Advertising*. New York: Harper, 1949.

NOTABLE CLIENTS/CAMPAIGNS

Arrow shirts

Blabon linoleum

Borden's

Campbell Soup

Fortune

Four Roses whiskey

General Electric

General Foods

Girard cigars

Grape-Nuts

Gulf Oil

International Correspondence Schools

International Silver

Jell-O

Johnson and Johnson

Life

Metropolitan Life Insurance

Packard

Parke-Davis

Postum

Rolls-Royce

Squibb

Steinway pianos

Swan soap

Travelers Insurance

Victor Talking Machines

MAXWELL SACKHEIM
(September 1890–December 2, 1982)

Leonard J. Hooper

David Ogilvy said, "I have learned a lot from Maxwell Sackheim." Robert F. De Lay, president of the Direct Mail Advertising Association, said, "Maxwell Sackheim is an unusual man. You name it, and you will find that Max either initiated it, improved it or sold it! He sold farm equipment by mail in the Midwest ... helped found Book-of-the-Month Club ... and proved that even lobsters could be sold by mail!" (Sackheim, *My First Sixty Years*, flyleaf).

Maxwell Byron Sackheim was born in September 1890 in Kovna, Russia, but moved to the United States with his family at an early age. In his first auto-biography, *My First Sixty Years in Advertising* (1970), he wrote, "I hated school. I don't know how I ever got through the eighth grade, but I did, and I have a diploma to prove it. I was graduated from the Goodrich School on Maxwell Street in Chicago's ghetto, at the bottom of my class, in June, 1905" (p. 27).

As a boy, Max loved baseball and other sports. He admired the sports heroes of the day, especially Walter Eckersall and Jim Jeffries, and the great sports writer Grantland Rice. He began to appreciate good reading and good writing during his middle teen years, after his mother gave him a set of Shakespeare's works for his 16th birthday. He absorbed most of the writings of Thackeray, Dickens, Shakespeare, and Mark Twain. Maxwell called mathematics his "downfall." He wrote, "Even simple arithmetic floored me. Computers came half a century too late" (p. 27).

His career in advertising and the media started just after he finished grade school. Max got a job as an errand boy at Barnes-Crosby, an engraving company across the street from the *Chicago-American* newspaper office. He delivered engravings to printers and advertising agencies, such as Lord and Thomas, the Mahin Company, H. W. Caster and Sons, Long-Critchfield, and the Gundlach advertising agency.

Max aspired to an agency job in an art department because he liked to draw, even though the ability to copy simple lettering was about the extent of his skills.

He was hired by the Long-Critchfield agency as an office boy and errand boy, with the understanding that he would be placed in the art department at the next "opening."

Long-Critchfield specialized in agricultural advertising, with clients such as International Harvester, John Deere Plow, Ohio Carriage and Harness, Studebaker Wagon, J. I. Case Threshing Machine, American Harrow, Hercules Stump Puller, "and several manufacturers of incubators, brooders, harnesses, animal remedies, stock feeders and other farm equipment" (p. 29). Advertising directed to farmers in 1905 and 1906 was, of course, aimed at family farms, where horses and mules pulled the plows.

Before 1910 the advertising message was pretty much the print advertising of today. There were no television or radio commercials, so copy appeared in newspaper, magazine, outdoor, and direct-mail advertisements. In smaller towns the postmaster and his employees knew most or nearly all of their postal patrons and their families, but delivering mail to families who lived on outlying farms was fairly random, inconsistent, and chaotic until the innovation of Rural Free Delivery (RFD mail), early in the twentieth century.

People who lived on farms and their city cousins were substantially different in life-styles and shopping patterns. Farm families grew much of the food they ate; some of the crops grown were converted into clothes and linens. Shopping trips, usually to the county seat, on weekends or three or four times a year were for replenishing stocks of paint, plumbing supplies, spices, medicines, hardware, fertilizers, and other necessities that could not be produced on the farm.

Young Maxwell Sackheim's first few weeks at the Long-Critchfield agency were mostly in the mail room, where he emptied sacks of checking copies of newspapers and magazines. He began by tearing the wrappers off these publications, unrolling and sorting them. Then he was promoted to the job of checking the advertising insertions, comparing "key numbers" with orders and watching for ad size discrepancies, poor positions, and poor printing.

Long-Critchfield had a composing room in the rear of the office and a small "kick" press. There, Max would see compositors set type by hand, lock up forms, and hammer out proofs. He learned how type was set, proofs were read, and how zinc etchings, half-tones, and electrotypes were produced. As a youth he read Walter Dill Scott's *The Psychology of Advertising*, where he discovered such basic truths as the classic four principles of successful advertising: attraction, interest, conviction, and action. By observing, comparing, and redrafting advertisements, then writing and rewriting copy, Sackheim trained himself to become a copywriter.

His first advertisement accepted for publication, in about 1906, was for a product known as Kendall's Spavin Cure, made by the Dr. B. J. Kendall Company in Enosburg Falls, Vermont. Under the headline, "When your horse goes lame," the copy, which included a testimonial message from a Canadian farmer and rancher, selected its prospects by such phraseology as: "When he develops a Spavin, Curb, Splint, Ringbone or any other lameness—don't risk losing him through neglect—don't run just as great a risk by experimenting with unknown remedies—don't pay a big veterinary bill. . . . Go to your druggist—get a couple of bottles to keep on hand'' (Sackheim, *My First Sixty Years*, pp. 30–31). He learned the definition of ''spavin'' in dictionary descriptions and pictures.

Soon he was writing advertising copy for horse collars, manure spreaders, steel toe shoes, barn-cleaning equipment, incubators, windmills, plows, buggies, and the Black Crow automobile. In addition, Max did some ''moonlighting'' advertising copywriting in 1909, 1910, and 1911 for the Patterson Civil Service School in Rochester, New York, and for the Brown Fence and Wire Company of Cleveland.

Max worked at two other agencies, returned to Long-Critchfield, then moved to Sears, Roebuck and Company in 1913 as an assistant to the advertising manager. He was paid $75 a week.

The year 1913 was a time of abrupt reversal in Sears's policy on patent medicine advertising. Starting with the 1913 catalog, there would be no more pages of copy about blood purifiers, countless laxatives, liver and kidney remedies, piles remedies, pink pills for pale people, worm killers, remedies for stomach complaints, obesity remedies, and aspirin tablets, which were offered as a new and beneficial remedy for rheumatic and uric acid conditions. At about the same time Sears adopted the policy of describing the exact percentage of worsted wool or cotton in every article of clothing sold.

''In selling furs, Sears stopped advertising rabbits as sables, foxes as minks, and cats as chinchillas, and began to describe every Sears fur garment as just what it was'' (p. 58). Sears's ''truth in advertising'' policy was adopted about a year before the establishment of the Federal Trade Commission in 1914.

Max began working at Sears at an innovative, exciting time. There were about 50 departments in the company, and he helped prepare advertising copy, direct mail, and catalog pages for all 50—much like 50 clients. He suggested his ideas about ''new and improved'' forceful, unprecedented, and effective advertising copy and techniques by means of a barrage of memos to the 50 department heads and to his mentor, Sears's advertising manager, Irwin S. Rosenfels.

Sackheim credited I. S. Rosenfels with helping to hone his retail copywriting skills, expanding his knowledge of production techniques, and introducing him to many other areas of advertising, such as catalog distribution and mailing lists, with which he had had little or no experience.

In 1914 Max and his new bride, Sarah Prockter Sackheim, moved to New York, where he began working as a mail-order advertising copy specialist at the J. Walter Thompson agency. He worked with Stanley Resor on a wide variety of accounts. In 1915 Max moved to the Ruthrauff and Ryan agency, also in New York, where he worked on such accounts as the Sherwin Cody School of English, Doubleday bookstore, Pelmanism, and the U.S. School of Music. At that time the Ruthrauff agency was practically the only one in New York producing mail-order or direct-response advertising copy.

While working at J. Walter Thompson, Max met Harry Scherman. In 1920 they combined their talents to form the Sackheim and Scherman advertising agency.

Sackheim and Scherman's successes began with the Little Leather Library, a forerunner of the Pocket Books idea, which the partners launched with an investment of $300. Between 1920 and 1924 their magazine advertising sales technique sold 40 million books by mail. They then proceeded to sell phonograph records by mail. In their first year of operation as National Music Lovers, they sold $1 million worth of records. The record business was great, but another great idea, radio, killed National Music Lovers.

In 1926 the Book-of-the-Month Club was formed by the partners, while Sackheim and Scherman was also functioning with some 25 advertising accounts and substantial billing.

Children in Aiken, South Carolina, learned ballroom dancing at a dancing school run by a young man named Arthur Murray. In the 1920s he got the idea of selling dancing lessons by mail. A visit to New York led to his being introduced to Max Sackheim. Together they produced advertising copy for mail-order lessons, which helped pave the way for the Arthur Murray Dance Studios that sprang up in many major cities.

In 1928 Harry Scherman and Max Sackheim decided to sell their New York agency to other advertising people in order to pursue different individual advertising interests. Max joined Brown Fence and Wire as a major executive, became president, and stayed in Cleveland until 1944. One year later he founded the Maxwell Sackheim and Company advertising agency in New York. His clients included American Express and the Columbia Record Club. He bought a house in Largo, Florida, near Clearwater, in 1956, and in 1960 he left New York and made Clearwater his home. He worked in Florida for public and community service causes as well as with local advertising clients. He and Sarah had two sons, Robert Benson Sackheim and Sherman Prockter Sackheim. He died in 1982.

FURTHER READING

Works by Sackheim

My First 65 Years in Advertising. Blue Ridge Summit, PA: TAB Books, 1975.
My First Sixty Years in Advertising. Englewood Cliffs, NJ: Prentice-Hall, 1970.

Work about Sackheim

Rowsome, Frank, Jr. *They Laughed When I Sat Down*. New York: Bonanza Books, 1959.

NOTABLE CLIENTS/CAMPAIGNS

American Express

Arthur Murray Dance Studios

Black Crow automobiles

Book-of-the-Month Club

Columbia Record Club

Doubleday bookstore

Kendall's Spavin Cure

Little Leather Library

Pelmanism

Sears Roebuck

Sherwin Cody School of English

U.S. School of Music

VICTOR O. SCHWAB
(1898–March 22, 1980)

Wayne W. Melanson

The name Victor O. Schwab is not well known outside the world of mail order and direct marketing, but his work set the imaginations of many ablaze. From boys who eagerly digested the comic strip–like advertisements picturing the powerful physique of Charles Atlas, who promised, "I can make you a new man . . . in only 15 minutes a day," to the millions of adults who dropped order forms in the mail, anxious to learn the secrets of how to win friends and influence people from Dale Carnegie, Schwab's skill as a copywriter and creative director will long be remembered. David Ogilvy named him as one of the three masters of mail-order advertising copywriting (*Confessions*, p. 91). Walter Weintz, direct-marketing consultant and author, called Schwab "the greatest mail-order copy writer of all time" (p. 48). Weintz was once an employee of the Schwab and Beatty agency, founded by Victor Schwab and Robert Beatty in 1928. Schwab was agency president until his retirement in 1962.

He was born in 1898 in Hoboken, New Jersey, to Letitia Cochrane (Irvine) and Albert James Schwab. Victor Schwab once said that he was born a "rathskeller guy," referring to the German community in which his family lived (Spielvogel, p. 10). In a 1957 letter to his daughter, Schwab said that his parents settled in Hoboken because his father had many friends there. He wrote that during World War I Hoboken was

because of its Germanic population—proscribed territory for American sailors, although some of our biggest troop transports were berthed there. At this time my father was also not looked upon too favorably by some of his friends because at the outset of the War he had belonged to a few societies which were Teutonic in membership.

In his youth, Schwab once worked on his uncle Edward Schwab's farm in Illinois. Apparently, farming was not a vocation that inspired him. He dropped out of high school and tried clerical and stenographic work. He became a skilled typist and learned to take shorthand. On the jacket cover of his 1962 book, Schwab described his early career attempts as "flat, stale and unprofitable vocations."

When he was 19 years old he enrolled in a composition course at Columbia University. It was here that he met a young man who would change his life. Maxwell Sackheim, a dapper young man nearly eight years older than Schwab, had also enrolled in the course. Sackheim was working as a copywriter at Ruthrauff and Ryan, a leading mail-order advertising agency of the day. He was looking for a personal secretary and hired Schwab because he could take shorthand. Beginning as secretary in 1917, Schwab soon became a copywriter and was on his way to becoming, in Sackheim's words, "one of the 'greats' in advertising" (Sackheim, "Passing of a Friend," p. 110).

Sackheim was highly skilled in the art of mail-order copywriting. He had worked for Sears, Roebuck and Company, J. Walter Thompson, and two advertising agencies that specialized in mail-order advertising before he went to Ruthrauff and Ryan. Schwab was in an excellent position to learn from the journeyman. Sackheim would pace the floor of his office, dictating copy to Schwab, who would take it down in shorthand, type it, and return it to Sackheim for editing. During one of these sessions, Sackheim's words flowed too quickly. John Brainbridge recorded Schwab's own account of the story.

He dictated very fast, and I couldn't get it all, so I filled in the gaps with my own words. One day he was reading some copy he'd dictated, and he said, "Say, this is all right. These aren't my words, but I like 'em." I said, "Well, maybe I'll get the next cub job in the copy department." And I did. (p. 351)

According to Sackheim, Schwab quickly "developed into a wonderful mail-order copywriter" (*My First 65 Years*, p. 110). It was in the copywriter's bullpen at Ruthrauff and Ryan that Schwab met John Caples, another advertising great, who was also at the beginning of his career.

Max Sackheim had met Harry Scherman when both were at J. Walter Thompson. The two had begun a side venture in 1915 called the Little Leather Library, which republished classic books in miniature form. They decided to form their own advertising agency in 1920 with their publishing company as a client. Sackheim brought Schwab with him from Ruthrauff and Ryan to assist in the copy department. The agency was successful, landing book publishing and correspondence school accounts, but it was their own ventures, spun off from the Little Leather Library, that brought the agency principals much of their income. The most successful was the Book-of-the-Month Club, started in 1926 with $40,000 in capital. By the end of 1927 it paid stockholder dividends of $90,000 (Lee, p. 30).

By 1928 Scherman had bought Sackheim's share of the Book-of-the-Month Club for $150,000 and was giving the club his full attention (Lee, p. 42). Sackheim had an attractive offer from the Brown Fence and Wire Company.

Thus, the two decided to give up the agency. They turned it over to two of their employees, Schwab and Robert Beatty. According to Sackheim, "The boys had no money, but Scherman and I, anxious to get into our respective new enterprises, turned the agency over to them at a price representing only the actual book value of the business, payable over a period of years" (*My First 65 Years*, p. 118).

Schwab and Beatty were unlikely looking partners. At six feet, two inches, Beatty towered over Schwab, who claimed he was five feet, five inches tall (former employees remember him as shorter by three or four inches). However, the talents of the pair were highly complementary. According to Beatty,

I handle the business and the administrative side of the operation. My partner is in charge of creative and copywriting activities. I sometimes venture an opinion about a piece of copy and maybe he'll say something about administration. But we bow to each other's special talents. (Spielvogel, p. 10)

Beginning with clients such as the Book-of-the-Month Club, Doubleday, and Walter J. Black, the agency prospered by specializing in mail-order advertising. They later added such clients as Charles Atlas and Dale Carnegie. By billing standards of neighboring agencies on Madison Avenue, the firm was quite small; when it was acquired by Marsteller in 1972, it was billing only $4 million. However, from the beginning it was among the top agencies specializing in mail order.

The agency kept meticulous daily records of mail-order returns. After years of review of these records, Schwab formed strong opinions regarding what made a successful advertisement. In December 1940 he addressed the New York Newspaper Promotion Group and shared some of his insights with them. He told the group that bad news adversely affects coupon returns. He explained that during coverage of the Lindbergh kidnapping, coupon returns dropped 30 percent. He revealed that Sunday papers work better than weekday papers for mail order, and good position of an ad, such as the back page, can yield better results ("News breaks," p. 46).

The following year Schwab published a series of five lengthy articles in *Printer's Ink*. All were titled "How to write a Good Advertisement." Each covered one of five parts of his now familiar copywriting formula. The first instructed readers on how to get attention. The second told readers to "show people an advantage" and listed several basic appeals that can be used effectively in copywriting. The third directed copywriters to "prove it" and provided a checklist of ways to offer proof of "what your product will do for people." The fourth article told copywriters to persuade readers to "grasp" the product's advantage. Finally, he instructed readers to "ask for action" and cited several ways to incite prospects to act on their purchase decision. One of special note was his suggestion to use a "hook," like offering a free booklet that "ties up in some way with the product itself."

The copywriting formula was not original to Schwab. Elements had been published earlier (e.g., Hopkins, *My Life In Advertising*, 1927). A similar formula had appeared one year earlier in a book by Clyde Bedell. In fact, Schwab reviewed Bedell's book before its publication, and his comments about the formula were published in a special section at the end of a chapter (p. 259). While the concepts behind the series of articles were not original, how the information was used was. Schwab put into practice what he preached, and the articles became the basis for a short book by the same title, *How to Write a Good Advertisement*.

The book was published in 1942 by the Schwab and Beatty agency, offered free to potential clients, and used primarily as a tool to "sell" the agency (Rose, p. 72). The content of the book was nearly a verbatim transcription of the five articles that had appeared in *Printer's Ink* with two additional sections intended to "incite action," the fifth step in Schwab's formula. One of the new sections was a revealing review of procedures used by the Schwab and Beatty agency to track coupon returns. The second was an appeal to potential clients to contact the agency. Schwab concluded, "If this book, which represents our own attitude toward advertising, has made you feel that our particular way of thinking can be of assistance in solving your advertising problems, then we would be happy to talk with you" (p. 61).

Schwab got additional mileage from the same material by publishing it in the form of advertisements both small and large in the *New York Times* and *New York Herald Tribune*. One full-page edition of the advertising series bore the familiar headline, "How to Write a Good Advertisement." It reviewed, in detail, the same five-step formula Schwab introduced in the 1941 *Printer's Ink* series. The advertisement also contained a brief agency "pitch" and logo. Other advertisements gave "the pit of their [Schwab and Beatty's] experience in finding the most successful headlines, and critical selling ideas and ways to produce direct response from advertising" (Rose, p. 72). Bill Benton, cofounder of Benton and Bowles, once told Schwab that the advertisements had added to "clearer thinking on the part of all advertising people" (p. 72). Schwab's strategy was to give "agency secrets" free, thereby causing potential clients to think the agency had even more to offer than it was revealing in the advertisements (Spielvogel, p. 10).

In 1962, the year that Schwab retired from Schwab and Beatty, Harper and Row published a major revision of *How to Write a Good Advertisement*. Added was a new subtitle, *A Short Course in Copywriting*. The first five chapters were based on the same five-step formula. Gone were the tiny line drawings that illustrated (and dated) the earlier versions, but added were rich examples, anecdotes, and research results. One particularly instructive new addition to the book was a delightful poem, penned by Schwab, titled "Tell Me Quick and Tell Me True (or Else, My Love, to Hell with You!)" (p. 63). From the perspective of a frustrated advertising reader, Schwab instructs copywriters in rhymed verse to include less copy about "how this product came to be" and more about "what the damn thing does for me" (p. 64).

Although Schwab had previously published portions of the book in articles in

Printer's Ink and other publications, including Barton's *Advertising Handbook* (1950), much of it was original material. Of particular note were new chapters on "How to Size an Advertisement," clearly based on his extensive experience, and "Fourteen Interesting and Instructive Split-Run Tests," drawn from part of the incredible data pool Schwab and Beatty had gathered during the previous 30 years.

Walter Weintz, former advertising manager of *Reader's Digest* and long-time direct-marketing consultant, believes that Schwab was a pioneer in modern copy research (p. vii). Schwab, who was a member of the American Marketing Association's Copy Research Council, was committed to answering questions about the effectiveness of advertising in terms of actual sales. From the beginning his agency tracked the results of every advertisement containing a coupon order form. To determine the number of orders in the daily mail, clients were contacted daily; coupons were coded so that on their return the agency could determine which advertisement they came from and where it was placed. Numbers were recorded on ruled cards. From these coupon codes, the agency could judge results by the headline used and track effective copy appeals, copy length, layout style, and action closings (Schwab 1942, p. 71). Schwab said, "The record of results entered on these 'case-history' cards is consulted by us for guidance in the preparation of new copy and in the purchase of new space" (p. 67).

To test copy, Schwab made extensive use of split-run tests, a standard methodology recognized by advertising researchers in the 1930s. The Advertising Research Foundation described this method: "A typical split run is where a publisher prints his magazine on different presses and will permit you to furnish him with several different versions of an advertisement" (p. 82). Thus, two or more versions of an advertisement could run in different editions of a single issue of a publication. Variations in elements such as illustrations, headlines, or copy appeals could be judged by actual response rates to the advertisement.

Due to the limitations of other popular testing procedures, Schwab contended that split-run tests "sound pretty much like the answer to the ad man's prayer" (Schwab 1962, p. 173). However, he was well aware of their limitations and in his book reported the results of only those tests that had return differentials of 15 percent or more.

Schwab began taking vacations to Europe with his wife, Vilma. The two were particularly taken with Spain and would often drive through the country. He decided to retire in an area between Malaga and Torremolinos on the Mediterranean Coast. Schwab said,

I spent forty-five years on Madison Avenue or its equivalent, either writing copy or fighting to get it out of copy men, and finally, after all those years, it really got to me. My nerves began to go, and I had trouble with my eyes. I was starting to take my ration of Tums at ten-thirty. That's when I said, "Well, I better get out of here. Forty-five years of the turmoil is enough." So, I did. (Brainbridge, pp. 351–52)

In 1962 Schwab left the agency. At first he attempted to keep his hand in its operation by corresponding and taking frequent trips back to New York, but that soon proved to be too much to handle.

Victor Schwab died on March 22, 1980, in Torremolinos from the effects of a stroke. He was survived by his only child, Vicky Aronoff. His legacy was as an author, teacher, and director of one of the most successful mail-order advertising agencies of its day. In 1972 the agency was acquired by Marsteller and later absorbed by Young and Rubicam. However, the influence of Schwab continued through the success of many who began their copywriting careers under his tutelage, then went on to become founders of their own agencies, consultants, and authors. Former Schwab employees include: Harry N. Abrams, Don Brown, Tom Collins, Ed Nash, Stanley Posthorn, Leonard J. Reiss, Bill Scherman, Frank Vos, and Walter Weintz.

In 1988 he was honored posthumously by being placed in the Direct Marketing Association Hall of Fame. At the presentation ceremony, Richard Wolter, president of Columbia House, said that from the Schwab and Beatty agency "came a whole generation of direct marketing leaders. Through them, Vic Schwab's talents and knowledge continue . . . in the words of the Hall of Fame Award . . . 'to make major contributions to the theory and practice of direct mail and direct marketing.' "

FURTHER READING

Works by Schwab

"How to Write a Good Advertisement." *Printer's Ink* (November 14, 1941): 18–22; (November 28, 1941): 58–59, 62, 64, 67–68; (December 5, 1941): 33–34, 38–39, 42, 46; (December 19, 1941): 38, 42–43, 46–47; (December 26, 1941): 31–33, 36–38.

How to Write a Good Advertisement. New York: Schwab and Beatty, 1942. 2d ed. 1945.

How to Write a Good Advertisement: A Short Course in Copywriting. Rev. and enl. New York: Harper and Row. Reprint. North Hollywood, CA: Hal Leighton Printing, 1962.

"Mail-Order Copy and Headlines." In *Advertising Handbook*, edited by Roger Barton. New York: Prentice-Hall, 1950, pp. 597–615.

Works about Schwab

Advertising Research Foundation. *Copy Testing: A Study.* New York: Ronald Press. Reprint. New York: Garland Publishing, 1985.

Bedell, Clyde. *How to Write Advertising That Sells.* New York: McGraw-Hill, 1940.

Brainbridge, John. *Another Way of Living: A Gallery of Americans Who Choose to Live in Europe.* New York: Holt, Rinehart and Winston, 1968.

Direct Marketing Association, New York. Script of DMA Hall of Fame Presentation, September 28, 1988.

"Famed Copywriter Vic Schwab Dies." *Advertising Age* (April 7, 1980): 78.

Hopkins, Claude C. *My Life in Advertising.* New York: Harper, 1927.

Lee, Charles. *The Hidden Public: The Story of the Book-of-the-Month Club.* Garden City, NY: Doubleday, 1958.

"News Breaks Affect Mail Orders." *New York Times* (December 5, 1940): 46.

Ogilvy, David. *Confessions of an Advertising Man*. New York: Atheneum, 1963.

———. *Ogilvy on Advertising*. New York: Crown, 1983.

Rose, Matthew. "Agencies: Riding the Third Wave." *Direct Marketing* (May 1988): 71–72, 74, 76–77.

Sackheim, Maxwell. *My First 65 Years in Advertising*. Blue Ridge Summit, PA: TAB Books, 1975.

———. "Passing of a Friend Who's 'Sorely Missed.' " *Advertising Age* (May 19, 1980): 110.

Scherman, William H. "Voice of the Advertiser." *Advertising Age* (April 28, 1980): 72.

Spielvogel, Carl. "Advertising: A Harmony in Separateness." *New York Times* (July 13, 1958): sec. 3, p. 10.

Weintz, Walter H. *The Solid Gold Mailbox: How to Create Winning Mail-Order Campaigns . . . By the Man Who's Done It All*. New York: John Wiley and Sons, 1987.

NOTABLE CLIENTS/CAMPAIGNS

Book-of-the-Month Club (1930s)

Doubleday (1930s, 1940s)

Dale Carnegie (1940s)

Sherwin Cody Course in English (1940s)

Charles Atlas (1950s)

Classics Club (1950s)

WALTER DILL SCOTT
(May 1, 1869–September 23, 1955)

Donald L. Thompson

Walter Dill Scott is best known for his career in educational administration. However, he was one of the first trained psychologists to apply that discipline systematically to the field of advertising. A remarkably productive scholar during his early years, Scott's works on psychology and advertising have become classics in the field. Scott's mid-life career change to the role of university president effectively ended his involvement with the fields of scholarship and advertising, but by then his reputation as a pioneer in the advertising field was already clearly established.

Walter Dill Scott was born on May 1, 1869, on a farm in Cooksville, Illinois. He was the son of James Sterling Scott, a farmer, and Henrietta Sutton Scott, a former schoolteacher who was instrumental in convincing her son that a teaching career was preferable to the limited opportunities then available in farming. In 1888 he entered Illinois State Normal University, where he spent three years to earn a degree, including time spent in remedial work and student teaching.

Upon graduation, with a state scholarship and relying on tutoring to help pay his expenses, he entered Northwestern University, where he held several offices in student organizations, taught at the Northwestern Settlement House, and played varsity football. He graduated from Northwestern in 1895 with his B.A. degree and subsequently enrolled in the McCormick Theological Seminary. His goal was to teach at a Presbyterian missionary college in China, a post he did not get upon being awarded the B.D. degree in 1898.

Influenced by his work in philosophy at Northwestern under George A. Coe and by his elder brother John's obtaining a doctorate at Johns Hopkins University, he then went to Europe to pursue postgraduate study at the University of Leipzig, from which he received his Ph.D. in 1900. There he studied the new science of psychology under Professor Wilhelm Wundt, and he also married Anna Marcy Miller, whom he had met at Northwestern. They were to have two children.

Upon his return to the United States, his brother, John, helped him obtain a position at Northwestern as an instructor in psychology. In 1901 he was promoted to assistant professor and was made director of the psychological laboratory. In 1902 he started teaching in the areas of advertising and applied psychology, and in 1905 he was promoted to associate professor, then to professor in 1908. He next spent 12 years as professor and head of the Department of Psychology at Northwestern, taking two leaves of absence which were significant factors in his pattern of career development. His first leave, 1916–1917, permitted him to establish and head the Bureau of Salesmanship Research at the Carnegie Institute of Technology.

Later, he was to serve for a year, 1917–1918, as director of a committee to devise methods for rating officers and classifying personnel for the U.S. Army. He was influential in developing the system used to classify some four million enlisted men in the First World War, and in developing tests for officer candidates. This led to a colonel's commission in the army during the period 1918–1919, and later in the reserves.

As his career developed, Scott's work tended to be more applied in nature than that of his colleagues. As early as 1901 he was lecturing to business groups on the psychology of advertising, which led to articles in advertising magazines. He focused on the importance of suggestion and annually reviewed literature on the subject in the *Psychological Bulletin*. Scott was not the first psychologist to study advertising, but he was one of the first to apply psychology to advertising. In this quest, he clearly looked on himself as a pioneer. Given his early training as a psychologist, he felt that he was the right person at the right time to provide a new, scientific approach to advertising. In a 1904 article in the *Atlantic Monthly*, Scott stated: "The day of reckless, sporadic, haphazard advertising is rapidly coming to an end as far as magazine advertising is concerned." Instead, Scott argued, "to advertise wisely, the business man must understand the workings of the minds of his customers, and must know how to influence them effectively— he must know how to apply psychology to advertising" (pp. 31, 36).

In arguing for a more scientific approach to advertising, one based on the systematic study of human behavior, Scott recognized that there were those in the field preoccupied with practice who were less than supportive of such an idea. One should keep in mind that at the turn of the century advertising practitioners were still very much concerned with technique, that is, making refinements in the use of color, type, paper quality, and producing better copy. Scott attributes to advertising professionals the same general attitudes that he felt lay persons held toward the young science of psychology:

[Psychology is] . . . something devoid of all practical application, related to metaphysics, and suited only to the recluse and the hermit. If ever there was a ground to expect sarcastic and pessimistic prophecies from the hard-headed business man, it was when it was proposed to establish advertising on a theoretical basis deduced from psychology. (Scott 1904, p. 32)

Scott, while a pioneer in the extent to which he developed the thesis, was not the first to argue strongly the potential benefits from applying psychology to advertising. In the profession he found support for his ideas from scientifically oriented advertising men such as John Lee Martin and Thomas Balmer. Cited as also supportive of his views were Harlow Gale, who in 1900 published the pamphlet *On the Psychology of Advertising*, monthly articles on the psychology of advertising in *Mahin's* magazine, an article in *Printer's Ink* in 1895 which stated, in part, "Probably, when we are a little more enlightened, the advertisement writer, like the teacher, will study psychology" and a March 1901 article in *Publicity* which argued, "The time is not far away when the advertising writer will find inestimable value of a knowledge of psychology" (Scott 1913, pp. 2–3). Scott also cited another article from *Printer's Ink* in 1907, which explored in detail the rationale for the application of psychology to advertising:

Scientific advertising follows the laws of psychology. The successful advertiser, either personally or through his advertising department, must carefully study psychology. He must understand how the human mind acts. He must know what repels and what attracts. He must know what will create an interest and what will fall flat. . . . He must be a student of human nature, and he must know the laws of the human mind. (pp. 9–10)

In his comprehensive treatment of the field of advertising, Scott went far beyond the narrow boundaries of his training as an experimental psychologist. One example of the direct transfer of knowledge from his discipline, found in his classic 1913 *The Psychology of Advertising*, is his discussion of the visual impact of geometric shapes used in advertising illustrations. He cites experimental findings relative to the impact of squares versus rectangles, and the fact that

a rectangle whose base is three per cent greater than the height is more pleasing than a perfect square. This is accounted for because we overestimate the height of a square by about three per cent. Thus the rectangle whose base is three per cent greater than its height appears to be a perfect square and so is more pleasing than the perfect square. (pp. 31–32)

Not all of Scott's applications of psychology to advertising were direct. On occasion, he was forced to adapt findings from his experimental work. For example, working from four principles he had used to help improve a person's memory, he developed an extensive model of the memory process and isolated "principles" that could be used to help ads be remembered (pp. 9–10).

Despite his concern with empirical data, Scott, in applying psychology to advertising, is not above recommendations based on subjective conclusions and personal opinion. For example, when deciding between the alternate approaches taken by two ads, he concludes: "Personally, I enter into the pleasure of the smiling young man more fully than I enter into the sorrow of the grief-stricken one" (p. 49).

To Scott, a scientific approach to advertising involved not only the application of the techniques of experimental psychology, when appropriate, but it also involved the collection, presentation, and analysis of empirical data relative to a wide range of advertising problems, some very far removed from psychology. Examples include: survey findings as to why several thousand respondents purchased various products; data from "all firms located West of Buffalo and advertising in the *Ladies' Home Journal* for a period of 8 years" on the number of lines of advertising purchased annually (p. 122); similar figures on space purchased by major advertisers in *Century* magazine for the period 1870–1907; a survey of magazine publishers asking their opinions of whether ads pull better when concentrated in a special section or mixed in with editorial matter; a study of the reasons several thousand men gave why they read newspapers; and observational data on the manner in which persons are exposed to and react to street railway cards.

In addition to his use of empirical data to support his work, Scott was also sensitive to the need for general, theoretical constructs to help better understand human behavior. For example, in his textbook discussion of instincts, Scott organized his discussion along essentially the same lines as Maslow, who later was widely cited for his development of the hierarchy of needs. While Scott did not present instincts in the context of a hierarchical model, he did isolate the following as relevant behavioral considerations: material possessions, food, clothing, hoarding, hunting, constructing, parenting, and the "social self" (equivalent to Maslow's self-actualization) (pp. 31–32).

At the same time that he actively pursued his research interests, Scott was also proceeding in developing his career in both the worlds of academe and business. In 1909, in addition to his regular university appointment, he became professor of advertising at Northwestern's School of Commerce, indicative of his long-range career interests. Coincidental with his teaching career he also pursued business interests through the Scott Company, a personnel consulting firm he and his associates operated in New York from 1912 to 1921. Scott was also director of the Division of Psychology and Anthropology of the National Research Journal (1919–1920), and in 1919 he was elected president of the American Psychological Association.

Throughout his early academic career, Scott was a prolific author, focusing on industrial psychology, with an emphasis on motivation. His first book, *Die Psychologie der Triebe*, published in 1900, was followed by many more on related subjects over the next 20 years.

In 1920 Walter Dill Scott was appointed president of Northwestern University, from which he had been on leave since 1916. This mid-life career change effectively ended Scott's research and his further development as a psychologist, but it was very much in the best interests of Northwestern University. His appointment as president reflected his vision of where the university might go, tempered by the realities of the present. Milestones of his presidency, which lasted until he retired in 1939, included $70 million in financial contributions to the university, the establishment of the Chicago campus, the construction of 57 new buildings in Chicago and Evanston, a doubling of the faculty, and a substantial increase in academic programs and course offerings. During his presidency the university's endowment increased from just over $5 million to nearly $27 million. Scott was also instrumental in establishing an extensive adult education program and the Medill School of Journalism.

After his retirement Scott remained active in pursuing his personal interests, by choice remaining out of the mainstream of academic and professional life. One of his interests was writing biographies of men important in the history of Northwestern and the Chicago area, such as John Evans, Walter Murphy, and Charles Deening.

He was also a trustee of a Century of Progress, Chicago (1933–1934) and a trustee of the Presbyterian Theological Seminary in Chicago. During World War II he served as chairman of the United States Solid Fuels Advisory War Council (1941–1946). Professionally, he remained active as a cooperating editor of *Psychological Bulletin*, and he worked with younger colleagues in revising his texts. He was also chairman of the editorial boards of the *American Reader's Encyclopedia* and the *American People's Encyclopedia*.

E. K. Strong, himself a psychologist of note, summed up Walter Dill Scott's professional life this way: "Scott was an applied psychologist, interested in solving practical problems rather than in developing psychological theory. He may properly be called the father of applied psychology for no one else applied psychology to such a variety of business problems as he did and at so early a date" (Strong, p. 682). Strong also provided a glimpse of Scott, the person, based on their long association over the years:

Scott was a lovable character, perceptive and kind. He was always mindful of the feelings of others, freely expressing approval of their behavior. His criticisms were privately expressed to associates when seeking advice as to how a situation could be approved. He engendered morale, keeping always before his associates the bigness, complexity and worth-whileness of the task and arousing their enthusiasm to its accomplishment. (p. 683)

Walter Dill Scott, a pioneer in the application of psychology to advertising and a distinguished university president, died on September 23, 1955, in Evanston, Illinois, where he is buried in Memorial Park Cemetery.

FURTHER READING

Selected works by Scott

Note: The most complete listing of Scott's early works is to be found in *The Psychological Register* III (1932). There is also a listing of selected articles in Leonard W. Ferguson, *The Heritage of Industrial Psychology (1962–1965)*. The most important collection of his papers is in the Northwestern University archives. Papers by Scott are also in the

Walter Van Dyke Bingham papers at Northwestern University and in the Robert M. Yerkes papers in the Yale University Historical Medical Library.

Aids in Selecting Salesmen. Pittsburgh: Carnegie Institute of Technology, Bureau of Salesmanship Research, 1916.

Charles Deering, 1852–1927: An Appreciation. Boston: Walter Dill Scott, 1929.

Die Psychologie der Triebe Historisch-Kritisch Betrachtet. Leipsig, 1900.

Increasing Human Efficiency in Business: A Contribution to the Psychology of Business. New York: Macmillan, 1911.

Influencing Men in Business: The Psychology of Argument and Suggestion. New York: Ronald Press, 1911.

John Evans, 1814–1897: An Appreciation. Evanston, IL: L. J. Norris, 1939.

Personnel Management: Principles, Practices and a Point of View, with Robert C. Clothier. Chicago and New York: A. W. Shaw, 1923.

"Psychology of Advertising." *Atlantic Monthly* 93 (January 1904): 29–36.

The Psychology of Advertising: A Simple Exposition of the Principles of Psychology in Their Relation to Successful Advertising. Boston: Small, Maynard, 1908.

The Psychology of Advertising in Theory and Practice: A Simple Exposition of the Principles of Psychology in Their Relation to Successful Advertising. Boston: Small, Maynard, 1913.

"A Research Concerning Next to Reading Matter; Facts and Opinions from 776 Advertisers and Agents." *Advertising and Selling* (January 1916).

Science and Common Sense in Working with Men, with Mary H. S. Hayes. New York: Ronald Press, 1921.

"The Scientific Selection of Salesmen: A Series of Tests Made by Big Corporations Representing the Most Important Development in Sales Management in the Past Dozen Years." *Advertising and Selling* (1916).

Society Today, with Edwin E. Slosson, F. S. Diebler, et al. New York: D. Van Nostrand, 1929.

The Theory of Advertising: A Simple Exposition of the Principles of Psychology in Their Relation to Successful Advertising. Boston: Small, Maynard, 1908.

Walter Murphy, 1873–1942: A Biography. Evanston, IL: Walter Dill Scott, 1932.

Selected Works about Scott

Camfield, Thomas M. *Psychologists at War: The History of American Psychology and the First World War*. Ann Arbor, MI: Dissertation Abstracts, 30/12, p. 5370.

Clothier, R. C. "Walter Dill Scott: Pioneer in Applied Psychology." *Science* 123 (1956): 408–9.

Jacobson, Jacob Z. *Scott of Northwestern: The Life Story of a Pioneer in Psychology and Education*. Chicago: L. Mariano, 1951.

Kuna, David P. *The Psychology of Advertising: 1896–1916*. Ann Arbor, MI: Dissertation Abstracts, 37/06, p. 3048.

Lynch, Edmund C. *Walter Dill Scott: Pioneer in Personnel Management*. Austin: University of Texas, Bureau of Business Research, 1968.

"Scott, Walter Dill." In *Biographical Dictionary of American Educators*. Vol. 3. Westport, CT: Greenwood Press, 1978.

"Scott, Walter Dill." In *Dictionary of American Biography*. Supp. 5, 1951–1955. New York: Charles Scribner's Sons, 1977.

"Scott, Walter Dill." In *Names in the History of Psychology*. New York: Wiley, 1975.
"Scott, Walter Dill." In *The National Cyclopedia of American Biography*. Vol. 42. Ann
    Arbor, MI: University Microfilms, 1958.
"Scott, Walter Dill." In *Who Was Who In America*. Vol. 3. Chicago: A. N. Marquis,
    1963.
Strong, E. K. "Walter Dill Scott." *American Journal of Psychology* 68 (December 1955):
    682–83.

DANIEL STARCH
(MARCH 8, 1883–FEBRUARY 5, 1979)

Donald L. Thompson

Daniel Starch is truly a household word in the world of advertising. Not only was he known widely for the firm he established and which still bears his name, but the Starch Advertisement Readership Service provided data that over the years was a major influence in shaping the mass media in America.

Daniel Starch was born on March 8, 1883, to Frank and Theresa Starch of La Crosse, Wisconsin. His father, a native of the Sudetenland in Bohemia, had emigrated to the United States in 1855. Starch grew up on his father's 420-acre farm, claimed to be the largest in La Crosse, with his three brothers (Emil, Benjamin, and John) and two sisters (Lydia and Anna).

Even before he started attending the one-room schoolhouse located on the farm, Starch had learned how to read from an older brother. He was a voracious reader all his life, although in his early years his time for books was limited by his chores on a working farm which produced wheat, corn, and dairy products. His love of literature, which was to last his entire life, was apparent early when he attended Charles City Preparatory School in Iowa, where he was involved in the literary and debating societies. Upon his graduation in 1899, he enrolled at Morningside College in Sioux City, where he relied on part-time employment to help defray his educational expenses. One of his jobs, tending a coal furnace, required him to get up at five o'clock in the morning.

At 19 he was the youngest in his class to graduate from Morningside, receiving a B.A. degree with a joint major in psychology and mathematics in 1903. He then enrolled at the University of Iowa to pursue his interest in the developing field of experimental psychology. He was the youngest student at the time ever to receive a master's degree at the university, in psychology and education in 1904, and he then proceeded on to doctoral study. In 1906 he defended his doctoral dissertation on the localization of sound, and he was awarded the Ph.D. in psychology. He stayed on as an instructor in psychology at the University of Iowa for the following year, moving on to an instructorship at Wellesley College.

At Wellesley he taught experimental psychology, while at the same time he also pursued post-doctoral work in the field at Harvard University.

In 1908 Starch moved back to his home state, taking a position as an instructor in psychology at the University of Wisconsin. He was promoted to assistant professor in 1912, and the following year he married Amy Jane Hopson, an attractive, vivacious girl he had met two years previously at a Madison, Wisconsin, Bible class.

Daniel Starch was to stay at the University of Wisconsin for 12 years, during which time he published numerous articles and four books in the field of applied psychology. These included: *Principles of Advertising: A Systematic Syllabus* (1910), *Experiments in Educational Psychology* (1911), *Advertising: Its Principles, Practice and Technique* (1914), and *Educational Measurements* (1916). He was promoted to associate professor in 1917, and two years later he was to leave Wisconsin once again for Massachusetts, when he received an appointment as a lecturer at the Harvard Graduate School of Business.

As a psychologist who early made advertising his major interest, Daniel Starch followed the lead of Harlow Gale and Walter Dill Scott, who also applied their talents to the business world. For example, in 1919 he conducted research for Gorton-Pew Fisheries on housewives' reactions to a new product: canned codfish flakes. Another early research project was one he undertook for the Liberty Mutual Insurance Company on the impact of various basic approaches to the advertising of automobile liability insurance. The theme recommended on the basis of his research, focusing on pictures of wrecked automobiles, was one used by the company for many years in its national campaigns.

One of Starch's early, compelling research concerns was the problem of how to measure ad readership—an effort that was looked on with skepticism by many contemporary practitioners working in the field of advertising. He rejected the widely utilized recognition method (pioneered by Walter Dill Scott and Edward K. Strong), which interviewed people on the recall of dummy ads to which they had been exposed, in favor of his readership-scoring method, which he expounded in his 1923 book *Principles of Advertising*. His method was designed to test recall of advertisements to which the respondents had been exposed in the daily course of their lives.

Starch's *Principles of Advertising* was concerned with far more than copy measurement techniques. In retrospect, it emerges as the first comprehensive treatment of the entire field of advertising, in a format that still influences the manner in which advertising is taught. Starch's book sought to come to grips with what he termed the five principal problems encountered by those seeking to use advertising as selling in print. These were: (1) To whom may the product be sold? (2) Using what appeals? (3) How may the appeals be presented most effectively? (4) Using what media? (5) What is a reasonable amount to spend on advertising? Despite his background in psychology, Starch realized that any comprehensive treatment of the field of advertising would take him beyond the boundaries of his discipline. He looked on problem (1) as part psychological and part economic in nature. His treatment of problems (2) and (3) was heavily psychological in its orientation. Problem (4), he acknowledged, required an integrated treatment, with perspectives from psychology, sociology, and economics. Finally, problem (5) was a problem heavily economic in nature.

Despite the fact that those in advertising were daily coming to grips with the problems cited, Starch felt that his contribution was to take a scientific approach. In his words:

The need of a thorough study of these problems is glaringly apparent. There is an urgent demand for the application of scientific methods to their solution, for the finding of facts and for the common-sense utilization of these facts in the preparation and execution of plans. Large sums of money are expended on the basis of a very limited knowledge of facts. (p. 13)

More so than any other author to that point in time, Scott's broad-based treatment of the field was heavily dependent on factual information. For example, in his treatment of the problem of how much to spend on advertising, he presented detailed figures showing the amounts spent by major firms, together with figures seeking to show the effect on prices and profits and data on seasonal and cyclical fluctuations. Not only did he present original findings from his own research, such as his early studies into the effectiveness of individual advertisements, but he also cited in great detail the results of a wide range of other studies, particularly those of Walter Dill Scott (pp. 224, 225, 315, 416).

Starch was also a pioneer in the descriptive, pragmatic approach he used to familiarize readers with the field, one which still characterizes contemporary textbook treatments. He was an innovator in his use of economic and demographic data to define the marketing environment. Overall, his choice of subject matter differs very little from contemporary textbooks; for example, he has chapters on survey research, copy measurement, advertising appeals, copywriting, layout and typography, use of color, posters and retail advertising, and even a separate chapter on ethics and truth in advertising.

Starch's 1923 book was an outstanding success, reportedly earning him more the year it appeared than he received from his teaching contract. To capitalize on his developing reputation in the field, in 1923 he had also established his own market research firm, Daniel Starch and Staff. The following year he was asked by the American Association of Advertising Agencies to heap up its newly established research department, a job he accepted only on a part-time basis. He spent two days a week in this position, while continuing to teach at Harvard and working to establish his own firm. These years were to be among the most busy and, at the same time, most productive in his life.

In 1926 he left his position at Harvard for the full-time task of running his young firm and developing his own emerging reputation as one of the nation's leading practitioners in the field of advertising and marketing research. Even though he did not make a lifetime commitment to an academic career, in his brief tenure at Harvard he counted among his students three who were to make their mark later in the advertising profession: Mills Shepard, C. E. Hooper, and Neil H. Borden.

Starch's applied research into the measurement of ad and media effectiveness served to involve him with all the major mass communications media of the time. His research for the American Association of Advertising Agencies projected him into quantitative studies of newspaper and magazine circulation, but Starch is probably best known for his pioneering research into the developing new medium of the 1920s, radio. He undertook the first comprehensive study of the size of the national radio audience—in 1928 for the National Broadcasting Company, then in its third full year of operations. He developed a probability-sampling procedure which obtained random samples taken from various areas and projected them to provide a nationwide estimate, a revolutionary concept at the time. When the Bureau of the Census in 1930 undertook a count of the number of radio sets nationally, Starch's earlier projection was within 4 percentage points of the final count. Later, his firm would do a replication of the original study—this time for the Columbia Broadcasting System.

The propietary nature of the majority of Starch's research projects means that the results were never reported in the literature. However, those he was free to share with others, and which were published, contributed materially to general understanding of the mass advertising media and their potential use and effectiveness. For example, his qualitative studies of newspaper and magazine circulation provided the first definitive information on duplicate circulation in these media, and many conclusions offered in his later published works were based on the thousands of ads with their original readership measurements which were contained in his firm's vast readership files (*Measuring Advertising Readership and Results*, 1966). Starch was open in sharing the results of his research using the NeTapps (net-ad-produced purchases) method, directed toward answering the basic question: How much does advertising increase sales? His research in this area was based upon data obtained from some 400,000 interviews on the readership of some 45,000 ads in two weekly magazines, and the later purchasing behavior of both readers and nonreaders of the ads.

In 1937 the Starch organization started to collect information for its ad files, and over the years it has accumulated thousands of print ads to which are attached the original readership findings. In 1940 it initiated a similar program for industrial magazines. By 1961 the Starch organization had grown to the point that it scheduled more advertising-readership studies on more issues of general magazines, business publications, and newspapers than any other research company in the world. Starch's active involvement with his firm continued well into his 70s, with him commuting from his home in Scarsdale, New York, to the offices his firm still occupies in a former department store in nearby Mamaroneck. His publications are too numerous to cite here, and they are remarkable for their diversity. For example, in 1934 he collaborated with Roger Barton on a book about the business cycle (*Faith, Fear and Fortunes*), and in 1943 he wrote *How to Develop Your Executive Ability*. At the time of his death in 1979, he was working on a book about great books.

The firm Starch founded survives as Starch, INRA and Hooper. It is the 17th largest research firm in America and still specializes in advertising readership studies. The firm is also a holding company for elements of the former Roper organization, and through its Friedman division it is still active in retail trade area analysis, another of Daniel Starch's interests. And, while computers have replaced the adding machines and calculators that were once used to tabulate data, the firm's uniqueness lies in the fact that it has the largest print advertisement data base in the world. The ad readership files, with the original stickers attached, are still an integral part of the data base that benefits present-day clients. And, while the emphasis has shifted from Starch's preoccupation with analyzing the precise impact of individual advertisements to the more contemporary computerized analysis of target markets, the company is still concerned with the integrity of its research designs and the quality of service to its clients—which was always a Daniel Starch hallmark.

In summarizing Starch's approach to advertising research, it is appropriate to cite his own words, as recounted in a *Printer's Ink* profile in 1962: "No one will ever be able to make the perfect ad. And I don't think this is bad. The making of an advertisement is a creative process—and it will always be. All that research can do is to help the creator do a better and a more precise job" ("Starch: The Man," p. 58).

Daniel Starch died at age 95 on February 5, 1979, in White Plains Hospital, and he is buried in Scarsdale.

FURTHER READING

Selected Works by Starch

Advertising: Its Principles, Practices and Technique. New York: Scott, Foresman, 1914.

Advertising Principles. Chicago and New York: A. W. Shaw, 1927.

An Analysis of Over 3,000,000 Inquiries Received by 95 Firms from 2,339 Magazine Advertisements. Cambridge, MA: Daniel Starch, 1927.

Buying Power of the American Market: National and Local Markets Measured by Family Incomes in All States: A Comprehensive Measure of America's Buying Power. New York: Daniel Starch, 1931.

Controlling Human Behavior: A First Book in Psychology for College Students, with Hazel M. Stanton and Wilhelmine Koerth, assisted by Robert A. Barton. Boston and New York: Macmillan, 1936.

Educational Measurements. New York: Macmillan, 1916.

Educational Psychology. New York: Macmillan, 1919.

Experiments in Educational Psychology. New York: Macmillan, 1911.

Factors in Readership Measurements. New York: Daniel Starch, 1946.

Faith, Fear and Fortunes: Why We Have Booms and Depressions. Must We Endure Them Again?, with Roger Barton. New York: R. R. Smith, 1934.

How to Develop Your Executive Ability. New York: Harper, 1943.

Look Ahead to Life: How to Be a Fine Person. New York: Vantage Press, 1973.

The Measurement of Efficiency in Reading, Writing, Spelling and English. Madison, WI: The College Bookstore, 1914.

Measuring Advertising Readership and Results. New York: McGraw-Hill, 1946.

Principles of Advertising. New York: McGraw-Hill, 1923.

Principles of Advertising: A Systematic Syllabus of the Fundamental Principles of Advertising. Madison, WI: The University Cooperative Company, 1910.

Psychology in Education, with Hazel M. Stanton and Wilhelmine Koerth. New York and London: Appleton-Century, 1941.

"The Use and Limitations of Psychological Tests." *Harvard Business Review* 1 (October, 1922): 71–80.

Works about Starch

Borden, Neil. "Daniel Starch." *Journal of Marketing* 21 (January 1951): 265–67.

"Starch: The Man Behind the Name." *Printer's Ink* (February 16, 1962): 54, 56, 58.

NOTABLE CLIENTS/CAMPAIGNS

In the early 1980s, 88 of the 90 American and Canadian advertising agencies billing $10 million or more subscribed to Starch readership reports. Other early clients/campaigns with which Starch was personally associated included:

American Association of Advertising Agencies

CBS

Gorton-Pew Fisheries

Liberty Mutual Insurance

NBC

J(AMES) WALTER THOMPSON (OCTOBER 28, 1847–OCTOBER 16, 1928)

Donald L. Thompson

J. Walter Thompson is best known for the advertising agency to which he lent his name, and which would eventually become the largest in the world. However, over the years he was also a pioneer in the development of agency practices and procedures. In the early years he instituted the practice of buying large amounts of advertising space in the print media, which he, in turn, resold to his clients. In this and many other ways his entry into the advertising field made a major impact on agency operations.

James Walter Thompson was born on October 28, 1847, in Pittsfield, Massachusetts. He was born in the old Henry W. Longfellow house, which his parents occupied at the time. At an early age he moved to Fostoria, Ohio, where his father, a building contractor, went to help build a bridge across the Sandusky River. He was educated in the public schools, and after his father's death he went to New York and joined the U.S. Marine Corps. He served on the U.S.S. *Saratoga*, which was engaged in the blockade of Confederate shipping.

After his discharge from the military, he eventually moved to New York, where he developed an interest in becoming an advertising agent. An early job interview put him in contact with the legendary George P. Rowell, then widely known as publisher of *Rowell's American Newspaper Directory*, who did not give him a position. Instead, Thompson went to work in 1867 for William J. Carlton, an advertising agent who operated under the trade style of Carlton and Smith, and whose main business was with Methodist magazines. In his book *Forty Years an Advertising Agent, 1865–1905*, Rowell later recalled the occasion: "Carlton . . . had in employ a young man named Thompson, given name J. Walter, to whom he paid a salary of $15 a week, and thought it rather munificent. . . . I once had an opportunity to engage the same clerk, Thompson, to work for me, but, after a talk with him, concluded he would be too easily discouraged to be an advertising man" (p. 202).

Thompson, with his go-out-and-get-the-business attitude, was a distinct contrast to his boss, a bookish type of fellow who liked to have the business come to him. The agency's main line of business was buying space in magazines, then reselling it to business clients who would use it to advertise. The agency's profits came from the sale of space; it did not provide any other service. Thompson changed this with his early focus on theatrical advertising, and it was he who started the practice of inserting advertisements in the playbills of the time, advertisements the agency helped prepare.

By 1878 Thompson had saved up enough money to make an offer to Carlton, who was, by then, eager to sell out. The price agreed upon was $1,300, consisting of $500 for the business and $800 for the office equipment and furnishings. As far as the sale and the early growth of Thompson's agency, Rowell recollected: "Carlton wanted to sell his business, and one day his assistant professed himself willing and able to pay the price. Carlton became a bookseller and the firm of J. Walter Thompson Co. started out, and became, a greater house than Carlton had dreamed of, and that from that day to this has had no setbacks, and about which no one hears anything but good words" (p. 202).

In evaluating the impact of the firm on the advertising agency business, one should keep in mind that advertising, at the time, was considered an unethical and less than respectable activity by many businesses. As a result, some magazines were less than enthusiastic about selling space in their publications for the purpose of advertising. Thompson, a handsome, bespectacled man with brown hair and beard, adopted an approach to these problems that was later to become a cornerstone of his firm's operating policies—that is, he looked on advertising as an independent force within society which could be used for productive purposes. The particular niche he established in the market centered around convincing publishers of national magazines to sell him the space on their back covers on a continuing basis and at a discounted rate, which he then resold at a higher price.

Thus started the practice of agents developing lists of publications in which they controlled space for advertising purposes, a major change from their traditional method of doing business by representing the interests of space users. Ralph Hower (p. 186) describes Thompson's exclusive "List of Thirty" magazines, which he argues "included practically all the magazines available in the United States. Mr. Thompson had persuaded the publishers to sell him the space on their back covers. He then proceeded to divide these covers into 1/4-page spaces and sell them to advertisers. He thus became the exclusive contractor of magazine advertising space for an extended period."

Thompson's dominance in the magazine field came at a propitious time, in that this was then a rapidly expanding advertising medium. Between 1888 and 1900, for example, magazine advertising increased by some 300 percent. However, the spectacular success and growth of the Thompson agency relied on far more than the virtual space monopoly the firm held in the magazine field. The agency was able to compete for major clients successfully when the industry's focus changed from space sales to the provision of services designed to help clients make use of the space. In the two year period from 1919 to 1921, for example, J. Walter Thompson increased its staff from 177 to 283 persons.

One key to Thompson's early success was his ability to sell mass marketers on popular magazines as a means of reaching women in the home. In this regard, he was one of the first advertising agents to appreciate the role that women played in purchasing goods and services, and the fact that magazines were one of the most cost-effective means of reaching the overall market.

In establishing his position in the media market, Thompson made profitable use of two early, very successful advertisements he placed for a client in *Godey's Ladies Book* and *Peterson's Magazine*, two popular women's magazines of the time. In his sales presentations, Thompson argued that there was a definite relationship between the quality of a magazine advertisement and its ability to sell goods and services. He was instrumental in getting publishers to upgrade the quality of their paper, utilize the half-tone process, and employ artists of the highest ability.

In 1885 Thompson added newspapers and thus entered the general agency business, incorporating under the trade style J. Walter Thompson the following year. Early clients included the Fleishmann Company, Eastman Kodak, Pabst Blue Ribbon beer, and the Prudential Company, for which JWT designed the famous Rock of Gibraltar logo. The company also achieved an early success with its development, from the ground up, of the Yuban brand of coffee for Arbuckle Brothers.

In terms of technique, the agency pioneered the use of the testimonial, which was adapted to a wide range of products and situations. An early campaign that was particularly successful in this regard made use of royalty and socialite endorsements to sell Pond's beauty-care products. The agency was also one of the first to offer clients an expanded range of support services, including help in the development of slogans, trademarks, and package designs. One of the firm's earliest successes, which attracted industry-wide attention and generated unprecedented sales, was the coordinated marketing program developed for Woodbury's facial soap, which made use of the enduring and highly effective slogan, "A skin you love to touch."

The J. Walter Thompson agency was also a front-runner in the use of demographic and economic data as the basis for its campaigns, and its fact book, *Population and Its Distribution*, was widely used both inside and outside the advertising field for media-planning purposes. This publication took basic demographic and economic data from the U.S. Census and other sources and recast it in a format better suited to the needs of those engaged in mass marketing and the definition of sales territories. The first edition was published in 1912, based on the 1910 census, with subsequent editions after each decennial census. In 1918 and 1919, intercensal editions were published. A particularly useful feature was the definition of some 679 retail trading areas in such a way as to reflect the area-wide commercial significance of the nation's largest cities. A major advantage of the publication was that the subcomponents of market areas based on population were clearly defined, to the point that users could produce their own customized market areas.

J. Walter Thompson was also one of the first agencies to be concerned with the application of a scientific approach to advertising. The company established a research department as early as 1915 and contracted, on a consulting basis, for the services of eminent behavioral scientists from the world of academe— for example, John B. Watson, widely known for his work in behavioral psychology. These professionals were instrumental in advancing the frontiers of marketing research by their use of scientific and medical findings as the basis for copy and campaign strategies. J. Walter Thompson was one of the first agencies to establish a consumer panel, composed of a representative group of families who were regularly surveyed and whose buying habits were studied.

In his *Advertising the American Dream* (p. 20) Roland Marchand offers this insight into a published statement of the fundamental, underlying philosophy of the J. Walter Thompson agency in its formative years: "To sell *goods* we must also sell *words*. In fact, we have to go further, we must sell *life*."

The effectiveness with which the firm applied this philosophy led to a series of longstanding relationships with clients, in an industry in which agencies and clients often measure the length of their association in months, rather than years. The company now reports continuous relationships with clients dating back 75 or more years, and 20-year clients are not uncommon. The latest figures, released in 1992, position Thompson as the fifth largest domestic advertising agency on the basis of 1990 billings of $1.88 billion.

In 1916, after taking stock of his achievements to date, Thompson, then 69 years of age, made the decision to sell his controlling interest in what still was a privately held company. Not illogically, he turned to 37-year-old Stanley Resor, who had opened the firm's Cincinnati office in 1908, and who in 1912 was moved to New York and made general manager of the agency. Resor raised the capital for the buyout from two partners, and in April 1916 the sale was completed. An article that later appeared in *Fortune* provides some insight into the state of J. Walter Thompson's mind at the time of the sale ("J. Walter Thompson," p. 205):

To cronies he confessed that the advertising business as he saw it had not much future, his billings had reached $3 million a year, and you couldn't go much further than that ... he felt that he had done a good day's work, for as he saw it the great days of advertising were gone forever. Since then, the firm to which he gave his name has multiplied from thirty to fifty-fold, by almost any yardstick of advertising which can be applied.

At the time of its sale, the agency was one of the largest in the country, with branch offices in Boston, Chicago, Detroit, Cincinnati, Toronto, and London. J. Walter Thompson was then the only U.S. agency with foreign branches, and it made a special point of establishing relationships with newspapers and periodicals in the worldwide market.

Unlike many of his contemporaries, such as Bruce Barton and Daniel Starch, Thompson did not seek the public spotlight, although he was conceded to be a master salesman. He was not a regular contributor to professional and trade publications, and there are few accounts of public appearances. What emerges is a picture of a relatively private person who was heavily concerned with the day-to-day operations of his agency. Statements of his philosophy and what comments he might have made on the contemporary advertising scene are largely limited to publications internal to the firm he created. His personal papers and early records of his work are housed today in the J. Walter Thompson Company Archives at Duke University. Of particular interest to scholars are board of directors minute books from 1896 on, tear sheets and proofs from 1875 on, competitive advertisement tear sheets from 1916 on, biographical files of Thompson employees from 1914 on, and the speeches and writings of Thompson employees from 1908 on.

After his retirement J. Walter Thompson devoted most of his time to his personal interests, especially his lifelong love of boats. Newspaper and other accounts of his activities in this regard referred to him as Commodore Thompson, of the New York Yacht Club. At one time he even went so far as to purchase a fleet of canal boats, which he managed for a hobby under the name Owl Transportation Company. He was also active in the New York Chamber of Commerce, the New York Athletic Club, and the Players' Club.

On October 16, 1928, J. Walter Thompson succumbed to the effects of a stroke he had suffered two weeks previously in his adopted home, New York. He was 80 years old. At his bedside were his wife of 47 years, Margaret, herself the daughter of James Bogle, a portrait painter and member of the National Academy of Design, and his only son, Walter Roosevelt Thompson. He is buried in Woodlawn Cemetery.

FURTHER READING

Works about Thompson

Fox, Stephen. *The Mirror Makers: A History of American Advertising and Its Creators.* New York: William Morrow, 1984.

Hower, Ralph. "The First Agents." In *Advertising in America*, edited by Poyntz Tyler. New York: H. W. Wilson, 1959.

"J. Walter Thompson." In *Encyclopedia of American Biography*. New York: Harper and Row, 1974.

"J. Walter Thompson." In *Webster's American Biographies*. Springfield, MA: G. and C. Merriam, 1974.

"J. Walter Thompson Company." *Fortune* 36 (November 1947): 94–101, 202, 205–6, 210, 212, 214, 216, 218, 220, 223–24, 226, 228, 230, 233.

Marchand, Roland. *Advertising the American Dream: Making Way for Modernity, 1920–1940*. Berkeley: University of California Press, 1985.

Mayer, Martin. *Madison Avenue, U.S.A.* New York: Harper, 1958.

———. *Whatever Happened to Madison Avenue?* Boston: Little, Brown, 1991.

National Cyclopedia of American Biography. New York: James T. White, 1967.

Rowell, George Presbury. *Forty Years an Advertising Agent: 1865–1905.* New York: Printer's Ink, 1906.

Ulanoff, Stanley M. *Advertising in America: An Introduction to Persuasive Communication.* New York: Hastings House, 1977.

NOTABLE CLIENTS/CAMPAIGNS

Eastman Kodak

Fleishmann Company

Ford Motors

Johns-Manville

Lever Brothers

Libby, McNeill and Libby

Owens-Illinois

Pabst Blue Ribbon beer

Pond's beauty products

RCA

Scott Paper

Shell Oil

Swift

JANE TRAHEY
(NOVEMBER 19, 1923–   )

Ann Maxwell Keding

During her 33-year career in the advertising industry, Jane Trahey became one of the few women to own a successful agency and the only one simultaneously to become an accomplished novelist, nonfiction writer, playwright, and screenwriter.

Born in Chicago on November 19, 1923, to David and Margaret Hennessy Trahey, Jane was raised Irish Catholic. Her early education was acquired at "an avant-garde grade school where learning piano on a silent keyboard and growing sweet potato (where is Quayle now that I need him?) plants were a significant contribution to family values" (Personal Correspondence, September 1992). After that, she attended the Providence Academy through high school graduation.

Early in life, Jane Trahey demonstrated a tendency toward the irreverence that eventually became her hallmark. As examples, she graduated from grade school using the pseudonym Adrienne Francine Trahey, surprising her family, her teachers, and her classmates. When she entered the Providence Academy, she and another new student again took pseudonyms. This time hers was an unlikely moniker for an Irish girl: Black Sock Pawnee.

In 1943 Trahey graduated from Mundelein College with a bachelor of arts degree. In 1975 she earned an M.F.A. from Columbia University.

Only two years after Jane Trahey began her career in advertising as a copywriter for the Chicago-based department store Carson, Pine, Scott, she was hired by Stanley Marcus as assistant advertising manager and copy chief for Neiman-Marcus, a specialty store in Dallas. Worried about leaving Chicago and moving to Texas, she accepted the job but negotiated with Marcus for a round-trip plane ticket in the event she chose to return home (*Jane Trahey on Women and Power*, p. 28). Happily, she never used it and remained at Neiman-Marcus until 1955, working first as copy chief before progressing to advertising/sales promotion director.

In 1955 she moved to New York as advertising director for the Kayser Corporation. At the time, Kayser was working with an advertising agency that did not produce the quality of work to which Trahey had become accustomed. "I was used to doing first rate stuff at Neiman-Marcus and I couldn't stand this agency bringing me twenty versions of the same bad concept" (Personal Correspondence, September 1992).

Having worked closely with Neiman-Marcus CEO Stanley Marcus for eight years, she thought nothing of approaching Abraham Feinberg, CEO of Kayser, to suggest that she take over the advertising and create an in-house agency for Kayser, something that was very much out of favor with the agency world at the time. "I told him that I could do the national ad stuff, and all the other stuff, as well as the agency he was paying a lot of money for. He might not have been sold on anything but saving money. I told him if it didn't work out he could fire me. What did he have to lose?" (Personal Correspondence, September 1992).

As a result of this successful endeavor, she even persuaded magazines such as the *New Yorker* and *Life* to accept advertising from an in-house agency for the first time. Two years later, when Feinberg sold his share of the business to Chester Roth, Trahey decided that "if I could make money for Abe in his shop, then I could make money for Jane in her shop" (Personal Correspondence, September 1992).

Jane Trahey Associates came into existence at the advent of one of advertising's most creative decades, the 1960s. Work from her agency contributed to the graphic and conceptual changes in the industry that resulted in the era's being dubbed "the creative revolution." Trahey used her wit to create swift, memorable messages that clearly positioned her clients and led to successful campaigns for many accounts, including those in the high-profile fashion industry.

Jane Trahey Associates and, later, Trahey/Cadwell and Trahey/Wolf were closely identified with fashion. The highly visible client list included Blackglama mink, Adele Simpson, Bill Blass, Calvin Klein, Mainstreet, Geoffrey Beene, Bonnie Cashin, and Pauline Trigère.

Trahey began her business with $200,000 in billings promised by her former employer, Abraham Feinberg of Kayser. When he sold his business to Roth, he gave her the hosiery line to advertise for one year. She also credits her opportunity for advertising agency ownership to Philip Sills, the manufacturer of Bonnie Cashin clothing. "I eventually bought out Philip Sills. But I did have mentoring from Philip and Abe as well as Stanley Marcus" (Personal Correspondence, September 1992).

Besides the direct and indirect financial support from Philip Sills and Abraham Feinberg, Trahey cites Stanley Marcus as another important mentor in her life, saying that he stood for the best in everything. He loved creativity and patiently allowed for any mistake, provided it was made only once. Referring to her mentors she wrote, "This is so important if a woman goes in business. She usually doesn't have the kind of knowledge that a young man gets from his scout club, his football coach, his pastor, his brother, his father, his uncle, etc.

We women go it alone most of the time and I was simply lucky as hell to have three brilliant men help me'' (Personal Correspondence, September 1992).

Of the many reasons for Jane Trahey's success as an advertising agency principal, her ability to communicate ideas powerfully and clearly is one of the most important. This ability is demonstrated in the following comment she made when asked to explain the success of the advertising campaign ''Foot-loose and Famolare!'' for Famolare shoes. She attributed it to the media buying strategy—heavy and consistent in a few select vehicles—saying, ''The alternative would be like the comment an American tourist in a hotel lobby in Syria made to me about his trip around the world. 'It's like a hoop skirt. It covers everything and touches nothing' '' (''Famolare's Face,'' p. 3).

In 1978, after 20 years at the helm of her own business, Trahey sold her advertising agency to one of her vice-presidents, Peter Rogers. The agreement allowed him to continue using her name, although they were never officially partners. For a few years after the sale, Trahey continued as a consultant to him. When their relationship officially terminated, she continued consulting for some clients, including Bergdorf Goodman, Neiman-Marcus, and Famolare.

By the time she left the business in the late 1970s, advertising had taken what some considered a dismal turn as a result of conservative reactions to an economy in recession. Jane Trahey's comments reflected the discouragement felt by many creative people at that time when she said, ''Most advertising these days is so bad I don't really believe it. I wonder about the sanity of clients. How can they buy such pulp?'' (Fox, p. 328).

When the observation was made that many of her clients were fashion-based with products oriented toward women, Trahey commented that a female agency has a price to pay. She related that her agency would have been happy to have taken on other products, but she was not invited to participate. She also cited Trahey advertising's successfully managed clients with gender-unrelated products such as Ogden, a multinational corporation with such varied businesses as dietetic foods, a shipyard, and a waste management company; Olivetti, manufacturer of office equipment; and Union Carbide, manufacturer of synthetic textiles used in everything from everyday clothing to space travel (interview with the author, May 1992).

From 1958 until 1978, while Trahey was the president of her agency in New York and Chicago, she created many recognizable advertising campaigns. Among them was the one for Blackglama, which included Richard Avedon photographs of famous women, each wearing a coat of Blackglama mink. The name of the well-known woman did not appear anywhere in the ad, and the only copy was the line, ''What becomes a legend most?''. Some of the women who appeared in this campaign were Joan Crawford, Leontyne Price, Lauren Bacall, Barbara Stanwyck, Maria Callas, Claudette Colbert, Brigitte Bardot, Rita Hayworth, Judy Garland, Carol Channing, and Barbra Streisand.

Other well-known campaigns and slogans include ''Danskins are not just for dancing!''; ''The Echo of an interesting woman'' for Echo scarves; ''It's not fake anything, it's real Dynel'' for Union Carbide; and ''Olivetti is the office.'' Highly visible fashion and cosmetic accounts included Elizabeth Arden, Charles of the Ritz, Borghese, Hamilton watches, Ma Griffe perfume, and St. Laurent perfume.

Jane Trahey is credited with making many breakthroughs for women in the advertising industry. She was the first woman to earn $1 million annually in the advertising industry (*Good Housekeeping*, September, 1967). She was the first woman to achieve a major success with her own agency in New York. She was the first woman to use humor in advertising. She is credited by Stephen Fox as one of a limited number of women who succeeded in advertising. According to him, other women who have made similar contributions include Mary Wells, Shirley Polykoff, Paula Green, Jo Foxworth, Janet Marie Carlson, Lois Geraci Ernst, Faith Popcorn, Joyce Hamer, Jacqueline Brandwynne, Adrienne Hall and Joan Levine, all of whom ran their own agencies (p. 323). However, it was Trahey who led women into the business of advertising agency ownership.

Schooled in retail at Neiman-Marcus, Trahey was encouraged to use her creative gifts broadly. She became the first advertising woman to use color in newsprint for a retail advertiser in 1947. In 1949 she became the first advertising woman to use scented ink in retail advertising for a special coffee. Trahey Advertising also innovated the first line of designer watches for Hamilton, employing her friend and client fashion designer Bill Blass.

In addition to these achievements and contributions, Jane Trahey has written over 16 books (both fiction and nonfiction), screenplays, and plays. She was a regular columnist for *Advertising Age*, the women's section of the *Chicago Tribune*, and *Working Women* magazine, and has written many articles for a wide range of other publications. She is currently writing a film adaptation of her most recent novel, *The Clovis Caper*.

Her first book, *A Taste of Texas*, a cookbook conceived by Stanley Marcus and published in 1955, launched her writing career outside of advertising. Other books followed in the 1960s, making it an exhaustingly productive decade. During this period her first novel, *Life with Mother Superior*, about life in a Catholic boarding school, was made into the movie *The Trouble with Angels* by Columbia Pictures. In 1968 *Where Angels Go, Trouble Follows* was filmed based upon the characters Trahey had created. *Life with Mother Superior* ran as a condensation in *McCall's* and *Reader's Digest*. It was also a Book-of-the-Month Club selection and was translated into German, Italian, Japanese, French, Dutch, and Swedish. Dell published the paperback, now in its 17th printing. After that, Trahey took on the tremendous task of editing *Harper's Bazaar: 100 Years of the American Female*, which was published in 1967. It took three years to read and research the material from which she was to choose.

In 1970 her first play, *Ring around the Bathtub*, premiered in Houston. Two years later, on April 29, 1972, it debuted not quite so successfully on Broadway at the Martin Beck Theater. She wrote, "The only way anyone could have seen "Ring" on Broadway was to be a 'first nighter!' " (Personal Correspondence, September 1992).

This prolific writing period culminated not only with a shelf full of books, a movie, and a play, but also with recognition for her achievements and contributions to the advertising industry. She was chosen Advertising Woman of the Year in 1970 by the American Association of Advertising Agencies.

During the 1970s Jane Trahey became more involved in the women's movement. She was interviewed by *Life* magazine as one of eight women who had succeeded in "a man's world." Each was asked to give her personal views of the women's movement. Trahey commented:

I think this whole movement is long overdue. I would have loved to have had it 20 years ago—it would have helped a great deal. . . . The basic thing is: how do you get a young woman to start thinking about a career early? That's really where it has to begin . . . women would be better off if they got out and worked and had something to say for themselves, something to achieve for themselves. . . . A lot of secretaries help guys a lot. The guy moves on into very good things because that's the system. The woman gets 25 bucks a year raise." ("On the March," p. 21)

Trahey directed her energy to her leadership role in the advertising industry, concentrating on issues related to women. She was not only an active member of NOW but began serving as vice president of the NOW Legal Defense and Education Funds, a branch in which she is still active.

She spoke to women's groups and organizations, often on the topic of equal pay for equal work. Women in her audiences responded so intensely that they asked how they might take action, while the same speech given to a predominantly male audience brought silence. Her reply to those who wanted suggestions on how to change things: "Teach your daughters—if you're going to spend $15,000 or so to educate them—that they must get out and fight and do something" ("Never Plain Jane," p. 3).

In 1973 Trahey, one of four women ad agency heads in the United States with yearly billings in the $4 million range, took note of more inequality, this time in her own industry. At a judging of the top 100 commercials of the year, she counted the announcer voice-overs and found that only 3 were women, 95 were men, and 2 commercials had neither. About this time she received the Super Sisters Award. She became one of 52 women who had each made a contribution to the women's movement that had earned them a place in a deck of cards entitled the "Super Stars." Other women chosen as Super Sisters were Gloria Steinem and Betty Friedan.

In 1977 *Jane Trahey on Women and Power: Who's Got It/How to Get It* was published. This highly acclaimed nonfiction book advises women interested in finding their share of the American dream in the world of business. The *Washington Post* called it "the best written and most personal of the titles on women and business" (November 10, 1977, p. 17).

In a 1979 address to women in Cedar Falls, Iowa, which later became part of the National Public Radio Educational Services' Option Series, Trahey said:

I came out of a society that wanted their daughters to have the spunk of Claudette Colbert, the whimsy of Jean Arthur, the goodness of Mrs. Miniver and the qualities of the girl next door, June Allyson. The best thing that could happen to a girl was to marry a rich man. And the second best thing was just to marry a man and raise little Miss Americas. . . .

These were the days when a woman—she'd spend two or three years clicking away on her Smith Corona hoping to have Prince Butonni whisk her off to White Plains and sweep her off her feet. What she didn't know was that he was going to hand her the broom forever.

These passages give a glimpse of Trahey's wit and humor and accurately reflect society's beliefs about a woman's role at the time Trahey moved into womanhood and began her life as a professional communicator.

Again in the 1979 Cedar Falls speech, she credited her mother with influencing her early decision to pursue her education.

I was lucky, I had an early suffragette in my life—my mother. She didn't buy Prince Butonni at all. One thing my mother was not—was an ad for marriage. She told my sister and I, "You get out and learn something—you get yourself a teacher's certificate so you can always leave your husbands."

Her mother also influenced her thinking with remarks such as, "Just remember this, there is no such thing as a wealthy discriminated against person" (NPR Option Series, April 14, 1979). Crediting her mother with her drive, Jane related in a May 10, 1973, *San Francisco Examiner* article that her father, an avid Chicago Democrat, died when she was young. Her mother raised her daughters on his pension. Jane said, "I came out of grammar school with drive. My mother wouldn't cook on Sunday—she said that even slaves had a day off a week. If you wanted to eat on Sunday, you learned to cook." When Jane was eight or nine she was cooking. Jane's mother also reminded her how much she owed her by referring to the pages of a ledger book she kept. "At 10, she figured I owed her $10,000 for all the board, dentists, clothing and upkeep ("Never Plain Jane," p. 3).

After being named Woman of the Year by the Westchester County Federation of Women's Clubs in 1973, Trahey commented that the single biggest influence in her life was her mother, who urged her to further her education and become self-sufficient. ("Jane Trahey," p. 8).

In her 1979 speech to the Cedar Falls audience, Trahey asked the women present to inventory their feminist behavior by examining whether or not they supported professional women. She said, "Do you have a female doctor, hair-stylist, dentist, bookkeeper, car dealer, jeweler, contractor, decorator? Or do you have underprivileged women in your life? Do you have a secretary, a clerk, a saleslady, a waitress, a domestic?''

Trahey seemed always to have the energy to sandwich two careers into one. During the 1970s she combined feminist activism and public speaking with the task of running her agency. Toward the end of that decade she returned to writing fiction.

Sought as a leader in business, not only advertising, Trahey was often asked to comment or write on a variety of issues. In an opinion article in the *Milwaukee Journal*, she wrote about the problems surrounding employees who called in sick. Her policy was to encourage someone who was tired and wanted a day off to ask for it. ''That way, we won't call you all day at home'' (''Take a Day Off,'' p 1).

As a regular columnist for *Advertising Age* during the 1980s, Trahey wrote an annual ''thumbs down'' column identifying the worst advertising campaigns in the industry. As a columnist for the *Chicago Tribune*, she was given license to write about anything she wanted related to women's issues.

During her career in advertising, Jane Trahey worked on volunteer projects from museum fund-raising to political campaigns. She had served as a member of the board of directors of the Fashion Group, New York. In 1978, she was one of the founders of the First Women's Bank of New York and was a member of its board of directors. As a member of the board of directors and as vice president of the NOW Legal Defense and Education Fund she created an advertising campaign to advance the ratification of the ERA. She was a member of the board of trustees of both Mundelein College and Seton college.

Additionally, she served on the Chicago Mayor's Advisory Committee for Private Industry Council; she was a member of President Carter's Advisory Committee on Families; and she was a consultant to President Carter's Advisory Committee for Women in Washington, D.C. Trahey also served as a member of the board of selectors for the Institute for Public Service in Washington, D.C.

In *Jane Trahey on Women and Power* she wrote that she received 213 awards during her career in advertising. Counted among those were numerous Andy Awards received by Trahey Advertising between 1960 and 1979. In *Contemporary Authors* it is noted that she was the recipient of the *Good Housekeeping* Award for her career accomplishments; she was chosen as one of 100 Women of Distinction by *Harper's Bazaar*; and she received the honorary Doctor of Humane Letters from Mundelein College in 1975.

Trahey is a member of the Advertising Women of New York, the Women's Forum of New York, and the Executive Women of New York. She has been a member of the Fashion Group, the Advertising Club of New York, and the American Institute of Graphic Arts. She continues her membership in the Authors League of America, the Writers Guild of America, the Dramatists Guild, and NOW.

FURTHER READING

Works by Trahey

Fiction

The Clovis Caper. New York: Avon, 1983.
Life with Mother Superior. New York: Farrar, Straus and Giroux, 1962.
The Magic Yarn. New York: Random Thoughts, 1960.
Pecked to Death by Goslings. Englewood Cliffs, NJ: Prentice-Hall, 1969.
Thursdays 'til 9. New York: Harcourt Brace Jovanovich, 1980.
The Trouble with Angels. New York: Dell, 1966.

Nonfiction

Harper's Bazaar: 100 Years of the American Female (editor). New York: Random House, 1967.
Jane Trahey on Women and Power: Who's Got It/How to Get It. Riverside, NJ: Rawson Associates, 1977.

Cookbooks/Humor

The Compleat Martini Cookbook, with Daren Pierce. New York: Random Thoughts, 1957 (under pseudonym Baba Erlanger).
Gin and Butter Diet: How to Lose a Pound a Day for a Year, with Daren Pierce. New York: Random Thoughts, 1960.
1000 Names and Where to Drop Them, with Daren Pierce. New York: Random Thoughts, 1960.
Son of the Martini Cookbook, with Daren Pierce. New York: Clovis Press, 1967.
A Taste of Texas. New York: Random House, 1955.

Plays

Life with Mother Superior, 1974.
Ring around the Bathtub, 1968.

Film and Video

Adrien Arpel's 30 Minute Makeup Lesson, 1985.
The Trouble with Angels, based on *Life with Mother Superior*, 1966 (screenplay by Blanche Hanalis).
Where Angels Go, Trouble Follows, based on Trahey's characters, 1968.

Radio Interviews/Recordings

On Women and Power. Iowa State University lecture, Women's Week Program, 1978.
Sex Objects, Saints, Homemakers but Not People. Minnesota Public Radio, St. Paul, 1979.
Women in Advertising. Options Series, National Public Radio Education Services, Washington, D.C., April 4, 1979.
Women on T.V. Minnesota Public Radio, St. Paul, 1980.

Columns

Advertising Age (1980s)
Chicago Tribune (1980s)
Working Women (1980s)

Works about Trahey

Bombeck, Erma. "100 Years of the American Female: What She Saw, Wrote, Dreamed, Devoured, Dieted on, Feasted on, Lived in, Fought for and Wore." *Book Week/ Chicago Sun Times* (October 22, 1967): 4.
"Clovis and Friend." *Harper's Bazaar* (March 1970): 254.
"Famolare's Face Becoming Famous via Ads." *Footwear News* (May 25, 1981): 8.
Foremost Women in Communications. New York: Foremost Americans Publishing, 1970.
Fox, Stephen. *The Mirror Makers: A History of American Advertising and Its Creators.* New York: William Morrow, 1984.
"Jane Trahey: An Image Maker." *Citizen Register* (Ossining, NY) (January 29, 1973): 8.
"Never Plain Jane—Trahey." *San Francisco Examiner* (May 10, 1973): 3.
"A New Look at Lady Millionaires." *Good Housekeeping* (September 1967): 88.
"On Madison Avenue, Women Take Stand in Middle of the Road." *New York Times* (July 3, 1973): 28.
"On the March for What They Still Haven't Got." *Life* (September 4, 1970): 18, 19.
"On Women and Power." *Book World/Washington Post* (November 10, 1977): sec. E, p. 8.
"Take a Day Off Because You Deserve One." *Milwaukee Journal* (May 31, 1981): "Lifestyle," p. 1.
Who's Who of American Women. 12th ed. Chicago: Marquis Who's Who, 1981–82.

NOTABLE CLIENTS/CAMPAIGNS

Adele Simpson

Bergdorf Goodman

Bill Blass

Blackglama (Great Lakes Mink Association)

Bonnie Cashin for Philip Sills

Calvin Klein

Charles of the Ritz

Danskin

D'Orsay of Paris perfumes

Echo scarves

Elizabeth Arden

First Women's Bank

Hamilton watches

Harper's Bazaar

Harzfelds (specialty store)

Johnson Publications (*Ebony, Fashion Fair*)

McDonald Sales (electronics)

Ma Griffe perfume

Mundelein College

NOW Legal Defense and Education Fund

Neiman Marcus

Ogden Corporation

Olivetti

Pauline Trigère

Princess Marcella Borghese cosmetics

Union Carbide, Fibers and Fabrics Division

Washington Star

Yves St. Laurent perfumes

WILLIAM D. TYLER
(1909–FEBRUARY 7, 1991)

Edd Applegate

William (Bill) Tyler worked in various positions in advertising for more than 20 years—from writing about products for a manufacturer to working as a copywriter and copy chief for several agencies. Tyler also contributed columns on writing copy to *Advertising and Selling* and *Advertising Age*. He was 82 years old when he died in 1991.

Although Tyler was born in Manhattan in 1909, he was raised in San Francisco, where he learned to play tennis. He desired to become a professional tennis player. He was offered an athletic scholarship by Yale University, which he gladly accepted, but within a year, he had grown disgruntled. He left Yale and the academic life-style it offered to teach tennis at the plush Miami Biltmore during the winter and at the Westchester Country Club during the summer, until 1929. When the stock market crashed, most of his students lost so much money that they could no longer afford to pay for private tennis lessons. Tyler was out of a job.

Tyler sold Jantzen bathing suits before he got a job in the advertising department of the Borden Company in Philadelphia. He wrote and created pamphlets about the company and its products. When he learned of a copywriting position at Young and Rubicam, he set up an interview with Bob Work. Work looked at the pamphlets Tyler brought with him and liked what he saw. Tyler was offered the job. According to Draper Daniels: "He had a fast-moving, stainless steel brain and tongue like a rusted razor blade. He did not suffer fools gladly and his voice made it evident. As a result, many who worked with him never discovered his warm heart, his honesty, or his decency" (p. 215).

While at Young and Rubicam, Tyler wrote copy for Simmons Beautyrest mattresses and Royal typewriters. One of the advertisements he wrote for the former was "Beautyrest goes to the circus," which depicted various performers, including a gorilla and an elephant, standing on the mattress.

Copy beneath the photographs described the tests the performers and animals conducted. According to Tyler, the advertisement was adapted, revised, and run for several years. "The assignment was to produce an answer to a whispering campaign that the Beautyrest, though soft and delectable, was lacking in guts and stamina. Exposing the mattress to the circus was my breath-held recommendation" (Schofield, p. 92). This advertisement was one of Tyler's favorites and appeared in the text *100 Top Copy Writers and Their Favorite Ads*.

Another advertisement, for Royal, was headlined "The 2258th part." An institutional ad, it was merely one in a campaign that appeared in *Fortune* magazine. As they appeared, sales personnel for the company wrote in to say that doors that had been closed to them were opened as a result of the campaign.

Tyler left Young and Rubicam to work briefly as copy chief for McCann. He then moved to Lord and Thomas, where he worked as a copywriter. Gaining valuable experience everywhere he worked, Tyler moved on to Kenyon and Eckhardt. About this time, he learned that the columnist who wrote " . . . and now concerning copy" for the periodical *Advertising and Selling* had resigned, so he applied for the job and got it.

Tyler discussed advertisements in this column, which appeared for years; more important, he included the names of the copywriters and art directors who had created the advertisements. This second feature attracted attention. Those unfamiliar with the column learned about it. The magazine captured additional readers and consequently its circulation increased. Tyler enjoyed praising and criticizing advertisements. The latter brought letters to the editor, however, who, in turn, told Tyler to tone down the criticism.

Tyler moved to Doherty, Clifford and Schenfield, a relatively new agency, as the agency's copy chief. He worked on several accounts, including Bristol Myers and Borden's. According to Draper Daniels, Tyler had to create advertisements that competed with Bristol Myers's other agency, Young and Rubicam. "He did this beautifully for a number of years until his inability to disagree with people agreeably betrayed him" (p. 216).

In 1947 Tyler moved to Chicago. He worked for Dancer, Fitzgerald and Sample, particularly on the Procter and Gamble account. A year later he moved to Leo Burnett, where he became the agency's first copy chief and later a vice president and member of the plans board. Tyler, much admired by his colleagues, helped the Burnett agency grow. As Daniels put it, "Bill Tyler helped teach Leo [Burnett] and Dick Heath to think big" (p. 217). He realized that the agency needed to grow, and he brought in several major accounts, including the Tea Bureau of Europe and Procter and Gamble. He also taught the agency how to deal with the latter account.

In response to the agency's growth, Tyler persuaded Dick Heath, the executive vice president, and Burnett to hire Howard Shank, Leo Higdon, John Matthews, Bob Reardon, and Draper Daniels, to name a few.

Although he was well paid for his services and expertise, seldom was Tyler given an operating budget to speak of. In order to give his staff more money, he would have to argue with Heath and Burnett. Sometimes he won these battles, sometimes he lost. The irony is he never lacked respect for Leo Burnett or Dick Heath, even if he criticized the former in public, which he did on occasion, as the following illustrates: "The most imposing voice Leo Burnett can muster to this day is a medium-low mumble with a slight gurgling overtone" (Fox, p. 219). As Stephen Fox mentioned, "The statement itself, along with its tone of affectionate teasing and the fact that Tyler felt free to say it in public, revealed something about life at the Burnett agency" (1984, p. 219).

Nonetheless, Tyler's bickering about salaries eventually forced Heath or Burnett or both to make him vice chairman of the plans board. This position would, they realized, remove him from overseeing the creative staff and possibly resign him from complaining about certain individuals' pay.

Tyler made contributions to the agency, even though he was no longer involved in the everyday creative executions. As Daniels pointed out, he was responsible for creative rationales. "He could button up a rationale more concisely and sharply than any man I have ever seen" (p. 219).

Tyler left Burnett in the late 1950s to take care of his wife, who had been ill. In 1958 he went to work for Benton and Bowles, where he became executive vice president and director of creative services. Four years later he left the agency to work as a consultant and critic. He contributed a column to *Advertising Age*. This column, which was similar to the one he had contributed to *Advertising and Selling*, discussed certain advertisements, particularly their strong points as well as their weak points, and informed readers about the copywriters and art directors who created them.

When Tyler died in 1991 he had been retired about ten years. His wife, the former Evelyn Marshall, son, and daughter are still living.

FURTHER READING

Works by Tyler

Columns on copy in *Advertising and Selling* and *Advertising Age*.

Works about Tyler

Daniels, Draper. *Giants, Pigmies and Other Advertising People*. Chicago: Crain Communications, 1974.

Fox, Stephen. *The Mirror Makers: A History of American Advertising and Its Creators*. New York: William Morrow, 1984.

Schofield, Perry, ed. *100 Top Copy Writers and Their Favorite Ads*. New York: Printer's Ink, 1954.

Watkins, Julian Lewis. *The 100 Greatest Advertisements—Who Wrote Them and What They Did*. New York: Dover, 1959.

NOTABLE CLIENTS/CAMPAIGNS

Borden's (Doherty, Clifford and Schenfield, 1940s)
Bristol Myers (Doherty, Clifford and Schenfield, 1940s)
Procter and Gamble (Dancer, Fitzgerald and Sample, 1940s)
Royal typewriters (Young and Rubicam, 1940s)
Simmons Beautyrest mattresses (Young and Rubicam, 1940s)
Procter and Gamble (Leo Burnett, 1940s–50s)
Tea Bureau of Europe (Leo Burnett, 1940s–50s)

CHARLES LEROY WHITTIER
(MAY 31, 1895–   )

Edd Applegate

Charles LeRoy Whittier worked for more than 35 years in advertising, first with the N. W. Ayer and Son agency in Philadelphia, then with Young and Rubicam in Philadelphia and New York.

Born May 31, 1895, in Toronto to parents who performed in vaudeville, Whittier was introduced to the stage at the age of three months. Although he traveled with his parents, he did not begin to act full-time until he was 13. As he writes in his memoir, *Dear Dad: Our Life in the Theater around the Turn of the Century*, "One of Dad's reasons for wanting to get into vaudeville was to keep the family working together" (p. 167). When the family was not working during the summer, they would stay at a cottage on Pushaw Lake in Maine, which Whittier's father eventually purchased. In about 1915 Whittier met a girl named Sydney Sewall during the family's annual stay at the cottage. Sydney, who married Whittier later, was unlike him in the sense that she had been raised to appreciate a formal education. Whittier, who sporadically attended schools in Ontario, Maine, and Utah, spent most of his first 22 years performing with his parents. One summer, however, he enrolled in two courses at the University of Maine. As he writes, "These are the only credits I have toward a college degree" (p. 173). Sydney, on the other hand, attended Simmons College in Boston.

In 1916, after seeing the Broadway play *Twin Beds*, Whittier got an idea for a new act, which he wrote and subsequently allowed his father to read. His father liked it, reworked it, and, according to Whittier, "made it better." The act was so successful that his father and mother used it from 1916 until 1929. Vaudeville had suffered for several years because of the increasing popularity of films. When the stock market crashed, vaudeville died.

Whittier enlisted in the naval reserves during World War I. He and Sydney were secretly married before he was called for duty, but the war ended while he was still in the Harvard Naval Officers School. Whittier, who had promised

Sydney before he married her that he would stop acting, did not return to the stage after the war ended. Instead, he wrote to the N. W. Ayer and Son advertising agency in Philadelphia, inquiring about a job as a copywriter. Alfred H. Higgins informed him that such a position did not exist, adding, "Should you ever be in Philadelphia, we would be pleased to have you drop in and see us" (p. 183). Whittier considered this to be an invitation, not necessarily a form reply, and immediately asked for two days leave so he could be interviewed for a job. He sent a telegram to Higgins and was in Philadelphia the next day. Hired as a cub writer, he learned from some of the best in advertising, including "Pop" Cramer, who handled Camel cigarettes and created the slogan "I'd walk a mile for a Camel." According to Whittier, John Orr Young and Raymond Rubicam joined N. W. Ayer and Son about a year later. Young worked as an account executive, Rubicam as a copywriter. Although Whittier considered Rubicam to be one of the best copywriters, Ayer could not keep him. In May 1924 Young and Rubicam left to form their own agency. Whittier joined them as a copywriter about six months later. Other members of the copy staff included Harold S. Barnes, Louise Taylor Davis, Lew Greene, Ted Patrick, Ted Repplier, John Rosebrook, Sidney Ward, and Robert Work. Young and Rubicam, primarily because of foresight and creativity, grew into one of the largest advertising agencies in the world.

At Young and Rubicam, Whittier wrote copy for A. G. Spalding and Brothers, including one advertisement that appeared in the *Saturday Evening Post* showing an Italian greens keeper saying in dialect, "Meesta munn, you no can cutta deesa Kro Flight ball." This ad and others increased Spalding's sales and consequently helped expand the company's business from football and baseball to golf. Whittier was promoted to copy supervisor and then to copy chief in 1927, soon after Young and Rubicam moved from Philadelphia to New York.

Whittier had been working as a vice president for two years when the Hearst newspapers opened their comics section to advertising in 1931. For Young and Rubicam's advertisements placed in this medium, Whittier supervised the copywriters, relying often on his dramatic experience in vaudeville to help them plot and execute the advertisements' messages. For Postum, for example, he created the humorous mustached character Mr. Coffee Nerves, which became one of the best-known cartoon characters in advertising history. For Grape-Nuts, he created Little Albie, another cartoon character, in a sequence of cartoon-like boxes. As Stephen Fox notes in *The Mirror Makers*, "The comic-strip technique was then applied to seemingly real people, engaged in an extended conversation about the product" (p. 139). For Pall Mall, Whittier was responsible for the visual comparison of a king-size versus a standard-size cigarette. This, too, became well-known and was used for several years. For the Travelers Insurance Company, he created the campaign in which "The House That Jack Built" was paraphrased. John Rosebrook wrote the poetic copy, "Harrison Hodge, the man you shouldn't dodge . . . ," and the campaign received national attention, primarily because the advertisements, specifically the copy, were unlike others being produced for insurance companies.

According to Draper Daniels, Whittier "had an exceptional command of the English language. This he combined with a quicksilver mind, a many-splendored imagination, and a sarcastic contempt for the ordinary." Indeed, Daniels recalls in *Giants, Pigmies and Other Advertising People* that clichés "made him choleric" (p. 64). Even as an advertising executive, Whittier believed it was his job to oversee every campaign, particularly the advertisements that were created. To him, words could not do a good job of selling unless they had a relative and arresting illustration to go with them. Memorability was important, he realized, so he made sure that memorable artwork appeared in every advertisement. If he saw something he did not like, he made sure everyone involved knew about it. He kept a file on every copywriter. As Daniels comments:

All who survived a year received a letter from him on their first anniversary and every anniversary after that. If it was your first anniversary, or if he had some misgivings about your ability, the note was signed, "C. L. Whittier." When he signed it "Roy" or "Whit," it meant you were part of the family and probably there to stay. (p. 65)

Several years later Whittier was promoted to chairman of the plans board and made a director of the company. In this capacity, he cleared new campaigns, including the creative strategies and accompanying advertisements. Advertisements created for older campaigns were not subject to his approval. Although the agency was growing faster than any in the history of American advertising, Whittier examined every proof and typed his comments on sheets of yellow paper, which were then attached. Periodically, he would route manila folders stuffed with advertisements to everyone in the copy department. As Daniels writes, "Copywriters and supervisors alike awaited the folder with mingled feelings of apprehension and hope" (p. 66). Whittier's comments were explicit. If he disliked an advertisement, he wrote why he disliked it and then explained how it could have been better. In this sense, he was an instructor. He taught his copywriters how to improve their writing. They became aware of faulty reasoning or organization, bromides, clichés, illustrative directions, confusing or awkward phrases. In short, they learned to create advertisements that were uncharacteristic for their day. Whittier emphasized:

The beginning of greatness is to be different. The successful production of great advertising is a never-ending resistance to similarity; a constant struggle to avoid the usual; a continuous effort to provide new ideas, to illustrate them with freshness and to express them with originality. ("Are Television Commercials," p. 59)

Consequently, originality was evident in every advertisement he touched.

When radio became an important medium, Young and Rubicam realized its importance. For their clients' programs, they secured numerous celebrities, including Ed Wynn, Peggy Wood, and Jack Benny. Benny's line "Jell-O again. This is Jack Benny speaking" became extremely popular, and as a result, Jell-O sales increased astronomically.

Whittier helped produce advertising campaigns for war bonds during World War II. In 1944 he served on a four-man commission for the Treasury Department charged with surveying the effects of soldier spending in England and France. A year later he was a consultant to the Committee for Economic Development.

Before he retired from Young and Rubicam in 1952, Whittier was asked to speak at meetings of various associations and organizations. On numerous occasions he encouraged top management to realize the importance of creativity. After all, Raymond Rubicam had not only allowed but had encouraged him to practice what he believed. As Whittier so candidly put it:

If better advertising is to germinate and grow in any agency, top management must supply the sun, soil and rainfall. The production of effective advertisements is the most important function of an agency. It is the only function that can keep an agency in business. Only when the pre-dominant importance of creative work is recognized and extolled by top management does creative effort find its greatest inspiration and incentive. ("Are Television Commercials," p. 59)

After retirement, Whittier and his wife moved to Maine. However, he did not leave advertising: He became a partner in a small advertising agency in Portland for which he wrote copy. Later, he served as a consultant to Campbell Soup's marketing department, for which he helped produce the campaign that began with the advertisement "Soup on the rocks!"

In an article that appeared in *Tide*, Whittier, who had earlier helped Young and Rubicam realize the potential of television as an advertising medium, severely criticized television commercials:

The impact of television is great. The memory of television is long. It doesn't take many repetitions of a commercial to become boring, and successive repetitions can make it insufferable. But repeating the same commercial is not the only kind of unpleasant repetition. Repeating virtually the same words, telling practically the same sales story week after week can become wearisome.

On the contrary, something new about a product each week—a story, a bit of news, a different use, for example—would be most welcome. ("Are Television Commercials," p. 27)

In 1955 his book *Creative Advertising* was published. Whittier not only explained what creative advertising meant, but informed the reader how to write it. The following from the book sums up what he believes creative advertising to mean:

An author can specialize in one kind of writing—"whodunits," novels, short stories, or articles. A poet can restrict his writing to thoughts that both burn and scan. A playwright can concern himself exclusively with plot, execution, business, and dialogue. A newspaper reporter fulfills his responsibility by writing, in as interesting a way as possible, facts divorced from interpretation or opinion.

A top-level advertising writer must combine to a professional degree all of these abilities. He cannot specialize. He must be able to write advertisements in short story form, in verse, in dialogue, and as news stories. And in quality of writing, each kind of advertisement should match its counterpart in other fields.

There is another distinction which makes the advertising writer's the more difficult task. His writing must not only interest, stimulate, inform, or excite its readers; *it must also make them want something.* (p. 121)

FURTHER READING

Works by Whittier

"Are Television Commercials as Bad as They Say?" *Tide* (February 13, 1954): 26–28.
Creative Advertising. New York: Henry Holt, 1955.
Dear Dad: Our Life in the Theater around the Turn of the Century. Freeport, ME: Bond Wheelwright, 1972.

Works about Whittier

"The Beginning of Greatness Is to Be Different." *Printer's Ink* (January 22, 1954): 38–39, 58, 60.
Daniels, Draper. *Giants, Pigmies and Other Advertising People.* Chicago: Crain Communications, Inc., 1974.
Fox, Stephen. *The Mirror Makers: A History of American Advertising and Its Creators.* New York: William Morrow, 1984.

NOTABLE CLIENTS/CAMPAIGNS

A. G. Spalding and Brothers athletic equipment (1920s)

Grape-Nuts (1930s)

Pall Mall (1930s)

Postum coffee (1930s)

Travelers Insurance (1930s)

Jell-O (1930s–40s)

Campbell Soup (1950s)

HELEN ROSEN WOODWARD
(MARCH 19, 1882–C. 1960)

Sharon S. Brock

Helen Rosen Woodward worked in advertising for 20 years before her retirement in 1924. She was one of the first women to be hired by an advertising agency to be a copywriter, and she pioneered creative techniques that are still popular. Her copy sold libraries of books for the *Review of Reviews* using teaser lines from story plots. She sold socially prominent women on the idea of endorsing products and developed friendly, persuasive letters to customers of early direct-mail catalogs. She also personalized messages about baby food to new mothers. Woodward developed a national network of housewives' clubs to sell magazine subscriptions for *Woman's Home Companion*, and through split-run advertisements she discovered that positive, emotional messages sell more insurance premiums than logic or fear.

Helen Rosen Woodward was born in 1882. In that era, the creators of advertising were overwhelmingly male, agency executives were primarily white, Christian, and male, and advertising messages were aimed at a mythical Middle America: WASP, white bread, and old-fashioned values (Fox, p. 274). In this setting, Woodward, a female, East Coast, working-class Jew, became a highly paid New York account executive who created imaginative advertising by placing herself inside the minds and emotions of consumers.

Woodward was born in New York to a German mother and Polish father. In her autobiography, *Through Many Windows*, she tells about growing up in a "hard-working, kindly, unemotional family." She describes herself as "red-cheeked, small, shy and wore heavily rimmed glasses," and she believed that she was unattractive and socially inept (*Windows*, p. 10). Vicariously, she enjoyed a social life by reading Dickens, Thackeray, (Horatio) Alger and about politics and national affairs. When she was 13 she moved with her family to Boston, where they lived for five years. Her education-minded parents regarded her as the most intelligent child among three, and sacrificed so that she could remain as long as possible at Boston's prestigious public Girls' Latin School. The curriculum was college-preparatory, even though no one expected her to go to college. She needed to find work and to contribute to her family, who returned to New York.

Woodward was 19 when she began to look for a job. She could read French and Latin, she had excellent math skills, and she knew that she could learn quickly. But these assets were not highly marketable for an inexperienced job seeker. The steady rejections during her job hunt hurt her already low self-esteem, and she tells how she craved to be "one of the worried looking people, sitting in an office or factory, who appeared powerful and secure" (*Windows*, p 15).

Her first two jobs, as a bookkeeper and then at a library helping patrons select books, ended quickly. The first taught her that she was not a good detail person; at the second, she learned that competence and humility are at least as important as enthusiasm and hard work.

In an effort to become more marketable, Woodward taught herself shorthand and typing and found a job running a training program demonstrating typewriters for Remington. She was always late but overcame criticism for her tardiness by doing excellent work as an enthusiastic, enterprising, reliable employee. She was a good teacher for her trainees and for potential typewriter customers.

Woodward's serendipitous path into advertising began after she left Remington and began working for Merrill and Baker, a subscription-book company which sold sets by mail or via door-to-door salesmen. The books were high-priced editions by well-known authors. The company sold slightly damaged books at large discounts to proud, wealthy consumers, using sales techniques that modern ethical practice and substantiation laws would challenge. The works of classic authors were beautifully bound to enhance polished-wood drawing rooms, and customers joined a "club" for the privilege of purchasing them.

Woodward explained, or rationalized, her part in the damaged-books schemes as being part of a great game. She wondered why consumers would not question how a book company could sell at great discounts, claim low profits, and still spend thousands of dollars on advertising. She "loved the game of business," she said, "and the responses people gave in the chase" (*Windows*, p. 39). She contributed to the enterprise by writing circular letters about Dickens and Dumas. Eventually, her supervisors stopped dictating and let her create the letters to customers because she did an excellent job. With this responsibility, she had created her own early experience in direct-mail copywriting by developing a persuasive writing skill she soon perfected. In later years, after she became disillusioned with the entire business of advertising, she was critical of this part of her career.

At 21, Woodward was secure in her job with Merrill and Baker, so she tried night classes again. It turned out that she was better read than her instructor and exhausted from working, so she stopped going to classes and began reading voraciously on her own. For example, she spent a year immersing herself in the French Revolution and was enamored of authors who described French peasants and their plight.

Woodward still did not share the neighborhood social life of her brother and sister or her peers because she felt self-conscious and awkward. Her inner-directedness allowed her to create unchallenged false ideas about herself while she watched and assessed others' more rewarding social behavior. She continued to hide her loneliness by escaping into books and adopting an attitude of intellectual superiority. Her mastery of the English language and careful observations of human behavior provided an ideal background for a master copywriter. However, to others, she seemed to be an intellectual prude.

Books and general household furnishings were the most popular items advertised in the early 1900s, and Woodward continued to help Merrill and Baker prosper by selling beautiful classics to people who liked to read and plush copies to people who "buy with money some certainty about their intellectual standing . . . they were snobs to whom the limited number of impressions in an edition and the high price gave some social satisfaction" (*Windows*, p. 74). Printing errors and misquoted authors did not disturb buyers of these expensive books; they did not examine them enough to discover the imperfections. Woodward, from her childhood a frugal, practical person, wrote in her autobiography, "No wonder we all developed a contempt for our customers" (*Windows*, p. 84).

Poor management caused Merrill and Baker to fold after five years, but during her 18 months there Woodward had moved beyond stenographic work to writing advertising as well as managing the mail department. She no longer dreaded job searches. In fact, she now believed regular job changes suited her temperament. She had grown to regard change as a stimulating way to make her life exciting and interesting.

Still only 21, Woodward began working for the Hampton advertising agency. She was happy to be at an agency, but this time she was in the wrong job, one that might resemble a modern-day traffic person and bookkeeper. Her adeptness with details had not improved, and she regarded the media commission system for paying advertising agencies to be illogical.

In the early days of advertising, agencies represented newspapers and magazines. As the field grew more complex and agencies began to write copy and plan strategies, the agencies worked for the advertiser and not the media. Yet, media continued to pay agencies for space used, so it would seem that the more advertisements an agency placed, the greater would be its income. Creativity or clever strategy would not matter. Like several advertising pioneers who succeeded her, Woodward thought this system of payment eroded the confidence that clients would have in agencies, yet it was the clients who wished to preserve the commission system. She believed that it gave clients a false belief that they were getting advertising services free. She thought that this kind of thinking kept American business from being great.

Although her six weeks at the Hampton agency were "a disaster amid chaos," her experience there convinced her that she wanted to be a copywriter, even though she was earning $18 a week for work she believed a man would earn $25. By 1930 she remarked that salaries for men and women in advertising had become equal, but still very few women were allowed to move into higher management positions.

Woodward moved to the J. A. Hill Company, a mail-order publishing house, as assistant to advertising manager W. E. Woodward. She married Woodward many years later, in 1913, but this romantic relationship was not evident at the time she joined Hill. She wrote advertising and managed a staff that wrote and mailed circulars about books. She developed mailing lists from previous customers, and even without the modern terminology, she made astute observations about the value of in-house lists and the merge/purge process. She loved her job and relished the responsibility it gave her, but the business of mail-order book selling had become unfashionable, and sales dwindled.

In her autobiography, Woodward discusses the ambiences of her work places and the personalities of the people who filled them. She was a confident and straightforward supervisor, who believed in constructive criticism and disliked having to fire anyone. She was uncomfortable with the office class system because she was not quite "one of the girls," nor was she strictly management. She envied the office women who, with little money, managed to look fashionable, while she had trouble converting her sensible fabrics and disinterest in sewing into chic business wear. But she continued to be a sharp observer of human behavior and noticed that although the women complained about punching a time clock, they continued to do it dutifully and punctually. "Free speech and contented slavery" (*Windows*, p 128) was how she described the female work place of the early 20th century.

Satisfied with her career at this time, Woodward felt it was her turn to become involved in a cause that would be good for society, so she joined the Women's Trade Union League. This modestly successful organization encouraged the formation of unions among women workers. Woodward helped with picketing, wrote some circulars, and gave a few speeches. She tutored English to immigrant factory workers to help them become office workers. However, she was keenly aware that she would have a job whether or not the league's protests worked, and she felt like an outsider.

She looked at the suffrage movement and believed that women would have a vote when they had economic clout, and that time was at hand. She did not think that women would change the political climate because she believed they would vote according to their social class, just as men did. This frustration was exacerbated by her lifelong aversion to being part of a social group, and she eventually gave up her causes and retreated to improving herself by reading.

At the Hill company, Woodward wrote advertising for the *Review of Reviews*, a magazine of book reviews. During her spare time she did free-lance work. When the Hill company went out of business (mail-order books were no longer a thriving business), Woodward began another job adventure, this time with

Woman's Home Companion. Her task was to elicit subscriptions for the magazine through women's clubs organized specifically to sell magazine subscriptions. Women sold subscriptions to their friends and neighbors and received small gifts or commissions, which usually amounted to little more than spending money. For many women of this era, their club was as close as they came to employment, and they cherished the modicum of independence. Many wrote to Woodward's "home office" about their aspirations and concerns. Helen Woodward continued her analysis of what drives people's behavior. For example, she tried to entice her club members to sell more subscriptions by launching a contest with a trip to New York for the winners. She learned that contests worked among salesmen, but not among her saleswomen in small towns. Women preferred to work for a specific reward: a brooch, a painting, or a sum of money.

Helen Woodward also was a student of management and human behavior in the work place. She enjoyed responsibility and the satisfaction of helping employees succeed. She identified office problems and personality conflicts and wondered, as business persons do today, how some people arrive in positions that were totally ill-suited to their training and personalities. Although she was a role model copywriter with her insatiable reading habit and thoughtful analyses of what motivates people, she was opposed to sending copywriters to the source of products about which they would write. She thought it unwise for a copywriter to see a factory or watch the assembly of consumer goods because these were not glamorous activities. The role of the copywriter, she believed, was to glamorize products, unhindered by images of where they came from. After a year and a half at the *Woman's Home Companion*, Woodward declared that a women's magazine was not for her. She was "homesick for the rougher methods" of direct criticism. She wanted to work again where people said, "This copy is no good," rather than, "This is a remarkably fine piece of work but don't you think it would be better if you substituted the word 'chatty' for 'garrulous' " (*Windows*, p. 180).

Woodward returned to the *Review of Reviews* to help develop advertising for thousands of recently discovered photographs taken by Civil War photographer Mathew B. Brady. The process of halftones had not been developed immediately after the war, so it had been too expensive to process the pictures then. Now the technology was available, and the *Review of Reviews* wanted to publish Brady's work for the American public. In 1910 Civil War veterans and their families were still alive, and the market looked good. The country had not yet experienced the horrors of two world wars, so photographs of prisons, injured soldiers, and the hardships of war were moving and dynamic. The pictures and her own literary background gave Woodward the action and drama she cherished for creating memorable advertising. For her, writing the copy for this series was like writing an adventure story.

The *Review of Reviews* sold hundreds of thousands of sets of the Brady Civil War pictures. They were made into an elaborate set of books, *The History of the Civil War*, by Robert Lanier. Woodward wrote advertising "with soldiers

dashing and flags flying and horses leaping all over it. And ringing words"
(*Windows*, p. 193). She credited Rudyard Kipling as her inspiration for the
rhythm and swing of her advertisements, and she mused about how enraged
Kipling would be to know he was an inspiration for jingoistic American
advertising.

After three years Woodward was tired of soldiers and Civil War pictures and
felt desperate for some relief from a job that had been exciting and challenging
when it began. History solved her problem tragically when World War I began.
People no longer wanted to see old war photographs, because fresh grisly scenes
were reproduced in the news daily.

In 1912 Woodward had also begun to freelance as a copywriter for a baby
food client of the Frank Presbrey Company, another advertising agency. Her
mandate was words that are familiar today: "make it different from all the
others." In Woodward's time, that meant no more pictures of overly fat, stuffed-
looking babies whose mothers filled them with the client's product.

Woodward drew on her *Woman's Home Companion* experience for talking to
women and developed messages that played on the fears and joys of mothers
with their babies. Her appeals were emotional and her copy good tearjerkers.
She dropped the gender neutral "it" when referring to a baby. Instinctively, she
knew that a mother would not be excited about a message that referred to her
child as "it." The baby food company liked her work so much that she was
hired permanently at the agency, and she became one of the first women to be
hired as a copywriter at a large advertising agency.

Woodward supervised a campaign presentation for Heinz showing appetizing
pictures of food prepared to eat. This obvious tactic was a novel idea at the time.
She then argued for an emotional approach to insurance advertising, even to
business executives, financiers, and bankers. She listened carefully to people
around her, and she believed that their concerns about accidents were no different
from those of working-class people. Woodward also learned when she tested
copy approaches for Hartford Insurance that upbeat messages worked better than
sad ones. She helped develop a split-run campaign, one ad showing a weeping
widow and her children, the other showing a bandaged man in a hospital bed,
happily receiving a check from his insurance company. Both ads were keyed
and couponed, and the latter ad won easily. Woodward worked happily at Presbrey until 1915.

That year, Woodward announced that she wished to work for a commission
rather than a salary, even though her supervisor assured her that she was earning
"a mighty good salary for a woman." She liked the risk and uncertainty of a
commission, and believed that she could earn more money while also enjoying
full responsibility for an account. This was a radical move for a woman in the
early 20th century, but the loyalty of clients to Woodward's work made the
agency want to keep her. Ideas came easily to her, and she was particularly
adept at talking to people about the things that were important to them. Agencies
realized that women did most of the shopping and that they seldom spoke about

intimate problems with anyone other than other women. Women copywriters had access to these conversations, and women researchers had access to women's homes (Marchand, p. 33). Woodward wondered why more agencies did not hire women to write advertising for women, when men spent so much time asking their stenographers about what motivated women.

Advertising was a new industry in the early 1900s, and its practitioners were feeling their way. They learned that positive copy works better than fear tactics, that emotion works better than logic for many products. Heads of agencies were creative people who took risks, not financiers who moved cautiously to protect the safest routes. Woodward recognized that copy needed to sell products. She regarded beautiful photographs, illustrations, trade characters, and jingles as clever only if they did not overshadow the name of the product. Clients, on the other hand, said they wanted the best advertising to sell their products, but, in fact, they wanted beautiful pages spread out with their name in magazines of large circulation (*Windows*, p. 360). Several times in her books Woodward bemoaned the fact that advertisers insisted on expensive pictures, clever sayings, pictures of their buildings or themselves, and "lost messages." David Ogilvy lamented the same problem in the 1970s.

Woodward pioneered teaser copy to sell books, a copywriting technique so common today that it is hard to imagine media without it. She quit describing the book jackets and sales records of O. Henry's modestly read stories and began writing enticing segments of the plots themselves. Sluggish O. Henry sales exploded, and advertising copywriting learned yet another successful technique. She sold Mark Twain, Richard Harding Davis and Robert Louis Stevenson with the same technique and success. Success for mail order was measured as it is today, by the number of returned coupons.

Woodward likened copywriters to preachers, teachers, and actors. "A really good copywriter requires a passion for converting the other fellow, even if it is to something you don't believe in yourself" (*Windows*, p. 289). Copywriters work with a cynical passion, she said, and they must have an almost painful moral earnestness about the subject of their writing. Woodward believed that copywriters were the most intelligent people in business because, in addition to a passion for conversion, they had "facility with the pen," active minds, insight, and emotional intelligence. She hired bright people who read and possessed a rich intellectual background, however they acquired it. A college education was not essential to her, and she preferred writers not "spoiled" by the style of another agency.

Woodward looked to classical writers for inspiration: Elizabeth Barrett Browning for baby food, Rudyard Kipling for the Brady pictures, Mark Twain and O. Henry for words to sell their own works. With her O. Henry approach to copywriting, she changed the method of advertising books by mail. She teased readers by introducing a plot and invited them to send in the coupon to order the book so they could find out how the tale was resolved. She was careful not to tell which of O. Henry's stories the plot came from so readers could not easily find it in a library.

She did not sell Twain as a literary genius; she sold his work by appealing to readers' childhood memories. The ad copy was young: "Recall that golden day when you first read *Huckleberry Finn*. How your mother said, 'For goodness sake, stop laughing aloud over that book. You sound so silly.' But you couldn't stop laughing" (*Windows*, p. 280). Woodward credited her knack for identifying what would sell to the public to intuition as well as years of experience. It is the kind of understanding about the public that she said could be attributed to editors and politicians.

Celebrity endorsements for cosmetics and women's clothing were a new idea for advertising in the early part of the twentieth century, but Woodward recognized their effectiveness and tweaked the egos of socially prominent women so they would go on record with praise for her clients' products. She appreciated the dose of fantasy that accompanied buying decisions for women's wear, and she used it masterfully.

In December 1924, at age 42, Woodward said she was too comfortable with her career and had begun to wonder if creating advertising had any long-term meaning. She left advertising and began her next career as an author and outspoken critic of advertising. She went to Paris to write an autobiography, and other books and magazine pieces followed. All of them drew on her life in advertising, and her criticism of the emptiness of the business fueled the rhetoric of the Consumer Movement, which was full-blown in the 1930s.

Woodward thought the industry's effort at self-regulation was meaningless and wrote *It's An Art*, a consumer's guide to Madison Avenue, in 1938. She believed that the goal of advertising was not good work or a better standard of living for consumers. The goal was to make money for the agency and for the advertiser, and she objected to that. She said that "advertising had at least an implicit power over newspaper editorial content" and that radio programs "snuck pitches deceivingly into programs" (Fox, p. 168).

In "Pocket Guide," a regular column she wrote for *Nation* magazine for two years, her themes regularly told readers the truth about advertising techniques. In longer articles she chided manufacturers like Chase and Sanborn coffee for its copy theme, "So fresh we date every bag" and that no date would be more than ten days old. Chase and Sanborn saved itself the cost of vacuum cans by packaging the "fresh" coffee in bags. Woodward explained that oxygen hastens aging and that coffee would be fresher at any age in a vacuum-sealed can, so cans should be preferred. She used the rest of that forum to tell readers how to buy and brew good coffee (*Nation*, December 25, 1937).

In another article Woodward explained how Bruce Barton, chairman of the board of BBDO, the sixth largest advertising agency at that time, used advertising techniques to win a state congressional seat in New York. She described how he wooed voters and how, like many products, he was not quite what he said he was (*Nation*, November 5, 1938).

One of her favorite topics was careers for women. She decried the lack of information and guidance available to women who wanted to enter business, and she did her best to fill the gap by interviewing successful career women, talking with employers, and drawing on her own 20-year experience in the business world.

Even her fiction, some of it whodunits, is set in the world of advertising, and her characters are recognizable from experiences she describes in her autobiography. Two early characters in *Queens in the Parlor* reflect the cynical attitude she developed toward advertising. A male advertising executive chides his female colleague for taking advertising seriously. The woman replies that she does not take advertising seriously, but she does take having a job seriously.

At the end of her life, Helen Woodward was working on a book about the years 1910 to 1919. Like all of her works, it would draw on her years in the advertising industry. "I am glad of those twenty years," she wrote. "I would not give up their blazing complex life. The diplomacy, the pulling of wires, the manipulating of people, the exasperations and hysteria, . . . But the wondering about motives and secrets of action will keep me busy for a long time" (*Windows*, p. 386). She was prophetic. The "secrets and motives" of what drives consumers to buy continue to challenge the wits and imagination of her successors.

FURTHER READING

Works by Woodward

The Bowling Green Murders, with Frances Amherst. New York: Random House, 1940.
General Billy Mitchell, Pioneer of the Air. New York: Duell, Sloan, and Pearce, 1959.
      (Children's literature)
It's an Art. New York: Harcourt, Brace, 1938.
The Lady Persuaders. New York: Ivan Obolensky, 1960.
Lances Down, with Richard Boleslavski. Garden City, NY: Garden City Publishing, 1932.
Money to Burn. Philadelphia: David McKay, 1945.
Queens in the Parlor. Indianapolis: Bobbs-Merrill, 1933.
Three Flights Up, with Sidney Coe Howard. New York: Charles Scribner's Sons, 1924.
Through Many Windows. New York: Harper, 1926.
200 Years of Charleston Cooking, with Blanche S. Rhett and Lettie Gay (eds.). New York: J. Cape and H. Smith, 1930.
Way of the Lancer, with Richard Boleslavski. Garden City, NY: Garden City Publishing, 1932.
Articles by Woodward appeared in periodicals including *Harper's*, *Woman's Day*, *National Review*, *Vogue*, *Nation*, *New Leader*, and *American Mercury*.

Works about Woodward

Fox, Stephen. *The Mirror Makers: A History of American Advertising and Its Creators*. New York: William Morrow, 1984.

Marchand, Roland. *Advertising the American Dream: Making Way for Modernity, 1920–1940*. Berkeley: University of California Press, 1985.

Norris, James D. *Advertising and the Transformation of American Society, 1865–1920*. New York: Greenwood Press, 1990.

NOTABLE CLIENTS/CAMPAIGNS

Hartford Insurance

Heinz foods

Remington typewriters

Review of Reviews

JAMES WEBB YOUNG
(JANUARY 20, 1886–MARCH 3, 1973)

Elsie S. Hebert

James Webb Young—advertising executive, author, educator, and public servant—was one of the great pioneers in American advertising. He was instrumental in instituting some of the advertising practices that have been utilized for more than a half century and was a prime factor in expanding the J. Walter Thompson agency into a worldwide operation. In addition to his leadership as an executive and director at JWT, his career involved him in book and magazine publishing; direct-mail and public service advertising; work with various government agencies, the Advertising Council, and the Ford Foundation; and a five-year stint as a professor at the University of Chicago. David Ogilvy called Young one of the five giants in the history of advertising copywriting (Dunn and Barban, p. 341).

Jim Young, as he was popularly known, was born in Covington, Kentucky, on January 20, 1886. His mother, Susan Anna Webb, was a native Southerner, and his father, James Davidson Young, was "a north of Ireland man who in his youth had gone steamboating on the 'western waters,' served in the Union Army's transports, and eventually settled down in the insurance business in Cincinnati" (Young, *Diary of an Ad Man*, frontispiece).

According to the custom of the day in Kentucky, a boy was praised for his ambition to become a "self-made" man by quitting school at an early age and getting a job. After completing the fifth grade, Young left school to become a "cash boy" at $2 a week for a Cincinnati department store. After a few months a truant officer caught up with him and sent him back to school. However, after three months in the sixth grade, the youth accepted a job with the Western Methodist Book Concern in Cincinnati and terminated his formal public schooling.

For the next ten years he worked successively as office boy, magazine mailer, shipping clerk, stenographer (after taking a night course), book salesman, and advertising manager. For one year during this period he joined with two partners in operating a printing business of their own, but he went back to Western Methodist because he could not make enough money.

For the next few years he sold books to ministers by direct-mail advertising for Western Methodist in Cincinnati and to businessmen for the Ronald Press Company in New York. He then went to Chicago to sell *System Magazine*.

In 1912 Young began his career with J. Walter Thompson, an association which would span 52 years. Stanley Resor, manager of the JWT office in Cincinnati, persuaded Young that the advertising agency was a better place than the book business to utilize his copywriting talents. During the next five years Young began to develop his own idea-generating approach to advertising creativity, about which he later wrote. His technique has been praised and utilized by some of the advertising greats who followed, including Leo Burnett and David Ogilvy (Dunn and Barban, p. 341).

During this period Resor went to New York as vice president of the agency, and Young was made head of the Cincinnati office. When Resor became president of J. Walter Thompson in 1917, Young came to New York as vice president. A year later he was sent to Chicago as vice president in charge of creative work for all of the western offices of JWT, and he became joint manager of western operations, a position he occupied for the next decade.

The agency launched an international expansion program in 1927, and Young played "an important role in the establishment of the worldwide network of J. Walter Thompson Co. offices," Sidney Bernstein wrote in 1973 (p. 4). Young was sent as part of a team to open eight European offices in 1927–1928. When he returned, he retired—for the first time—to his Rancho Canada in Pena Blanca, New Mexico, near Santa Fe. But he never remained far from advertising and "continued to be involved in a number of JWT projects, among them setting up offices in Australia and New Zealand" (Bernstein, p. 76).

In 1931 Robert Hutchins, president of the University of Chicago, persuaded Young to join the faculty of the School of Business as professor of business history and advertising. For the next five years he taught during the winter and spring and spent his summers on his ranch.

In the introduction to Young's *How to Become an Advertising Man*, published in 1963, John Crichton wrote:

Jim Young's advertising career began more than 50 years ago, and covered nearly every phase of the developing advertising business in this country. This long experience has made him a superb teacher, and Young's whole career is typified by dual roles—practitioner and teacher. (p. 5)

In addition to college teaching, the decade of the 1930s was a busy one for Young before he returned to J. Walter Thompson in 1941. He became involved in a number of advertising, publishing, and public service projects, including becoming a principal stockholder of *Sunset Magazine* of San Francisco. He also conducted a study of the magazine industry for a group of principal publishers and made six trips abroad for special work in JWT's foreign offices (Young, *Diary of an Ad Man*, frontispiece).

Combining public service and his interest in Indian affairs, Young conducted a study of the marketing of Indian arts and crafts for Secretary of the Interior Harold Ickes. Using his advertising creativity and experience, he supplied the American Indians with advice and financing to help make and market their goods. With his son, Webb, he developed a mail-order business for New Mexican handwoven neckties. The Indians, in gratitude, named him "Man-Who-Points-at-Rainbows" (*New York Times*, March 5, 1973, p. 32).

At the request of Secretary of Commerce Harry L. Hopkins, Young served in Washington from 1939 to 1941 as director of the Bureau of Foreign and Domestic Commerce and was appointed director of communications to assist Nelson A. Rockefeller, coordinator of Inter-American Affairs, combat German propaganda in South America (*New York Times*, March 5, 1973, p. 4).

One of his major contributions to the advertising industry during this period was his study of the agency compensation system for national advertisers, the media, and agencies. He found the commission system, which is still widely used, was not perfect but one that seemed to work. His recommendations were published in *Advertising Agency Compensation* in 1933.

Young returned to J. Walter Thompson in 1941 as vice president and chairman of review boards, later becoming senior consultant. For the next 23 years, he divided his time between the agency and his apple orchard and ranch in New Mexico.

Shortly before Pearl Harbor, Young presented his plan for a public service program sponsored by the advertising industry, a plan which grew into the formation of the War Advertising Council and later into the founding of today's Advertising Council. Young outlined his plan before the first joint meeting ever held of the American Association of Advertising Agencies and the Association of National Advertisers, pointing out the problems advertising faced before the public. It was largely through his efforts that all facets of the advertising industry were organized to create and disseminate campaigns through the War Advertising Council, supporting government programs during World War II at no cost to the government.

Young never hesitated to criticize his advertising colleagues if he thought they were not putting forth their best efforts for public service advertising. At a meeting in November 1943 he told members of the Association of National Advertisers that at least $10 million more advertising space was needed immediately to meet the needs of the war program and that "bragging copy" should be avoided. He declared that 40 percent of the jobs on the docket of the War Advertising Council had either no advertising sponsorship or inadequate sponsorship:

We have mobilized the men and women of advertising, but we have not succeeded in mobilizing enough of the dollars. This is particularly true in printed advertising. . . . I am sure there is no advertiser in this room who does not cherish the desire to make every possible contribution to the war effort. But I think there is no escaping from the fact that many of us have been very inept about doing this in advertising. . . . I think we agencies are ultimately responsible for it, when we have lacked the vision, the courage or the ingenuity to suggest the better ways to use that space. (*New York Times*, November 19, 1943, p. 33)

To counter his own criticism of the advertising that was being produced, Young once again proved his genius as an outstanding copywriter by publishing *A Technique for Producing Ideas*, first published by *Advertising Age* in 1940 and reprinted in six editions through 1949, with 33,000 copies sold. He felt that every form of communication should have a functional purpose, so he used his creative ability to combine words and pictures with the marketing objective of selling goods and services.

Young's organized approach to generating creative ideas involved five stages: (1) gathering all available information pertinent to the subject or problem—"ingestion"; (2) exploring different facets of the information gathered for possible relationships—"digestion"; (3) putting the problem out of the mind for a while to let the subconscious work—"incubation"; (4) grasping the new ideas or associations which came to mind—"illumination"; and (5) developing the ideas—"verification" (Dunn and Barban, p. 341).

Young followed this effort to help advertising students and practitioners understand the fundamentals of copywriting and the advertising business with an anonymous column in *Advertising Age*, beginning in June 1942. A collection of these columns was published in 1944 as *The Diary of an Ad Man*.

James Webb Young was elected chairman of the War Advertising Council on March 9, 1945. Having served as a director since its inception, he quickly outlined plans to focus public attention on the U.S. role in peacetime and on the proper treatment of returning service personnel, recognizing their military experience as increasing their value as employees and citizens. He pointed out that the work of the council "shows among other things that it pays advertisers to cooperate with home-front information campaigns in terms of increased advertising effectiveness" (New Series of Ads," p. 18).

The War Advertising Council became the Advertising Council on November 1, 1945, with Young as its first chairman. Continuing its public service mission, the council expanded its services to include not only work with government departments in developing information programs, but assistance to nongovernmental organizations dealing with national problems. Speaking of the transition to peacetime public service operations, Young explained:

Business leaders and owners of advertising media, . . . have learned from their war experience that public service advertising is the best public relations advertising. . . . This action is only one more expression by business of its intent to continue into peacetime that recognition of its social responsibility which it so magnificently displayed in war. (*New York Times*, November 1, 1945, p. 28)

Less than a year later Young reported that more than $100 million worth of advertising space was being contributed by American business to support public service projects (*New York Times*, September 19, 1946, p. 38).

Young added to his own public service record by being elected to successive terms on the board of trustees of the Committee for Economic Development (CED), a national organization of businessmen, economists, and educators which had been formed to promote full employment after World War II and to develop national policies for that purpose. The CED is credited with having been a major influence in securing congressional approval of the Marshall Plan. Young served until May 1958 (*New York Times*, July 11, 1955, p. 33).

Jim young was recognized on February 7, 1946, as advertising Man of the Year, and the annual Advertising Awards jury presented him with their gold medal for "outstanding achievements of a lifetime and most particularly for his notable contributions during the war" (*New York Times*, January 15, 1946, p. 28; February 8, 1946, p. 32).

In 1951, at the age of 65, while still serving as senor consultant and director of J. Walter Thompson, Young was appointed consultant to the Ford Foundation in the fields of communications and education. He quickly became involved in studying the potential for educational radio and television through cultural and information programming, but felt that commercial broadcasting would have a greater social importance. He felt that the key problem was the cost of programming and wrote:

There may develop specialized uses for television in instructional and cultural material for which we need noncommercial support, just as we need it in other institutions of our society. But the important fact remains that we are committed to a commercial competitive system of broadcasting in this country, and that through it we will eventually be spending not less than a billion dollars a year in time and talent costs for the commercial television. (*New York Times*, June 13, 1951, p. 1)

He advocated setting up cooperative workshops, involving the Ford Foundation, station owners, and networks, to see what contribution could be made within commercial broadcasting operations to provide a better level of educational and cultural programming.

In the decade that followed, American advertising continued to learn from James Webb Young's professional experience and wisdom. He told an Advertising Council group that "an economy of abundance had reduced the differences between competing products," causing advertising copywriters to magnify minute product differences (*New York Times*, November 18, 1954, p. 53). He advocated giving advertising in public print the same kind of criticism given to other major aspects of our culture, such as music, literature, and the visual arts. Young suggested that publications create an editorial position of "advertising critic" to keep an eye on all advertising "praising the good, exposing the meretricious, and lambasting the bad" (*New York Times*, April 18, 1960, p. 46).

The *Saturday Review* took Young up on his suggestion and commissioned him to write a monthly column beginning October 8, 1960, devoted to advertising, public relations, press, radio, television, publishing, and public opinion polling:

His task will be to report how well his associates go about their business, how well they communicate with the American public and to suggest improvement or praise noteworthy performances in the advertising field on the yardstick of public interest and professional competence. (*New York Times*, September 22, 1960, p. 44)

James Webb Young closed out his publishing career in 1973, at the age of 77, with advice on *How to Become an Advertising Man*. He dedicated the book to the advertising men and women of JWT around the world. He retired as a director of J. Walter Thompson on January 28, 1964. He died on March 3, 1973, in Santa Fe at age 87.

Reinhold Niebuhr wrote in the foreword of the 1949 edition of *A Technique for Producing Ideas*:

There is an elusive quality in the creative individual which defies analysis and imitation. Yet there are techniques and modes of procedure which can be learned and transmitted; and Mr. Young has given us a very clear exposition of them. . . . Only an advertising man could have written with such brevity and clarity; but not every advertising man or any other kind of specialist could have written with such depth of comprehension.

FURTHER READING

Works by Young

Advertising Agency Compensation. Chicago: University of Chicago Press, 1933.
The Compleat Angler. Coapa, NM: Pinon Press, 1953.
The Diary of an Ad Man. Chicago: Advertising Publications, 1944.
Ego-Biography. Coapa, NM: Pinon Press, 1955.
A Footnote to History. Coapa, NM: Pinon Press, 1950.
Full Corn in the Ear. Coapa, NM: Pinon Press, 1959.
His Girl and His Dinner. Coapa, NM: Pinon Press, 1956.
Hometown Boy Makes Good. Coapa, NM: Pinon Press, 1958.
How to Become an Advertising Man. Chicago: Crain Books, 1963.
The Itch for Orders. Coapa, NM: Pinon Press, 1957.
Mirror for a Lady. Coapa, NM: Pinon Press, 1954.
Pills for the Angels. Coapa, NM: Pinon Press, 1952.
A Story Still Untold. Coapa, NM: Pinon Press, 1951.
A Technique for Producing Ideas. Chicago: Advertising Publications, 1940.
Note: The books published in the 1950s were autobiographical anecdotes on the life and times of James Webb Young, produced in private printing, 600 each year, to be sent to friends at Christmas.

Works about Young

"Advertising 'Man of Year' Selected by Awards Jury." *New York Times* (January 15, 1946): 28.

Bernstein, Sidney R. "A Remembrance of James W. Young." *Advertising Age* (March 12, 1973): 4.

Dunn, S. Watson, and Arnold M. Barban. *Advertising—Its Role in Modern Marketing.* 6th ed. New York: Dryden Press, 1986.

Fox, Stephen. *The Mirror Makers: A History of American Advertising and Its Creators.* New York: William Morrow, 1984.

"Grand Old Man of Advertising, James Young, Dies." *Advertising Age* (March 12, 1973): 3, 76.

"New Series of Ads to Back War Front." *New York Times* (April 21, 1945): 18.

Ogilvy, David. *Confessions of an Advertising Man.* New York: Atheneum, 1963.

———. *Ogilvy on Advertising.* New York: Crown, 1983.

"War Advertising Council Elects Him [Young] as Chairman." *New York Times* (March 10, 1945): 23.

Wells, William, John Burnett, and Sandra Moriarty. *Advertising: Principles and Practice.* Englewood Cliffs, NJ: Prentice-Hall, 1989.

Who Was Who in America. Vol. 5. Chicago: Marquis Who's Who, 1973.

"Young to Aid Ford Fund." *New York Times* (April 3, 1951): 15.

NOTABLE CLIENTS/CAMPAIGNS

James Webb Young was involved in many campaigns throughout his long career with J. Walter Thompson, the War Advertising Council, and the Advertising Council. He is credited with introducing the first deodorant campaign for JWT, for a product called Odorono, in 1919. The headline read, "Within the curve of a woman's arm." Although the ad brought public commentary and reportedly offended some readers, sales of the product increased more than 100 percent the next year. In 1928 he launched the first campaign for Maxwell House coffee after extensively researching the history of the Maxwell House Hotel in Nashville (Fox, p. 88).

David Ogilvy, in his book *Ogilvy on Advertising*, reproduces an ad for Young's Santa Fe mail-order business, conducted under the name "Webb Young, Trader." The ad, for handwoven ties, ran one time in *Life* and sold 26,000 ties (p. 147).

JOHN ORR YOUNG
(JUNE 25, 1887–MAY 1, 1976)

Carolyn Tripp

John Orr Young founded Young and Rubicam with Raymond Rubicam in 1923 on a shoestring. The fledgling agency's first account was the Quick Tipper, a gadget to put tips on shoelaces. From that modest beginning, the firm grew into one of the world's largest advertising agencies. In 1990 Young and Rubicam ranked sixth, with nearly $1.1 billion in billings and 324 offices worldwide.

Born June 25, 1887, in Leon, Iowa (a town of 800), Young was the son of a farm couple, Major John Lewis and Elizabeth Woodbury Young. He was always proud of his Iowa heritage, especially the farm. As a youth, Young took a trainload of hogs from Chicago to Hoboken, New Jersey, then earned his way overseas by working on cattle boats. His agricultural roots resurfaced much later in 1938, when he was named president of the Atchison Agrol Company, Atchison, Kansas. Agrol, a motor fuel of gasoline and alcohol, was manufactured from farm products such as corn, wheat, and sorghum.

Educated at Lake Forest College in Illinois (1906–1908), Young paid his way through school by working as the business manager of the college newspaper and clerking at a drugstore. His entry into big-time advertising occurred in Chicago with the Lord and Thomas agency. Following a two-year stint in the advertising department of the *Salt Lake Herald Tribune*, he accepted a position with Lord and Thomas as a cub copywriter for $60 a week.

At Lord and Thomas, Young worked on the Sunkist and Palmolive accounts and rubbed shoulders with such advertising legends as Claude Hopkins and A. D. Lasker. According to Stephen Fox in *The Mirror Makers*, Hopkins was unimpressed with the succulent pictures of oranges Young devised for the Sunkist campaign (p. 132). Fox further states that Young's departure from Lord and Thomas may have been hastened when he circulated a parody of the agency's letterhead around the office. Under the masthead of Loud and Promise Badvertising, Young had listed Lasker as A. D. Rascal, President, and Hopkins as Fraud Hopkins, V.P. (p. 133).

From Lord and Thomas, Young went to Procter and Gamble as the advertising manager of the Crisco division (1913–1914). He left Procter and Gamble after two years to become a partner at Young, Henri and Hurst (1914–1915), then moved to New York to begin his own agency, the John Orr Young Company. In 1918 Young moved to Philadelphia to work as an account executive for F. Wallis Armstrong. Two years later he moved to N. W. Ayer and Son, where his account executive skills became linked with the talented copywriter Raymond Rubicam.

In *Adventures in Advertising*, Young relates how he and Rubicam declared their independence from N. W. Ayer following a noon walk to Independence Square. Interestingly, the two young men promised not to take any Ayer accounts with them, nor to solicit any Ayer accounts for a period of one year. Thus, on May 23, 1923, Young and Rubicam was founded.

Young had a gregarious personality (Fox, p. 132) and the contacts for attracting clients; hence, he worked on attracting new business. Young's solicitation philosophy was to ask for the most difficult job first. He called on large companies and challenged each to let Young and Rubicam work on that firm's most troublesome product. His assumption was that if Young and Rubicam was successful, the client would reward the agency with additional accounts.

Postum, a decaffeinated beverage with deteriorating sales, was obtained from General Foods in this manner. As noted by Fox, Rubicam wrote a campaign that emphasized the soothing effect drinking Postum would have on nervous, sleepless people. "The series of ads—'Why Men Crack' and 'When the Iron Man Begins to Rust'—revived Postum sales, won a Harvard-Bok prize, and established Young and Rubicam as an agency" (p. 133). Following that initial work, Young and Rubicam agreed to open an office in New York in order to work on additional General Foods accounts, in particular, Grape-Nuts, Jell-O, Sanka, Minute tapioca, and Baker's coconut.

According to Fox, Rubicam considered leaving the firm early in its existence to pursue writing fiction. Young convinced him to stay on in the capacity of president. Thereafter, given controlling interest in the firm, the power and initiative flowed toward Rubicam (p. 135). Nevertheless, the two partners and their families remained close friends.

In *Adventures in Advertising*, Young recounted leaving Young and Rubicam due to his deteriorating health. Blaming his own predisposition as a "worrier," he admitted he was a workaholic who never had difficulty *envisioning* his own success. He cautioned young advertising professionals to *plan* for success by allocating specific time for relaxation, family, and service to others. According to Young, "By the time we had passed the $12 million mark of annual billings, we had broken some records for acquiring new business, but I had also broken my health" (*New York Times*, October 13, 1957, p. 10f).

An alternative explanation for Young's departure from Young and Rubicam is presented in *The Mirror Makers*. Fox provides evidence that Young may have been pressured out of the agency for not pulling his weight. Reports indicate that he took long vacations and did not work too hard when on the job. Once a client specifically requested of Rubicam that Young *not* attend a critical meeting (p. 136).

Upon leaving Young and Rubicam, Young spent the next seven years traveling through Europe and raising and riding horses in the Shenandoah Valley. He liked his hobbies and free time and was not motivated to accumulate riches (Fox, p. 136). In fact, Fox attributes the following quote to Young: "Remember that some of the best years are passing while you prostrate yourself at the feet of the idol of Success" (Fox, p. 136).

Following this hiatus to restore his health, Young's participation in advertising, public relations, and consulting continued. In 1939 he announced a new agency under his name. An ad in the *New York Times* (May 25) read as follows:

Some springs ago my then partner and I decided to leave a large advertising agency— to build our own . . . a fortunate decision for us—and for the advertisers who had the sense of values and courage to retain us.

Now after a vacation from advertising, I seek again the action and constructive opportunity I have found only in advertising.

This preliminary statement will be followed by the announcement of an agency, now building, to be devoted to a custom-built service for a highly restricted number of only Class A accounts. (p. 38)

The new company was not an advertising agency but, rather, a supplement to the client's advertising agency. The firm's special emphasis was on wartime problems. In particular, Young wanted to advise firms concerning new products and revised products that would result due to the curtailment of materials.

Young also lent his promotional expertise to political issues. In 1940, under the guise of a businessman who had paid for the ad space himself, he took out a full-page ad in the *New Yorker* to support Wendell Wilkie as the Republican presidential nominee against incumbent Franklin Roosevelt. The ad's hook asked for donations from those who cared to join in bringing Wilkie to the magazine-reading public. The ad further explained that 1,000 readers could be reached for only $2. This approach was successful in funding Wilkie's campaign, but it also raised some controversy.

At that time, the Hatch Law limited national presidential campaign expenditures to $3 million and individual contributions to $5,000. Shortly after the campaign broke, Young and Oren Root, Jr., chairman of the Wilkie Club, were called before the Senate Campaign Expenditure Committee to explain their methods and purposes in raising contributions for Wilkie. During his testimony, Root told of a mix-up with the Wilkie Magazine Fund, directed by Young. "The latter has inserted in one advertisement that Mr. Young's advertising campaign was approved by the Root committee. This was dropped after Root complained" (*New York Times*, September 21, 1940, p. 10).

In his testimony, Young admitted that one ad (the one stating that the profits would be given to the Wilkie campaign) was illegal. However, he noted that this statement was removed from subsequent ads. He also indicated that no profits had been made. With regard to the motive behind the advertising campaign, Young indicated that he wanted to bring Wilkie's qualifications before the voters because he opposed the reelection of President Roosevelt.

Although Young's ad campaign was not successful in electing Wilkie, in 1947 he attempted a similar strategy for Dwight D. Eisenhower. "I want Eisenhower! How about you?" headlined a series of ads that first appeared in the *Westport* (Connecticut) *Herald*. The ad presented the general's qualifications and said none of the declared Republican candidates could defeat Harry S. Truman.

In 1945 Young formed a public relations agency with Harold C. Meyers, former head of Institutional Relations. Young and Meyers was designed to represent industrial, commercial, municipal, and institutional clients. Young was a strong believer in public relations advertising. In a speech given to the advertising chapter of the American Veterans Committee, he held,

I should like to see more product ads flavored by the public relations ingredient. There can be and there should be a spot, or section, of public relations in 90 per cent of the medium-to-large ads you read and those you listen to on the radio. (*New York Times*, June 17, 1948, p. 42)

Young went on to stress a firm distinction between sincere public relations advertising and institutional ads that are "four parts tax dodge and one part sincerity."

In 1949 Young published *Adventures in Advertising*, an autobiography written while riding the New Haven Railroad daily between his Westport, Connecticut, home and Manhattan. Using his briefcase as a table, he wrote, edited, and rewrote the 199-page book in longhand. Working twice daily, it took one year to complete. According to the *New York Times* (May 3, 1976, p. 34), 11 of Young's fellow commuters gave him a surprise party on the train one morning. The occasion was to congratulate him on the book's publication.

In later years Young maintained a simple two-person office on Park Avenue. As one of the best known advertising consultants in the industry, he became involved in mergers and acquisitions, served as a consultant on many ad campaigns, and assisted in agency selection and executive placement processes. He took credit for merging D'Arcy Advertising with the Federal agency; Cowan and Dengler with Donahue and Coe; Ivan Hill with Cunningham and Walsh; and Brisacher, Wheeler and Staff with C & W (*New York Times*, October 13, 1957, p. 10F).

Commenting on his role as a consultant, Young stated:

When companies come to me and say that they think they should change their agency, 50 percent of the time I counsel them not to. The biggest problem I have found is a lack of communications between client and agency. In most instances they just do not have a clear cut idea of what they want to accomplish. If this were corrected there would be a lot less switching of accounts. (*New York Times*, December 7, 1958), p. 10F)

An interesting aside to Young's career was his stance on alcohol and tobacco advertising. During his career he had refused to accept alcohol manufacturers as clients. In 1964 he upbraided his colleagues for their handling of cigarette advertising. In a column of his monthly newsletter, he said:

A few months ago, the industry appeared to agree that they should be less aggressive in appealing to young readers, young listeners, and young TV viewers, but I have not been aware of any lessening of attractive boys and girls serving as decoys in cigarette advertisements. . . .

Advertising agencies are retained by cigarette manufacturers to create demand for cigarettes among both adults and eager youngsters. The earlier the teenage boy or girl gets the habit, the bigger the national sales volume. . . . The agency proceeds to do a smashing big job for its client in building sales volume. Results: bigger sales, serious health difficulties for the smoker, Government intervention brought about by cigarette manufacturer and advertising agency teamwork. (*New York Times*, January 29, 1964, p. 49)

Young himself began smoking at the age of 14 and stopped smoking only after age 70.

Among Young's hobbies were collecting farms and antiques. At the time of his death on May 1, 1976, his family included his wife, Bernice Renner; a daughter, Helen Jackson; two sons, John, Jr., and Raymond; five grandchildren; and two great-grandchildren.

FURTHER READING

Work by Young

Adventures in Advertising. New York: Harper, 1948.

Work about Young

Fox, Stephen. *The Mirror Makers: A History of American Advertising and Its Creators.* New York: William Morrow, 1984.

NOTABLE CLIENTS/CAMPAIGNS

Crisco (Procter and Gamble, 1910s)

Palmolive (Lord and Thomas, 1910s)

Sunkist (Lord and Thomas, 1910s)

Quick Tipper (Young and Rubicam, 1920s)

Heinz rice flakes (Young and Rubicam 1920s–30s)

Jell-O (Young and Rubicam, 1920s–30s)

Johnson and Johnson baby powder (Young and Rubicam, 1920s–30s)

Rolls-Royce (Young and Rubicam, 1920s–30s)

Sanka (Young and Rubicam, 1920s–30s)

Wendell Wilkie presidential campaign (John Orr Young, 1940s)

Dwight D. Eisenhower presidential campaign (John Orr Young, 1940s)

BIBLIOGRAPHY

Advertising Today/Yesterday/Tomorrow. New York: McGraw-Hill, 1963.

Appel, Joseph H. *Growing Up with Advertising*. New York: Business Bourse, 1940.

Barton, Bruce Fairchild, and Bernard Lichtenberg. *Advertising Campaigns*. New York: Alexander Hamilton Institute, 1930.

Bates, Charles Austin. *Good Advertising*. New York: Holmes Publishing, 1896.

Belding, Mollie. *Mollie Belding's Memory Book*. Los Angeles: Ward Richie Press, 1945.

Bowles, Chester. *The New Dimensions of Peace*. New York: Harper, 1955.

———. *Promises to Keep*. New York: Harper and Row, 1971.

Brainbridge, John. *Another Way of Living: A Gallery of Americans Who Choose to Live in Europe*. New York: Holt, Rinehart and Winston, 1968.

Broadbent, Simon, ed. *The Leo Burnett Book of Advertising*. London: Business Books, 1984.

Brower, Charles Hendrickson. *Me, and Other Advertising Geniuses*. Garden City, NY: Doubleday, 1974.

Brown, Helen Gurley. *Sex and the Office*. New York: B. Geis Associates, 1964.

Burnett, Leo N. *Leo: A Tribute to Leo Burnett through a Selection of the Inspiring Words He Spoke*. Chicago: Leo Burnett Company, 1971.

Buxton, Edward. *Creative People at Work*. New York: Executive Communications, 1975.

———. *Promise Them Anything*. New York: Stein and Day, 1972.

Cahn, William. *Out of the Cracker Barrel: The Nabisco Story from Animal Crackers to Zuzus*. New York: Simon and Schuster, 1969.

Calkins, Earnest Elmo. *Advertising*. Chicago: American Library Association, 1929.

———. *The Advertising Man*. New York: Charles Scribner's Sons, 1922.

———. *"And Hearing Not."* New York: Charles Scribner's Sons, 1946.

———. *The Business of Advertising*. New York: D. Appleton, 1915.

———. *Business the Civilizer*. Boston: Little, Brown, 1928.

———. *"Louder Please!": The Autobiography of a Deaf Man*. Boston: Atlantic Monthly Press, 1924.

———, and Ralph Holden. *Modern Advertising*. New York: D. Appleton, 1905.

Caples, John. *Advertising for Immediate Sales*. New York: Harper, 1936.

————. *Advertising Ideas: A Practical Guide to Methods That Make Advertisements Work*. New York: McGraw-Hill Book Co., 1938.

————. *How to Make Your Advertising Make Money*. Englewood Cliffs, NJ: Prentice-Hall, 1986.

————. *Making Ads Pay*. New York: Dover, 1957.

————. *Tested Advertising Methods*. 4th ed. Englewood Cliffs, NJ: Prentice-Hall, 1974.

Clark, Eric. *The Want Makers. The World of Advertising: How They Make You Buy*. New York: Viking Penguin, 1988.

Cone, Fairfax M. *With All Its Faults*. Boston: Little, Brown, 1969.

Cummings, Bart. *The Benevolent Dictators: Interviews with Advertising Greats*. Chicago: Crain Books, 1984.

Daniels, Draper. *Giants, Pigmies and Other Advertising People*. Chicago: Crain Communications, 1974.

Della Femina, Jerry. *From Those Wonderful Folks Who Brought You Pearl Harbor*. New York: Simon and Schuster, 1970.

Dobrow, Larry. *When Advertising Tried Harder*. New York: Friendly Press, 1984.

Durstine, Roy Sarles. *Making Advertisements and Making Them Pay*. New York and London: Charles Scribner's Sons, 1921.

————. *This Advertising Business*. New York and London: Charles Scribner's Sons, 1928.

Fitz-Gibbon, Bernice. *Macy's, Gimbels and Me: How to Earn $90,000 a Year in Retail Advertising*. New York: Simon and Schuster, 1967.

Foremost Women in Communications. New York: Foremost American Publishing, 1970.

Forty Years in Advertising. Philadelphia: N. W. Ayer and Son, 1909.

Foster, G. Allen. *Advertising: Ancient Market Place to Television*. New York: Criterion Books, 1967.

Fox, Stephen. *The Mirror Makers: A History of American Advertising and Its Creators*. New York: William Morrow, 1984.

Foxworth, Jo. *Boss Lady: An Executive Woman Talks about Making It*. New York: Thomas Y. Crowell, 1978.

————. *Boss Lady's Arrival and Survival Plan*. New York: Warner Books, 1986.

———— *Wising Up: The Mistakes Women Make in Business and How to Avoid Them*. New York: Delacorte Press, 1980.

French, Elbrun Rochford. *The Copywriter's Guide*. New York: Harper, 1958.

Glatzer, Robert. *The New Advertising*. New York: Citadel Press, 1970.

Gossage, Howard Luck. *Is There Any Hope for Advertising?* Edited by Kim Rotzoll, Jarlath Graham, and Barrow Mussey. Urbana: University of Illinois Press, 1986.

Graham, Irvin. *Advertising Agency Practice*. New York: Harper, 1952.

Gunther, John. *Taken at the Flood: The Story of Albert D. Lasker*. New York: Harper, 1960.

Higgins, Denis. *The Art of Writing Advertising: Conversations with Masters of the Craft*. Lincolnwood, Ill.: National Textbook Company, 1965.

Hinckle, Warren. *If You Have a Lemon, Make Lemonade*. New York: Putnam, 1973.

Hopkins, Claude C. *My Life in Advertising*. 1927. Reprint. Lincolnwood, IL: National Textbook Company, 1987.

————. *Scientific Advertising*. 1923. Reprint. Lincolnwood, IL: National Textbook Company, 1987.

Hower, Ralph M. *The History of an Advertising Agency: N. W. Ayer and Son at Work, 1869–1949*. Rev. ed. Cambridge: Harvard University Press, 1949.

Hyman, Sidney. *The Lives of William Benton*. Chicago: University of Chicago Press, 1969.

In Behalf of Advertising: A Series of Essays Published in National Periodicals from 1919 to 1928. Philadelphia: N. W. Ayer and Son, 1929.

Jacobson, Jacob Z. *Scott of Northwestern: The Life Story of a Pioneer in Psychology and Education*. Chicago: L. Mariano, 1951.

Johnston, Russ. *Marion Harper: An Unauthorized Biography*. Chicago: Crain Books, 1982.

Kennedy, John E. *The Book of Advertising Tests*. New York: Lord and Thomas, 1905.

Lasker, Albert D. *The Lasker Story . . . As He Told It*. Chicago: Advertising Publications, 1963.

Lee, Charles. *The Hidden Public: The Story of the Book-of-the-Month Club*. Garden City, NY: Doubleday, 1958.

Lieberman, Joseph I. *The Power Broker*. Boston: Houghton Mifflin, 1966.

McElvaine, Robert S. *The Great Depression: America, 1929–41*. New York: New York Times Books, 1984.

MacManus, Theodore F. *The Sword-Arm of Business*. New York: Devin-Adair, 1927.

Marchand, Roland. *Advertising the American Dream: Making Way for Modernity, 1920–1940*. Berkeley: University of California Press, 1985.

Mayer, Martin. *Madison Avenue, U.S.A.*. New York: Harper, 1958.

———. *Whatever Happened to Madison Avenue?* Boston: Little, Brown, 1991.

Meyers, William. *The Image-Makers*. London: Orbis, 1984.

Mott, Frank Luther. *American Journalism: A History: 1690–1960*. 3d ed. New York: Macmillan, 1962.

Norins, Hanley. *The Compleat Copywriter*. New York: McGraw-Hill, 1966.

Norris, James D. *Advertising and the Transformation of American Society, 1865–1920*. New York: Greenwood Press, 1990.

Ogilvy, David. *Blood, Brains and Beer, The Autobiography of David Ogilvy*. New York: Atheneum, 1978.

———. *Confessions of an Advertising Man*. New York: Atheneum, 1963.

———. *Ogilvy on Advertising*. New York: Crown, 1983.

Osborn, Alex F. *Applied Imagination: The Principles and Procedures of Creative Thinking*. New York: Charles Scribner's Sons, 1953.

———. *How to "Think Up."* New York: McGraw-Hill, 1942.

———. *Short Course in Advertising*. New York: Charles Scribner's Sons, 1921.

———. *Wake Up Your Mind*. New York: Charles Scribner's Sons, 1952.

———. *Your Creative Power*. New York: Charles Scribner's Sons, 1948.

Packard, Vance. *The Hidden Persuaders*. New York: David McKay, 1957.

Pollay, Richard W., ed. *Information Sources in Advertising History*. Westport, CT: Greenwood Press, 1979.

Pope, Daniel. *The Making of Modern Advertising*. New York: Basic Books, 1983.

Presbrey, Frank. *The History and Development of Advertising*. 1929. Reprint. New York: Greenwood Press, 1968.

Reeves, Rosser. *Reality in Advertising*. New York: Knopf, 1961.

Rowell, George Presbury. *Forty Years an Advertising Agent, 1865–1905*. 1906. Reprint. New York: Franklin Publishing, 1926.

Rowell, Roland. *Biographical Sketch of Samuel Rowell*. Manchester, NH: William E. Moore, 1898.

Rowsome, Frank, Jr. *They Laughed When I Sat Down*. New York: Bonanza Books, 1959.

Runyon, Kenneth E. *Advertising and the Practice of Marketing*. Columbus, OH: Charles E. Merrill, 1979.

Sackheim, Maxwell. *My First 65 Years in Advertising*. Blue Ridge Summit, PA: TAB Books, 1975.

————. *My First Sixty Years in Advertising*. Englewood Cliffs, NJ: Prentice-Hall, 1970.

Schlesinger, Arthur M., Jr. *The Age of Roosevelt: The Politics of Upheaval*. Boston: Houghton-Mifflin, 1960.

Schofield, Perry. *100 Top Copy Writers and Their Favorite Ads*. New York: Printer's Ink, 1954.

Schwab, Victor O. *How to Write a Good Advertisement*. New York: Schwab and Beatty, 1942.

————. *How to Write a Good Advertisement: A Short Course in Copywriting*. Rev. and enl. New York: Harper and Row. Reprint. North Hollywood, CA: Hal Leighton Printing, 1962.

Scott, Walter Dill. *Increasing Human Efficiency in Business: A Contribution to the Psychology of Business*. New York: Macmillan, 1911.

————. *Influencing Men in Business: The Psychology of Argument and Suggestion*. New York: Ronald Press, 1911.

————. *The Psychology of Advertising: A Simple Exposition of the Principles of Psychology in Their Relation to Successful Advertising*. Boston: Small, Maynard, 1908.

————. *The Psychology of Advertising in Theory and Practice: A Simple Exposition of the Principles of Psychology in Their Relation to Successful Advertising*. Boston: Small, Maynard, 1913.

————. *The Theory of Advertising: A Simple Exposition of the Principles of Psychology in Their Relation to Successful Advertising*. Boston: Small, Maynard, 1908.

Starch, Daniel. *Advertising: Its Principles, Practices and Technique*. New York: Scott, Foresman, 1914.

————. *Advertising Principles*. Chicago and New York: A. W. Shaw, 1927.

————. *Measuring Advertising Readership and Results*. New York: McGraw-Hill, 1946.

————. *Principles of Advertising*. New York: McGraw-Hill, 1923.

Tebbel, John. *The Media in America*. New York: Thomas Y. Crowell, 1974.

Trahey, Jane. *Jane Trahey on Women and Power: Who's Got It/How to Get It*. Riverside, NJ: Rawson Associates, 1977.

Tunstall, Jeremy. *The Advertising Man in London Advertising Agencies*. London: Chapman and Hall, 1964.

Tyler, Poyntz, ed. *Advertising in America*. New York: H. W. Wilson, 1959.

Wakeman, Frederic. *The Huckster*. New York: Rinehart, 1946.

Watkins, Julian Lewis. *The 100 Greatest Advertisements*. New York: Dover, 1959.

Webber, Gordon. *Our Kind of People*. New York: Benton and Bowles, 1979.

White, Gordon. *John Caples: Adman*. Chicago: Crain Books, 1977.

Whittier, Charles LeRoy. *Creative Advertising*. New York: Henry Holt, 1955.

————. *Dear Dad: Our Life in the Theater around the Turn of the Century*. Freeport, ME: Bond Wheelwright, 1972.

Who's Who in Advertising. New York: Haire Publishing, 1963.

Wood, James Playsted. *The Story of Advertising*. New York: Ronald Press, 1958.

Woodward, Helen Rosen. *It's an Art*. New York: Harcourt, Brace, 1938.

———. *The Lady Persuaders*. New York: Ivan Obolensky, 1960.

Young, James Webb. *Advertising Agency Compensation*. Chicago: University of Chicago Press 1933.

———. *The Diary of an Ad Man*. Chicago: Advertising Publications, 1944.

———. *Ego-Biography*. Coapa, NM: Pinon Press, 1955.

———. *How to Become an Advertising Man*. Chicago: Crain Books, 1963.

———. *A Technique for Producing Ideas*. Chicago: Advertising Publications, 1940.

Young, John Orr. *Adventures in Advertising*. New York: Harper, 1949.

INDEX

Page numbers in **bold** refer to main entries.

ABOUT THE EDITOR AND CONTRIBUTORS

EDD APPLEGATE is an associate professor in the Department of Journalism, College of Mass Communication, at Middle Tennessee State University. Applegate (with Sharon Brock, Joseph Pisani, and Eric Zanot) edited the text *Advertising: Concepts, Strategies, and Issues*. His articles and other pieces have appeared in *The Media in America*, *Corporate Magazines of the United States*, and *Dictionary of Literary Biography*.

THOMAS A. BOWERS is professor and associate dean of the School of Journalism and Mass Communication at the University of North Carolina at Chapel Hill. A past president of the Association for Education in Journalism and Mass Communication, he is coauthor (with Alan D. Fletcher) of *Fundamentals of Advertising Research*.

SHARON S. BROCK developed the advertising program at the Ohio State University in 1985, when she was assistant director of the School of Journalism. Brock teaches in that program and advises the student AAF chapter. In addition, she is a public member of the National Advertising Review Board as well as a member of the executive committee of the Advertising Division of the AEJMC. She chaired the Teaching Standards Committee of the AEJMC and, for outstanding service to journalism and mass communication, won the AEJMC Presidential Award in 1992, when she was also named "Headliner of the Year" by the Columbus chapter of Women in Communications, Inc. Brock has had professional internships at several advertising agencies and has lectured on advertising at Moscow State University. She has written articles about subliminal advertising, puffery, and advertising education, and she edited (with Edd Applegate, Joseph Pisani, and Eric Zanot) the text *Advertising: Concepts, Strategies, and Issues*. She frequently chairs site teams for the Accrediting Council in Journalism and Mass Communication.

LESLIE COLE teaches in the Marketing Department, Hankamer School of Business, at Baylor University.

MARJORIE J. COOPER is a professor in the Marketing Department, Hankamer School of Business, at Baylor University. She has published numerous articles in such journals as the *Journal of Advertising* and the *Journal of Advertising Research*. She is also coauthor of the text *Direct Marketing, Direct Selling, and the Mature Consumer*.

SAMMY R. DANNA is a professor of communication at Loyola University of Chicago. Danna has authored over 70 articles, ranging from business and educational pieces to book chapters and monographs. Regarding the latter, the University of Missouri School of Journalism's Freedom of Information Center published five of these treatises on historical and problem areas in the FOI realm. Danna edited the text *Advertising and Popular Culture: Studies in Variety and Versatility*, to which he also contributed two essays.

J. NICHOLAS DE BONIS is an adjunct associate professor of marketing in the School of Business Administration at Emory University and a marketing/communications consultant.

RICHARD W. EASLEY is an assistant professor in the Department of Marketing, Hankamer School of Business, at Baylor University, where he teaches consumer behavior and marketing research. Easley's research interests are primarily in the area of marketing communications and how consumers process the information in advertisements. He is currently studying deceptive advertising practices in the mail-order industry and the effects of negative information in marketing, and strategies used to minimize such effects.

ELSIE S. HEBERT is an associate professor and head of the Advertising/Public Relations sequence of the Manship School of Journalism at Louisiana State University, Baton Rouge.

LEONARD J. HOOPER is a former professor in the Department of Advertising, College of Journalism and Communications, at the University of Florida, and is a past president (1982–1983) of the Gainesville Advertising Federation (4th District—Florida and Caribbean—of the American Advertising Federation).

ARTHUR J. KAUL is an associate professor and chairman of the Department of Journalism, School of Communication, at the University of Southern Mississippi. His scholarly interests include media ethics and history and literary journalism. His work has appeared in *Critical Studies in Mass Communication, Journal of Mass Media Ethics, Dictionary of Literary Biography*, and other publications.

ANN MAXWELL KEDING is an assistant professor of advertising in the School of Journalism at the University of Oregon and is the author (with Thomas Bivins) of the text *How to Produce Creative Advertising: Proven Techniques and Computer Applications.*

CHARLES S. MADDEN is the Ben H. Williams Professor of Marketing in the Hankamer School of Business at Baylor University. He is the author (with David Stewart and Joseph T. Plummer) of the text *Advertising Management.*

ROBERT McGAUGHEY III is a professor and chairman of the Department of Journalism and Radio-TV at Murray State University, Kentucky.

WAYNE W. MELANSON is an associate professor in the Department of Advertising, College of Journalism, at the University of Nebraska, Lincoln. Melanson earned his Ph.D. from the University of Tennessee, Knoxville. He has presented his research at meetings of the American Academy of Advertising, Western Marketing Educators, and Popular Culture Association.

WILLIAM RAY MOFIELD is professor emeritus of the Department of Journalism and Radio-TV at Murray State University, Kentucky.

DEBORAH K. MORRISON is an assistant professor in the Department of Advertising, College of Communication, at the University of Texas at Austin. She is the coordinator of the Creative Program. Her creative advertising students have won numerous national and regional awards.

KAY M. NAGEL is a reference librarian in the main library of the University of Georgia.

ROXANNE E. NEUBERGER-LUCCHESI is an assistant professor in the Department of Journalism and Mass Communication at South Dakota State University in Brookings.

JOHN R. OSBORN is the grandson of Alex F. Osborn and is a vice president and associate media director at BBDO.

DONALD E. PARENTE is an associate professor in the Department of Journalism, College of Mass Communication, at Middle Tennessee State University.

BILLY I. ROSS is a Distinguished Visiting Professor in the Manship School of Journalism at Louisiana State University. He is also a professor emeritus of Texas Tech University, where he was chairman of the Department of Mass Communications for 17 years.

KIM B. ROTZOLL is the dean of the College of Communications at the University of Illinois at Urbana-Champaign. He is the coauthor of several books on advertising and a coeditor of the works of Howard Gossage.

TOMMY V. SMITH is currently serving as director of the Advertising Program at the University of Southern Mississippi in Hattiesburg. Smith is the editor of the AEJMC's Advertising Division's newsletter and enjoys teaching advertising creativity, principles, and campaigns. He formerly directed the advertising and public relations program at Texas Tech University and was on the faculty at Kansas State University.

TED CURTIS SMYTHE, Ph.D., is a Distinguished Scholar in Residence at Sterling (Kansas) College. He is an Emeritus Professor of Communications, California State University, Fullerton. Smythe is the editor (with Michael C. Emery) of *Readings in Mass Communication: Concepts and Issues in the Mass Media*, now in its eighth edition.

CAROLYN STRINGER is an associate professor in the Department of Journalism, College of Arts, Humanities and Social Studies, at Western Kentucky University, and is the editor of *The President's Handbook*, a guide for AAF chapter presidents and faculty advisers. She also is the editor of *Adviser*, a bimonthly newsletter for advertising professors, published by the American Advertising Federation.

DANAL TERRY is an assistant professor in the Department of Mass Communication at Southwest Texas State University, and the owner of Visual Communications, a creative advertising service in Austin.

DONALD L. THOMPSON is a professor and head of the Department of Marketing, Georgia Southern University. He is the author of five books and numerous articles in business and professional journals in the field of marketing.

CAROLYN TRIPP is an assistant professor of marketing in the College of Business at Western Illinois University. Her research has appeared in the *Academy of Consumer Research Proceedings* and the *American Marketing Association Proceedings*. She has ten years experience in advertising management and specializes in direct marketing.

BONNIE VANNATTA was an instructor in the Department of Journalism, College of Mass Communication, at Middle Tennessee State University. Her research has appeared in the *Newspaper Research Journal* and *Art Education*.

JOHN VIVIAN is a professor of journalism at Winona State University in Minnesota, and is the author of the text *The Media of Mass Communication*.

His research interests are media history, news-gathering practices, media ownership patterns, and media law.

E. R. WORTHINGTON is an associate professor in the Department of Journalism and Mass Communications at New Mexico State University.